History

for the IB Diploma
Causes and Effects of 20th Century Wars

Mike Wells and Nick Fellows
Series editor: Allan Todd

Cambridge University Press's mission is to advance learning, knowledge and research worldwide.

Our IB Diploma resources aim to:

- encourage learners to explore concepts, ideas and topics that have local and global significance

- help students develop a positive attitude to learning in preparation for higher education

- assist students in approaching complex questions, applying critical-thinking skills and forming reasoned answers.

CAMBRIDGE
UNIVERSITY PRESS

CAMBRIDGE
UNIVERSITY PRESS

University Printing House, Cambridge CB2 8BS, United Kingdom

One Liberty Plaza, 20th Floor, New York, NY 10006, USA

477 Williamstown Road, Port Melbourne, VIC 3207, Australia

4843/24, 2nd Floor, Ansari Road, Daryaganj, Delhi – 110002, India

79 Anson Road, #06–04/06, Singapore 079906

Cambridge University Press is part of the University of Cambridge.

It furthers the University's mission by disseminating knowledge in the pursuit of education, learning and research at the highest international levels of excellence.

Information on this title: education.cambridge.org

© Cambridge University Press 2016

This publication is in copyright. Subject to statutory exception and to the provisions of relevant collective licensing agreements, no reproduction of any part may take place without the written permission of Cambridge University Press.

First published 2011
Second edition 2016
20 19 18 17 16 15 14 13 12 11 10 9 8 7 6 5 4 3 2

Printed in the United Kingdom by Latimer Trend

A catalogue record for this publication is available from the British Library

ISBN 978-1-107-56086-4

Cambridge University Press has no responsibility for the persistence or accuracy of URLs for external or third-party internet websites referred to in this publication, and does not guarantee that any content on such websites is, or will remain, accurate or appropriate.

NOTICE TO TEACHERS IN THE UK
It is illegal to reproduce any part of this work in material form (including photocopying and electronic storage) except under the following circumstances:
(i)   where you are abiding by a licence granted to your school or institution by the Copyright Licensing Agency;
(ii) where no such licence exists, or where you wish to exceed the terms of a licence, and you have gained the written permission of Cambridge University Press;
(iii) where you are allowed to reproduce without permission under the provisions of Chapter 3 of the Copyright, Designs and Patents Act 1988, which covers, for example, the reproduction of short passages within certain types of educational anthology and reproduction for the purposes of setting examination questions.

This material has been developed independently by the publisher and the content is in no way connected with nor endorsed by the International Baccalaureate Organization.

Contents

Contents

Introduction

This book is designed to prepare students taking the Paper 2 topic, Causes and Effects of 20th Century Wars (Prescribed Subject 11) in the IB History examination. The book is focused on five key conflicts: two of them major international wars; in addition, two civil wars, and one regional war – all of which had some input from other countries – are examined. Each war is considered in terms of:

- Causes, both long- and short-term, of the war
- Practice of the war – the main events, how the war was fought and the role of technology
- Effects and results of the war – military, political, social and economic.

Each of the detailed case-study chapters will have units dealing with these three themes, to help you focus on the main issues. This approach will allow you to compare and contrast the wars and to identify similarities and differences. Each of the case studies is divided into a number of key questions, which focus on the issues that you need to study in order to answer the Paper 2 questions.

IB History and regions of the world

The wars covered by the five case studies are:

- Chapter 2 – The First World War 1914–18 (all regions)
- Chapter 3 – The Spanish Civil War 1936–9 (European region)
- Chapter 4 – The Second World War 1939–45 (all regions)
- Chapter 5 – The Chinese Civil War 1927–49 (Asian region)
- Chapter 6 – The Iran–Iraq War 1980–8 (Africa and the Middle East region)

Remember, when answering a question that asks you to select examples from **two** different regions, you must be careful – failure to comply will result in limited opportunities to score high marks.

You may well, of course, study some other examples of civil or limited wars identified in the IB History Guide, such as the Nigerian Civil War or the limited wars between India and Pakistan.

For the purposes of study, IB History specifies four regions of the world. Where relevant, you need to be able to identify these regions.

Fact: The Nigerian Civil War (1967–70) was caused by the breakaway of southern provinces to form the new republic of Biafra.

Fact: India and Pakistan fought wars in 1947–8, 1965 and 1971. The two countries dispute ownership of Jammu and Kashmir, which are ruled by India but have a largely Muslim population.

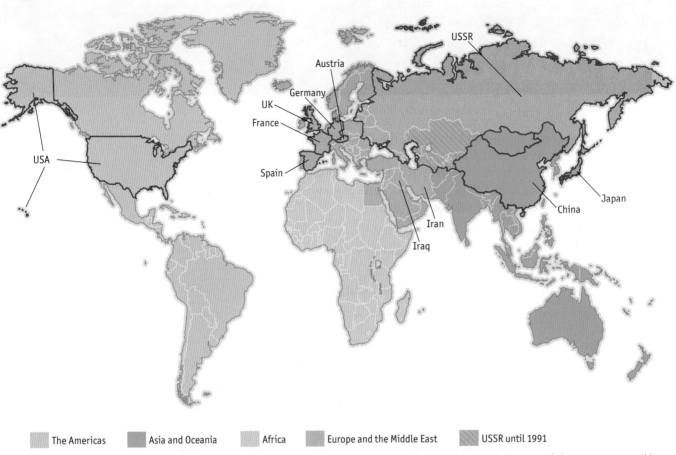

The Americas   Asia and Oceania   Africa   Europe and the Middle East   USSR until 1991

Figure 1.1   The four IB regions are shown on this map, along with some of the states covered by this book

Exam skills needed for IB History

Throughout the main chapters of this book, there are various activities and questions to help you develop the understanding and the exam skills necessary for success. Before attempting the specific exam practice questions at the end of each chapter, you might find it useful to refer to Chapter 7 first. This suggestion is based on the idea that if you know where you are supposed to be going (in this instance, gaining a good grade) and how to get there, you stand a better chance of reaching your destination!

Questions and mark schemes

Mark schemes: These are drawn up by IB for examiners to ensure that the same standards are applied to each question. It is important to know what qualities your answers are expected to have to gain the best possible marks.

To ensure that you develop the necessary understanding and skills, each chapter contains a number of comprehension questions in the margins. In addition, three of the main Paper 1-type questions (comprehension, value/limitations, and cross-referencing) are dealt with at the end of Chapters 2–6. Help for the longer Paper 1 judgement/synthesis questions, and the Paper 2 essay questions, can be found in Chapter 7 – the final exam practice chapter.

For additional help, simplified **mark schemes** have been put together in ways that should make it easier to understand what examiners are looking for in examination answers. The actual IB History mark schemes can be found on the IB website.

Finally, you will find examiners' tips and comments, along with activities, to help you focus on the important aspects of the questions and answers. These should help you avoid simple mistakes and oversights which, every year, result in even some otherwise good students failing to gain the highest marks.

Terminology and definitions

When studying the background to and consequences of wars, you will need to understand the meaning of terms used by military historians and also more general historical terminology. Words like 'strategy' and 'mobilisation' are important, as are general terms like 'left' and 'right', 'communism', 'anarchism' and 'fascism'. You will then be able to focus on the similarities and differences between the causes, course and consequences of different wars.

The key definitions are those of 'total war', 'civil war' and 'limited war'.

Total war

In a total war, all the resources of a nation – human, economic, even spiritual – are used by the state to achieve complete victory. There is no real distinction between the 'home front' – where people produce war materials and food to supply troops, as well as providing the soldiers for mass armies – and the 'fighting fronts' where the war is waged. Increasingly, the state has to take over, or at least control, production, imports and exports, and the allocation of resources – for instance, by rationing food and raw materials. The whole nation is encouraged by **propaganda** to support the war. It becomes difficult to oppose the conflict, as total commitment is needed to win total victory. Every means is used to portray the war as vital to the survival of the nation. There is an expectation that the spirit of the people will be totally behind the war. There can be no compromise for peace; total war is fought until the enemy surrenders. To achieve that, almost any means become justified: any new weapon, for example an **atomic bomb** or poison gas; economic warfare to starve the enemy; bombing raids to destroy their means of production, or just to kill the people who are producing the means to go on fighting. There may still be limits – for example, taking prisoners rather than simply killing those captured – but these are only observed under some circumstances and for fear that the enemy may retaliate in the same way. In some areas of conflict in total war, no prisoners are taken and sometimes states may even resort to genocide (the murder of whole peoples or racial/national groups whom they see as threatening survival).

In 1943, the German propaganda minister Josef Goebbels announced that Germany would need to wage total war (Source A).

Propaganda: The means used by a state to persuade its citizens to support it or its policies. In the 20th century this included posters, leaflets, state newspapers and press, state-sponsored films, radio and TV.

Atomic bomb: The most destructive weapon ever used. It is derived from the power created by splitting uranium atoms and has been used only twice – in August 1945 on the Japanese cities of Hiroshima and Nagasaki.

SOURCE A

The total war effort has become a matter of the entire German people. The people are willing to bear any burden, even the heaviest, to make any sacrifice, if it leads to the great goal of victory. [*Lively applause*]

Rich and poor, high and low must share the burdens equally. Everyone must do his duty in this grave hour, whether by choice or otherwise. The alarm must sound throughout the

(continued)

SOURCE A (*continued*)

nation. Millions of hands must get to work throughout the country. The individual may have to make great sacrifices, but they are tiny when compared to the sacrifices he would have to make if his refusal brought down on us the greatest national disaster.

Extract from 'Nation, Rise Up, and Let the Storm Break Loose', a speech by Josef Goebbels delivered at the Sports Palace in Berlin, broadcast to a large but carefully selected audience on 18 February 1943. Quoted at www.calvin.edu.

The idea of a total war dates from before the 20th century, but can only really be applied to the First and Second World Wars. In these conflicts, the entire population was expected to contribute to the war effort, and the war affected both soldier and civilian alike. By the Second World War, mass bombing of civilians brought the front line to ordinary people. The civilian deaths by bombing in Germany between 1939 and 1945 were four times the number of British soldiers killed during the First World War. Increasingly, the line between combatant and non-combatant was blurred.

Civil war

Civil wars are not fought between people of different countries, but between people within the same country. A civil war may have characteristics of total war and, in practice, few civil wars end in compromise, but rather are fought until one side or the other is victorious or gains its aim. This may be the break-up of a 'country' – for example, when East Pakistan broke away from Pakistan in 1971 to become a new country, Bangladesh, leaving just West Pakistan as 'Pakistan'.

The civil wars of the 20th century have been fought with the same ferocity and involvement of whole peoples as international total wars. In a civil war, bitterness may be much greater and the distinction between soldier and civilian is often less clear. If people in a country fight between themselves, then the enemy is likely to be the whole of the opposing side, not merely its troops. In both civil wars covered in this book, civilians suffered greatly, both during the war and in its aftermath. In both cases, the result of war was prolonged **dictatorship**.

This is not unusual in history, as civil war has often resulted in the militarisation of communities and the rise to power of a strong leader. Many past civil wars have also seen intervention by other countries – sometimes to take advantage of the divisions in a neighbouring country, at other times to support the side that might prove favourable if it emerged victorious. What was unusual in the case of the Spanish and Chinese Civil Wars was the degree of political ideology involved, which was far greater than in other civil wars. In Nigeria in the 1960s, for example, war was fought less for political principles than for reasons of hostility between different peoples in different regions. Civil war can arise:

- because people in certain regions of a country feel oppressed or neglected;
- because of political divisions;
- because of different religious ideas in a country.

In Spain, where all three factors contributed, the civil war was particularly intense (see Chapter 3). In China, regional differences were less significant than political ideas (see Chapter 5).

Dictatorship: The rule of one person, uncontrolled by parliaments or democratic elections. Before the 20th century, most European dictators had been military leaders, but the most famous of the European dictators came to power through radical political groups, such as Hitler's Nazis in Germany and Mussolini's fascists in Italy.

However, behind the ideas there is often a considerable amount of social conflict: to fight one's own countrymen is a major step, and one that usually results from significant social pressure. In the world wars, once the decision to fight had been taken by the leaders of a country, the people had to follow. A civil war, however, is more 'personal' and often involves people choosing a side and making a commitment for a variety of reasons.

Limited war

The two world wars spread to include a large number of countries in different continents. Not all 20th-century wars spread in this way, and some were limited to a small group of countries – sometimes just two participants, as in the case of the Iran–Iraq War (1980–8). One of the issues covered in this book is why, in the world wars, conflict did not remain limited and why it spread. The opposite question could be asked of limited wars – why, for instance, did the wars between Iran and Iraq, or between India and Pakistan (1947–8, 1965 and 1971), not turn into world wars, despite both sides having links with other powers? Why did Austria's decision to invade Serbia in 1914 lead to a world war, while Britain's decision to send a military force to contest Argentina's occupation of the Malvinas (the Falklands) in 1982 remained a war fought between just two countries? Iran and Iraq fought a very costly and bitter war between 1980 and 1988, but it remained limited in the sense that it did not develop into a regional or international conflict (see Chapter 6). The struggle between Poland and Germany in 1939, however, led to a war that involved millions worldwide.

Differences in fighting methods

Within different types of war – total, civil, limited – fighting can take different forms. Wars fought mainly with soldiers are known as 'conventional wars'. There may also be fighting on foot (infantry). A war can take the form of sieges – where the enemy attempts to surround, cut off and starve strong points before attacking. Battles can be fought in open-order warfare, in which both sides move their forces until they meet in conflict. Armies can fight using combined arms – infantry, vehicles (or cavalry) and aircraft. For an army:

- the main fighting may be defensive (holding positions) or offensive (attacking positions);
- they may use different strategies – the whole concept and planning of wars and campaigns (the 'big picture');
- they may use different tactics – methods to make the strategy a success.

Thus the strategy (grand plan) of Germany in 1914 was to defend on the Eastern Front and attack rapidly in the West. To achieve this, Germany used the tactic of bringing up forces rapidly by railway, dividing its forces and attacking with infantry supported by cannon (field artillery). When the strategy became more defensive, the tactics of using machine guns, barbed wire and heavy big guns (artillery) were used to defend the lines. However, sometimes both strategy and tactics required the use not of mass armies or sieges, but of smaller groups operating independently to attack the enemy wherever possible – sometimes behind its own lines. These groups could not achieve a massive victory, but could attack essential communications and supply lines, and unsettle enemy forces by lightning raids. Sometimes these groups were units of regular soldiers; sometimes they were groups of civilians who took up arms to attack the enemy. These non-military groups were called, among other things, 'partisans'. This type of warfare is known as guerrilla warfare – from the Spanish *guerra* ('war').

Fact: The Malvinas, off the coast of Argentina, are known in Britain as the Falkland Islands. They were occupied by Britain after an armed invasion in the 18th century. When the Argentinian military Junta pressed a historic claim to the islands in 1982, the British prime minister, Margaret Thatcher, sent a task force to recapture the islands. They remain a British possession.

Fact: Guerrilla warfare became famous when Spanish irregular forces attacked the regular armies of France in the Peninsular War (1808–14), fought when Napoleon I of France invaded Spain. This type of warfare has been practised since ancient times.

QUESTION

Why has 20th-century warfare seen much less of a distinction between soldiers and civilians than the warfare of previous centuries? For example, one reason could be technology, i.e., the development of aircraft and bigger bombs. Pool your ideas and explanations, and think about which you find most convincing. You could return to this after you have finished studying the book to see if your conclusions are still the same.

1

Introduction

Guerrilla warfare was a notable feature of the war in Russia from 1941 to 1945, and German forces faced guerrilla armies in several of the countries they occupied in the Second World War. Guerrilla warfare could also be a feature of civil wars, notably in the Chinese Civil War, where much communist success was due to small-scale fighting rather than large, open-order conflict. The Chinese communist leader Mao Zedong felt that guerrilla warfare played an important part in achieving revolutionary goals (Source B).

Figure 1.2   Modern guerrillas – the Mujahedin in Afghanistan in 1980

SOURCE B

What is the relationship of guerrilla warfare to the people? Without a political goal, guerrilla warfare must fail, as it must, if its political objectives do not coincide with the aspirations of the people and their sympathy, co-operation, and assistance cannot be gained. The essence of guerrilla warfare is thus revolutionary in character. On the other hand, in a war of counter-revolutionary nature, there is no place for guerrilla hostilities. Because guerrilla warfare basically derives from the masses and is supported by them, it can neither exist nor flourish if it separates itself from their sympathies and co-operation.

Mao Zedong. 1937. 'On Guerrilla Warfare'. From Selected Works of Mao Tse-Tung. *Vol. IX. Quoted at www.marxists.org.*

Fact: Algeria had been a French colony since 1830, but a liberation movement among its native North African inhabitants (as opposed to European colonists) demanded independence and fought French forces from 1954 to 1962. A civil war took place in Algeria from 1992 to 1999 between Islamic and secular groups.

Guerrilla warfare also featured heavily in the Algerian War (1954–62), in which Algerian guerrillas (freedom fighters from one point of view, terrorists from another) fought French troops. Guerrilla warfare was of vital importance in the Vietnam War. It took a heavy toll on civilian populations, who were often punished by regular forces for sheltering guerrillas – and by guerrillas for refusing aid and shelter.

This book cannot deal with every war in the 20th century, but the questions it raises will help you consider individual wars in a wider context, and to make comparisons that help you understand that few historical events can be understood simply by looking at them in isolation.

Activities

1 The table shows the wars specified for study by IB. Decide whether each one is total, limited or civil.

War	Total, limited, civil?
First World War, 1914–18	
Chinese Civil War, 1927–49	
Spanish Civil War, 1936–9	
Second World War, 1939–45	
Indo–Pakistan Wars, 1947–8, 1965, 1971	
Algerian War, 1954–62	
Nigerian Civil War, 1967–70	
Nicaraguan Revolution, began 1978	
Falklands/Malvinas War, 1982	
Iran–Iraq War, 1980–8	
Gulf War, 1990–1	

2 Explain briefly the difference between the following:

• total war and limited war
• national war and civil war
• conventional war and guerrilla war
• strategy and tactics
• defensive and offensive warfare.

War and historical debate

In order to score highly in Paper 2 you will need to show awareness and understanding of the **historiography** surrounding the wars you have studied. Historians – like most other people – are rarely completely neutral when dealing with important or controversial issues. Debates about the causes of both world wars have divided historians. This book refers to a major discussion that has divided opinion since the time of the First World War itself – the responsibility of Germany. Germany was officially blamed for the First World War by the victors in 1919. German historians were eager to show that the war came about for many different reasons, and that blame could not be placed with a single nation. In the inter-war period, German nationalists attributed

Historiography: This is literally the study of the writing of history, but the term has also come to be used to describe the different ways that historians have written about particular aspects of the past.

blame to all the main powers involved. The post-Second World War work by historian Fritz Fischer caused a storm in Germany, by suggesting that there was continuity between Hitler's desire for nationalist expansion and the desire of his pre-1914 predecessors for a war that would open up valuable areas in Eastern Europe to Germany and remove restrictions on German growth.

The key element in considering such debates is to look at the evidence being offered by historians. **Marxist historians** saw the war as an inevitable consequence of the final phase of the development of capitalism (Lenin regarded imperialism as the final phase of capitalism, and assumed that the war stemmed from imperial rivalry over global markets). Diplomatic historians relish the detailed study of crises. Sceptical historical writers like A.J.P. Taylor saw Europe blundering into war as statesmen were led by over-optimistic military leaders obsessed with timetables.

> **Marxist historians:** Marx saw class struggle as determining history, with communist revolution being possible in developed countries. Marxist historians focus on economic factors and class conflict, and relate other elements in history to underlying economic issues. For some Marxists, therefore, the First World War was the result of contradictions in capitalism rather than diplomatic decisions.

> **Fact:** A.J.P. Taylor (1906–90) was a controversial British historian who offered deliberately challenging interpretations of diplomatic history, famously arguing that Hitler behaved like a normal, rational statesman, taking advantage of the mistakes of other leaders rather than following a plan. This view seemed to make Hitler less responsible for war and thus became very controversial.

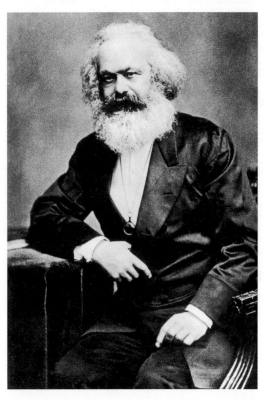

Figure 1.3 Karl Marx (1818–83)

After the Second World War, the situation seemed much more clear-cut. Blame was largely placed with Hitler and his pursuit of the ideological goals of conquest and racial supremacy. However, modern German historians have shown that Hitler was not a lone voice and that the Nazi ideology had more widespread support than was previously supposed.

Some historians have questioned whether Hitler's aims were dictated by mad ideas or a rational consideration of Germany's long-term interests. Again, A.J.P. Taylor, in his 1961 study *The Origins of the Second World War*, opened the way for a flood of debate.

There is no consensus on whether appeasement, for instance, was a disastrous policy that contributed directly to the outbreak of war, or a sensible course of action given the alternatives. The opening of British **cabinet papers** has shown why the policy was followed, but information on how decisions are taken cannot replace judgements about their effects.

> **Cabinet papers:** These are the records of discussions between leading British government ministers, who sit in a committee called the Cabinet. The papers were not available to historians until 30 years had elapsed.

Reputations in war wax and wane. The British generals of the First World War, particularly Sir Douglas Haig, were seen as incompetent and old-fashioned by many. However, **revisionists** have seen Haig as a thoughtful and educated soldier doing what he could in impossible circumstances, and developing the British army and its fighting techniques in such a way as to make victory possible in 1918. Mao Zedong, often seen as the architect of communist victory by his brilliant guerrilla warfare, is now viewed by revisionists as an erratic leader, motivated by personal ambition more than the good of his followers or his cause.

Even where there is limited debate in the sense of deeply opposed positions, historians have to weigh the relative importance of different factors – they have to consider how to explain the outcome of the Spanish Civil War, for example, and decide what weight to give to different explanations. Historians must constantly assess evidence and test judgements. This book contains some accounts of major controversies, but it also invites you to consider what the best explanations are for wars and their outcomes by looking at the evidence.

> **Revisionists:** Historians who challenge accepted views are sometimes called revisionists. For example, there was a generally accepted view that Stalin and the Soviet Union were to blame for the Cold War. This was challenged by historians who blamed the USA. This 'revisionist' view was then developed by those who saw it as a mixture of elements – these historians became known as 'post-revisionists'. Generally, labelling views like this is of little real use in understanding the past, but you will come across these terms in historical writing.

Key Concepts

To perform well in your IB History examinations, you will often need to consider aspects of one or more of six important Key Concepts as you write your answers. These six Key Concepts are listed below:

- Change
- Continuity
- Causation
- Consequence
- Significance
- Perspectives.

Sometimes, a question might require you to address two – or more – Key Concepts. For instance: 'Evaluate the reasons why the Spanish Civil War broke out, and explain the main consequences it had for European diplomacy during its duration.'

It is immediately clear with this question that the Key Concepts of Causation and Consequence must be addressed in your answer. However, it is important to note that although the word 'cause' doesn't explicitly appear in the question, words such as 'reasons' or 'why' nonetheless are asking you to address Causation. To help you focus on the six Key Concepts, and gain experience of writing answers which address them, you will find a range of different questions and activities throughout these chapters.

Theory of Knowledge

Alongside these broad key themes, all chapters contain Theory of Knowledge links to get you thinking about aspects that relate to history, which is a Group 3 subject in the IB Diploma. The Route 2 topic Causes and effects of 20th century wars (Topic 11 of 20th century world history) has clear links to ideas about knowledge and history.

Questions relating to the availability and selection of sources, and to interpretations of these sources, link to the IB Theory of Knowledge course. Issues are raised such as whether or not historians should approach interpretations of wars by considering the role of national leaders. The scope of historical writing on aspects of social history during periods of war is also discussed. There are interesting philosophical questions relating to causes and consequences, and there is some discussion about whether a historian should be drawn at all to consider 'what if', or counter-factual, history. This is very tempting when wars do seem to depend on key decisions and are often triggered by dramatic events.

For example, when trying to decide on aspects of the origins of wars, or why they turned out as they did, historians must decide which evidence to select and use – and which to leave out – to make their case. But in selecting what they consider to be the most important or relevant sources, and in making judgements about the value and limitations of specific sources or sets of sources, how important are these historians' personal political views? Is there such a thing as objective 'historical truth'? Or is there just a range of subjective historical opinions and interpretations about the past that vary according to the political interests and leanings of individual historians?

You are therefore encouraged to read a range of books offering different interpretations and, where revisionists are putting forward challenges to accepted views, to look critically at the bases for those views. If using contemporary evidence, are historians paying attention to its provenance? This is a major skill for any historian at every level, so practice is offered in considering a range of sources.

Summary

By the time you have read this book:

- You should be familiar with the causes, conduct and results of two major total wars; along with two civil wars, and one regional war, each from a different region.
- You should understand that the wars had some features in common and some that were very different, and you should be able to offer some explanation as to why this is the case.
- You should be aware of broad categories in which the causes and results of war have been seen – for example, political, social and economic.
- You should be aware of aspects of war over which there is historical controversy, as well as understanding the reasons for this. You should start to make judgements about disputed areas, as well as about the relative importance of varying explanations for the causes, outcomes and results of conflicts.
- You should understand key historical terms and concepts, and use them with confidence in writing answers that are genuinely analytical and focused on the question, rather than merely descriptions related to the general topic.
- You should have considered a range of different sources and developed an increasingly critical assessment of evidence.

Causes of the First World War

KEY QUESTIONS
- What were the main long-term causes of the war?
- What were the main short-term causes of the war?
- What were the economic, political, ideological and territorial causes?

Overview

- In the late 19th century, rivalry developed among the 'Great Powers' of Europe, which competed to enhance their empires and expand their colonial possessions. European states also found themselves in economic competition, battling for control of trade and markets. This rivalry was fuelled by national insecurities and enmities arising from 19th-century conflicts.

- From 1870, an arms race developed, which saw most countries increasing their armies and turning to more sophisticated weapons and tactics. The growth of nationalism was accompanied by an upsurge in militarisation, as countries prepared to mobilise for war. Meanwhile, a system of alliances and treaties evolved, which meant that any conflict was likely to lead to a war throughout Europe and beyond.

- In the early 20th century, the break-up of the Ottoman Empire was followed by upheaval and unrest in the Balkans, as the Great Powers sought to establish their interests in the region. Tensions were heightened by a series of crises, including the Balkan Wars of 1912–13.

- The final trigger for war took place in the Balkans, when the heir to the Austro-Hungarian Empire was assassinated while on a state visit to Serbia. When Austria's subsequent demands were not fully met by Serbia, Austria declared war. The international system of alliances meant that Europe, and indeed much of the rest of the world, was soon involved in a full-scale war.

TIMELINE

1871 A united German Empire is proclaimed after war with France; Germany takes Alsace-Lorraine from France.

1879 Dual Alliance between Germany and Austria-Hungary.

1882 Triple Alliance between Germany, Austria-Hungary and Italy.

1894 Franco–Russian alliance.

1898 First German naval law; construction of fleet challenges Britain.

1904 Anglo–French colonial entente.

1905 First Moroccan crisis.

1907 Anglo–Russian entente.

1908 Bosnian crisis.

1911 Second Moroccan crisis (Agadir crisis).

1912–13 Balkan Wars.

1914 Assassination of Archduke Franz Ferdinand and outbreak of the First World War.

2

Introduction

This is the first case study of a cross-regional war between states. In this – as in the following chapters – there are three sections:

- the first deals with the causes of the war;
- the second covers the practices of war and their impact on its outcome;
- the final section looks at the effects of the war.

Until 1939, the war of 1914–18 was called 'The Great War'. There had been world wars before, but nothing on the scale of the fighting of 1914–18 – and no war that had affected the civilian populations of so many different countries. It was with some justification, therefore, that it became known, before its even more destructive successor of 1939–45, as not just a great war, but the Great War.

The nature of warfare changed considerably between 1914 and 1918. The belief in war as decisive manoeuvre gave way to the realisation that modern industrial war was one of **attrition** – that victory depended on wearing down the enemy's resources rather than relying on brilliant military tactics.

Weapons and armaments developed on a new scale throughout the war. Theorists rightly argued afterwards that aircraft and tanks were the weapons of the future, and that wars would become more mobile and faster-moving. However, it was not only military change that made the First World War so distinctive from wars that had come before.

Civilians were involved in this war more than ever before, both in assisting the war effort and as targets for enemy attack. In occupied areas, such as Belgium and Poland, stringent military rule was established over civilians. For example, the Turks carried out what amounted to genocide against the Armenians, who were thought to be a risk to security, and because the war had unleashed hatreds that were directed towards an unpopular ethnic minority. Civilians of enemy origin were often persecuted – a sign that this was a war between peoples as well as armies. The war undoubtedly had profound consequences in terms of lives lost, but also in terms of political, territorial, social and economic change.

The casualty rates of the war were devastatingly high – not only as a result of the fighting, but also because of factors such as food shortages and the influenza epidemic that hit a weakened Europe in 1918. The emotional impact of the war is hard to comprehend today. For years afterwards, the terrible wounds suffered by so many were visible everywhere, and mental disturbances among survivors lasted a lifetime.

Attrition: The process of wearing down the enemy by steady killing. With very large armies and so much heavy artillery, the element of surprise was often lacking and armies found it difficult to manoeuvre. Thus the war became more a matter of wearing down the enemy by causing losses of manpower and resources than winning by strategic attacks that were decisive in themselves.

2.1 What were the main long-term causes of the war?

Imperial rivalry

The 'Great War' was a war between the 'Great Powers' of Europe and their empires – the Austro-Hungarian Empire, Britain and its empire, France and its empire, Germany and its empire, and the Russian Empire. The Ottoman Empire (Turkey) joined the war in 1914; Italy and its imperial possessions in 1915. Of the major non-European powers, Japan joined in 1914 and the USA in 1917. Both these countries had overseas possessions.

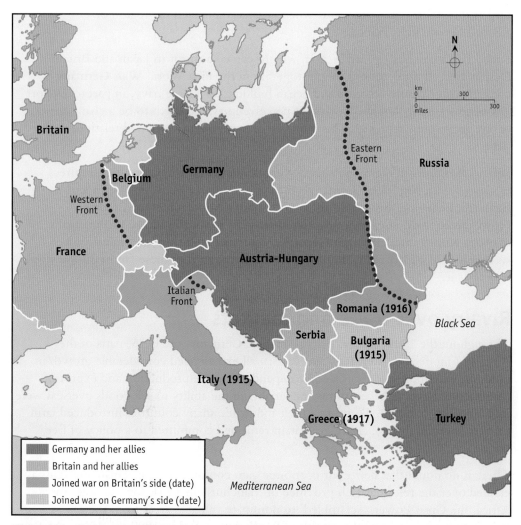

Figure 2.1 The First World War, showing its two sides; note that Italy joined France and Great Britain, despite its previous alliance with Austria and Germany; Turkey had not been in the alliance system before 1914

The fact that the key nations ruled over vast empires guaranteed that the war was worldwide, in the sense that all continents saw some fighting. However, unlike the Second World War – a struggle for mastery in Europe and Asia, in which North America played a prolonged part – the First World War was centred on Europe. Fighting outside Europe was a result of the imperial possessions and the naval strength of the European powers.

Prior to the outbreak of the First World War, there had been several conflicts between the Great Powers over colonial possessions. However, these conflicts did not all lead to war. France and Britain were bitter rivals in North Africa, for example, and nearly went to war in 1898 over ownership of the southern Nile. However, these disputes were settled. Russia was also in danger of going to war with Britain over ambitions on the north-west frontier of India. In the end the disputes were resolved and Britain, France and Russia all fought on the same side in the First World War. France objected to Germany interfering in its interests in North Africa and two major crises, known as the Moroccan Crises, resulted in 1905 and 1911 (see Section 2.2, 'The Moroccan Crises'). However, the main source of disagreement between France and Germany went back further than these crises – to 1871, when Germany annexed the region of Alsace-Lorraine from France.

Russia had a colonial empire in Asia, which seemed a threat to Japan and Britain. Despite this, all three nations fought together in the First World War. Germany certainly craved more colonies and began building up a large navy, in part to support its overseas empire, but also because it perceived naval strength to be a characteristic of any great colonial power. This build-up of naval might worsened relations with Britain.

Britain also disliked Germany's increasing contact with the Ottoman Empire. It viewed with suspicion Germany's plans for a railway between Berlin and Baghdad, believing this would threaten Britain's Middle-Eastern Empire. However, the two countries negotiated sensibly about the future of Portugal's overseas empire and, although Germany's colonial ambitions and naval power were unpopular in Britain, there was little indication that these factors alone would lead to war.

Rivalry over trade and markets

Throughout the 19th century, Britain, France, Germany, the USA, parts of the Austrian Empire and, later, Italy and Russia, all experienced considerable growth in industry, with more and more people dependent on the production and export of manufactured goods. Access to raw materials and the ability to sell goods overseas were undoubtedly important. To protect their industries, many countries introduced tariff barriers (customs duties), although Britain remained committed to a policy of free trade.

There is no doubt that desire for economic gain could incite war. Japan and Russia clashed over the resource-rich province of Manchuria in 1904, for example. In Africa, the Great Powers 'scrambled' to dominate valuable areas from the 1870s. Britain wanted to control the wealth of South Africa, and in 1899 this led to the Boer War, a conflict with the independent Dutch-speaking states in the region. Germany may have harboured ambitions to take over the rich area of the Ukraine in Russia. However, the main motives for conflict were not primarily economic, nor were they rooted in a desire for land (as they were to a much greater extent in the Second World War).

The roots of French discontent dated back to the loss of Alsace-Lorraine. This area did have natural resources that were valuable to the French, but of far greater significance was the humiliation they felt at two 'French' areas being ruled by Germany.

Austria's invasion of Serbia proved to be the trigger for the war. However, this move was not driven by economic needs, but rather to secure what Austria felt was a threat to its empire. If there was any economic basis for the invasion, it was simply that economic

Fact: Britain had ruled Egypt since the 1880s, and had also conquered the Sudan. A British expedition travelling south to find the source of the Nile met a French expedition from the French colonies in West Africa. There was a hostile encounter at Fashoda (today's Koda, in southern Sudan) in 1898, which nearly led to war.

Fact: The border provinces of Alsace-Lorraine in France contained mostly German speakers. When France was defeated in a war against the German states in 1871, the German chancellor, Otto von Bismarck, absorbed the two provinces into the new German Empire, proclaimed in occupied Paris in 1871. France never accepted this, and it became a major cause of anti-German feeling in the lead-up to the First World War.

Fact: The Berlin–Baghdad Railway was begun with German funding and engineering in 1903, although it was not completed until 1940. By cooperating with the Ottoman Empire, the Germans hoped to establish a port on the Persian Gulf with direct rail links to Germany. This angered Britain, which saw it as a threat to both Egypt and India and to its own influence in the Middle East.

growth in Austria had created more powerful weapons and armies, which led to heightened feelings of national power and pride.

Militarism

After 1870, nearly all the European powers increased the size of their armies, the sophistication of their weapons, and the technology used to wage war on land and sea. Developments in transportation meant that more railways could carry greater numbers of troops. Every country had detailed war plans.

The peoples of Europe were proud of their armed forces, and the growth of mass nationalism often went hand in hand with increasing militarisation. There were longer periods of **conscription,** and more praise for military values in schools and in youth organisations such as the Boy Scouts and military cadets. Military parades were a feature of most countries, as were 'naval days', at which the populace cheered new battleships. The press praised military virtues.

As will be shown, the much larger military forces needed time to get ready for war, so the concept of mobilisation came about. This involved putting the armed forces on a war footing – calling up reserves and organising trains and transport to move troops to the battle fronts. Once mobilisation was underway, it was difficult to stop, and it thus came to be seen as a declaration of war. Political leaders were also aware that detailed war plans were of enormous importance, making conflict both a distinct option and a risk worth taking.

However, whether or not mobilisation was a major cause of war must be considered carefully. It is, after all, the job of military leaders to prepare for war. There have been many occasions on which plans for war have been drawn up but never executed. In the 1920s, Britain and the USA had plans for war with each other. After the Second World War, all-out war between the USSR and the West never broke out, despite detailed plans being drawn up by both sides. National feeling was often intensely hostile between countries that did not actually go to war with each other – for example, between France and Italy or Britain and France.

Alliances and treaties

Imperial rivalry, economic pressure for more markets, militarism and nationalism all led to feelings of hostility between countries and contributed to the build-up of tensions. However, what linked all these contributing factors was the network of alliances that emerged from the late 19th century. By 1914, there appeared to be two distinct 'sides': Austria, Germany and Italy (the Triple Alliance), and France, Russia and Britain (the Triple Entente).

The first agreement, between Austria and Germany, emerged in 1879. Germany sought an alliance against France, which wanted revenge for defeat in a war of 1870–1. Italy joined in 1882 because at that point it was anti-French. Initially, Germany had also made an agreement with Russia, but this was discarded after **Kaiser Wilhelm II** came to the throne in 1888. France managed to gain an alliance with Russia in 1894, and both countries made agreements (**ententes**) with Britain over colonial possessions (1904 and 1907).

Fact: The Boer War (1899–1902) broke out when Britain defended its citizens in South Africa, who had been denied rights in the Dutch-speaking Republic of the Transvaal. The British suffered a series of defeats to begin with, but emerged victorious in 1902. During the war, Britain used concentration camps to imprison the families of the Boers (Dutch speakers). Despite its victory, Britain's conduct in the war made it unpopular in Europe, especially in Germany.

Conscription: The 'call up' or drafting of men for compulsory military service.

Entente: An understanding (as opposed to a firm alliance) between nations. Britain and France made agreements about colonial borders: for example, Egypt. Russia made agreements about Afghanistan and Persia (Iran). The ententes improved relations but did not bind Britain to support either France or Russia. They did, however, make it more likely that Britain would join in a war.

Sphere of influence: The Great Powers while having some areas under their direct control saw themselves as having virtual control over other areas while not actually owning them. These were called 'spheres of influence'

The alliances were all defensive and would only operate if a country was attacked. Despite its ententes, Britain had no firm commitments with Russia or France – in fact it was Italy that fought alongside France and Britain when the war broke out. However, the agreements encouraged the powers to think in terms of two opposing sides and certainly made Germany feel 'encircled' or surrounded by potential enemies. When conflict arose, this network of alliances ensured that it did not remain localised.

Figure 2.2 Kaiser Wilhelm II (1859–1941)

He ruled Germany from 1888 to 1918. He parted company with the veteran statesman Bismarck and pursued a new and aggressive course of foreign policy. He was a militaristic leader, and dropped the Reinsurance Treaty with Russia, relying instead on alliance with Austria-Hungary for defence. His support for a new fleet upset Britain, as did his claims that Germany should have more colonies ('a place in the sun'), as did his general assertion of Germany's influence and power in Europe and the world. His tactlessness and blustering speeches led to international tensions over the building of a German navy, Morocco and the Balkans. However, he did try to maintain good relations with Russia, and was prepared to negotiate about colonial issues. He was hesitant over war in 1914, but could not prevent it. He abdicated in 1918 and lived as a private citizen in Holland.

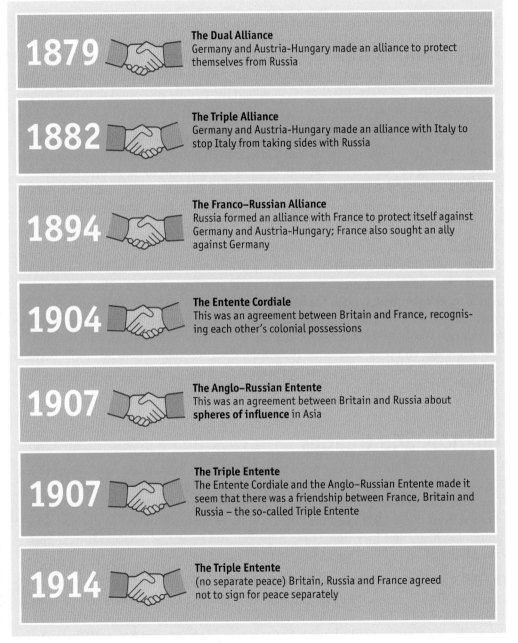

1879 The Dual Alliance
Germany and Austria-Hungary made an alliance to protect themselves from Russia

1882 The Triple Alliance
Germany and Austria-Hungary made an alliance with Italy to stop Italy from taking sides with Russia

1894 The Franco–Russian Alliance
Russia formed an alliance with France to protect itself against Germany and Austria-Hungary; France also sought an ally against Germany

1904 The Entente Cordiale
This was an agreement between Britain and France, recognising each other's colonial possessions

1907 The Anglo–Russian Entente
This was an agreement between Britain and Russia about **spheres of influence** in Asia

1907 The Triple Entente
The Entente Cordiale and the Anglo–Russian Entente made it seem that there was a friendship between France, Britain and Russia – the so-called Triple Entente

1914 The Triple Entente
(no separate peace) Britain, Russia and France agreed not to sign for peace separately

Figure 2.3 The alliances and ententes from 1879 to 1914; Britain's only formal alliance before 1914 was a 1902 treaty with Japan, promising mutual assistance if either were attacked by Russia

2.2 What were the main short-term causes of the war?

Unrest in the Balkans

The Balkans was an area of Europe that was of huge importance to two great European empires – Austria-Hungary and Russia. Originally part of the Ottoman Empire, this largely Christian region had broken away and established independent states. These states were not always stable, however, largely because not all members of the same national groups were included in the new states. For example, many Serbs found themselves settled in areas that were part of the Austrian Empire rather than the new state of Serbia. Not only was there a complex mix of nationalities, some in their own countries and some under foreign rule, but this situation was also grounds for rivalry between Russia and Austria.

Austria

The Austrian Empire was not a nation-state but rather a collection of peoples and regions that owed allegiance to the Habsburg emperor. This in itself was not unusual. The Russian, British, French and German empires were also made up of people of varying nationalities, with different languages, cultures and religions. However, their 'subject peoples' were mainly non-European, while the Austrian Empire ruled many different European peoples. Another difference was that Austria had lost more of its empire in the 19th century than the other Great Powers. In 1815, the Habsburg monarchy dominated Germany and Italy, as well as having control of much of south-east Europe. In 1859–60, Italy was lost in a war waged against France and the northern Italian kingdom of Piedmont.

Italy was still divided into a number of states, but a nationalist movement led by Giuseppe Garibaldi invaded Sicily and Naples, which were ruled by a separate Bourbon king. This led to Piedmont gaining control of the whole of Italy except the central area, which was ruled by the pope. In 1870, this region was also overcome, leaving the pope the ruler of only the Vatican City – a small area of Rome.

Austria suffered defeat again in 1866, this time in a war against Prussia, in which it lost its dominance over Germany. The Austrian Empire was now largely confined to south-east Europe, and in 1867 Austria was forced into offering Hungary equal status in the form of a 'dual monarchy' – Austria-Hungary. If national feeling elsewhere led to any further break-up of the empire, it would swiftly lose its status as a serious power on the European stage.

The subject peoples grew increasingly resentful of the Austro-Hungarian control. The Czechs in particular disliked the domination of the German- speaking emperor. However, the different nationalities were too divided to form any type of cohesive opposition to their rulers, nor were they likely to be able to produce the military power necessary to challenge Austria on their own. However, if they had the support of neighbouring powers, then the situation might be different.

Fact: In 1866, Prussia's leader, Otto von Bismarck, went to war with Austria over disputed territory, hoping to end Austrian influence in Germany. He was successful: the superior Prussian army won, resulting in Prussian domination of northern Germany. Austria lost its power and became much more an Eastern European monarchy. From then on, Austria was determined to keep its remaining lands.

17

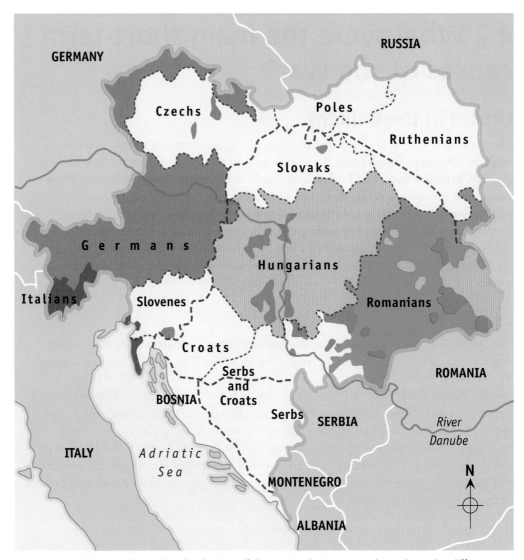

Figure 2.4 This map shows the distribution of the main ethnic groups throughout the different regions of Austria-Hungary in 1914

The great danger for Austria was that Russia might step in to support the demands for independence being made by the different nationalities living under Austrian rule in the Balkans. Austria was a Catholic power ruling many Orthodox peoples in its Balkan territories, and culturally these groups were closer to Russia. These tensions surfaced in the Bosnian Crisis of 1908.

The Bosnian Crisis, 1908

Austria had occupied the two Balkan provinces of Bosnia and Herzegovina since 1878. In September 1908, Russia and Austria agreed that at some point in the future Austria might officially absorb these provinces into the Austrian Empire. In return, Austria would support Russia's demand to move warships from the Black Sea into the Mediterranean through the Turkish Straits – the waterway between the two seas near which Constantinople (today's Istanbul) was situated. Russia had been banned from using this route by an international agreement of 1841.

Fact: During the medieval period, the Christian Church split into two distinct forms – Catholic in the West and Orthodox in the East. Russia became Orthodox, while most of Europe became Catholic. However, many groups in the Balkan territories were Orthodox Christians.

In October 1908, Austria went ahead with the annexation of Bosnia and Herzegovina – but without keeping to its side of the agreement. The two provinces were largely populated by Serbians, so the annexation angered Serbia, and Russia gave support to its protests. However, Germany backed Austria and in 1909 Russia was forced to give way and to stop supporting Serbia, which in turn had to accept the Austrian annexation. Russia was humiliated at being forced to back down and Serbia was resentful at the outcome of the crisis. Austria, however, was encouraged by Germany's support.

The Balkan Wars, 1912–13

Serbia was another independent country that posed a threat to Austria. It had gained independence from **Ottoman** control in 1830, and grew considerably as a result of wars against the Ottomans in 1912 and 1913.

In 1912, Serbia, Bulgaria, Greece and Montenegro formed the Balkan League. This alliance aimed to drive the Turks from Europe. The Ottoman (Turkish) Empire was distracted by an internal revolution (1908–9) and a war with Italy over control of North Africa (1911–12). Seizing this opportunity, in October 1912 the Balkan League attacked the Turks and began what became known as the Balkan Wars (1912–13). There were militant anti-Austrian groups in Serbia.

> **Ottoman:** The Turks and their empire were ruled by a dynasty called the Ottomans. The terms 'Turkish' and 'Ottoman' tend to be used interchangeably, but strictly 'Ottoman' refers to the ruling dynasty. The empire owed personal allegiance to the Ottoman sultans.

The rapid success of the League made the Great Powers anxious, and Austria in particular was concerned by Serbia's growth. A settlement was negotiated in the Treaty of London, but some of the Balkan States were unhappy with the terms of this agreement, and this led to friction among the Balkan allies. The Bulgarians, who felt most cheated, declared war on both Greece and Serbia, but they were defeated by Serbia, Greece, Turkey and Romania.

The territorial changes that resulted saw an expansion of Serbia into the Kosovo region and northern and central Macedonia. Turkey was expelled from Europe, except for the area around Adrianople, and its navy was defeated by Greece. Austria insisted on an independent Albania to restrict Serbia's access to the Adriatic Sea. Bulgaria had been badly defeated and lost its gains; it turned to Austria as an ally and away from its former partner, Russia. With 122 000 dead, the scale of the wars had not been large. The Great Powers had acted together and had not joined in the fighting. However, there were major consequences:

- Austria saw Serbia as a threat and an enemy. It was concerned at the rapid growth of Serbian territory and power as a result of the war.
- Russia had not directly backed Serbia, but with the defeat of Bulgaria it needed to maintain good relations with Serbia for influence in the Balkans.
- Serbia resented having to give up its gains and the creation of the new state of Albania, so nationalist feelings in Serbia against Austria ran high.
- Austria had approached Germany for support against Serbia and, if necessary, Russia, and the idea had been planted that this was a possibility.

The assassination of Archduke Franz Ferdinand – an international crisis

The immediate trigger for the outbreak of the war was an assassination. On 28 June 1914, the heir to the Austro-Hungarian Empire and his wife were killed by a terrorist on a state visit to the Bosnian capital of Sarajevo. The Serbs in Bosnia had

2

resented Austria's annexation of the region in 1908, and wanted to see Bosnia joined to the independent country of Serbia. Several terrorist groups worked against Austrian rule in Bosnia and one of these, the Black Hand Secret Society, went to Sarajevo with the intention of killing Archduke Franz Ferdinand. A first attempt failed, but a wrong turning by the driver of the royal car offered Black Hand member **Gavrilo Princip** another chance, and he shot the archduke and his wife.

Austria responded to the outrage with a series of demands that Serbia perceived as compromising its independence. It refused to meet them, setting the stage for war. Austria was allied to Germany and counted on its support. Serbia relied on support from Russia, the greatest of the **Slav** powers, and Russia itself was allied to France. Thus both parties had powerful friends. The system of international agreements meant that a local quarrel could easily spread to become a general European war.

The military plans of the major powers involved putting their armies on a war footing as early as possible – in other words, they began to mobilise. Once this began it was hard to stop, and when the deadline for Serbia's acceptance of Austria's ultimatum passed, the danger of conflict was so great that Russia mobilised. Austria called on Germany. Germany had plans in the event of a war with Russia to attack Russia's ally France and to defeat it quickly to avoid war on two fronts. Russia would not halt its war preparations, and this prompted the French to begin mobilising.

When Russia refused to demobilise, Germany declared war on Russia. France declared war on Germany. Britain feared isolation, but its only formal alliance was with Belgium. However, German war plans involved an invasion of Belgium, which ultimately led to Britain declaring war on Germany.

Gavrilo Princip (1894–1918)

He was a fanatical Serb nationalist born in Bosnia. He was part of a three-man assassination squad sent by the terrorist group the Black Hand to kill Franz Ferdinand. He failed to kill himself after shooting the royal couple, and was imprisoned until his death from tuberculosis in 1918.

Slav: Russia was a Slav power – its peoples were descended from the Slavonic tribes of what are now Poland and western Russia. Other Slav areas were Poland, Bulgaria and Serbia. In the late 19th century, there was a pan-Slavonic movement to encourage all Slav peoples, who shared a similar Orthodox religion, to come under Russian control. This worried the Germanic powers, Austria and Germany, especially as both had Slav peoples in their empires.

Fact: In May 1911, ten men in Serbia founded the Black Hand Secret Society. The Serbian army intelligence chief was involved with the group, whose main objective was the creation, by violent means, of a Greater Serbia: 'To realise the national ideal, "the unification of all Serbs" ... this organisation prefers terrorist action to cultural activities.' There were plots to kill the emperor and the head of the military government in Bosnia before 1914. No more than 2,500 Serbs were members, but these did include army officers.

TIMELINE

Key events that led to war in July–August 1914

23 July	Austria issues an ultimatum to Serbia.
28 July	Austria declares war on Serbia after Serbia only accepts eight of Austria's ten demands.
29 July	Russia orders partial mobilisation of its forces.
30 July	Germany mobilises and demands that Russia demobilise.
1 August	France mobilises; the German ultimatum to Russia expires at noon; Germany declares war.
2 August	Russia declares war; Germany issues an ultimatum to Belgium to allow the passage of German troops.
3 August	Germany declares war on France.
4 August	German forces invade Belgium shortly after 8am; the British government issues an ultimatum to Germany stating that it must withdraw by midnight; Britain declares war on Germany.
6 August	Austria-Hungary declares war on Russia.
10 August	Britain and France declare war on the Austro-Hungarian Empire.

Why Austria declared war on Serbia

On 23 July 1914, the Austro-Hungarian imperial council issued an ultimatum to Serbia that was unlikely to be accepted. It blamed Serbia for failing to control terrorism and demanded that Austria monitor security measures. The ultimatum was a threat to Serbian independence, and it was based on no evidence that the Serbian government had been responsible for the assassination.

The Austrian commander in chief, Conrad von Hötzendorf, urged the government towards a preventive war against Serbia to deal with Austria's enemies. Austria had been building up and modernising its armed forces, and the military planners were certain they would achieve victory.

There was a risk that Russia would be involved, but Austria hoped that the alliance signed with Germany in 1879 would guarantee its support, and there was anyway no certainty that Russia would act. The tsar was not in sympathy with Serb terrorism and had been shocked at the death of an eminent member of a fellow royal family. Even if Russia did act, there was no guarantee that France would step in to support it.

The Serb problem would not go away – with Serbia's expansion, the nationalist excitement in the Balkans in 1912–13 and growing terrorism, it was likely that there would be further threats to Austrian control of Bosnia. The loss of Bosnia might threaten the whole Austrian Empire. A short, decisive war would solve the problem and allow Austria to both maintain its empire and make a federation with the southern Slavonic areas a possibility. The foreign minister, **Count Leopold Berchtold,** urged war as the solution to the problem of growing Serb power.

Austria – the key factors

There were several key factors behind Austria's decision to declare war:

- the preservation of the Austro-Hungarian Empire;
- the reliance on the Triple Alliance and particularly on links with Germany;
- the belief that Austria could manage a quick, decisive victory;
- the influence of the growth of military power and military planning;
- the desire to prevent Serb nationalism spreading;
- the willingness of its statesmen to take risks.

Austria started the process that led to war because its statesmen took a calculated risk, based on the advice of diplomats and generals, to resolve a situation that they saw as threatening their national existence.

SOURCE A

An extract from a note sent to all major European powers by Austria, explaining its actions.

In the presence of this state of things the Imperial and Royal Government have felt compelled to take new and urgent steps at Belgrade [the capital of Serbia] with a view to inducing the Serbian Government to stop the incendiary movement that is threatening the security and integrity of the Austro-Hungarian monarchy.

The Imperial and Royal Government are convinced that in taking this step they will find themselves in full agreement with the sentiments of all civilised nations, who cannot permit

(continued)

QUESTION

Significance: How important were events in the Balkans in bringing about the First World War, (a) in the long-term and (b) in the short-term?

Figure 2.5   Count Leopold Berchtold (1863–1942)

He was a wealthy Austrian diplomat and served as Austrian foreign minister from 1912 to 1915. After the Balkan Wars he became convinced that Austria should invade Serbia. The events of July 1914 gave him the ammunition he needed to persuade the Austrian imperial powers to declare war.

SOURCE A *(continued)*

regicide to become a weapon that can be employed with impunity in political strife, and the peace of Europe to be continually disturbed by movements emanating from Belgrade.

C.F. Horne (ed.). 1923. Source Records of the Great War, *Vol. I. National Alumni.*

QUESTION

Does Source A show that Austria did not expect war if it took strong action against Serbia? Think about this – should a historian take this at face value or do you think Austria was trying to justify its actions?

Tsar: The Russian rulers took their title from the Roman 'Caesar'. Originally they had been princes of Moscow, but they had come to rule all of Russia. The last tsar, Nicholas II, was descended from the Romanov family, who took the throne in 1613. He believed that God had appointed him to rule, and had little time for parliaments, though he was forced to establish one after a revolution in 1905. He took personal charge of his armies in 1915 and was blamed for their failure. He was forced to abdicate in March 1917 and he and his family were killed by the Bolsheviks in 1918.

Why Russia mobilised its forces

Russia was the largest of the Great Powers. Like the others, it was an empire, and the **tsar** ruled over many non-Russian nationalities. Russia had the reputation of being backward because of its large peasant population (most of whom had been slaves until 1861) and its autocratic monarchy, which believed in the God-given authority of the tsar.

Russia had suffered a major military defeat in a war with Japan in 1904–5 and this had provoked a serious rebellion against the tsar. However, the situation changed after 1905. Russia had one of the fastest-growing economies in Europe. After the 1905 revolution, the tsar introduced a form of constitutional monarchy with a national parliament. Major changes took place in agriculture and there were more peasant landowners. Finally, the army underwent modernisation and expansion.

The extent of these changes has been questioned, but there is no doubt that Russia was seen to be a growing power, and military preparations were expected to be at their height by 1915. There was a considerable amount of investment from overseas, particularly from France, and the monarchy seemed more popular by 1914 than it had been for years.

However, Britain still distrusted Russia, despite the agreement the two countries had made in 1907 in an effort to end conflicts in Asia. Austria and Russia were rivals in the Balkans, and Russian desires to control the Turkish Straits and gain access to the Mediterranean through Ottoman territory were cause for concern. Germany was worried about the growth of Russian power, and relations between Russia and Germany had not been good since 1890, when the treaties in existence between the two countries since 1882 broke down.

The expansion of Russia in the Far East had been halted by the unsuccessful war against Japan in 1904–5, but after this Russian interest returned to the Balkans. Russia had initially encouraged the Balkan League in 1912, but it did not give any help to the Slav nations in the Balkan Wars. Its main ally, Bulgaria, was defeated, and Russia had to accept the creation of a pro-Austrian state in Albania by the terms of the Treaty of London in 1913. Russia's major source of influence in the area was Serbia, so when Serbia was threatened it was a matter of grave concern to Russia.

The Slavonic countries were linked to Russia culturally and through a shared religion, the Eastern Orthodox Church. However, Russia was not close to Serbia. Russian leaders did not necessarily like or trust Serbian leaders, and the tsar and his ministers greatly disapproved of Serbian terrorist activity. If Austria invaded Serbia, however, this would be a major blow to Russian power and prestige. It would end any hopes of expansion into the Mediterranean and, more importantly, it would suggest that Russia was powerless to support a fellow Slav state. The tsar would be seen as too weak to defend Russia's interests. Tsarism depended on its image and support from the army, the Eastern Orthodox Church and from Russian nationalists. In Serbia, fellow Slavs – fellow Orthodox Christians – were being bullied and oppressed. The pressure for

Figure 2.6 Two military monarchs – Nicholas II of Russia (left) and Wilhelm II of Germany (right). In this photo, they seem friendly enough but, though related, their countries fought each other bitterly in the First World War

action was enormous. In addition, the Bosnian Crisis of 1908–9 had humiliated Russia, and the country's leaders were determined that such an event should not happen again.

It was not at all clear whether Russia's military ally, France, would help, as the alliance between the two was only defensive. Nor was Britain's sympathy and support assured. However, there was at least the possibility that these nations would support the Russians, and this encouraged them to act. France's attitude certainly led Russia to believe that it would support the country in the event of war. The key to any action was to begin preparing Russia's large military resources for war. Military plans existed, but the forces needed to be mobilised in order for these plans to be executed. Without this, Russia could exert no real pressure – mobilisation would send a message to enemies and allies alike that the country intended to act. On 31 July 1914, the general mobilisation of the Russian army and navy was officially announced.

SOURCE B

After Count Berchtold has declared to Russia that Austria does not aim at any territorial acquisitions in Serbia, but only wishes to ensure security, the maintenance of the peace of Europe depends on Russia alone. We trust in Russia's love of peace and in our traditional friendly relations with her, that she will take no step which would seriously endanger the peace of Europe.

Telegram from Theobald Bethmann-Hollweg, the German chancellor (prime minister), to Russian foreign minister Sergei Sasonov, 26 July 1914.

QUESTION

Do you think Source B shows that Russia, rather than Germany or Austria, was to blame for the First World War? What are the value and limitations of this source for historians studying the causes of the First World War?

In fact there is some debate about Russia's intentions. Some historians argue that Russian military technicalities meant that mobilisation was necessary but did not necessarily mean that the country was determined on war. However, it is difficult to argue that Russia believed there was any real distinction between mobilisation and an intent to wage war. There was no genuine possibility that Russia could accept Austrian domination of Serbia. Given that Russia had the largest army in Europe and the likely support of France, war had become an acceptable risk.

Russia – the key factors

There were several key factors behind Russia's decision to declare war:

*   national feeling – support for fellow Slavs in Serbia ran high;
*   military power and preparation – Russian military expansion had given its statesmen the confidence to act, and military planning required early mobilisation;
*   the alliance network, which offered the chance of France and possibly Britain giving support;
*   the need to support the Russian Empire, which depended on the prestige and power of the tsar;
*   humiliation in foreign affairs in 1904–5 had led to revolution but success in war would strengthen the empire and unite the country behind Tsar Nicholas II;
*   the willingness of Russian leaders to take a risk and their expectations of a quick victory, with overwhelming numbers of troops, better railways and improved weapons.

Why Germany supported Austria

One of the great historical debates since the ending of the First World War has been whether or not Germany was to blame for the conflict. In 1961, the German historian Fritz Fischer produced a controversial book, *Germany's War Aims in the First World War*. Fischer's views are broadly outlined below:

*   Germany had plans for a war before the crisis of 1914 and used the assassination of Archduke Franz Ferdinand as an excuse to put them into practice.
*   There was a general aim to make Germany a dominant world power, as well as more specific aims, produced by the chancellor, Theobald Bethmann-Hollweg, for annexations of Belgium, part of France and European Russia.
*   There were strong links between the decision to go to war and domestic pressure groups urging expansion. Also, the imperial government wanted to stop internal discontent and the rise of socialism by an expansionist and nationalist foreign policy.
*   Germany deliberately encouraged Austrian war plans to provoke a crisis in which it could solve the problems of **'encirclement'** by France and Russia, dominate Europe and expand its territories.

Later, Fischer argued that there was more continuity than difference between German nationalist expansion in the Second World War under Hitler and the policies pursued by Kaiser Wilhelm II and his government in 1914.

Encirclement: This refers to a situation in which a country is surrounded by hostile states – in the event of war, this would prevent supplies and reinforcements reaching the encircled country, and face it with attacks on different fronts. Such a situation would lead to a fight to the death or surrender. German statesmen and military leaders expressed fears from the 1890s that Germany was being trapped in a ring of potentially hostile powers.

The counterargument in the 1960s was provided by another German historian, Gerhard Ritter. His views, in *Staatskunst und Kriegshandwerk: das Problem des 'Militarismus' in Deutschland* (*Statesmanship and War*, 4 volumes, 1954–68), were as follows:

- Germany was mainly motivated by the desire to keep Austria as a great power and to prevent Russia dominating the Balkans.
- Austria was determined on a risky war and pulled in Germany.
- There was no long-term plan, but rather a response to the particular crisis of Russian mobilisation.
- The evidence for Bethmann-Hollweg's support of annexations is questioned, as he actually opposed ideas put forward by the military for this.
- Germany miscalculated, expecting that Britain would not join the conflict and that support for Austria would not mean war, as other nations would be appalled by the murder of the heir to the throne.
- Military necessity was more important – there were plans to meet the threat from Russia, which involved war on France. Once Russia seemed intent on war then those plans had to be implemented.

The debate has been pursued by historians ever since. There is no general consensus about blame, but there are several factors to consider:

1 **Germany was a recent creation.** It had emerged only in 1871 as a result of wars against Austria and France. It then became a major industrial power with a strong army, which upset the whole balance of power in central Europe. With no natural frontiers, Germany was vulnerable to attack from other powers: it had to avoid fighting a war on two fronts.

2 **Germany needed alliances.** In 1879, the German chancellor, Bismarck, signed a defensive alliance with Austria-Hungary and balanced this with a Reinsurance Treaty with Russia. However, as Austria and Russia were rivals in the Balkans, this was bound to be difficult to maintain.

3 **There was little hope of a treaty with France.** France resented the defeat of 1870–1 and the seizure of Alsace-Lorraine by Germany. Germany had to be constantly aware of the French desire for revenge.

4 **In 1892–5, France and Russia signed a full military defensive alliance.** This opened up the possibility of a two-front war, which Germany would be likely to lose.

5 **The Schlieffen Plan.** To meet the threat of a two-front war, from 1898 the German army developed a plan devised by Count von Schlieffen. Assuming that Russia would be slower to mobilise, it argued for a rapid attack on France, which would lead to victory in weeks, after which forces would be taken to meet the threat from Russia. The plan was developed in such a way that it involved a rapid thrust through Belgium into northern France, using large forces. Without this, German troops would be divided between east and west and could lose the war.

6 **German naval expansion.** Germany built up its armed forces considerably after 1870, and in 1898 it decided on naval expansion. This caused significant anxiety in Britain. There was a costly naval race between the two powers to build the most modern type of battleship.

Face: The Schlieffen Plan was named after Count Alfred von Schlieffen (1833–1913). Schlieffen became head of the German army in 1891 and, following the Franco–Russian alliance, worked on a plan from 1895 to deal with war against France and Russia at the same time. The plan was circulated in high army and government circles from 1905. It relied on a quick defeat of France and rapid movement of troops by rail to deal with Russia.

Fact: Germany had big armies, but small naval forces. In 1898, plans were announced, masterminded by Grand Admiral Tirpitz, for a great German navy. This expansion would link Germany to its colonies and give it a place among the great naval powers of the world. It would also help German heavy industry and be popular at home. However, the building of the fleet, especially the battleships, was seen by Britain as a direct threat and was a major cause of war.

Fact: The German Socialist Party (SPD) grew rapidly after 1869, despite being persecuted by the state. It believed in greater power for the working class and reforms to help the people. The kaiser toyed with suppressing it, but in fact when war began most of the party supported the government.

The First World War

Figure 2.7 *The British battleship HMS* Dreadnought, *1906*

7 **German colonialism.** From the 1880s, Germany developed a colonial empire in East, West and South Africa, as well as in China and the Pacific. After 1888, Kaiser Wilhelm II spoke frequently about Germany's colonial role and the need for 'a place in the sun' alongside other European colonial powers. German policy seemed to be aggressive. Incidents in Morocco in 1905 and 1911 alienated French and British opinion, and revealed that Germany's only reliable ally was Austria.

8 **German fear of encirclement.** In 1909, Germany lent support to Austrian policy in the Balkans, alienating Russia. Germany itself was alienated by the colonial agreements between Britain and France in 1904, which settled existing differences but did not amount to a firm alliance, and by similar colonial agreements between Russia and Britain in 1907. There was talk of Germany being 'encircled'. In theory, Germany was allied to Italy as well as Austria, but it was clear that its only meaningful alliance was with Austria.

9 **Internal change.** The growth of German cities and industry after 1870 had led to urban problems and the rise of socialism. The German Socialist Party (SPD) became the leading party in the German parliament in 1912. However, there was also a rise in German nationalist and patriotic feelings. Many in the lower middle class supported German power, and the German army enjoyed huge prestige within the nation.

To sum up, war was very hazardous for Germany given its geographical position between two very powerful enemies. The plan it had evolved was a high-risk one and if it failed would result in a war on two fronts – an event likely to result in defeat. Also, Germany was a much divided nation – the working classes had strongly opted for socialism, but this ideology had little attraction for rural Germany, for the large lower middle class or for the richer industrialists and landowners. The predominantly socialist parliament might not support war. Germany's main ally, Austria, had been defeated in previous wars and its multinational armies were not necessarily reliable. Germany had pulled back from supporting Austria in 1913 and there is evidence that its statesmen tried to resolve the July 1914 crisis peacefully. Germany was not incapable of reaching agreements on naval expansion and colonial disputes. The generals were a powerful voice, but Germany was not a totally military state and in fact spent less per head on its forces than other powers before 1914.

Activity

Split into two groups.

- One group should identify possible reasons why Germany was more to blame than any other power for the war.
- The other group identifies as many reasons why Germany was not to blame.

Each group provides a tennis champion: the players can be helped at any time by the whole group. The first player 'serves' by sending an argument over the net (e.g., 'Germany is to blame for being militaristic and building up its forces to worry other countries'). This serve has to be returned by the opposing player, helped by the team (e.g., 'Germany was not the only country to build up its forces – Britain built up its navy and Russia built up its army').

The game is scored like a tennis match. When the opposing side cannot meet the argument, the point is won and they have to 'serve' a new argument.

The links between Balkan issues and the Moroccan Crises

Germany was greatly concerned by Russia's military expansion and the growth of its industry, transport and armed forces. It was also troubled by the economic and diplomatic links between Russia and France. Germany was conscious that in the disputes over Morocco it was isolated among the Great Powers, supported only by Austria.

The Moroccan Crises

There were two incidents centring on Germany's attempt to block France's control of Morocco and to restrict French power. As France had the neighbouring state of Algeria under its control, it saw Morocco as a vital area for its security. In 1904, Britain and Spain had accepted greater French control over Morocco. However, while visiting Tangier in 1905, Kaiser William II issued a statement of support for Moroccan independence. In doing so, he seemed to be challenging the colonial friendship treaty of 1904 between France and Britain. The crisis was resolved at the international Algeciras Conference (1906), which recognised both France and Spain's special political interests in Morocco.

The second crisis occurred in 1911, when a German gunboat arrived in Agadir, seemingly to protect German economic interests during a local uprising. Anti-European rioting in Morocco had caused France to send in more troops and the German naval action seemed to challenge this. The French objected and made preparations for war, as did Britain – which was horrified to see a German naval presence on the Atlantic coast of Morocco, as this threatened British approaches to the Mediterranean. A settlement was negotiated that gave France rights to a formal protectorship over Morocco. In return, Germany acquired part of the French Congo. These incidents left Germany isolated and made Britain and France distrustful.

By 1914, therefore, Germany felt it must support its ally Austria or risk serious consequences. If Russia drove Austria out of Serbia and established itself in the Balkans,

Fact: Although the agreement reached at the end of the Algeciras Conference accepted French interests in Morocco, it also acknowledged the independence of the sultan. More significant in the context of the First World War, however, were the sides various nations backed during the conference. Only Austria supported Germany. Notably, Britain and the USA supported France – foreshadowing their roles in the coming war.

Historical debate:
Was Germany mainly
responsible for the First
World War? Germany was
blamed for the war in the
peace treaty which ended
it in 1919 and there was a
specific 'War Guilt' clause.
Some historians like A.J.P.
Taylor in *The Course of
German History* saw German
aggression as part of a
long-term development.
The German historian Fritz
Fischer argued that there
were plans for expansion
eastwards and saw German
leaders as aggressors.
However, most historians
see the responsibility being
more shared and more
typical of modern views
is Christopher Clark *The
Sleepwalkers: How Europe
Went to War in 1914* (2012),
which sees European
statesmen drifting into
conflict.

**KEY CONCEPTS
ACTIVITY**

Causation:
Draw up a list, in
order of importance,
of which countries
you think contributed
to the outbreak of
war. Then write a
couple of paragraphs
to explain whether
or not any country
can be realistically
blamed for the First
World War.

then Germany's security would be seriously undermined. If France gave support and retook Alsace-Lorraine, then Germany would never be secure again. If the kaiser showed weakness then war might well follow anyway and the chance to use the Schlieffen Plan would be lost forever. If war had to be faced, Germany felt, it was better to face it now than in 1915 or 1916, when Russia would be stronger. War with France would probably come sooner or later as the issue of Alsace-Lorraine had been ongoing for more than 30 years. Nationalism and militarism were strong in France, and if socialism spread then it might weaken Germany and prevent any effective action in the future.

Above all, however, Germany realised that Russian mobilisation was an action that could not be ignored, and the German leadership could not avoid supporting its only major ally.

Germany – the key factors

- German militarism and nationalism meant there would be enthusiasm and support for war, as well as strong military forces to wage that war.
- Detailed plans existed, which led to hopes that the war would be as quick and decisive as Germany's wars of the 1860s had been.
- The security of the German Empire seemed to depend on war. Imperialism had increased conflicts with other powers and there may have been plans to expand Germany's imperial territory by conquests in Russia, where the Ukraine offered a tempting prospect of food supply for a growing German population.
- The 1879 alliance with Austria was a major consideration. Germany could not let Austria be defeated. It is arguable whether Germany gave too much support early on rather than restraining Austria.
- German statesmen took a number of risks. They risked supporting Austria in the hope that action against Serbian terrorism would not lead to general war; they risked war against France and Russia on the basis that a well-trained and well-equipped German army following a careful plan would bring a swift victory. It would have been a greater risk, however, to allow Austria to be defeated.

Why France mobilised its forces

The French Third Republic, which was established in 1870, was born out of defeat. The emperor, Napoleon III (ruled 1852–70), was captured by Prussian forces during the war that France was led into fighting against the newly expanded state of Prussia. By the terms of the peace treaty signed at Frankfurt in 1871, the new French Republic had to pay a large fine, as well as relinquish two of its historic provinces in eastern France, Alsace and Lorraine, to the new German Empire which was, humiliatingly, proclaimed at the palace of Versailles near Paris.

France had been one of the great military powers. Its conquests under Napoleon I (ruled 1799–1815) had made it virtual master of continental Europe. Its great military tradition was a major factor in its desire to regain both honour and its lost lands. In the French parliament, black-wreathed chairs were left vacant for absent representatives of the lost border provinces. The great city of Strasbourg was a particularly grievous loss and no French leader could abandon the idea of 'revenge'. Far from fading, nationalist feeling had grown in the years immediately before 1914. Military expenditure and the size of the armies had grown. France had cultivated its ally Russia, lent it money, engaged in military and diplomatic dialogues with the Russians, and had encouraged cultural links as well as better relations between Russia and Britain.

French military planning had focused on rapid and decisive attacks on Germany. Plan XVII (the French plan to attack decisively and robustly on the eastern frontier) envisaged a dramatic assault supported by the effective 75mm artillery and carried by the sheer willpower of French troops fighting in the French Revolutionary tradition. Better relations with Britain allowed French forces to be concentrated for a thrust against Germany: the French fleet was moved to Toulon in 1912 on the understanding that the British fleet would look after the Channel.

German actions since 1900 had reinforced the view that there could be little chance of a friendly rapprochement. The two Moroccan crises had seemed to show German aggression and had brought France and Britain closer. There were few jointly developed military plans, but the idea that Britain and France would cooperate after years of strained relations had followed the signing of the colonial agreements known as the Entente Cordiale ('friendly understanding') in 1904. France could risk taking action with the strong possibility of British support; it also had its military alliance with Russia to rely on. Action against Germany without this Russian help would not be possible so, with the July 1914 crisis over Serbia, with Russian mobilisation, and with the likelihood of a major European war between Russia, Austria and Germany, France saw its opportunity to reclaim its lost lands.

Despite industrial unrest and divisions between right and left in France, there were many indications that a war would gain strong nationalist support. There was a belief in the power of the French forces, and every expectation from the advice of the generals of a rapid victory against an enemy preoccupied with a two-front war.

France – the key factors

- France had been concerned by Germany's challenge to its empire.
- It had been building up its military power.
- The French hoped for support through their country's alliance with Russia and its friendship with Britain.
- Nationalism was strong – opinion in France supported the return of Alsace-Lorraine.
- Confidence in France's plan of attack made war a risk worth taking.

Why Britain declared war on Germany

Unlike the other major powers, Britain had little to gain in terms of land or influence by becoming involved in the war. It already had a vast empire and had no desire for territory in Europe. It had no firm alliances, except with Japan (1902) and one obligation to defend Belgium under a treaty of 1839. Britain's army was small, although it boasted a large and expensive navy. In 1914, Britain was ruled by progressive reforming statesmen whose party, the Liberals, had always stood for peace and negotiated settlements of international disputes.

Fact: Plan XVII was developed after the Franco–Prussian War by the French commander Ferdinand Foch. It was instigated in 1913 by the commander in chief Joseph Joffre with the intention of recapturing Alsace-Lorraine. When Germany began its invasion through Belgium, the plan was modified. However, the scale of the German offensive and the numbers of troops involved were totally miscalculated, and Plan XVII was swiftly abandoned.

QUESTION

What were the long- and short-term causes of France's actions in 1914?

Fact: Britain has always been concerned with Belgium and Holland, as these areas are points from which an invasion of England could be launched. However, the main concern had been with France. Britain would not accept the French invasion of Belgium after 1792 and this was a major cause of war with France between 1793 and 1814. In 1839, when there was more danger, Britain signed the Treaty of London guaranteeing the independence of Belgium.

2

Prior to the 1890s, Britain had not seen Germany as an enemy. However, a number of factors changed that:

- the aggressive statements of Kaiser Wilhelm II and his apparent jealousy of and hostility towards the British Empire;
- the hostility of Germany to Britain's dealings with the Boer republics in South Africa and the subsequent Boer War (1899–1902);
- the development of a German navy, which was seen by British leaders as an action directed mainly against Britain and that brought about a costly naval race;
- the attempts of the kaiser to undermine Britain's friendship with France in the Moroccan Crisis of 1905;
- the seeming danger of a German naval presence on the Atlantic coast of Morocco in the second crisis, in 1911.

In popular British imagination, Germany was now seen as a threat – evidenced by the number of spy stories featuring German secret agents in the years before the war. Germany was regarded as an economic competitor and a naval rival. The Kaiser Wilhelm II was considered to be a disturber of European peace, and German militarism was viewed as an unhealthy and threatening development.

However, despite all this, there was no certainty that Britain would go to war in 1914. Arms races in the past had not led to conflict. Relations with Russia were still not strong, and British policymakers had been more worried about Russian expansion in the Balkan Wars than about Germany. However, when a European war became a serious possibility by 3 August 1914, there were two overwhelming questions to consider:

- What role would Britain have in Europe or the world in the event of either France and Russia or Germany being victorious?
- Could Britain stand by while Belgium was occupied and France defeated?

Events since 1904 had given Britain a moral obligation to support France. Germany's invasion of Belgium offered Britain not only an excuse to intervene, but a genuine cause. In the long term, Britain hoped that any action would settle the outstanding issue of instability caused by Germany and its naval, colonial and commercial rivalry. As with the other countries, public opinion would support a war. Britain could count on its empire for support, and the risk was much lessened by the likelihood that Russia and France would do most of the fighting while Britain followed its traditional policy of using its navy to blockade Germany and restrict its trade.

Britain – the key factors

- Treaty obligations – even if these were not directly linked to firm alliances, they were important. The ententes with France and Russia gave Britain moral obligations, and the 1839 treaty with Belgium had to be enforced if Britain was still to be seen as a major power whose word could be trusted.
- National feeling could be counted on. Patriotic crowds rallied to 'King and Country'.

- The security of Britain – the chance to end the threat of the German fleet and the need to avoid any one power controlling the coastline of Europe from Germany to western France.

- Military power – in Britain's case naval power, which would prevent any invasion and enable Britain to wage war with limited casualties.

- The need to maintain a **balance of power** in Europe without one power being dominant.

- An acceptable risk – both France and Russia had very large armies; Germany would be encircled and it seemed unlikely that large British forces would need to be involved on land.

> **Balance of power:** This concept is concerned with the idea that one power or combination of powers should not dominate a region or continent but its/their influence should be balanced by other powers.

2.3 What were the economic, political, ideological and territorial causes?

General factors

Many analyses of the First World War have blamed various general factors as causes. These include:

- economic
- political
- ideological
- territorial.

Economic

Many analyses of the war were produced that blamed economic factors. For communists such as Vladimir Lenin, the war was the inevitable outcome of the final stage of capitalism – imperialism – where the capitalist countries of Europe fought for markets and resources. The empires of the great powers had been expanding in the 19th century and this had led to tensions. Britain and France nearly went to war over North Africa. Russia and Britain were rivals on the north-west frontier of India. Germany wanted imperial expansion and built a fleet to support this, which led to British hostility. Germany's economic expansion after unification led to an expansion of armaments and may have encouraged its rulers to seek greater power in Europe. There is evidence of German ambition to expand into Eastern Europe to expand markets and to secure grain supplies. Also economic decline in Austria-Hungary may have made it even more determined not to lose control over its territories in the Balkans.

Territorial

The main territorial issue was the loss of Alsace-Lorraine by France in 1871. Although there was some economic importance in the region in the form of metal ores, the main reason why this was important was because these were historic provinces that included the major city of Strasbourg and their loss was a blow to French national pride. A major aim for France was the recovery of lost territory. Austria by its policy towards Serbia showed its determination to resist any South Slav threat to its Balkan territories. The historian Fritz Fischer has argued that some elements in Germany favoured territorial expansion eastwards. Italy was motivated by a desire to gain the Italian-speaking areas still held by Austria – Italia irredenta – and was persuaded to join the allies in 1915 by promises of more territory here and in the Adriatic. Japan was an expansionist power and its motives in joining the war included the acquisition of German colonies in the Pacific and China.

Political

There was mass support for war in the growing nationalism that had been a feature in many countries. Russian support for fellow Slavs was strongly supported; Britain feared that it would appear weak and isolated if it did not support France and that such apparent weakness would have political consequences. French politics had been increasingly nationalistic in the years before the war and nationalist feeling for supporting Russia and starting a war to regain Alsace and Lorraine was strong. Austria feared the political effects on its empire if it did not take a strong line against Serbia. War may also have been seen as a means of escaping domestic political problems and unifying the nation. Britain faced great political problems in Ireland; Germany was concerned with the rise of socialism; in most of the countries there was a rise in working-class militancy brought about by industrial expansion and poor conditions. War was a popular option, politically.

In terms of international politics, it was the network of alliances that turned a local crisis into a European war, as countries felt they had to support allies or countries to which they had grown closer as a result of agreements. Countries would lose the confidence of allies and their own prestige if they did not act in support of their allies. International prestige was a powerful political factor. There was also the wider political issue of the balance of power in Europe. For Britain, victory by Germany and Austria would lead to a dangerous concentration of power. The rapid growth of Russian military and economic strength was a political threat to Germany. France and Russia depended on their alliance for political influence in Europe and neither could afford to let the other be defeated. Russia also had been supported politically by French loans.

Other causes

For some historians, such as A.J.P. Taylor, it was a war brought about by military plans and railway timetables – as soon as a crisis arose, the generals insisted that governments put mobilisation plans into operation and then the politicians lost control and war developed its own momentum.

Evaluation

Economic factors and imperialism

Imperial conflict certainly existed. However, some of the most difficult areas were between the countries that ended up as allies – Britain and Russia, and Britain and France. The German colonies did not cause much conflict, and imperialist ambitions do not explain the conflict in the Balkans. The struggle for resources does not explain the fervent desire of France to regain Alsace-Lorraine, whose natural resources, although they played a part in France's decisions, were not the driving force. Neither does the imperialism argument really explain British policy, as Britain was not short of colonies or resources in 1914. In addition, it does not explain the later American entry to the war. Neither Austria nor Russia could be seen as 'capitalist' powers in the way that Britain or America were. Austria did not attack Serbia to gain resources or for reasons of capitalist competition. There is limited evidence for desire for expansion for economic reasons in the decisions taken in 1914. The more compelling link to economic factors is that the rapid economic development of Europe and Japan in the Industrial Revolution gave countries the means to build up great stocks of weapons that they were convinced would lead them to victory.

Territorial causes

Italy and Japan were more obviously eager to use war to gain territory and France certainly wanted to recover Alsace-Lorraine. However, Britain had more than enough imperial territory and found it costly to defend. Germany and Austria were more intent on meeting threats – Germany of encirclement and Austria of the possible break up of its empire – than on a war of conquest. France was less concerned about the intrinsic value of Alsace-Lorraine than about the loss of prestige and standing as a great power that any loss of territory represented.

Political factors

The pictures of cheering crowds and the reminiscences of contemporaries all reveal a huge enthusiasm for war in 1914, without which the statesmen might not have risked military solutions. However, the élite diplomats, statesmen, politicians and rulers were not known for being responsive to the general populace and could have ignored the public mood if they had wished – instead they exploited it. Political enthusiasms and nationalism were unlikely to bring about war by themselves.

More compelling are explanations that focus on the importance of international politics, alliances and agreements. Statesmen felt obligations to support their allies or countries to which they had moral obligations, in the case of the Triple Entente. Failure to do so might have meant future isolation, loss of prestige and criticism at home. It could be argued that, without them, what was essentially a local crisis might not have led to a general war. However, this is doubtful. Most of the agreements were defensive and did not commit countries to any support if their ally took the initiative. Germany was not bound to support Austria when it invaded Serbia. France was not bound to help Russia when it mobilised in preparation for an attack on Austria to defend Serbia. Italy, although allied to Austria and Germany, remained neutral in 1914 and joined France and Britain in 1915. Britain had no obligation to help France. Even without alliances, could Russia have stood aside while Austria occupied Serbia? If Russia had gone to war with Austria, could Germany have remained neutral and allowed the Russians to penetrate the Balkans and Eastern Europe? If war had broken out in Eastern Europe, would France not have been tempted to attack Germany even without a formal alliance with Russia? Turkey, the USA, Romania, Bulgaria, Greece, Portugal and China all joined the war even though they were not part of the pre-war alliance system.

Military plans

The influence of military plans is an explanation based on practicalities rather than Marxist theory, but the decisions taken in July and August 1914 must be placed in a wider context. Military plans became acceptable because the alternative to using them

Theory of Knowledge

History and determinism:
'History abhors determinism, but cannot tolerate chance' – Bernard de Voto (1897–1955)

Can historical events be convincingly explained by a single factor that is more important than other factors, or is the nature of historical explanation bound to be 'multi-causal'? Does a historian have a duty to consider the relative importance of different causes or is this an artificial and unrealistic exercise because causation is, in practice, a web of long- and short-term factors? How does a historian discriminate between the relative importance of different factors and will this inevitably lead to subjectivity (i.e., the historian's own opinion)?

was unacceptable. Why statesmen rejected compromise and what they felt was at stake is a broader issue, and the plans themselves cannot be the whole explanation. The statistics of military expenditure do not show constant growth and not all nations armed themselves to the same degree. Militarism as an ideology had increased, but there is no suggestion that it dominated policy. For example, the great powers managed the Balkan Wars of 1912–13 by international diplomacy.

Activity

Look again at the information in this chapter about the assassination of Archduke Franz Ferdinand and consider how it brought all the countries together in the short term. Austria decided to invade Serbia; Serbia looked to Russia, which mobilised to help; France decided to mobilise in support of Russia; Germany decided to mobilise to support Austria and to risk war against France and Russia, which involved invading Belgium; Britain declared war on Germany to support France and protect Belgium. But these decisions had roots in longer-term factors.

It is important to understand how the long-term tensions link to the short-term events of 1914, and you must know what part each major country played in bringing about the First World War.

End of unit activities

1   Consider the following view:

    All these causes have some justification, but no single cause is likely to explain the war except perhaps that no country enters a war that it thinks it will lose or it believes will destroy it. What the decisions that led to war had in common was that the risk was seen to be worth taking and the chances of victory were good. These assumptions were shown to be grievously mistaken in the war to come.

    How convincing do you find it?

2   Create and complete a table like the one below to analyse the importance of long-term causes of war.

3   Decide for yourself on the order of importance for these general causes and explain your reasons for this order. This could be a class activity, with different students or groups of students gathering evidence for each general cause and presenting it to the class for discussion about its importance.

General cause of war	Evidence for the importance of the cause (you will need more space than this)
Economic	
Political: alliances and entente	
Political: nationalism	
Political: power balance	
Miscalculations by statesmen	
Other causes	

4 Look at the list of short-term causes in the table below. Copy the table and then complete it. Rank the importance of the event on a scale of 1–4 (1 = unimportant, 2 = not very important, 3 = important, 4 = very important). You do not have to restrict yourself to this format. Instead, you could use cards, putting a summary of an event's importance on one side and the 'mark' with a brief explanation on the back.

Incident	Why it was important	Its importance on a scale of 1–4
The Moroccan Crisis, 1905		
The Bosnian Crisis, 1908–9		
The Moroccan Crisis, 1911		
The Balkan Wars, 1912–13		
The assassination of Archduke Franz Ferdinand, 1914		

TIMELINE

1914 Germany implements Schlieffen Plan and invades France through Belgium; first use of gas as a weapon (by French troops).

Germany defeats Russian advances at the Tannenberg and Masurian Lakes.

German advance halted at the Battle of the Marne; both sides establish a defensive line through Belgium and France – the Western Front.

1915 German attacks in Russia – Eastern Front formed; British and French attacks on Western Front fail; British and French fail to take Constantinople in Gallipoli attacks.

Italy joins war against Austria and Germany; stalemate on all fronts.

1916 Battle of Verdun – Germany attempts to 'bleed France white'.

British attacks on Somme – little advance; first use of tanks; indecisive naval battle at Jutland.

Russian Brusilov offensive fails.

1917 Russian Revolution – last Russian attacks of war fail; some British successes in the west but the Battle of Passchendaele fails.

French attacks at Chemin des Dames fail.

Italian defeat at Caporetto.

USA joins war.

1918 Major German offensive (Operation Michael).

Allied counterattacks in France.

Turkish defeats in Middle East.

Austria defeated on Italian front.

11 November: Germany signs armistice.

KEY QUESTIONS

- What was the nature of the practices of the war of 1914–18?
- What were the main events?
- How important was technology in determining tactics and outcome?
- How important was the mobilisation of human and economic resources and the home front?

Overview

- Although it was a 'world war', the struggle of 1914–18 was largely carried out on two fronts. The so-called Western Front extended from the English Channel to the Swiss frontier. The Eastern Front was much more extensive, stretching from the Baltic to the Black Sea.

- The war was characterised by opening moves of intense activity and the deployment of millions of men. However, for much of the war, movement was restricted and both sides 'dug in' behind increasingly complex lines of defence.

- Beyond the two main theatres of war some more fluid campaigns took place – in the Middle East, in the Balkans and in Africa. Fighting also took place in Italy after it joined the war in support of France and Britain in 1915; however, the nature of the conflict in Italy was slow and static.

- A key feature of the war for much of its duration was attrition:

  Neither side found it possible to achieve a decisive outcome on the battlefield, so they had to wear down the enemy by draining it of men and resources.

  The war at sea saw few decisive encounters and was characterised by blockades and attacks on merchant shipping as each side tried to starve the other.

  The use of air power pointed the way to future developments, but the technology of the time was not far enough advanced for air warfare to play a decisive role.

- The final part of the war saw rapid changes that anticipated the nature of the Second World War, and indeed some of the post-1945 conflicts.

- The war led to the development of weaponry on a new scale. Artillery was larger and more precise; air power advanced far beyond the primitive combat of 1914. The great battleships had not proved significant, but submarines had nearly won the war for Germany. The tank was a major military development. After the war, it was accepted that future conflicts would rely heavily on both tanks and aircraft.

- The war relied on a great deal of public support and endurance. Civilians supported the war effort in many ways, including working in factories. Propaganda maintained popular support; the public accepted much greater controls by the state, such as rationing and conscription. The difference between soldiers and civilians was also less obvious than in previous wars – civilians themselves became the targets of military action as aircraft were used to bomb cities.

- There was some resistance to occupation by enemy forces, for example in Belgium and northern France, but this was met with severe repression and did not develop in the way it did in the Second World War. Nor was resistance promoted by the Allied powers. Overall, guerrilla warfare and organised resistance movements were not a major feature of this war.

- The war resulted in significant revolutions – two in Russia (in February and October 1917) and the attempted revolutions in Hungary and Germany. It also encouraged the growth of the communist and nationalist movements in China.

- Indirectly, the war encouraged a greater awareness of the need for political change – for example, in Italy and Germany, in the rise of the Labour Party in Britain, in demands for more rights for women, and in African and Asian nationalism.

2.4 What was the nature of the practices of the war of 1914–18?

A new type of war

The First World War was conducted on a scale unknown to previous generations:

- much larger armies were involved;
- casualties were much higher;
- the whole population was involved in the war effort;
- the state controlled the people and the resources of every country to a much greater extent than ever before;
- weapons were more destructive and more varied than previously, and included gas, flame-throwers, aircraft, huge artillery and more developed machine guns.

Factors that had revolutionised warfare since 1815 included the **Industrial Revolution,** the growth of modern science and technology, larger populations, a revolution in transport (especially railways), the growth of mass communication and national feeling. The industries developed in the 19th century allowed the production of weapons on a scale exceeding any previous war. Mass armies could be raised, supplied and transported. The whole nation could be involved in sustaining war.

Industrial Revolution:
The Industrial Revolution, which began in Britain in the late 18th century and spread to most of Europe and to Japan, involved mass production in large factories of engineering products using new forms of power; first steam then electricity. The development of steel allowed for new weapons and new battleships. Technological growth led to new transport and aeroplanes. It also led to a larger population, so industrial growth meant large armies equipped with machine-made weapons and increasingly powerful artillery. It also meant the growth of railways, which transported troops and motor vehicles and military aircraft.

Figure 2.8 A Belgian troop train leaving Ostend on the way to the front in 1914

KEY CONCEPTS

Change and continuity: According to Source C, how was the First World War different from previous wars? How does this source explain the changes? What other elements influenced changes in warfare by 1914?

SOURCE C

The scarlet-and blue-coated infantrymen of Napoleon's age advanced into battle with colours streaming and bands playing. The combatants of 1918 were clad in khaki or field grey, their faces obscured by steel helmets and gas masks had lost their humanity and individuality in fighting industrial warfare. The dramatic change in warfare can be linked, in the first place, to national economic development. ... Between 1815 and 1914, for example, Germany's production of coal increased 200 fold and of pig iron 18 times. From these raw materials were fashioned the steel and then the guns and rifles which affected a revolution in fire-power.

H. Strachan. 1996. The Oxford History of Modern Europe. *Oxford: Oxford University Press, pp. 170–1.*

2.5 What were the main events?

The war of movement, 1914 – the battle for the frontiers

The early stages of the war were dominated by the German Schlieffen Plan and its failure. This bold concept was based on certain key facts:

- Germany needed to avoid a long war on two fronts, given its lack of natural frontier defences.
- The coming war would be waged against France and Russia, both of which had large forces.

- Russia's poor railway system, inefficient military organisation and the large distances its troops would need to travel to reach the battlefronts meant that the country would need time to mobilise.
- Germany's railways were efficient and its military planning was well-developed.
- Germany needed to defeat France first. The rapid defeat of France in 1870 gave the military planners confidence that the same could be achieved now.

The Schlieffen Plan thus concentrated large forces against France, leaving smaller forces to defend the East. The key points of the plan were:

- The main German attack on France would take place in the north, on the assumption that France would attack Germany in Alsace-Lorraine.
- A massive drive by the German right wing would encircle Paris, taking the French by surprise.
- German forces would hold the French attacks until the right wing had taken Paris and moved to attack the French from the rear.
- The railways that had been used to concentrate forces against France would then carry German troops to the East, where they would defeat Russia – again by concentrating a large proportion of manpower in one place.

The Schlieffen Plan had been developed in great detail, but as the German offensive began, some major problems appeared:

- By the time the plan was put into operation, Russian railways and organisation had improved, and Russian forces were available for action far sooner than Germany had anticipated.
- Railways could concentrate forces in one area, but the German armies had to march to battle. As they travelled further from their own bases and supplies, they lost the advantage to the defenders.
- The Schlieffen Plan did not anticipate resistance from Belgium, nor did it make any provision for British forces stepping in to resist the advance.
- The plan did not take into account France's use of aircraft observation to track German movements and allow countermeasures to be taken.
- The planners had underestimated the impact of modern weaponry. Relatively small numbers of defenders could hold up large numbers of attackers by the use of automatic weapons.

Behind many of these issues lay a fundamental misunderstanding of modern warfare. Victory would not be achieved by brilliant strategic moves or the fall of capital cities, but by the side that destroyed the enemy armies in the field. In a war between peoples, victory could only be achieved by the complete destruction of the enemy's will to win. Germany had achieved remarkably swift and decisive victories against Austria in 1866 and France in 1870, but it was unlikely that the Schlieffen Plan could achieve success in a matter of weeks. Too much had changed by 1914.

In the event, the plan failed for a number of reasons. First, the timetable broke down as the Germans faced unexpected resistance in Belgium, holding up the all-important advance at Liège. Further delays occurred as the British forces fought fiercely at the battles of Mons and Le Cateau, before being forced to retreat in the face of greatly superior numbers. Hot weather also contributed to the slow progress of the advance. Thus, the Schlieffen Plan ran into difficulties from the outset.

Fact: The German advance was held up by the unexpected appearance of the small British Expeditionary Force (BEF) at Mons. The expert rifle fire of these well-trained troops caused heavy casualties in the ensuing battle, on 23–24 August 1914. A legend later spread – exploited by British propaganda – that angels had appeared at Mons to support the British. Despite this, British troops were still forced to retreat.

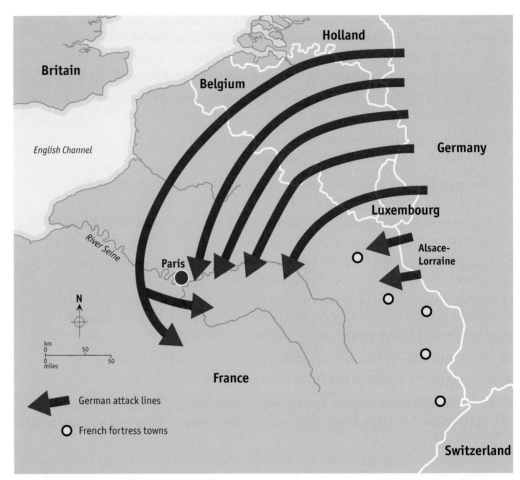

Figure 2.9 Map showing the Schlieffen Plan

In addition, pre-war changes had weakened the numerical strength of German troops in the key thrust through Belgium. The unexpected appearance of Russian forces in eastern Germany threw out the calculations of the planners. Greater numbers of troops than originally intended were dispatched to the East to guard against a Russian invasion.

Finally, a fatal decision was taken to adapt the plan: instead of encircling Paris as originally conceived, the German armies would change direction and attack Paris from the east. This caused confusion on the ground, and the French were able to monitor German movements from their reconnaissance aircraft. Seeing the German flank exposed, the French rallied their forces for a counterattack and defended Paris on the River Marne. The Germans were forced on the defensive and withdrew to stronger positions.

The war of movement – the next phase

The war of movement now entered a key phase. French attacks further south resulted in heavy casualties and prevented a German breakthrough. The German offensive ground to a halt. Russia invaded eastern Germany but was unable to exploit its advantage by a drive on Berlin. Austrian advances into Serbia had not been as rapid as hoped. As war plans across Europe broke down, both sides resorted to rapid improvisation.

In the West, each side tried to outflank the other – i.e., to extend their lines in the hopes of getting behind the enemy. A race to the sea began, and the front line extended to its furthest point in the south – the Swiss frontier. Each side struggled to gain the most advantageous positions, especially high ground. Once these had been achieved, troops 'dug in' and awaited further instructions. In smokeless battlefields, soldiers on the ground were easy targets, and they simply had to remain out of sight. Temporary trenches became more developed as increasing amounts of men and equipment were brought up to the front line. Engineers constructed more extensive defences. Heavy artillery was also brought up to the battle fronts.

The development of a long, fortified front line, with both sides putting large numbers of troops in trenches and erecting barbed-wire defences, was not something military planners had anticipated, and it resulted in a totally new form of warfare. By November 1914, the rapid-movement phase of the war in the West was over and a new phase began, which dominated the events of the war until March 1918.

In the East, Germany employed traditional tactical warfare to expel the Russians. At the battles of Tannenberg and the Masurian Lakes, Russian forces were outmanoeuvred and encircled. The Russian failure to exploit its initial successes was the greatest lost opportunity of the war and cost Russia dearly. Driven back, the Russian armies had to regroup and defend, and the conflict on the Eastern Front, like that in the West, became one of trench warfare.

The war expands – Turkey, the Far East and Africa

Meanwhile, the geographical scope of the war had expanded. Turkey joined when British naval forces chased two German warships, the *Goeben* and the *Breslau*, into Constantinople.

Although traditionally pro-British, Turkey's new reforming government leaned towards Germany, which had trained its armed forces and seemed more likely to help Turkey resist Russia.

Fact: In the Battle of Tannenberg, 25–28 August 1914, the German forces encircled and destroyed the Russian troops that had invaded Germany, taking 95 000 prisoners and killing 30 000 people. The German commanders Hindenburg and Ludendorff became famous, and dominated the war effort from 1916.

Fact: British attacks were made on German South-West Africa and colonies in East and West Africa. The German commander Paul von Lettow-Vorbeck, together with 30 000 men, evaded capture and waged effective war against Britain right up to November 1918, despite being outnumbered. However, most German overseas possessions were taken by the Allies and never regained by Germany.

KEY CONCEPTS ACTIVITY

Significance: Static trench warfare was very important in this war. Find five reasons why this was so and put them in order of importance.

Figure 2.10 New weapons of war – gas and machine guns; here British machine gunners are firing during the Battle of the Somme, wearing gas masks

Japan took advantage of the defensive alliance it had signed with Britain against Russia in 1902 to declare war on Germany, and to overrun German colonies in the Pacific and the German port of Kiaochow in China. The overseas empires of the European powers were now involved in the war, and campaigns began in Africa as attacks were made on German colonies in 1915. Italy was persuaded to join France and Britain by promises of gaining Italian-speaking areas under Austrian control and extending its empire. However, although the war was spreading, it was clear that the most decisive battles would occur in Europe.

Characteristics of the war on the Western Front

- The early fighting had shown that defence was easier than attack. Artillery and machine guns, together with rapid-fire magazine rifles, had a devastating effect on attackers.
- Once trenches and support trenches had been dug, barbed wire established and light railways built to carry more men and supplies to the front lines, attack became even more difficult.
- Large numbers of troops and a great deal of heavy artillery and weaponry were concentrated in quite a limited area. The entire industrial capacity of advanced modern states was focused on producing heavy weapons and supplying mass armies. But the troops could not manoeuvre and instead they faced each other over devastated strips of land.
- To win, forces had to break though the trench lines, then engage with the enemy, destroy the opposing armies and move through to take key strategic points to prevent further resistance.
- Breakthrough alone would not achieve victory, but if the war could become more mobile then cavalry could once again be used, and there was the possibility of traditional warfare in which armies were surrounded and destroyed. However, breakthrough was the first step and there were considerable problems in achieving this.

Why was it so hard to break through?

Commanders were faced with large concentrations of enemy forces in developed trench lines, supported by heavy artillery, machine guns, mortars, barbed wire and accurate long-range automatic rifles. The lines could not be outflanked and aircraft were not developed enough for precision bombing. The situation was more like siege warfare, but because of the improvised nature of the battle for the frontiers, the lines were established in open country or in small villages (apart from the large French forts at Verdun). The line was formed quite randomly at points in the French and Belgian countryside where the armies had fought and could advance no further.

The only real plan in 1915 was to accumulate heavy artillery to inflict devastating damage on the enemy line, then to advance troops to gain control of the gap in the line and push forward. These attacks failed to achieve a major breakthrough. The heavy casualties of 1915 continued into 1916, with British attacks in Flanders, French attacks in the Champagne region and German attacks in the East. Italy's entry into the war opened up new, heavily defended lines, while Romania's entry brought it a crushing defeat by Germany. An attack by Britain on Constantinople to knock Turkey out of the war ended in more trench warfare on the Gallipoli Peninsula and eventual British withdrawal.

Fact: Australian, New Zealand and British forces were landed on the Gallipoli Peninsula in April 1915 to take Constantinople after a naval attack failed. The Turks, under the command of the future leader Kemal, held the high ground and forced the so-called ANZAC forces to dig in on shallow hillsides, where they were trapped. After heavy casualties, the British decided to evacuate. It was a humiliation for Britain, and particularly for Winston Churchill, who had been the architect of the attacks.

A key example – the Battle of the Somme, July 1916

In 1916, one of the most infamous battles in the history of warfare took place – the Battle of the Somme. British and some French forces faced well-established German positions on the River Somme in France. The Allies were anxious to break through to relieve the pressure on France, which was being attacked by the Germans at Verdun, and to support a major Russian attack. For the first time, Britain had amassed a large army and its industries had supplied great amounts of heavy artillery.

The attack was focused on 13km (8 miles) of front, and millions of shells were fired onto the German line in what was probably the greatest artillery bombardment in history. Aerial photography revealed the position of the German lines and the British gunners focused on these targets. An attempt to destroy the German defences by mining under their lines and setting off high explosives was made. Such large amounts of explosive were used that the explosions could be heard in Britain. The crater left behind German lines by this bombardment amazes even today.

Planning had been intense – attacks were made in both the north and south, intended to divert the Germans. The main attacks had well-defined objectives and the troops were well briefed. There was enormous enthusiasm and high morale on the British side. The commander, **Sir Douglas Haig**, was both experienced and well-respected. Yet these attacks did not achieve a decisive breakthrough any more than those made in 1915 or the German attacks at Verdun in February 1916. There were several reasons for this:

- The artillery bombardment was terrifying and did destroy a lot of the front-line positions, but the defences were deep and they extended to the rear. With troops well dug in defensively, it was impossible to destroy every German unit.

- There was no element of surprise. The Germans knew that when the bombardment stopped an attack would begin, so they were ready to deploy their defenders and use their own long-range artillery behind the lines to pour fire on the attackers.

- The crucial time was the gap between the end of the bombardment, the detonation of the mines, and the start of the assault. Seconds were vital, as once the big guns stopped, the Germans would rush their machine guns to the front. Huge forces acting together could not go 'over the top' quickly. Commanders allowed minutes to pass before an attack was launched.

- The mass armies were not long-serving professional soldiers, many of whom had been killed in the initial fighting. The view was that keen, but essentially amateur, troops needed to stay together and effect a concentrated attack. They therefore provided easy targets for the defenders.

- The actual attack – a rush towards a broken and demoralised enemy – had seemed easy in theory, but in practice it was more difficult. The ground between the two sides had been churned up by artillery. Shelling had also caused barbed wire to be distributed throughout **'no-man's land'**, forcing troops to bunch together rather than being spread out.

- There was no effective radio communication between the commanders and their forces. Once the attack began, the troops were effectively on their own. If a unit was successful, it could not radio in and bring other units to the key area. The commanders had a limited idea of what was happening. Forces in areas that met heavy resistance, therefore, did not stop attacking and shift to areas where resistance was light.

Figure 2.11   Sir Douglas Haig (1861–1928)

A cavalry officer who took over the command of British forces in France in 1915 from Sir John French, Haig was a well-educated but withdrawn commander. He was responsible for the major attacks of the Somme (1916) and Passchendaele (1917), for which he has been seen as a 'butcher', careless of casualties. Haig also commanded the victorious forces in 1918 and rallied his men after the German attacks in March of that year. He founded the Royal British Legion after the war, which continues to look after former soldiers.

No-man's land: The name given to the land between the opposing trenches on the Western Front.

- Once the attack began and the British moved further from their starting point, the Germans had the advantage as they were able to bring up forces from the rear and use their massive heavy artillery. The only way an attack could be successful was if the initial assault achieved all its objectives and the gains were quickly consolidated. The Germans had to be driven back before they could begin an effective counterattack. However, conditions on the front line made this very unlikely.

- In later wars, even later in the First World War, attacks by small groups with a more flexible command structure managed to break through. Only with more modern field communications could attacks have been successful on the Somme. In later wars, for example, commanders were able to call in strategic air attacks, but these were not available in July 1916.

The only successes on the first day of the Battle of the Somme were the diversionary attacks to the south. Enemy troops in these areas had not been forewarned by heavy bombardment, so the generals maintained the element of surprise and gained their objectives. Elsewhere, little was achieved but heavy losses – 60 000 dead, wounded and missing on the first day on the British side. The resources produced by the great industrial powers were too much to be overcome by bravery alone, but technology had not yet produced the key weapons that might have broken the deadlock – military aircraft, tanks with heavy armour and powerful cannon, and modern communications.

Figure 2.12 Infantry going to war, circa 1916; this image shows German troops going 'over the top'

Were the generals to blame?

The case against the generals

- The generals were too rigid in their thinking. The same tactics were tried again and again, even after they had failed.
- They were 'butchers', careless of human life, remote in their headquarters away from the battlefield and unaware of the awful conditions in which their men were fighting and dying.

- They were often too old and thinking of past wars. They did not understand modern warfare, and instead dreamed of great cavalry charges and Napoleonic victories.
- They were overly concerned with matters of military honour and allowed battles to continue even when there was little hope of winning.
- They were unrealistic in their plans, preferring grand strategies to more achievable aims.
- They were often remote and dictatorial, and refused to take advice.

The British commander Sir Douglas Haig has been particularly singled out for blame, but other leaders have not escaped. Erich von Falkenhayn, the German commander in 1916, earned a poor reputation after the attacks on Verdun in which the Germans aimed to 'bleed France white' by simply killing as many French troops as possible. The Italian commanders were seen as upper-class Piedmontese militarists, sending masses of Italian troops to their deaths in pointless conflicts in the mountain regions between Austria and Italy, and then showing their incompetence by allowing a full-scale disaster in 1917 when the Germans and Austrians attacked at Caporetto.

The German General Erich von Ludendorff has been regarded as over-ambitious in his attacks of 1918, and then being weak and hysterical when they failed. Both he and his fellow commander Paul von Hindenburg have been criticised as dictators, dominating the civilian government of Germany. When the US joined the war, its commander John J. Pershing seemed unwilling to learn anything from the events that had taken place, and has been accused of throwing inexperienced troops into poorly planned battles. The French general Robert Nivelle has one of the worst reputations for ordering a suicidal attack in 1917, which led to a mutiny in the French army. Russian generals have also been accused of incompetence and failing to supply their armies properly.

Biographies and campaign histories find military incompetence everywhere. In the inter-war years, this view was common, curiously more among the victorious powers, and it explains much of the reluctance by Britain, France and the USA to fight another war. The viewpoint was less common in Germany, which, although it had lost more men than Britain, did not see such a reaction against its military leaders. Paul von Hindenburg was even elected president in 1925.

Fact: The Battle of Caporetto began on 24 October 1917 and was one of the biggest Allied disasters of the war. Italy had joined the war in 1915 on the promise of regaining Italian-speaking areas still under Austrian rule. Italy lost 600 000 men in the war, but achieved little. The defeat at Caporetto forced the Italians back almost to Venice, and Italy had to be saved by French, British and US forces.

Historical debate:
Historian Norman F. Dixon, in his famous study, *On the Psychology of Military Incompetence*, offers a general theory of poor leadership. John Laffan's *Butchers and Bunglers of World War I*, and Denis Winter's *Death's Men* both argue that commanders on the Western Front needlessly condemned their troops to suffering and death. However, such views were later challenged by other historians.

Figure 2.13 (From left to right) Haig and Joffre, the French commander, appeal to the future British prime minister, David Lloyd George, 1916; Lloyd George became increasingly sceptical about Haig's plans and abilities

Figure 2.15 David Lloyd George (1863–1945)

He was a radical politician who took charge of munitions in 1915 and rose to be prime minister in December 1916. He led a determined war effort by increasing the power of the state. He remained prime minister until 1922, but never held office again.

Figure 2.14 The burial site at Verdun – Falkenhayn's aim to 'bleed the French white' succeeded here, but the bones are also those of German troops who were killed in their thousands from February to November 1916

The counter-view

Revisionist historians, such as John Terraine in *Haig: The Educated Soldier* and Gary Sheffield in *The British Army in the First World War*, have challenged the hostile view of commanders for a variety of reasons.

1 Although there was incompetence, it strains credibility to blame all generals in all countries for the war's high cost and indecisive nature.

2 The idea of rigidity in military tactics has been challenged. There could not be major developments because of the nature of the weaponry and the strategic situations, but the way in which war was fought did develop.

- The use of artillery became more sophisticated, with 'creeping barrages' that fired shells to positions just ahead of the attackers. Tunnels and mines were used effectively to achieve surprise attacks (for example, in the Allied attack on Germany at Vimy Ridge, 1917).

- Both Germany and Russia developed more flexible tactics, using smaller units with local commanders who had greater freedom to show initiative and avoid pointless assaults on strong points. This can be seen in the Russian Brusilov offensive of 1916, for example, or the German attacks in March 1918, which used 'storm troop' tactics developed on the Eastern Front by the German colonel, Oskar von Hutier. Here, a short bombardment was followed by attacks by smaller, highly trained units, which probed for weaknesses in the defence and, once a breakthrough had been made, quickly followed up with mass infantry directed at key points.

- The Allies developed a united command and coordinated their attacks far more in 1918 using planes, tanks, flexible artillery bombardment and infantry in a way that anticipated the fighting of the Second World War.

- All sides welcomed new technology: poison gas (although this proved an ineffective weapon); mines; the tank – first used by Britain in 1916; military aircraft. Horses

Fact: Poison gas accounted for 1.25 million casualties. Although initiated by French forces in 1914, the first major use was by the Germans in 1915 using chlorine. This triggered reprisals and regular use by both sides. In 1917, mustard gas was used against the Russians on the Eastern Front. Gas masks became a regular feature of war, but gas was not an effective weapon, being dependent on favourable winds.

were important for transport but it is not true that commanders were wedded to cavalry charges.

3   The issues of heavy losses and military incompetence need to be decoupled. Given the mass armies, the development of heavy weapons and the insistence of national leaders on complete victory, rather than negotiated peace – a view by and large supported by the populations – heavy casualties were bound to occur. The casualties of the Second World War, with better weapons and skilled commanders far more under the control of the political leaders, were higher, yet the generals are not blamed in most historical writing. Napoleon is regarded as a military genius, yet the casualty figures for his battles are huge. Mobile warfare is not less costly than static trench warfare.

4   It is not true that generals were remote and did not fully understand the conditions on the front lines. However, military intelligence was not as developed as it was later, and it was difficult to know what was happening once action started. The death rate in battle among generals was high, but in modern war it was not the place of high-ranking officers to be involved at direct operational level.

5   Although many of the leaders had unattractive character traits, nevertheless they were prepared to take advice. When the French forces mutinied in 1917, Marshal Pétain did not punish excessively and he was cautious in the attacks of 1918. New ideas were adopted and – a point that is often overlooked – there were considerable successes. The German attacks of 1918 might well have achieved victory had there been more reserves available. After initial failures, the British campaigns in the Middle East in 1917–18 successfully defeated Turkey. The final campaigns of Britain, France and the USA brought Germany to an **armistice,** and Austria and Germany were successful in their attacks on Italy in 1917. The Germans and Austrians were able to knock the much larger forces of Russia out of the war by 1917. Not all aspects of the war were characterised by failure or stalemate.

Concluding the main events

In broad terms, after the initial advances and retreats of 1914, 1915 was characterised by German successes in the East and Allied failures in the West.

By 1916, nations had increased the size of their armies and had mobilised their resources for war on a much larger scale. Industrial countries were gearing themselves to produce more and more ammunition and heavier weapons. Militarily, the advantage seemed to lie with Germany and its allies.

*   Germany had advanced well into Russia.
*   German **U-boats** were posing a serious threat to Britain's shipping and its vital links with North America, which was producing a lot of Britain's supplies.
*   British and French attacks in France had failed to achieve breakthrough.
*   Italy had joined the Allies but had made little progress in attacking Austria.
*   Britain had failed to eliminate Turkey by attacking at Gallipoli, and had been defeated in Mesopotamia (Iraq) by the Turks.

In 1916, the Germans decided to concentrate on the Western Front. In theory, the strongest point here was the fortified area in and around Verdun. The great forts there

---

Theory of Knowledge

History and morality: *'Suffer no man and no cause to escape the undying penalty which history has the power to inflict on wrong' – St Thomas Aquinas (1225–74)*

Moral judgements belong to the philosopher, not the historian – do you agree? Is it part of the historian's task to make moral judgements and to condemn historical figures such as Haig, or is this unhistorical? If a historian explains decisions that cost thousands of lives, must he or she go further and make a moral standpoint clear in order to prevent the recurrence of such tragic events, or is this merely exercising hindsight and introducing an element that the reader should bring as he/she thinks appropriate? However, if a historian is morally neutral, does he or she run the risk of condoning loss of life?

Armistice: An agreement to stop fighting. This may lead to a formal surrender but is not the same thing. By accepting that hostilities should cease, the Germans did not realise that they would have peace terms imposed on them without the right to attend the peace talks. The word is thus important in understanding future conflict.

U-boat: Unterseeboot, meaning submarine. Most U-boat attacks occurred on the surface in the First World War, when the submarine would come up, attack and then submerge.

were thought to be impossible to take. France would never surrender them, as they represented security and historic French honour. It was at Verdun, therefore, that the Germans decided to attack – not for a strategic breakthrough but to 'bleed France white' by drawing increasing numbers of troops into battle and causing French strength to ebb away in a bloodbath. It was the fullest expression of the war of attrition – a war that would be won by wearing down enemy resources.

The Battle of Verdun began with unexpected German successes at Fort Douaumont and Fort Vaux. It continued as a bloody conflict of mass artillery and costly attack and counterattack. The battle lasted most of the year, and cost the Germans almost as many lives as the French. To relieve the pressure, Britain attacked on the Somme. This similarly became a drawn-out battle of attrition, in which little ground was gained and thousands died. A more promising Russian advance under General Alexei Brusilov began well but ended in deadlock. The one great naval battle of the war – Jutland – ended with both the British and German fleets returning to port after a costly exchange of fire that settled little. There were British gains in the Middle East, but by the end of 1916 little had been gained in return for the huge expenditure of life and equipment.

The different arenas of war

The war at sea

At the start of the war, Germany attacked Allied shipping with destroyers, but these were defeated by the British and Australian fleets, and Britain was able to blockade German ports. Germany increasingly relied on its U-boats (submarines), but this changed after the U-boat *U20* sank the liner *Lusitania*, killing 128 Americans. This prompted the US, not yet drawn into the conflict, to instruct the Germans to restrict their submarine warfare. In 1916, the Germans planned to lure a smaller part of the British fleet into the North Sea and destroy it with a great fleet that would sail out of the major German naval base at Kiel. However, the plan was discovered by British intelligence and instead the Germans faced the might of the entire British grand fleet, which sailed from its base in the Orkney Islands. The ensuing naval battle of Jutland, however, was inconclusive. Technically, the Germans won, but their surface fleet retreated back to base and did not re-emerge for the rest of the war.

Once again the Germans relied on submarines, but to stop the British trade with the USA more and more US seamen were being killed in unrestricted U-boat warfare, which recommenced in 1916. The battle against the submarines was waged first by British and then US naval forces escorting convoys after April 1917, when German naval policy brought about US entry to the war. However, as in the Second World War, the U-boats were a severe threat. In April 1918, the U-boat base at Zeebrugge was successfully attacked and blocked by a British naval raid. The German sailors were restless in Kiel and mutinied in 1918 when they were ordered out for a last great battle with Britain.

Britain had used its navy to maintain trade links with North America, to ensure war supplies, to keep the link with France open and to transport and supply troops fighting in the Middle East. However, after its initial successes against German surface raiders (armed ships made to look like ordinary merchant vessels) in 1914, the British navy had been less successful in direct conflict with the Germans. Naval warfare was significant in bringing the US into the war. In itself, however, naval warfare was not decisive. The limitations were shown when British warships could not defeat the Turks at Gallipoli

Fact: The *Lusitania* was a famous Cunard Line ship that was sunk off the Irish coast by U-boat *U20* on 4 May 1915. Some 128 Americans on board died, and the USA issued a warning that led the Germans to restrict U-boat warfare until 1917. In fact, the *Lusitania* was carrying 4000 cases of ammunition. The incident worsened relations between the USA and Germany, and was one reason for the USA's entry into the war in 1917.

in 1915. The great battle between the British and the German fleets proved indecisive. The German submarine campaign – although it led to shortages and caused great concern – was not able to starve Britain out of the war. The British naval blockade – although it hit German supplies and morale – did not in itself bring an end to the war.

The war in the air

In 1914, the use of planes in war was limited to reconnaissance. The troop movements in the Schlieffen Plan were visible from the air, for instance, and aerial photography rapidly improved. The primitive use of bombing and weapons fired from planes quickly developed. The Germans dropped bombs on Liège from aircraft as early as August 1914. From this developed attempts to shoot down enemy planes, and all countries increased their production of military aircraft. Individual 'dog fights' became a feature of warfare, with the emergence of 'air aces' like the German airman Baron Manfred von Richthofen and the British flyer Albert Ball (both of whom were killed in action). The poorly armoured planes were vulnerable and casualty rates were high. However, as machine guns were mounted on planes, and as bombing capacity increased, the potential for aircraft as weapons of war developed rapidly, as did the numbers of planes. In 1914, France possessed 162 aircraft. By 1918, it had 11,836, including 3,437 on the front lines. Britain established an effective Flying Corps, which became the RAF. Such developments made it possible to carry the war much further afield, to the enemy home front. The effectiveness of such air warfare was seen dramatically during later conflicts such as the Spanish Civil War and the Second World War.

The Germans terrorised London and Paris by Zeppelin (gas-filled airships) raids until 1916, when inflammatory bullets and better air defences made them less effective. The Germans' heavy Gotha bombers and the subsequent Giants could carry 2000lb bombs, and by 1918 London's air defences included anti-aircraft guns and barrage balloons. Both sides developed air technology but the Allies took the lead in using their planes in conjunction with infantry, tanks and artillery, anticipating the coordination of air and land warfare that was a more significant feature of wars after 1939.

The situation in 1917

The massive losses did not lead to any significant demand for peace, and it was remarkable that the powers sustained such heavy fighting without greater unrest at home. However, this changed in 1917.

In Russia, the disappointments of the campaigns of 1916, the shortages caused by poor management of the war and unexpectedly large demonstrations in the capital, Petrograd (as St Petersburg had been renamed), brought about a crisis in February 1917. Tsar Nicholas II was away from the capital, commanding his own troops, and he lost the confidence of Russian military, industrial and political leaders. His soldiers would not fire on the protesting crowds in Petrograd, and shortly afterwards the tsar abdicated. Germany took advantage of the disruption and encouraged Russian political unrest. The Russian Front virtually collapsed, though it was not until a second revolution brought the Marxist Lenin to power in October 1917 that Russia officially withdrew from the war, in March 1918.

Russia's collapse put considerable pressure on France and Britain to increase their war effort. In an attempt to keep Britain short of materials and vital imported food, the Germans stepped up their submarine campaign. However, in order to make the blockade effective, the U-boats were forced to attack US and neutral shipping as well as

Fact: The war in the air, while significant, did not really decide the outcome of a war of attrition in which very large armies struggled to break through on a narrow front. In phases of greater mobility, aircraft played a part in providing intelligence and eventually by 1918 in supporting offensives. However, not until the Second World war did air technology develop in such a way as to play a major part in the final outcome.

Figure 2.16 T.E. Lawrence (1888–1935)

Known as 'Lawrence of Arabia' – he was a scholar who was recruited to act as liaison officer with the Arab tribes who had rebelled against their Turkish ruler. He took part in guerrilla warfare in Arabia and became a national hero. Lawrence opposed the poor treatment of the Arabs after the war and went into private life, changing his name and joining the RAF. He died in a motorcycle accident in 1935.

Storm troopers: Small groups of highly trained German soldiers who sought out weak points and used maximum force to break through. Some became Nazis after the war, and Hitler took the name for his own paramilitary forces. They were first used by the Germans in Russia.

Railheads: The points to which the railways brought troops and supplies for the front. Capture of the railheads would disrupt the entire supply line.

British ships – in defiance of the warning the US had issued in 1915 after the sinking of the Lusitania. This reversion to unrestricted submarine warfare was seen as provocative by the USA, which was also angered at the discovery that Germany had been plotting with Mexico to wage war against the USA. In April 1917, a combination of these factors led the USA to declare war on Germany.

US forces were small but the country's manpower and industrial potential was huge. With America preparing for war and with Russia on the point of dropping out of it, there was a furious race to settle the conflict in the West. Futile French attacks in the Chemin des Dames offensive led to a mutiny in the French army that effectively reduced its participation. Against all pre-war expectations, the deciding struggle would be between Germany and Britain.

British tactics seemed to be making headway, and the first part of 1917 saw more realistic attacks with limited aims, carefully planned, and achieving surprise. The Battle of Vimy Ridge, though costly, was short, attained its objectives and achieved surprise by using flexible tactics. Inexplicably, Haig then reverted to previous tactics of heavy bombardment and a frontal attack on the German high ground above the town of Ypres. In doing so, he hoped to break through and reach the Flanders coast in preparation for a grand attack on Germany. In rain and mud, the attacks here at Passchendaele floundered. Casualties mounted in possibly the most futile and unimaginative attack of the war. To make matters worse, Germany managed to strengthen Austrian forces and to break the Italian lines at Caporetto and threaten Venice (see page 48). Allied troops had to be diverted to save Italy. The only Allied success was the British advance in the Middle East, aided by Arab irregulars and Colonel **T.E. Lawrence's** guerrilla forces. Damascus fell to the British on Christmas Day 1917.

By early 1918, Germany had transferred large forces to the West, although millions were still held in the East, occupying great areas of former Russian territory. The British had been weakened by the losses at Passchendaele and by having to divert forces to Italy. The French army was too weak and unreliable to be useful in attack. American forces had arrived in France but were inexperienced. All now depended on a final attack by Germany, which began in March 1918. The German offensive, codenamed Operation Michael, broke the stalemate and the Western Front shifted for the first time since 1914. Small groups of **storm troopers** supported by accurate artillery fire broke through the Allied lines.

Amiens – the turning point on the Western Front, 1918

German successes were followed by the arrival of larger forces, and the Allies were driven back. Britain once again found itself defending against large-scale attacks. However, a consequence of concentrating large forces in a relatively small area was that the attackers moved further from their **railheads** and support, while the defenders were closer to theirs. To win, Germany would have needed all the soldiers killed in the great battles of 1916 and 1917. It had neither the men nor the resources to achieve victory.

The industrial might of Britain and the USA now began to tell. Three huge bulges were made in the Allied line, but Paris was saved. The German attacks stalled, and a well-equipped and coordinated Allied counterattack began that deployed fresh American troops, large numbers of tanks, sophisticated artillery able to lay down barrages to support advances, and aircraft used in conjunction with tanks, artillery and infantry.

The defeat of the Germans at Amiens in August 1918 was the turning point in the West, but despite the subsequent advances through the heavy German defences, a considerable amount of fighting would have been required to reach Germany itself. It was only by the standards of the Western Front since 1914 that this could be considered a rapid advance.

Why then did Germany fail?

By 1918, Germany was facing problems on all fronts:

- The Turks had been decisively defeated by British forces in the Middle East in 1918. The great Battle of Megiddo in Syria was decisive.
- Austria had been defeated in another major battle on the Italian Front – Vittorio Veneto – and, with the continual drain of the campaigns in Russia, it was not in a position to continue its involvement in the war.
- Greece was persuaded to abandon its neutrality and an Allied force that had landed at Salonika, but which had been inactive since 1917, began to advance through the Balkans.
- The U-boats had been overcome by superior tactics, which protected Allied shipping by convoys, and they had been weakened by a British naval raid on the U-boat base at Zeebrugge.
- The Allied naval blockade, together with the disruption of agriculture by wartime requisitioning, had created serious food shortages in Germany. These led to growing discontent in German cities. There was a fear that Germany would experience a revolution similar to that in Russia.
- The arrival of American troops and equipment, together with US credit for the Allies to purchase war supplies, left the Germans in an unequal position: they could not match the manpower and production available to the Allies.
- The nerve of the German high command broke at a crucial time, and they handed over power to the civilian parliament and advised that the war could not be won.
- US president **Woodrow Wilson's** offer of peace terms suggested a way out for a war-weary Germany, isolated by the defeat of its allies and fearful of internal unrest and revolution.

QUESTION

Why was Amiens such a significant battle?

Figure 2.18   Woodrow Wilson (1856–1924)

He was a former professor who was elected US president in 1912. A Democrat, he was re-elected in 1916 after the success of his progressive domestic policy and because he had kept the US out of the war. However, he felt obliged to declare war in 1917 because he wanted to ensure that a lasting peace built on a new international morality and co-operation resulted. He suggested peace terms in 1918 and worked towards a fair settlement at Versailles. He was forced to compromise, and the US Congress did not approve the peace treaty or agree to the USA's membership of the League of Nations.

Figure 2.17   This Austrian poster blames the Jews on the home front for defeat

QUESTION

Why do you think the cartoon on the previous page is so bitter? Is it true that German military failure alone was not to blame for the defeat? Who should the cartoonist have been blaming?

In March 1918, Germany had acquired great areas of agricultural land and industry in western Russia, but had no time to develop them. German forces were, professionally, superior to those of its enemies, but it was increasingly clear that, although Germany could go on fighting, it could not actually win the war. The armistice was signed on 11 November 1918 without Allied troops on German soil, and with Germany still in possession of large amounts of other nations' land. Germany still had a large and effective army; it still had an intact fleet and it had outgunned and outmanoeuvred the British in their one great naval battle; it still had a largely supportive civilian population; it had potentially large food supplies from its conquered territory. Compared with the situation in 1945, therefore, Germany was not desperate and the Allied victory was not especially decisive. For many in Germany, including Corporal Adolf Hitler, defeat came completely unexpectedly.

Practice and outcome

How far did the way that the war was practised affect its outcome? The war was essentially one of attrition and was static on the key Western Front for much of the time, resulting in heavy losses with small territorial gain. The greater resources of the USA, therefore, had a major effect, but even then the final campaigns were not decisive. The war of movement that resumed in 1918 failed to see Germany break through and the counterattacks failed to see allied forces on enemy territory. There was no huge final battle or invasion of Germany. The collapse of her allies Austria and Turkey made Germany vulnerable. Thus the war ended when the German leaders decided that further fighting could not achieve victory rather than because of Germany being decisively defeated. The way the war had been fought – as a long drawn out slogging match – determined its outcome.

2.6 How important was technology in determining tactics and outcome?

The Industrial Revolution transformed both weapons and the state. By 1914, there had been many significant changes in the equipment, weaponry, organisation, planning and support for Europe's armed forces.

The main developments lay in the speed and accuracy with which both small arms (rifles and pistols) and artillery (cannon, mortars and howitzers) could fire. Rifles had developed considerably from the old muskets in the course of the previous century.

The deadliest development was that of rifled artillery. Much more powerful shells could be fired longer distances, more rapidly, with cannon developed as a result of the engineering of the Industrial Revolution. The shells could be packed with explosive and could have a devastating effect from a long distance. In addition to this, mines and mortars with considerable destructive power had been developed during the long period of peace after 1815. The huge advances in modern science and engineering meant more destructive weapons were designed. The mass production of steel turned these designs into reality, and the emergence of huge factories meant that these weapons could also be produced in large quantities.

Fact: The word 'rifle' refers to a groove in the barrel which sends the bullet out spinning, not, as in the case of the musket, out of a smooth bore. The spin gives greater accuracy. The greater charge in the cartridge case gives longer range. So attackers had to face a much greater number of bullets from a much closer range. Those bullets could be aimed specifically at them, not just fired in their general direction.

A major development was the machine gun, which could fire hundreds of rounds a minute from relatively long distances. The new weaponry also produced much less smoke. Attacking forces were no longer obscured by masses of smoke and thus became targets for heavy artillery, rapid-firing rifles and machine guns. A dash over open ground to attack the enemy offered little chance of success.

Naval technology had also progressed rapidly after 1815. The age of sail gave way to the age of steam; ships were equipped with formidable long-range guns and armoured with the latest steel plating. When modern European ships encountered older navies, such as those of China and Japan in the mid-19th century, their superiority was overwhelming. European empires expanded on the basis of technological superiority – non-industrialised peoples could not resist the revolution in military power. Also by 1914, military aircraft were being used by all sides, mainly for reconnaissance, but also for limited attacks. Aircraft made surprise attacks difficult to achieve, as troops on the ground could be monitored from the air.

Another significant development was the tank, first used in 1916. However, this did not lead to the breakthrough that was hoped for. The technology available to the generals was not sufficient to break the deadlock of the war. Larger-scale artillery could not destroy all the defences; the machine guns favoured the defenders; air power was not strong enough to destroy trenches. No side possessed a 'wonder weapon' and both relied on similar weaponry. Tactics either did not or could not take enough consideration of the heavier weapons for most of the war. It was not until 1918, when the war of attrition finally took its toll on manpower and resources, that tactics were sufficiently adapted to allow more mobile and decisive warfare.

Fact: The tank was developed by Major Ernest Swinton of the British army, and the first one was produced in 1915 – an armoured container with tracks to overcome the trenches. Tanks were first used in 1916 at Flers during the Battle of the Somme, but they broke down and, because they were slow-moving, they were vulnerable to artillery. However, they were used effectively in conjunction with flexible artillery barrages in 1918, when the Allies had superior numbers. Their potential was recognised by theorists and tank development was a major part of inter-war military thinking. Tanks played a significant part in the Second World War.

2.7 How important were the mobilisation of human and economic resources and the home front?

ACTIVITY
List as many features of the First World War that are characteristic of total war as you can.

In many past wars, there had been a clear distinction between fighting done by professional forces and normal civilian life. This had been less true of civil wars, which had become struggles between the whole population of competing sides. However, the First World War came to be a 'total war' where there was less distinction between soldiers and civilians; for example, when cities were bombed and where the total resources of the countries were employed in winning the war by devoting resources to war production, rationing goods and using women and children to produce war resources. Total war also led to a belief in outright victory as the only aim, not a compromise peace.

In a total war, there is less distinction between the actual fighting fronts and what came to be known as the home front. The huge demand for weapons meant that industry was vital, and as more and more men were called up to the front lines, women took their place. Women had always worked, but mainly in the textile industry and in agriculture. Women working in engineering and arms manufacturing and, to some extent, in transport – which was a new development. British women were also urged to join the **Land Army**.

Land Army: The Women's Land Army was set up in the First World War, when a great deal of farm work had been done by men. With so many young men called up for the armed services, there was a shortage of farm workers. Hence, the government called on women to fill this gap. Women worked 50 hours a week in the summer and 48 hours a week in the winter. They also wore a special uniform.

QUESTION

What does this poster suggest about the involvement of the population in war? Why do you think it was necessary for nations to use this sort of propaganda? How would you explain the possible impact of this poster in the light of what you know about the situation in 1917?

Figure 2.19 A British recruitment poster urging women to join the Women's Land Army

By the later stages of the war, women were also in uniform. In Britain this was in the army and navy, although not as combatants. Russia went further by forming a women's battalion in 1917. The work women did in the war was a strong impetus towards greater women's political rights and the right to vote in several countries.

The state increased its control over the economic resources as well as the human resources of the countries involved. All participants had had conscription before 1914 except Britain and the USA which relied on small volunteer professional armies. Conscription was introduced in Britain in 1914 and the greatest army in British history was assembled in which more than 4 million people had served by 1918. The US had had conscription during the Civil War, but the introduction of conscription in 1917, after a disappointing number of volunteers, was much greater – with 24 million men registered and 3 million called up. Other powers had a conscription system with a large reserve pool of former soldiers, but the scope of conscription increased considerably.

The state utilised economic resources both by placing orders for munitions with existing firms and also by establishing new government factories, such as happened with the British ministry of munitions and by the widespread control of economic life established in Germany under a virtual military dictatorship established by the generals Hindenburg and Ludendorff. Rationing of resources was common as shortages caused by the diversion of horses and men from agriculture resulted and as blockades hit imports. National enthusiasm had played a part in bringing war about and it was necessary to sustain this enthusiasm when the conflict proved to be longer and more costly than expected. The participating nations did not face serious anti-war unrest at home. Propaganda was often effective in rallying morale. Posters tended to stress the need for service to the nation. When images of the war were shown in cinemas, they were either of troops preparing for action or very limited footage of action. A newsreel of the Battle of the Somme by the official British cameraman Geoffrey

Malins was seen by half the population of Britain, so great was the interest, but although it showed the massive explosion that preceded the attacks, it depicted only limited coverage of the fighting itself. It is significant that Malins was given a special concrete shelter from which to film his piece, and that the film was expected to be used as part of a record of victory. The propaganda value of film was being recognised for the first time. **Censorship** prevented anti-war feelings gaining prominence, and conscientious objectors to the war faced persecution, not only from the state but also from their fellow citizens. Britain was unusual in having a legal concept of conscientious objection.

The war increased the power of the state in most countries. Taxes rose, communications were controlled, goods requisitioned and men conscripted. Maintaining the home front became a major aspect of fighting the war. Bombing brought the war home to civilians in a way that no one had experienced before. The scale of civilian casualties, together with the economic hardships endured on the home front, meant that this war touched ordinary people as no other had before. In Britain, the policy of encouraging people from the same town to enlist together brought considerable hardship to local communities when losses occurred on the battle fronts.

However, countries or states were largely successful in adapting to the needs of modern industrial warfare – even Russia was able to overcome early problems and sustain a major offensive in the summer of 1916, although the pressure began to show after that.

Naval **blockades** and the wholesale use of horses and manpower caused severe shortages of food and rationing in some countries. By 1916, much of Germany was suffering food shortages, and by 1918 Britain faced official rationing of food and raw materials, as well as the compulsory cultivation of agricultural land. War was deeply linked to the erosion of personal liberties and an increase in state power.

Censorship: The control by the state of communications of all sorts – books, newspapers, journals, even letters sent from combat zones. Later wars also featured censorship of radio, film and television.

Blockades: In this case, using naval power to prevent the enemy trading and bringing in essential supplies. This was a traditional British weapon because of the country's naval superiority. The Germans applied it by using submarines. Both blockades were dangerous, but the British blockade caused much hardship in Germany by the winter of 1916, and was one of the reasons why Germany could not carry on the war in 1918.

Significance of the home front

The ability of states to mobilise resources for war was thus one of the key elements in the outcome of the First World War. Russia was much less successful in maintaining a supply of munitions and equipment for its forces than Germany and losses were high as a consequence. Although efficiency improved during the war, there were significant shortages. Germany, however, came under pressure from shortage of food and fuel on the home front and its troops were less well fed than those of Britain, France and the USA by 1918. This contributed to loss of morale. The human resources of the Allied side were boosted by the promise of large numbers of US troops from April 1917. Given the very large losses suffered by Germany, this was highly important. Germany was forced to keep large numbers of troops in Russia and the attacks it made in 1918, while strategically effective and well executed, suffered from lack of manpower. Allied counterattacks were boosted by the fresh US forces and the ability of Britain and France to keep raising fresh troops, albeit of poorer physical quality. In a war of attrition, the access of Britain and France to supplies from North America and then the injection of men and war material from America's entry into the war was of considerable importance. Also the morale on the home front was maintained more successfully in Britain than in Germany, where shortages were causing discontent and there were outbreaks of social and revolutionary unrest in 1918. The home front proved decisive in the withdrawal of Russia from the war in 1918 following revolution. A total war can only be won with the continuing commitment of domestic resources. The counter attacks on the Western Front in 1918 depended for their success on the resources in terms of tanks and aircraft available to the Allies.

End of unit activities

1 What evidence is there in this chapter to show that the First World War was a war of attrition? Look again at what this means and find material that shows how this term might be justified.

2 Why was there rapid movement only at the beginning and the end of the war and not in the middle years?

Effects of the First World War

KEY QUESTIONS

- What political and territorial changes resulted from the First World War?
- What economic and social changes arose?
- What were the successes and failures of peacemaking?

Overview

- The exposure of so many millions of people to modern warfare and the nearness of death, destruction, pain, loss, fear and much heightened emotion had profound and long-lasting effects. It should be remembered that the casualties are not simply statistics – they had a dramatic effect on the nations involved and the people left behind.

- The war also had considerable impact on the political boundaries of Europe, and there were changes worldwide as the victorious powers gained, and the vanquished powers lost, overseas possessions. More significant, however, was the profound political effect of such losses and the experience of war. The emergence of extreme right-wing and left-wing regimes and the desire for political change in some democracies can all be attributed to the war.

- The war also brought major social and economic changes – in attitudes to women, in the relationship between the individual and the state, in the balance of world trade and in the disruption of the old pre-war economy.

- Such an unprecedented experience also affected the world economy, international relations, nationalism and imperialism, and culture, science and technology. It signified a great turning point in world history, after which the previously unthinkable became the norm. Prior to the First World War, there was a widely held belief in Europe that humanity was progressing through industry, the arts, scholarship and even physical development. Such a view took a considerable blow in the aftermath of the war, as people dwelt on the vast – and, many argued, pointless – loss of life. To some it seemed akin to a medieval plague.

TIMELINE

1917 February: Tsar overthrown in Russia.

October: Communists take power in Russia.

1918 November: Armistice is signed.

1919 June: Treaty of Versailles and other Paris Peace treaties.

August: Socialist revolution in Germany fails.

1920 January: League of Nations is formed.

1922 October: Mussolini becomes prime minister of Italy.

1923 January: France occupies the Ruhr.

1925 December: Locarno Pact.

1928 August: Kellogg–Briand Pact.

1929 Great Depression begins.

1933 January: Hitler becomes chancellor of Germany.

2.8 What political and territorial changes resulted from the First World War?

Resistance and revolution

Conscientious objection:
'Conscientious objector' was a name given in Britain to those who refused to join the armed forces because they had moral objections to war. Some religious groups, such as the Quakers, considered the taking of human life unjustified under any circumstances. The philosophical and/ or religious grounds for objection were investigated by special tribunals. The right to object was reluctantly recognised, but there was considerable stigma attached to it in both world wars.

Fact: Petrograd was the name given to the Russian capital St Petersburg during the First World War. It was there that the fate of Russia was decided in 1917, but the communists moved the capital to Moscow in 1918. Petrograd was renamed Leningrad in 1924, before reverting to its tsarist name, St Petersburg, after 1989.

Theory of Knowledge

'In the long term, we are all dead' – John Maynard Keynes (1883–1946)

How can historians distinguish between long- and short-term factors and weigh their relative importance?

There was a great deal of criticism about the war, especially as losses rose. The British Prime Minister Herbert Asquith was forced to resign in 1916 in favour of a stronger war leader, David Lloyd George. Even Lloyd George faced strikes, the rapid rise of trade unions and support for socialism. In Germany, shortages on the home front resulted in discontent and there was widespread dislike of a virtual military dictatorship. The disturbances in the German fleet and among the workers by the end of the war led to attempts at revolution. Food and fuel shortages in Russia and discontent among the élite at the poor management of the war by Tsar Nicholas II led to a revolution in Petrograd in 1917 and the abdication of the tsar. There was recognition of the concept of **conscientious objection** to war in Britain, but those who claimed exemption from service on grounds of conscience often faced considerable hardship in prison, or were placed in dangerous roles in military service while not actually fighting. In the main, organised religion lent its support to the war effort. Newspapers took a pro-war stance and it was difficult to escape involvement.

The Russian Revolution was possible because the tsar's troops did not obey orders to suppress discontent. In 1917, even some front-line troops were refusing to attack. French support for the war had been strong during the initial battles for the frontier and the Verdun campaign of 1916, but the futile Chemin des Dames offensive of 1917 gave rise to the only significant large-scale mutinies of the war. In the end, order was restored by a mixture of concession and severe but limited punishment – targeting only a selection of mutineers rather than whole regiments. However, the French ability to sustain heavy fighting into 1918 was diminished. Arguably, the French army had not recovered by the time of the Second World War, and it did not show the determined resistance to Germany then as it had in 1914 and 1917. There was much excitement about the Russian Revolution, and a strong radical movement emerged in the German navy – the sailors at Kiel mutinied in 1918 and refused to sail out for a final 'death or glory' battle with the British. Mutineers also took part in disturbances in Berlin and Munich in 1919 and 1920.

What seems remarkable is that in many countries, for a long period, there was relatively little demand for an end to the war. Even the more educated and politically aware peoples of Europe simply accepted hardship on both the fighting fronts and home fronts.

The greatest political change during the war was the Russian Revolution of 1917. The war brought to light the many problems and weaknesses of the Russian regime. The heavy casualties, the shortage of food and the decision of the tsar to command his own forces – and therefore take on the blame for Russia's military defeats – led to mass discontent by February 1917. In Petrograd tens of thousands took to the streets in protest, and the tsar's troops refused to fire on the crowds. Nicholas II was at Pskov with his forces and was advised by leading generals and politicians to abdicate.

The new provisional government decided to carry on with the war, creating even more discontent. The one group that supported peace was the Marxist party, called the Bolsheviks and led by **Vladimir Ilyich Lenin**. Their slogan 'Peace, Bread and Land' won them increasing support, and they achieved power by a sudden takeover of Petrograd in October 1917. Lenin withdrew from the war and signed away large areas of Russia at the Treaty of Brest-Litovsk. Although some areas, such as the Ukraine, were later recovered, other areas were not taken back by Russia until after the Second World War.

The Great Powers and empires that entered the war did not all survive it.

- Germany saw the abdication of the kaiser in November 1918 and the establishment of the first lasting republican democracy in German history, with a constitution announced in the city of Weimar.
- Russia experienced two revolutions in 1917, one of which ended the Romanov dynasty that had ruled since 1613 and the whole institution of tsarism. The second, masterminded by Trotsky and Lenin, ended the parliamentary democracy that had been set up in its place and brought about the first communist state, which lasted until 1991.
- The Austro-Hungarian Empire fell apart at the end of the war. Instead of preserving the monarchy, the war brought about its downfall.
- The French Third Republic survived, but it faced increasing instability in the years leading up to the Second World War and finally fell in 1940.
- The British Empire survived but was faced with growing nationalism in its colonies and social unrest at home.

The war brought about the growth of the political left in the victorious powers, which was met by a counter-movement from the political right. In Italy, after a disturbed post-war period, a right-wing dictatorship emerged from 1922 under the fascist **Benito Mussolini**, which owed much to the discontent brought by war. Mussolini's dictatorship lasted until 1943. A nationalist, right-wing racialist dictatorship, headed by the Nazi Party, emerged in Germany after 1933, which again owed much to post-war discontent. The defeats suffered by Turkey inspired a revolution in the central homeland against the Ottoman sultans. This led to a new, secular, reforming regime under Kemal Atatürk, a successful military commander of the First World War who modernised the country.

Of the rulers who had been so enthusiastic for war in 1914, the Russian tsar Nicholas II was murdered along with his family; the German Kaiser Wilhelm II became an exile in Holland; the Ottoman sultan Mehmed VI was overthrown; the Austro-Hungarian emperor Karl I was forced to abdicate in 1918 and watched his empire broken up.

Failure also awaited the democratic wartime leaders: in the US, Congressional elections went against the Democrat president Woodrow Wilson, and he fell from power. The Democrats remained out of office until 1933. In Italy, political power went to a new nationalist party and the parliamentary system came to an end. David Lloyd George, the British wartime prime minister, was forced from power in 1922 and never held office again. His party, the Liberals, suffered a long-term decline and never again formed a government, although their successors, the Liberal Democrats, did form a coalition with the Conservatives in 2010.

Figure 2.20 Vladimir Ilyich Lenin (1870–1924)

He was the leader of a minority group of communists which favoured a small conspiratorial party dedicated to revolution, and which adapted Marxist theory to suit Russia. Its members argued that it was possible to go from a feudal monarchy to a workers' revolution without going through a transitional capitalist phase – provided the new government then received assistance from more economically developed workers' states. Lenin took power by force and was a beneficiary of the First World War. He played on anti-war feelings, but was faced with a civil war in 1918, which he won by showing the ruthlessness and strong organisation that tsarist Russia lacked. He masterminded the imposition of communism in Russia but was forced to make concessions to the peasants that were later reversed by Stalin, his successor after 1928. Lenin laid the basis of a one-party dictatorship that lasted until 1989.

2

Figure 2.21   Benito Mussolini (1883–1945)

He was leader of the right-wing fascist movement in Italy, and the country's ruler from October 1922 to 1943. He became a dictator and aimed to make Italy a new sort of totalitarian state in which the state controlled hearts, minds and all aspects of life. He failed, and his decision to support Hitler in 1940 brought defeats and his own dismissal by the Italian king, Victor Emmanuel III. He was executed in 1945 by communist opponents.

KEY CONCEPTS QUESTION

Causation and consequences: War was undoubtedly a cause of political change, but how significant were longer-term situations in many of the countries affected? For example, the losses of the war helped to bring down the tsar of Russia, but the regime had suffered many problems before the war.

The peace treaties

Germany had signed an armistice in November 1918 but did not expect to have peace terms imposed upon it as though it had unconditionally surrendered. As a result of a conference of victorious powers in Paris, this is exactly what happened and, as will be shown in Chapter 4, it was a major cause of the next world war. The Treaty of Versailles was imposed on Germany after lengthy and often acrimonious discussions between the Allies, all of whom came with different agendas: the French wanted revenge and future security; the British desired imperial gain; the USA wanted world peace and future international co-operation and trade; Italy and Japan were seeking territorial gains. Other Parisian suburbs gave their names to separate treaties with Austria (St Germain), Hungary (Trianon), Bulgaria (Neuilly) and, in 1920, Turkey (Sèvres) – although this treaty was challenged by Turkey, which drove Greece from its allocated colony in Smyrna and forced the Allies to renegotiate at Lausanne in 1923. Turkey, Germany, Austria, Hungary, Bulgaria and Russia were not invited to the Versailles discussions, but merely informed of the results.

The new Europe

The map of Europe was transformed by the peace treaties, as the nationalities of Europe struggled to establish independent states. In 1914 there were some small states, but Europe was dominated by the Great Powers. After 1919, there were considerably more small independent states.

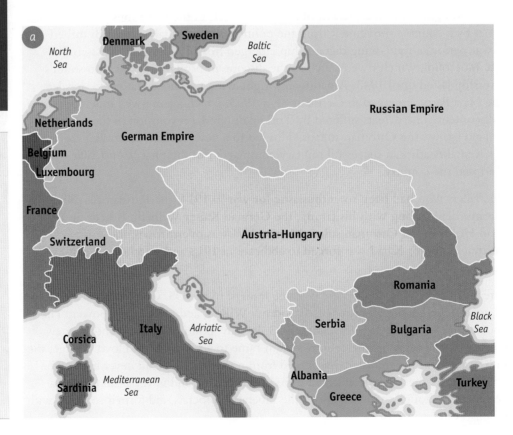

Figure 2.22 Political maps of Eastern and Central Europe (a) in 1914 and (b) in 1925

QUESTION
What major changes do these maps show? Do you think the territorial changes shown here were good for European stability?

Winners and losers

Some countries had the support of the victorious powers and gained their dream of independence: a new Poland; a new Czech state in alliance with the Slovaks; the new states of Latvia, Lithuania, Estonia and Finland, freed from Russian control. This was because the victors decided that the lands taken from Russia by Germany were available to redistribute.

The southern Slavs got a federation, dominated by Serbia, called Yugoslavia, which lasted until the 1990s.

Turkey became a modernised state but lost its lands in Arabia and the Middle East.

Italy gained some of the lands it had desired and had been promised – Istria, Trentino, Trieste and the South Tyrol – but not all. Italy had to seize Fiume by force and there were still Italians living under Austrian, German and Yugoslav rule.

Austria and Hungary became independent – but instead of dominating a great empire they were now small, weak states. In Austria's case, its great capital Vienna now ruled over only German-speaking rural areas and small towns and cities.

Russia had recovered some of its lost lands, but not the Baltic territories, or Bessarabia, or eastern Poland. It found itself isolated behind a number of small independent states, a so-called cordon sanitaire – a barrier against plague, in this case the political 'plague' of communism. Like Germany, Russia never accepted that its post-war situation of weakness and loss was permanent.

2

Germany lost considerable lands in the east and the contentious provinces of Alsace and Lorraine in the west (to France). It was physically divided in the east by a strip of Polish territory. It had lost lands to Denmark and Belgium and all its overseas colonies.

Japan, which had supported the Allies, found itself only able to rule over new territories it had gained in China as a trustee, reporting to the new League of Nations. It did not win control of the Chinese Shandong province as it had wished, and had to give up the gains it made in the east of Russia after the Russian Revolution. After the war, Japan was forced by the USA to give up its alliance with Britain and to agree to a pact guaranteeing the territorial status quo in the Far East, thus restricting its ambitions in the region. It was also forced to keep its navy smaller than those of Britain and the USA.

Thus Russia, Germany, Italy and Japan saw themselves as losing powers. Other losers were the national minorities in the newly created independent states – the Poles and Ruthenes; Germans and Slovaks in a Czech-dominated Czechoslovakia; non-Magyars in Hungary; Ukrainians in eastern Poland; Germans in the Baltic States; minority groups in Estonia, Latvia and Lithuania. The newly dominant nationalities often discriminated against **ethnic minorities**, and as the new states came into being there was frequently a great deal of violence.

The balance of power

The balance of power had been seriously altered by the war. With Austria-Hungary broken up, Russia outcast and Germany defeated and humiliated, there was a vacuum of power at the heart of Europe. Once Germany became strong again and Russia had recovered, there was bound to be a struggle to alter the new balance of power. The losers would want to take what they felt they had been denied – but would the winners be strong enough to hold on to their victory?

2.9 What economic and social changes arose?

Economic effects

The trading networks of the pre-1914 world were dislocated by war, with its blockades and economic disruption. In Europe, the heavy spending of countries at war and currency manipulation by their governments resulted in severe **inflation**. This was particularly true in Germany and Russia. Direct war damage caused economic problems; overseas investments were sold to pay for the war; the economies of the Great Powers had been turned over to war production and producing food; marginal land was put into cultivation. The loss of so many men meant a shortage of labour, and more women entered the workforce.

In terms of relative power and wealth, what was most noticeable was a shift in economic advantage to the USA in the West and Japan in the East. These countries were able to take advantage of the war to increase profits and gain a greater share of world markets. Before 1914, British sterling had been the key international currency

Ethnic minorities: People who belong to different racial or language groups from those who predominantly populate and run a state. For example, in Czechoslovakia there were around 3 million German-speakers in a country dominated by Czechs who were of Slav racial origin and whose language was closer to Russian.

KEY CONCEPTS ACTIVITY

Significance: The peace treaties that ended the war clearly disappointed many of the states involved – including some of the 'victors'. Select one 'victor' and one 'loser', and list the main ways in which the peace treaties left both these states dissatisfied.

Inflation: A rise in prices. Europe suffered severe inflation during the First World War.

and Britain was the greatest financial lender, shipper, insurer and investor. After 1918, the USA began to gain economic dominance. The profits to the USA from the First World War were so huge that they came to dominate money markets. US production was the key to Allied victory and the US became the financier of the Allied powers.

Agriculture

After the war, the world needed to get back to a peacetime economy, but agriculture had produced so much that the prices of raw materials and food could not recover. There was less demand, yet so much land had gone into cultivation worldwide that a large gap had arisen between the amounts produced and what could be sold. The depression in world agriculture was to be a major feature of the inter-war period and a source of considerable hardship and political instability.

Industry

Heavy industries were at a peak during the war. By 1917, US steel was producing four times its pre-war output to meet the needs of war. In countries like Britain, the war had reversed a pre-war fall in production in the great industries of the Industrial Revolution, such as iron, steel and coal. However, after the war there was reduced demand and heavy industry faced falling profits and sales. Problems were made worse as large numbers of people had worked in these industries during the war and now found themselves unemployed.

Social changes

Population and demographic changes

Table 2.1 Some military casualties of the First World War

Country	Killed	Wounded	Total	Percentage
Australia	59 000	152 000	211 000	64%
Austria-Hungary	1 200 000	3 620 000	4 820 000	74%
Canada	67 000	173 000	241 000	39%
French Empire	1 385 000	4 266 000	5 651 000	75%
Germany	1 718 000	4 234 000	5 952 000	54%
Great Britain	703 000	1 663 000	2 367 000	44%
India	43 000	65 000	108 000	7%
Italy	460 000	947 000	1 407 000	26%
Japan	250	1000	1250	0.2%
New Zealand	18 000	55 000	73 000	66%
Russia	1 700 000	4 950 000	6 650 000	55%
Serbia	128 000	133 000	261 000	37%
Turkey	336 000	400 000	736 000	46%
USA	117 000	204 000	321 000	8%

QUESTION

What does this graph show you about the effects on war on fertility and birth rates? What do you think explains the changes shown in the graph?

The table above outlines the losses suffered by the key nations involved in the First World War. It also shows some surprising variations among casualty rates as a percentage of those mobilised, with those of Russia and Germany, for instance, being much higher than those of Britain, yet lower than those of Austria and France. As the losses fell heavily on men of military age, the long-term demographic effects were considerable.

Figure 2.23   European birth rates

Women

As the industrial countries mobilised their forces for total war, so they needed to bring more women into the workplace to keep up production levels as men went away to fight. With greater participation in the national effort, women gained confidence and it became harder to sustain the view that women were essentially part of home life and lacked the strength and abilities to play an equal role with men in the world of work. Without participation in the war it would have been more difficult for women to obtain the right to vote and greater social equality. The war brought freedom and mobility for women, who often moved away from home and lived as independent workers, enjoying a degree of social and sexual freedom that would have been difficult in the pre-war years. Much of this freedom did not carry on into peacetime, but it was hard to turn back the clock, and women's role had undeniably changed. The role and status of women did not change evenly throughout the countries affected by war and the changes were not all permanent. For example, women did not gain the vote in France. In Britain in 1918 only women over 30 married to householders or householders in their own right got the right to vote. The emergence of right-wing dictatorships in Italy and Germany as a result of war retarded women's rights. The notional equality of women increased far more in the new communist Russia. In terms of work opportunities, the return of men from war and opposition from organised labour meant that women did not continue to do the range of work in large numbers that they had done during the 'total war'. The emancipation of women in towns and cities in the 1920s was often not seen in rural areas. Male attitudes changed more slowly and women still faced discrimination and double standards.

Figure 2.24 Change in the status of women was not merely a European phenomenon, here women in the US are voting in 1920 after they gained the right to vote in the 19th Amendment to the Constitution

The working classes

The same might also be said of the urban working classes. Their participation in major wartime industrial production was so vital that after the war they were able to exert more bargaining power as the workforce grew and changed. Migration to urban centres was common. In Russia, there was a big influx of peasants to the cities. In the USA, black workers from the south moved into northern factories and into a new world of attitudes and freedom, despite the prejudice and the race riots that they faced. In Britain, trade union membership doubled from 4 million to 8 million. In Italy, workers moved from the **Mezzogiorno** to the northern factories and, like their Russian, American, English, French, German and Austrian counterparts, learnt more about the radical social and political doctrines of socialism.

In Russia, the effects were apparent in the revolutionary situation in the large cities, but radical and socialist ideas had become common throughout Europe. Italy experienced a wave of strikes and the growth of the socialist movement after the war. In Germany, the Social Democratic Party (SPD) was already the largest party and the war caused the change that would bring it into government; ironically, the SPD also crushed the more extreme socialist groups in a brief but bloody civil war. In Britain large-scale strikes culminated in the first effective general strike of 1926. In France, post-war society was polarised between right and left. The war increased the confidence and hopes for change of European workers and also introduced a new radicalism to the USA.

The idea of a fairer society

The enormous sacrifice made by so many people in the war years led to hopes for a new society – often encouraged by wartime propaganda. There were dreams of a new society in which war would not be needed and justice would prevail.

The comradeship of the trenches had brought the classes together. In the face of extreme danger, class consciousness often disappeared. As so many young officers from the upper classes died, their places had to be taken by soldiers from lower down the social scale.

The growth of industries brought greater urbanisation, which eroded traditional class barriers and reduced the distinction between town and country. Russian communism,

Mezzogiorno: The name for the agricultural south of Italy, which included many large estates where the peasants and agricultural workers were poor and often illiterate.

Prohibition: A ban on the production and sale of alcoholic drinks. In the USA, national Prohibition came about in 1919 but some individual states had introduced it earlier than this.

Anarchism: A belief that government is oppressive and corrupt, and that the state exists only to oppress the ordinary people. This justified attacks on the state, its rulers, administrators and police.

Fact: There had been much talk before 1914 of an international parliament of nations to keep peace. The proposal to form a League of Nations was made by US President Woodrow Wilson as part of his peace proposals in 1918. It was set up in 1920, but the USA never joined and other leading countries, such as Russia, Germany and Italy, were not members throughout its existence.

Historical debate:
The famous economist Keynes wrote *Economic Consequences of the Peace* in 1919, criticising the reparations and the disruption of European economic life that would make a lasting peace difficult. Against this, the treaties have had their defenders, notably Margaret MacMillan in *The Peacemakers* (2003).

Chinese Marxism, Nazi nationalism and Italian fascism's belief in a corporate state in which all classes and sectors of the economy worked together, the British Labour Party's socialist programme of 1918, the Japanese belief in working together on behalf of the God-Emperor – all were part of the movement sometimes known as '1919-ism' in which the old capitalist, imperialist and class-ridden societies seemed outdated and a new, more idealistic world order was called for. **Prohibition** in the USA was part of this desire for social change and for new standards. On the other hand, violent **anarchism** and frantic pleasure-seeking were also reactions to the war. Both responses could also be seen as rejections of traditional values.

This was evidenced in the new morality in the 1920s, which was part of the effect of the war's dislocation of traditional values. In the USA there were the 'Roaring Twenties' and guilt-free consumption of alcohol and cigarettes. Women enjoyed the freedom of less restricting clothing. Music became more 'abandoned' – the new jazz and swing was thought by contemporaries to be 'wild'. Sexual freedom and experimentation were common. It was as though the war had shown that life was fragile and the post-war generation wanted to make the most of it while they could.

2.10 What were the successes and failures of peacemaking?

The peace settlement came in for a lot of criticism. Many in Britain saw in the 1920s and 1930s that Germany had been treated harshly. It had been blamed for a war that most countries bore some responsibility for. It had stopped fighting on the understanding of a fair peace and then it had been forced to pay reparations and lost territory. Other nations had been allowed 'national self-determination' but Germans were living outside Germany under foreign rule. A nation with a fine military tradition had been forced to reduce its defences so that it was vulnerable to attack while general European disarmament had not taken place. The existence of new small weak states in Eastern Europe was not enough to provide a balance against any resurgence of German power. Discontent about the peace helped the rise of an extreme nationalist dictator, Adolf Hitler, who started another war in 1939.

The peace treaties had resulted in more discontent than satisfaction. Italy had not gained the lands it wanted and was especially angry about Fiume going to a new Yugoslavia. This paved the way for the rise of a fascist dictatorship that was a danger to Europe. Japan was discontented and this led to the development of nationalism and a desire to expand together with resentment at the racial prejudice of the West. Russia was excluded and did not regain the lands lost to Germany in 1918. This led to a long-term discontent and the determination to regain lands and to end the 'cordon sanitaire' that the Allies imposed. The new states of Eastern Europe often contained ethnic diversity, which caused tensions that resulted in ongoing conflicts; for example in Yugoslavia, which continued into the 21st century. The League of Nations produced by the treaties was ineffective because neither the USA nor Russia joined. In the end, the peace conference did not have the confidence of the European powers and they undermined it by separate agreements in the 1920s and 1930s; also the settlements were not popular with the public in France, for not going far enough, and in Germany and Britain for going too far. Russia saw the treaties as a capitalist plot against communism and land-grabbing by imperialist powers eager to get their hands on former German colonies.

The terms have been said to have been reasonably lenient given the losses of the war, the hostility to Germany among the victors and the savage terms imposed by Germany on Russia in 1918. The suffering caused by the reparations has been said to have been exaggerated and the amount paid not high enough to have caused damage to the German economy. German territorial losses have been said to be exaggerated. Losses in North Slesvig and Upper Silesia reflected the popular will. Alsace-Lorraine had not been German since 1871. There was every chance that problems could be decided by peaceful revisionism. The new countries of Eastern Europe were not all failures and given a more favourable economic and political situation between the wars might have become well-established and dealt with their internal problems. In any case, the peacemakers faced the reality that the Austrian and Turkish empires were collapsing and that Russia had withdrawn into revolution and civil war. They had to make a settlement that balanced the public's desire for revenge in the victor countries with the need to offer a fair and lasting settlement, and they had to try and meet the complex needs of a variety of different people in Eastern and Central Europe. To have set up a League of Nations at all was a considerable achievement and the peacemakers could not foresee the isolationism of the USA.

Activity

Find evidence from the chapter to allow you to make a decision about whether the failures of the Paris peace settlement outweighed its successes.

PEACE AND FUTURE CANNON FODDER

The Tiger: "Curious! I seem to hear a child weeping!"

Figure 2.25 This cartoon shows the Allied leaders leaving the Versailles peace conference and casts doubt on the permanence of their work

QUESTION

What is the message of this cartoon? How does the cartoonist try to get this message across? Is the cartoonist's view a fair representation of the Versailles Treaty?

Peace and reconstruction

The war had forced men and women into greater communal life. Millions fought together in the armed forces and there were larger numbers working in factories. Wartime patriotic associations and total war encouraged a view of national activity. For example, greater numbers joined trade unions. More people became interested in political associations to achieve national aims after the war. In the post-war period, this communalism was extended to the international sphere as the first international peace organisation, the League of Nations, was formed in 1920 with a permanent headquarters in Geneva. It went some way to meeting the dream of idealists before the war for an international parliament. Members met to discuss international affairs and problems in an assembly, and there was a ruling body, the Council, and a permanent civil service. There was, however, no standing army and not all countries were members, notably the USA and communist Russia. Germany did not join until 1926.

The old alliance system was blamed for the war and the pressure was on post-war leaders to avoid bilateral treaties and to rely on international agreements and complete openness. Under US pressure, the Anglo–Japanese treaty was replaced by an international agreement – the Treaty of Washington – to maintain the existing state of affairs in the Far East. The Locarno Pact of 1925 between Britain, France, Italy and Germany guaranteed the existing western frontiers of Germany. The Kellogg–Briand pact of 1928, signed by 65 nations, outlawed war. The League of Nations brought the powers of the world together in a permanent organisation and led to international bodies on refugees and world health. There were also international disarmament conferences. Although the USA was not a formal member of the League, it was involved in its activities as an observer. Nations cooperated far more, and even when pacts were made – such as the French agreements with the countries of Eastern Europe – they were open and included a group of countries: the so-called 'Little Entente' of Eastern Europe (Czechoslovakia, Romania and Yugoslavia).

Many countries had peace organisations, like the League of Nations Association in Britain. Ex-servicemen's associations were established, and the Russians revived the international conference of socialist parties – the Third International. There was an interest – albeit limited – in pan-Africanism (a movement to unite Africans and encourage a sense of African identity), and in America the beginnings of what would become the civil rights movement emerged in the form of the National Association for the Advancement of Colored People (NAACP).

A popular idea in some Catholic countries was corporatism – the belief that social harmony could arise if all elements of economic life came together to plan progress and avoid conflict. This was put into operation in Italy in a limited way, when Mussolini's fascist dictatorship brought together representatives of employers and workers with the government to discuss economic matters – although the interests of workers were largely ignored.

Shinto: Traditional Japanese spirit worship, which includes the concept that the emperor was descended from the sun goddess.

Bushido: The code of conduct of the samurais that, among other beliefs, held that the samurai's obligation to his lord was more important than anything, even family and life itself.

Another less positive form of communal activity was the development of nationalist and racialist groups. Japan saw a new interest in traditional culture that stressed the special position of Japan, its emperor and its **Shinto** religion, and revived interest in its ancient warlike codes such as **bushido**. Large Japanese business organisations – collectively known as Zaibatsu – also stressed communal economic activity and the needs of the state and large organisations above the needs of the individual. This was also the philosophy of fascism in Italy – the nation came before its inhabitants.

The most developed racial community theories emerged among the right-wing nationalist groups in Germany. They had ideas of a pure 'Aryan' race, binding together all Nordic peoples with hierarchies of race, placing the pure-bred Nordic types at the top and the supposedly inferior, 'sub-human' Jews at the bottom. The war did not create these ideas, but the discontent it brought gave them more popularity.

Similarly, by bringing about communist revolution in Russia, the war helped the spread of socialist, community-based ideas in China and other Asian countries, as well as in Europe. Left-wing ideas were particularly influential and attractive to the workers and peasants in Spain, in France, with its own revolutionary tradition, and even in Britain, which had a far less socialist and radical history.

In practice, reform and reconstruction were not implemented in such a way as to fulfil people's hopes and dreams. Economic problems prevented large-scale reforms, and traditional attitudes reasserted themselves. Countries put their own interests before internationalism. Dictatorships were more common than democracies in the new countries of Eastern Europe and, by 1928, Russia was dominated by Joseph Stalin's personal power rather than by a socialism that liberated and benefited the Russian people as a whole. Women did win more voting rights in some countries – Britain, Austria and Germany gave women the vote in 1918. In Russia, votes for women had been introduced in 1917 and the USA followed suit in 1920, but France did not give women the vote until 1944. However, the goal of complete equality (political, economic, social and sexual) remained, and possibly still remains, some way off.

Empires and nationalism

The Great Powers had needed the subject peoples from their empires to fight in the war, and they were considered essential in maintaining and supporting their homeland. For many of these people, the experience of war had meant increased travel and greater contact with the mother country. They were brought into contact with each other and given promises of a brighter future. In some cases the war weakened the ability of the dominant ruling power to maintain political control. The rulers of Austria-Hungary, for example, lost control of their subject peoples and had to accept the break-up of their empire.

Another example is Turkey, whose Middle-Eastern possessions gained independence with the support of the enemies of the Ottoman Empire. Russia too saw the loss of its western empire and had to accept a federation of its far-flung territories in the east. Initially, this took the form of autonomous national regimes and then, when communist authority was restored, a federation – a Union of Soviet Socialist Republics (USSR). However, communism proved to be a means of controlling the nationalities and the 'empire' was reborn in a different form. By 1945, even the western lands of pre-1914 Russia had been regained, with the exception of Finland.

Britain and France faced unrest in their empires too. Most notable was the emergence of a strong movement for independence in India, Britain's key imperial possession. Following a massacre of demonstrators in the holy city of Amritsar in 1919, the nationalist leader **Mohandas Gandhi** led a resistance campaign of non-violence that anticipated and inspired the later civil rights campaign in the USA.

Closer to home, the British faced armed resistance in Ireland. A semi-independent south emerged in 1922 – effectively leaving the empire – although it did not gain full independence as the country of Eire until 1949.

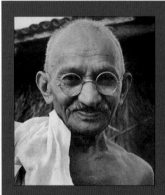

Figure 2.26 Mohandas Gandhi (1869–1948)

He was an Indian lawyer who campaigned for the rights of Indians living in South Africa. He returned to India to campaign for Indian self-government and freedom from British rule. He adopted a policy of non-violent resistance and his simple lifestyle attracted wide support. He was imprisoned by the British, but took part in conferences in London which led to greater self-government for India. He continued to press for independence and was again imprisoned during the Second World War. India was granted independence in 1947, but Gandhi was horrified by the violence between Hindus and Muslims. He was assassinated by a Hindu fanatic in 1948.

Zionist movement: A movement whose members believed that the Jews needed to establish their own state. At first, Zionist leaders considered parts of Africa and Latin America – it was only later that they decided to focus on Palestine, which they saw as 'their' biblical homeland. The modern movement dates from the late 19th century and was founded by Austro-Hungarian journalist Theodore Herzl.

Theory of Knowledge

'We study the past to understand the present; we understand the present to guide the future' – William Lund (1886–1971)

How far should historians see their main role as explaining contemporary issues and problems by looking at past causes? Should their main role be to be 'relevant' or should they simply study the past for its own sake?

Palestine

The greatest impact of the war on future international issues, which emerged out of changes in empires, took place in Palestine. This had been part of the Ottoman Empire, but in 1920 it was given to Britain to rule as a mandated territory nominally under the control of the League of Nations, together with Iraq and Transjordan. France gained Syria and the Lebanon in this division of the Middle East.

However, in 1917, Britain and the USA made a promise to establish a Jewish national homeland in Palestine. The Jews had been expelled from their biblical homeland by the Romans in 79 CE and the **Zionist movement** had pressed the Allied powers to restore this land to them and to offer the Jews a chance to resettle their original 'Promised Land'. In the Balfour Declaration (2 November 1917), the British offered this, partly with an eye to pleasing influential Jewish opinion in the USA at a time when Britain desperately needed American support and credit for vital war supplies. The delivery of this promise resulted in Jewish immigration to Palestine, and laid the basis for the independent state of Israel. However, Britain had also promised the Arabs in the region independence if they rose against their Turkish rulers in support of Britain, and that Palestinian Arabs would not be subject to Jewish rule. When clashes between Jews and Arabs in the inter-war years broke out, the British were forced to intervene. After the Second World War, Britain was made to relinquish control and hand back its mandate to the United Nations. This led to the formation of an independent state of Israel in 1948. This created a huge problem of Palestinian refugees and provoked wars between Israel and its Arab neighbours. The problems in this region remain unresolved today.

Europe and the US

The First World War increased the size of the empires of the victors. For some – Italy and Japan – the gains were insufficient and served only to increase their desire for expansion. For others, increased empire meant increased costs and responsibilities as well as greater resources – particularly Middle-Eastern oil supplies in the case of Britain. Thus the war both strengthened imperialism and weakened it. Ultimately, the losses by the European powers during the war opened the way for non-European powers to gain greater control and made the defence of overseas empires more difficult. This was later demonstrated dramatically in the Japanese attacks on European and US colonies in late 1941 and 1942.

Before the war, Europe had been the dominant global influence economically. After the war, however, the US became a much more significant economic influence. US pressure was one of the factors that led to the end of the European empires. Colonised peoples realised how much their controlling powers had relied on them in the war. This gave them a sense of empowerment and encouraged ideas of liberty. In the long term, this made it difficult for the colonial powers to maintain their overseas empires.

A continuing cycle of violence

The so-called 'war to end all wars' did not live up to its name. It ushered in a new era of violence that continued after 1939, after what seems in retrospect more like an extended 20-year truce. The scale of the war was so massive that it had widespread consequences, but the obvious one – to shock the world into never fighting a world war again – was short-lived. The pacifist writings and organisations, the influential anti-war poems, books and films were less durable than the desire for revenge, the intense nationalism and militarism, and the belief that national power and racial utopias were worth risking war again.

An Austrian corporal heard the news of the 1918 armistice when he was in hospital. In 1925, he recorded his reaction in his political memoirs. The hatred expressed here – a feeling shared by so many – made a lasting peace unlikely. 'In these nights [after Germany's surrender had been announced] hatred grew in me, hatred for those responsible for this deed' (*Mein Kampf*, 1925). This feeling was made worse by the Treaty of Versailles and especially Clause 231.

QUESTION
What message is conveyed by Source D?

SOURCE D

The Allied and Associated Governments affirm and Germany accepts the responsibility of Germany and her allies for causing all the loss and damage to which the Allied and Associated Governments and their nationals have been subjected as a consequence of the war imposed upon them by the aggression of Germany and her allies.

Treaty of Versailles, Article 231, June 1919.

End of unit activities

1 In groups, prepare a poster on the different aspects of the effects of the First World War. This could be done in terms of broad themes: political repercussions, economic and social change, the role of women – or it could be done in terms of individual countries. The poster should include an image (not from this book) that sums up its content. Put the posters on the wall and discuss, if these were part of a museum exhibition, which poster should come first when the members of the public enter the exhibition.

2 Make cards of the major results of the First World War. Arrange the cards in order of importance and think about why you made your choice. This can be done in groups or individually.

3 Debate the issue of the success or failure of the peace treaties.

4 In groups, read and discuss a memoir of the fighting and explain in a brief presentation how the experience of war affected the writer.

5 Find out how women were affected by war in at least four countries and organise your findings into a table like the one below. Rank each example according to how lasting is was on a scale of 1 (temporary) to 5 (long-lasting).

Change	Examples from different countries	How lasting was it?
Different types of employment		
Women in the armed forces		
Social change in the way women lived		
Political change – any new rights or increased political awareness		

End of chapter activities

Paper 1 exam practice

Question

What reasons are suggested by Source A below for Germany's decision
to go to war in 1914?   [3 marks]

Skill

Comprehension/understanding of a source

SOURCE A

Germany was fearful of being encircled. Since Russia's defeat in 1905, the Franco–Russian
alliance had not given cause for concern. But now Russia was recovering its military
strength, drawing on huge manpower resources, and in March 1914 the Duma [Russian
parliament] had voted massive credits for a three year military programme. This aimed to
increase the standing army to almost two million men by 1917. A strategic railway network
was being built to facilitate mobilisation.

The German Chief of Staff Moltke was for a pre-emptive strike against Russia.

R. Gildea. 1987. Barricades and Borders: Europe 1800–1914. *Oxford: Oxford University Press,
p. 423.*

Examiner's tips

Comprehension questions are the most straightforward questions you will face in Paper 1.
They simply require you to understand a source and extract two or three relevant points
that relate to the particular question.

As only three marks are available for this question, make sure you don't waste
valuable time that should be spent on the higher-scoring questions by writing a long
answer here. All that's needed is a couple of short sentences, giving the necessary
information to show you have understood the message of the source. Basically, try to
give one piece of information for each of the marks indicated as being available for the
question.

Common mistakes

When asked to show your comprehension/understanding of a particular source, make
sure you don't comment on the wrong source! Mistakes like this are made every year.
Remember, every mark is important for your final grade.

Simplified mark scheme

For each item of relevant/correct information identified, award one mark – up to a maximum of three marks.

Student answer

Source A shows that Germany was afraid of Russia because it had been building up its military strength and its army was much bigger. Germany was worried about Russia organising its huge manpower resources and threatening Germany.

Examiner's comments

The candidate has selected one relevant and explicit piece of information from the source and has clearly understood the point being made in relation to German fears about the Russian army – this is enough to gain one mark.

However, as there is no point/information relating to the encirclement, desire of the German military leader for a pre-emptive plan, or to the increase in railways, the candidate fails to gain the other two marks available.

Activity

Look again at the source, and the student answer above. Now try to identify some other pieces of information from the source, and try to make an overall comment about the source's message. This will allow you to obtain the other two marks available for this question.

Summary activity

Complete the spider diagram below by giving information on each of the events listed. Use the material you have read in this chapter and any other sources available to you.

1 What were the key causes of the First World War?

- The disagreements over the Balkans, 1908–13.
- The Moroccan Crises, 1905 and 1911.
- The assassination of Franz Ferdinand, 1914.

The First World War

3 Why did the First World War have such great consequences?

- The Peace Treaties and the problems they caused.
- The link between the First World War and revolution in Russia, 1917, and the rise of political extremism in Germany and Italy.

2 What were the key elements of the fighting in the First World War?

- The way that technology prevented breakthrough.
- The mistakes of the generals.
- Trench warfare.

2

Paper 2 practice questions

1 Evaluate the importance of economic factors as a cause of the First World War.
2 'Political factors were the most significant cause of the First World War.' To what extent do you agree with this statement?
3 Examine the ways in which mobilisation of resources affected the outcome of the First World War.
4 Evaluate the impact of the First World War on international relations in the first few years after 1918.
5 Compare and contrast the impact of the First World War on the role and status of women in any two participating states.

Further reading

Try reading the relevant chapters/sections of the following books:

Clark, Christopher (2013) *The Sleepwalkers*, New York: Harper.

Ferguson, Niall (2006) *The Pity of War*, London: Penguin.

Gildea, Robert (1987) *Barricades and Borders: Europe 1800–1914*, Oxford: Oxford University Press.

Henig, Ruth (1995) *Versailles and After*, London: Routledge.

Joll, James and Martel, Gordon (2006) *The Origins of the First World War*, London: Longman.

Philpott, William (2014) *Attrition: Fighting the First World War*, New York: Little Brown.

Sheffield, Gary (2005) *Forgotten Victory: The First World War, Myths and Realities*, London: Headline.

Strachan, Hew (2006) *The First World War: A New History*, New York: Free Press.

Tooze, Adam (2014) *The Deluge*, London: Allan Lane.

Wawro, Geoffrey (2014) *A Mad Catastrophe*, New York: Basic Books.

3

Causes of the Spanish Civil War

KEY QUESTIONS

- What were the main long-term causes of the war?
- What were the main short-term causes of the war?
- What were the political, ideological and economic causes of the war?

Overview

- Spain had a history of political instability, with deep divisions dating back to the 19th century and beyond between different regions and also between the forces of change and those of conservatism.

- The rise of a militant left wing in Spain intensified divisions, and conservative forces in the Church and the army resisted change.

- There was growing unrest in town and country, and worsening economic conditions led to more extremism.

- The dictatorship of Primo de Rivera failed to solve the underlying problems, and he was replaced by a republic in 1931. This is usually called the Second Spanish Republic (the first was between 1873 and 1874).

- By the 1930s, Spain was deeply divided between left and right. The efforts to reform between 1931 and 1933 increased the divisions, and on both sides there was hostility towards any form of democratic and parliamentary government.

- The creation of a left–wing coalition, the Popular Front, and the murder of a leading right–wing politician (Sotelo) provoked a military coup in 1936. The initial success of the coup led to a prolonged civil war between those who supported it and those who opposed it.

TIMELINE

1923 September: King Alfonso XIII installs a military dictatorship under General Miguel Primo de Rivera (the king ruled until 1930).

1931 April: Second Spanish Republic established; left-wing election victories; Manuel Azaña becomes prime minister at the head of a reforming government.

1933 Formation of CEDA (mass Catholic right-wing party).

1934 October: right-wing government takes office; revolt of Asturias.

1936 15 January: Popular Front pact of left-wing parties.

16 February: Popular Front wins election.

April: General strike in Madrid, spreading throughout Spain; street fights occur between left and right; rumours of a coup.

13 July: Assassination of right-wing leader José Calvo Sotelo.

17–18 July: Military revolt.

19 July: Armed workers control Barcelona.

26 July: Arrival of German Nazi and Italian fascist planes to support Franco.

SOURCE A

American journalist John Whittaker wrote of an encounter with the Moroccan nationalist General Mohammed Mizzian.

'I met this general near Navalcarrero when his troops threw two girls of less than 20 years to his feet. He discovered in the pocket of one of them a trade union card. He took her to the public school of the village where 40 Moorish soldiers were resting. He threw her to them.' A huge cry resonated in the building, writes Whittaker, horrified by what he saw. General Mizzian smiled and dismissed Whittaker's protest by saying, 'She will not survive more than four hours.'

J. Whittaker. 1942. Prelude to World War: A Witness From Spain. *Council on Foreign Relations.*

> **QUESTION**
>
> What are the value and limitations of Source A as evidence of the nature of the civil war?

Introduction

The First World War was a major cross-regional war. In this chapter, you will be investigating another type of war – civil war. You should approach the study of this war in a similar way, by thinking about why it happened, the practices (how it was fought), and what effects it had. By now you should be accustomed to thinking in terms of asking and answering key questions, as well as analysing and explaining events and their impact. Chapter 5 deals with another civil war in a different region, and you will be able to make comparisons of key issues. There are more political terms to understand in this chapter, but you should be able to build on your knowledge of military events and vocabulary, and start to see connections between these civil wars and the cross-regional wars.

Civil wars are fought by different groups within the same country. They are often characterised by greater bitterness than wars between states, and the effects are sometimes greater – the wounds take longer to heal, and families and communities are often divided. The feelings that give rise to civil war are often stronger than those that bring about national war. Wars between states can be fought for territory, in support of allies, to gain security or in response to an outrage committed against a country. Decisions may be taken for war between states without the people of a country feeling any particular animosity towards their opponents. This is much less true of civil wars. The Russian Civil War (1918– 21) saw great bitterness, many atrocities and a heavy toll taken on civilians. The Chinese Civil War (1926–49), which had already been raging for nearly ten years when the civil war began in Spain in 1936, was one of the most prolonged and divisive wars of the 20th century. Later civil wars, such as those in Mexico, Nigeria, the Congo, Rwanda, North Yemen and Vietnam, resulted in similar sustained violence and unwillingness to compromise.

Fact: Rwanda's civil war (1990–3), was based on tribal hatreds between the Hutus and the Tutsis, and involved mass killings that may have led to as many as 800 000 deaths.

Republic: A state without a monarch as its official head.

The Spanish Civil War (1936–9) came about as a result of an attempted military coup (takeover) against the elected government of the Second Spanish Republic. The **republic** had existed since the abdication of the Bourbon king Alfonso XIII in 1931. What sparked the revolt was the electoral victory of a coalition government of left-wing parties called the Popular Front in 1936. The military leaders, who started the revolt in Spanish Morocco and then crossed to the mainland, were concerned that a radical government would destroy traditional Spain. However, unlike the coup that had occurred in 1923, the revolt encountered prolonged resistance.

In 1936, Spain had a population of 24 million. In all, the war may have directly touched a million Spaniards and indirectly many more – those killed, wounded, mutilated, exiled or rendered homeless. The violence persisted well after the end of the war. In some areas there was continuing guerrilla activity, and Francisco Franco was signing death warrants for political enemies right up to 1975. The war was fought with considerable brutality on both sides, and the divisions took many years to heal.

Figure 3.1   Republican volunteers

3.1 What were the main long-term causes of the war?

Long-term divisions in Spain's history

Spain itself was no stranger to civil war. Between 1803 and 1936, no fewer than 19 military coups had taken place. Three civil wars, called the Carlist Wars, were fought between 1833 and 1876. The Carlists were members of a conservative political movement in Spain. They fought bitterly against more liberal opponents over succession to the throne. Unlike other mid-19th-century wars, the Carlist Wars, were fought with a fervour and brutality derived from deep divisions within Spain. They also lasted longer than national wars and were more difficult to resolve. They anticipated the Spanish Civil War in a number of respects.

There was a strong element of different and conflicting beliefs within the country:

- profound traditional Catholicism against modern liberal thought;
- regional independence against traditional central control;
- political liberalism against deep conservative monarchism.

The rise of the left

The left had few roots in Spain and its rise in the 20th century came as a surprise to many. In the mid-19th century, when **Marxism and socialism** emerged in Europe, there was little to suggest that Spain would soon have its own flourishing revolutionary movement. Spain was predominantly agricultural, and in many areas of the Spanish countryside, traditional customs and values and the power of the Catholic Church were strong. Capitalist industry had not developed in the same way as it had in Germany, Britain and America, and Spain had little in the way of organised labour.

After small-scale beginnings in 1868, **anarchism** came to be a major revolutionary influence of the 20th century, and was more widely embraced in Spain than other left-wing ideas. The movement first gained notice in the 1870s. After a violent incident at the town of Alcoy in 1873, when anarchists took advantage of a strike to spread radical ideas, causing the police to fire on the gathered populace, a clampdown was enforced that sent the movement underground. Consequently, it became largely based in rural areas, which were more difficult to police. Anarchism was reduced to individual acts of terrorism, which in turn were met by repression and torture by the state throughout the 1880s and 1890s.

By the early 20th century, terrorism had given way to a belief in anarcho-syndicalism. This was the theory that the state could be challenged by cooperative action by the workers in strikes. The Federation of Workers' Societies of the Spanish Region was formed in 1900. This movement organised strikes to exercise political power, and was again suppressed. Wage cuts and closures of factories in Barcelona in 1909, together with the call-up of men for a colonial war in Morocco, led to a **general strike** in the city on 26 July. This turned out to be a major event, with 1700 arrests, attacks on railway lines and anti-clericalism (hostility to the Church). Eighty churches and monasteries were attacked. The government response was swift and merciless, and five leaders were executed.

The Confederación Nacional del Trabajo

The need for stronger organisation was clear, and in 1910 the Confederación Nacional del Trabajo (CNT, the National Confederation of Labour) was founded.

Its loose structure meant that there were local organisations unencumbered by a central bureaucracy. The group quickly called another general strike. Troops were rushed to cities and the organisation was banned. The CNT allied with the **Unión General de Trabajadores (UGT)** and in 1917, a significant general strike was called. The city of Barcelona was the scene of clashes between workers and police and army units.

Marxism and socialism: This was the belief based on the writings of the German theorist Karl Marx (1818–83) that all human history was the history of class struggle. The workers were bound to take over and dominate the state, and their rule would bring true social justice and the destruction of capitalism and the ruling class who owed their wealth to exploitation. Socialist groups and parties had spread across Europe by the 1880s.

Anarchism: This is a belief associated in the 19th century with the Russian thinker Mikhail Bakunin (1814–76). It rejected the need for disciplined revolutionary organisation and looked to a working-class revolution that would bring an end to state rule and usher in government by the people. Anarchism was particularly influential on the Spanish revolutionary movement.

General strike: A strike not just in one industry but throughout the economy, with the aim of demonstrating the power of workers in bringing the country to a standstill.

The **Unión General de Trabajadores (UGT):** was a trade union initially founded by the Barcelona printing workers in 1888, which supported republicanism and socialism. It led a general strike in 1909, was responsible for the first trade union member being elected to parliament, and had 100 000 members by 1913.

Post-war unrest

After 1917, the example of the Russian Revolution and the post-First World War depression increased unrest. In 1919, another general strike broke out in Barcelona involving more than 100 000 workers. For the first time, significant concessions were gained – union recognition and an eight-hour day. The latter became law in 1919. However, political violence continued and was a contributory factor to the establishment of a right-wing military dictatorship by General Primo de Rivera in 1923.

The Federación Anarquista Ibérica

Anarchism was banned between 1923 and 1930. The movement split – the more radical Federación Anarquista Ibérica (FAI, Spanish Anarchist Federation) was formed in 1927 to prevent ideological backsliding by the CNT. Although membership was initially low (fewer than 30 000), it rose rapidly later on. The group was militant, and organised bank robberies and assassinations.

Activity

Write a brief explanation of each of the following organisations:

- CNT
- FAI.

The Catholic Church

Fear of industrial revolt, socialism and anarchism, and rural unrest were potent reasons for the support by many Spaniards for the coup of 1936, but these factors were bound together by fears for the position of the Catholic Church. Catholicism was deeply embedded in Spanish life and history. It had spearheaded the stand against the Islamic invasions of the Middle Ages and the subsequent re-conquest (*Reconquista*) of southern Spain from the Moors, which was not completed until the late 15th century. The Church was associated with the survival of Christianity and racial purity; it was also deeply linked to the power of the state – with the association between Crown and Inquisition – and also with the prestige of Spain in Europe, as the Spanish kings of the 16th and 17th centuries stood against Protestant enemies. Catholic Spain had defeated France during the Napoleonic wars. Love of nation and love of Church were thus deeply connected by history. The Catholic Church held a powerful and privileged position in Spain, and had not suffered the attacks by secular authorities that had been common in other Catholic countries since the 18th century.

The Catholic Church had been alarmed at the growth of **anti-clericalism**, anarchism and socialism, all of which took a hostile attitude towards religion. Politically, the Church had aligned itself with the landowners, the army and the Crown. It had supported the dictatorship of Primo de Rivera and had formed agrarian organisations to combat anarchism in the countryside. Church leaders were appalled by the reforming legislation proposed by the Republic after April 1931.

The army

Military coups were not a novelty in Spain. In 1874, the First Spanish Republic had been overthrown by a liberal general, Arsenio Martínez Campos. The military

Fact: The post-First World War depression occurred because most European countries were economically damaged by the disruption to international trade and payments caused by the war. Agriculture worldwide was hit by falling prices and the demand for food and raw materials. Even before the Great Depression of 1929, farmers around the globe were suffering from reduced incomes.

Fact: The *Reconquista* was the re-conquest by Christian forces of lands taken by the Islamic Arab forces that swept through North Africa and Spain in the 8th century. This long struggle ended with the fall of the Islamic state of Granada to Queen Isabella I of Castile and her husband King Ferdinand of Aragon (*Los Reyes Católicos* – the Catholic Monarchs) in 1492. The wars encouraged a fierce fighting Catholic spirit in Spain, which was still prevalent more than 400 years later.

Anti-clericalism: Hostility to organised religion, particularly to the Catholic Church, which was common in Europe in the 19th century and sometimes encouraged by governments. Otto von Bismarck led a campaign in Germany against the church in the 1870s, and laws were passed against the church in France in 1902–5. In Spain, the new Republic passed anti-clerical measures between 1931 and 1933.

The Spanish Civil War

Fact: The First Spanish Republic lasted from February 1873 to December 1874, when King Amadeo I abdicated and Spain came under parliamentary rule. The First Republic was politically unstable. It was overthrown by military action, after which the monarchy was restored.

Figure 3.2 Holy Week in Seville in the 1930s

Figure 3.3 Miguel Primo de Rivera (1870–1930)

He was born in Jerez. He joined the army and took part in the colonial wars in Morocco, Cuba and the Philippines. With the support of King Alfonso XIII and the army, he led a military coup in September 1923. He promised to eliminate corruption and to regenerate Spain after the defeats in Morocco and the rising tide of left-wing agitation. To achieve this, he suspended the constitution, established martial law and imposed a strict system of censorship. He was faced with increasing discontent in the late 1920s and was forced to resign in 1930.

governor, Camilo Polavieja of the Philippines, contemplated a coup after the Spanish defeat by the USA led to the loss of the colony in 1898. Another colonial defeat in Morocco in 1923 led to a coup by the king and **Miguel Primo de Rivera**, who was commanding the army in Catalonia. The constitution was suspended and the general's own party – the Spanish Patriotic Union (Unión Patriótica Española) – was the only one permitted. When Rivera was dismissed in 1930 he was followed by another general, Berenguer, and then an admiral, Aznar, before Spain returned to constitutional rule and a second republic was established.

Like the Church, the army had enjoyed a privileged position in Spain before 1931, and also like the Church it felt threatened by the Republic. The republican government of Manuel Azaña was quick to announce anti-military measures. Military judicial tribunals no longer had authority over civilians; the army was to swear an oath of loyalty to the Republic rather than being separate to the state and outside its control. The length of military service was reduced to a year, the size of the army was reduced and the Zaragoza military academy – source of much elitist military thinking – was closed. There was a renewed inquiry into military failures in Morocco and officers were put on trial. This particularly infuriated those who had served in Africa.

In return for diplomatic support for France and Britain, Spain won the right to control northern Morocco in 1906. This led to a full-scale rebellion against Spain by the Moroccan people. Ambitious young Spanish officers took advantage of the colonial war to demonstrate their merit, but they were frustrated by an old-fashioned corrupt and bureaucratic army. Enlargement of the forces was met with popular discontent in 1909. Conventional officers took the unusual step of forming an association called the Juntas Militares (military councils) during the First World War, which won some concessions towards reform. The Juntares (members of the Juntas) took a leading role in crushing left-wing revolts.

However, in 1921, the army suffered a major and humiliating defeat at Annual in Morocco, losing thousands of men. From this emerged a new and reformed Spanish African army, scorning civilian government and using brutal methods to suppress the Moroccan opposition. These forces were known as Africanistas and saw themselves as a new élite. By 1927, they had conquered Morocco, with the help of German advisers and chemical weapons. A gap emerged in the army between the Juntas and the Africanistas – between career officers in Spain and a new reckless brutal 'storm trooper' colonial force. Both opposed the reforms of the new Republic, but by 1936 it was largely the Africanistas who were spearheading the revolt, while the Juntas supported the Republic.

The most brutal element was the Foreign Legion – nicknamed the 'Bridegrooms of Death' – under the leadership of Francisco Franco. They were intensely nationalistic and saw themselves as Spain's saviours. The Moorish troops were no longer the enemy, but rather the means to suppress more deadly threats from communists, anarchists, freemasons and opponents of the Catholic Church. The Africanistas were infuriated by the reforms instigated by Azada, the minister of war, in promoting the Junteros and holding enquiries into the mismanagement of the Moroccan campaign. The Africanista general Sanjuro launched a premature coup in 1932, but it was to these fanatical and brutal troops that the conservative republicans turned in 1934 to suppress the risings in the Asturias, a region in northern Spain. Encouraged by **martial law** and the elimination of leftist opposition, the officers of the Africanistas began to plot. Circumstances gave the rebellion of 1936 support from landowners, industrialists, Catholic traditionalists, and the opponents of separatism.

Separatism

The revolt of 1936 was a reaction to the threat of the break-up of Spain – a fear that dated right back to the formation of a united country in 1469 by the marriage of Ferdinand of Aragon and Isabella of Castile. The historic kingdoms did not successfully merge, and retained much of their own identities as well as different languages. The acquisition of Andalucía from the Moors (1492) and Navarre from France (1513) added territories with different traditions.

Despite the centralising activities of these powerful monarchs, Catalonia in particular proved difficult to integrate. A major rebellion occurred in 1640, and France intrigued to maintain **Catalan separatism**. In the War of the Spanish Succession in the early 18th century, Catalonia resisted the accession of the **Bourbon** dynasty in Spain, but in 1714 it was completely subjugated by the forces of the Bourbon Philip V, who abolished the Catalan constitution and autonomy.

Catalan separatism re-emerged in the 19th century, and Catalan nationalists gave their support to the conservative Carlist side to win concessions from the liberal nationalists. The resurgence really began in the 1850s, however, when serious efforts were made to revive the Catalan language.

The Esquerra Republicana de Catalunya

The separatists had some success in gaining a measure of self-government by 1913, but it was repealed in 1925 by Primo de Rivera, who insisted on the unity of Spain. By then Catalonia had adopted a more left-wing stance, and the anarchists were regarded as the best hope of liberty. Rivera's policy led to the formation of a left-wing coalition party in Catalonia – the Esquerra Republicana de Catalunya (ERC), or the Republican Left. The Esquerra won a sweeping victory in the municipal elections of 1931, and two

Martial law: The imposition of military discipline and courts on a country's civilians.

QUESTION

What evidence is there in the chapter so far that Spain was becoming increasingly divided politically between 1931 and 1936? Do you think it was likely that the Second Republic would be as short-lived as the First?

Fact: 'Spain' is a concept rather a reality because of the diverse nature of the different areas. The biggest distinction is the language divide between Catalonia and the Basque region. Both these areas had a long history and culture of their own. They hoped for greater self-government after the Republic was proclaimed in 1931. 'Separatism' refers to the desire for regions to have more control over their own affairs and, in this case, to have their language accepted as official.

Catalan separatism: Now an autonomous region of modern Spain, Catalonia in the north-east was initially linked to France but came under the kings of Aragon in 1258. It kept its local customs and resisted integration into Castile when Spain became united in the 15th century. With a separate language, history and culture, and one of Spain's great cities – Barcelona – it was proud of its heritage and pressed for self-government.

Figure 3.4 The historical regions of Spain

Bourbon: The Spanish royal family from the 18th century were a branch of the French Bourbon family after the last Habsburg ruler of Spain died childless. The present king, Felipe VI, is a member of the Bourbon family.

KEY CONCEPTS ACTIVITY

Significance: Draw up a list of the main long-term causes of the Spanish Civil War, then use this list to construct a table, providing brief details of each factor. Finally, write a couple of paragraphs to explain which factor you consider to be the most significant.

days later its leader proclaimed a Catalan Republic. A compromise was worked out with the new Republic, and in September 1932 the statute of autonomy (self-government) for Catalonia became law. The association of an independent Catalonia, together with radical land reform and industrial and social unrest in the city of Barcelona, meant that the forces of conservatism bitterly opposed local rights, and national unity became one of the rallying cries of the nationalist rebels.

3.2 What were the main short-term causes of the war?

Religious discontent

The Catholic Church was deeply angered by the initial reforms introduced by the new Republic. The Church lost control of divorce and marriage, as the state installed divorce procedures and civil marriages. The ecclesiastical orders were barred from teaching under Article 26 of the new constitution. Religious symbols were removed from public buildings. The Church lost its subsidy from the state, phased out over two years, and its property and assets had to be declared and were liable to taxation.

An outburst of anti-clericalism in Madrid, in which 50 convents were attacked, seemed to confirm that the presence of socialists in the government was tantamount to a godless attack on the Church, and that a fate awaited it similar to that suffered by the Russian Church under communism or the French Church at the height of the French Revolution. Clerical support for political groups culminated in the formation in 1933 of the Confederación Española de Derechas Autónomas (CEDA, Spanish Confederation of Independent Rightists) – akin to the Catholic Centre Party in Germany. This was a mass political movement of the right to protect Catholic interests. Spain's religious and political divisions began to entwine, and many Catholics felt that they were under threat and needed to take political action.

Figure 3.5 People voting in the November 1933 election, Spain

The elections held in November 1933 resulted in a coalition between the moderate radicals and the CEDA led by **José Maria Gil Robles**, and when CEDA ministers entered government in 1934 it seemed that Catholic influence might prevent radical change. However, it also provoked fury from the left, which was afraid that a situation might develop similar to that in Italy and Germany – when extreme right-wing ministers entered government and subverted the constitution from within. The new right-wing government then proceeded to undo most of the reforms passed from 1931 to 1933. It also used the police and army to repress any signs of protest or opposition. The left called these years the *bienio negro* ('two black years').

The Popular Front

When Robles failed to be appointed prime minister in 1936, he negotiated with leading generals for a coup, but failed to convince them. The reunification of the left in the Popular Front, and their election victory in 1936, marked the end of any hopes for Catholic political influence, and opened the way for a renewed campaign against the Church. The early radicalism of the Republic now seemed likely to return and, as in

José Maria Gil Robles (1898–1980)

He was a right-wing Catholic journalist who supported the dictatorship of Primo de Rivera and opposed the Second Republic. He formed the CEDA in 1933, which was basically anti-democratic and backed Franco. Robles was forced to dissolve his party in 1937, and played little part in post-war Spain.

**Causation and
Consequences:** How
did the increasingly
CEDA-dominated
coalition of 1934–5
help polarise politics
in Spain? What was
the immediate impact
on the left?

France, the Popular Front appeared to be linked to international communism and the
influence of the USSR. In May 1934, the USSR gave official approval to alliances
between communists and other left-wing groups (the Popular Front) – from the extreme
anarchists to the moderate reforming liberals – to enable them to gain office. This had
previously been regarded as going against Marxist theory. The result was that left-wing
alliances gained power in France and Spain. The coalitions were bitterly opposed by
conservatives, who recognised the threat of Soviet-influenced communism. The alliances
were also difficult to maintain – in France they did lead to reforms; in Spain the coalition
led to military revolt and civil war. The more united nationalist forces were at a greater
advantage in the end because of the disunity among members of the Popular Front parties.

Divisions between left and right in Spain had now become part of an international
battle. The right-wing parties polled 4 505 524 votes in the election but gained only
124 seats; the Popular Front polled 4 654 000 and gained 278 seats. It is not altogether
surprising that many conservative Catholics were prepared to support the military coup.

Activities

1   Divide into groups and make a poster for the anarchists; the Catalan separatists;
the FAI; and CEDA.

2   Make up a slogan for each poster. Do your posters help to explain the growth of
political extremism? The poster here is from the semi-Trotskyist POUM party. How
useful is it as evidence for the situation that led to civil war?

Figure 3.6 'Farmers, the land belongs
to you': Spanish poster, 1936, from the
republican forces

Divisions in Spain by 1936

By 1936, the rifts in Spanish society had become dangerous. Rising leftist activity had provoked a rise in right-wing extremism. The army had become increasingly involved in politics. There was a fear of anarchist revolution and concerns about the Popular Front.

When this coalition came to power, popular unrest in the countryside exploded into land seizures encouraged by radical anarchists. There was little attempt by the anarchists to moderate their behaviour, and no demands to allow the Popular Front to reassure moderate elements in Spain. A CNT conference held in May 1936 was full of revolutionary language. It seemed that the new Republic had not been able to control the major revolutionary group.

The trigger for war

The murder of former finance minister José Calvo Sotelo on 13 July 1936 was the trigger for the war, in much the same way as the assassination of Archduke Franz Ferdinand had sparked the First World War. Sotelo had been in exile from 1931 to 1934, but had returned to become a leading right-wing figure associated with the Spanish fascists (the Falange) and a deputy for the Renovación Española (Spanish Revival) group. He clashed with the socialists in the assembly and was murdered by left-wing members of the Civil Guard. His death hastened the preparations for a military coup by generals Sanjuro and Mola, and by the Foreign Legion. It may have prompted **Francisco Franco**, then in the Canary Islands, to join the coup as an influential right-wing general.

Figure 3.8   Francisco Franco (1892–1975)

He was a general who joined the military revolt in 1936 and emerged as the leader (*El Caudillo*). After victory in 1939, he introduced elements of fascism but was more a military dictator. He brutally punished his former opponents. Spain became isolated and impoverished in the post-war years. However, there was some relaxation and economic recovery by the 1960s. Franco made Prince Juan Carlos his successor in 1969.

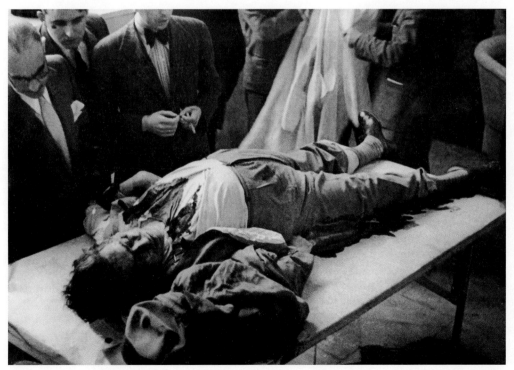

Figure 3.7   The body of José Calvo Sotelo, July 1936.

3.3 What were the political, ideological and economic causes?

When the army of Africa began its revolt in July 1936, Spain was already deeply divided. On one side were the landowners, monarchists, the small Spanish Fascist Party, the Catholic Church, much of Castile and north and north-west Spain. On the other side were the anarchists, the socialists, the republicans, Catalan separatists, landless labourers of the south, the small Spanish Communist Party and the trade unions, especially the UGT. On one side, a secular, reforming constitutional Spain; on the other, militaristic, authoritarian, conservative, Catholic Spain. On one side, admirers of Soviet Russia and Western democracy; on the other, admirers of Nazi Germany and fascist Italy.

The international element was an important factor. Like many other civil wars, the Spanish Civil War was driven by global influences as well as ideas that were unique to Spain. What made this war special was that by 1936 Europe had become deeply divided ideologically between communism and the nationalistic fascist and Nazi dictatorships of Mussolini and Hitler, as well as their imitators in smaller states. In the middle lay the path of parliamentary democracy, and added to the mix was anarchism and Trotskyism (named after its founder **Leon Trotsky**). The establishment of militaristic right-wing dictatorships in Italy and Germany had influenced the growth of a fascist movement in Spain founded by Jose Antonio Primo de Rivera and called the **Falange**. This was modelled on early Italian fascism and was another sign of growing political extremism.

Political and ideological causes

Spain became a battleground for opposing ideologies characterised by some strained alliances – 'fundamentalist' Catholics allied with militarists, nationalists and fascists; democrats allied with anarchists, separatists, communists and Trotskyists – in a bewildering mixture of ideals. The war was complicated by the desire of some areas to break away from central domination. For example, Catalonia fought not only for political ideas but for regional freedom. Supporters of these ideas – or perhaps more commonly opponents of these ideas – came to Spain to fight for their beliefs. The war took on an international flavour, with volunteers from different countries enjoying a higher profile than in the other civil wars of the previous 100 years.

Just as with the other civil wars, however, the European powers could not ignore what was happening. The Mediterranean was of vital interest for many of them and, ideologically, the war affected communist Russia, fascist Italy and Nazi Germany. Ideology prompted intervention, just as it had done for the British, French, Americans and Japanese in the Russian Civil War in their desire to crush communism. The USSR sent supplies, weapons and political advisers; Germany largely contributed air power, perhaps in a desire to test its bombers; Italy sent large-scale ground forces. Britain and France attempted to enforce non-intervention and the only direct action was an effective British threat against Italian submarines, tactfully referred to as belonging to a 'mystery power' whose presence in the western Mediterranean was seen as being undesirable.

Figure 3.9 Leon Trotsky (1879–1940)

He was a Russian revolutionary who aided Lenin in the Russian Revolution of 1917. He broke with his fellow revolutionary, Stalin, after Lenin's death, believing in worldwide revolution and rejecting the personal power of Stalin. He was assassinated on Stalin's orders in Mexico in 1940, after having been exiled in 1928.

Falange: A fascist movement in Spain founded in 1933. It was an idealistic mix of Christian nationalism and an alternative to communism for the working classes. Its founder was sentenced to death by the Republic in November 1936. It attracted a great deal of intellectual support, and its members were fervent opponents of the Republic. Some 60 per cent died in the war.

Thus, a prolonged, brutal and costly conflict in Spain was fuelled by official and unofficial foreign intervention. Like other civil wars, it had a considerable effect on the ordinary people of Spain and determined the nation's development for a generation afterwards.

Economic causes

Long term rural unrest

Land ownership in Spain was concentrated among relatively small numbers of people. During the 19th century, a great deal of former royal land and Church land had been sold, and – especially in the south – large estates exploited cheap labour from a mass of landless labourers. In Córdoba province (southern Spain), for example, 7 per cent of landowners controlled 52 per cent of the land. In other regions, a greater proportion of peasant proprietors existed, but rural wealth and landholding were still unevenly distributed. As the population grew and inflation rose, agricultural wages were kept down. It was difficult to form any kind of protest because of the close relationship between the landowners and local police and government.

By 1919, there were frequent episodes of rural unrest and violence. Socialist and anarchist ideas spread, as did the demand for land reform. Rebellion was suppressed in the 1920s, but the establishment of the Republic in 1931 caused a considerable outburst of unrest, as the rural workers hoped for change. However, falling agricultural prices and exports led to wage cuts. Rural unemployment also rose. Attempts at land reform were blocked by the conservative parties and the countryside became radicalised. There was a considerable rise in membership of the socialist-led peasant workers' union, the **Federación Nacional de Trabajadores de la Tierra** (**FNTT**, National Federation of Land Workers), which went from 27 000 members in 1930 to more than a million by 1932. Land seizures and estate occupations became more frequent.

At the same time that the rise in industrial unrest was alarming conservatives, the danger of rural revolution also reared its head. This had been a potent element in the Russian Revolution in the summer of 1917. There had been a growing influence of CNT anarchism in Andalucía (southern Spain) and migration had spread it to other regions. When the Spanish Civil War began, substantial numbers of anarchist collectives were already established in the south, but also in Aragon in the west and Castile (central Spain).

Unrest after 1931

Rural unrest

In April 1931, Spain became a republic, raising the hopes of the landless labourers of the south. Agrarian reform was a major feature of the new regime; working hours were reduced and overtime had to be paid if they were exceeded. Landowners were compelled not to bring in cheaper labour if workers were available in their own municipality. They were forced to cultivate all usable land on pain of their land being **requisitioned** and redistributed to the landless workers. This had a major impact on the wealthy landowners of the south, who depended on cheap labour. In Castile and northern Spain, where there was more small-scale peasant land ownership, the new Republic had much less appeal because, alongside agrarian reform, measures were introduced to restrict the power of the Catholic Church. Thus, Catholic farmers were

Fact: The Russian government was overthrown by the Bolsheviks (communists) in October 1917. However, they were a minority in Russia and their opponents organised forces against them after their leader Lenin signed a humiliating peace with Germany (the treaty of Brest-Litovsk). The Russian Civil War (1918–20) brought together a wide variety of anti-communist forces – democrats, monarchists, those who wanted regional independence. These forces were known as the Whites. France, USA, Japan and Britain sent help to the Whites against the Reds (communists). But internal disunity, the unwillingness of foreign powers to sustain aid, and the effective leadership of the communists, led to the Whites' defeat.

Federación Nacional de Trabajadores de la Tierra (FNTT): The socialist-led peasant workers' union of the National Federation of Land Workers.

QUESTION
Why did anarchist ideas spread so widely in Spain?

Fact: Similar to Spanish rural unrest in 1931, the summer of 1917 – after the abdication of Tsar Nicholas II in March – saw a wave of attacks on landowners in the Russian countryside, and seizures of land by peasants who had been tenants or workers on the land. In November 1917, the new communist government recognised this by legalising land seizures.

3

The Spanish Civil War

Requisitioned: When property is taken over by the state.

Coalition: When two or more political groups join together to form a government.

attracted to the CNCA (1917) – Confederación Nacional Católico-Agraria (National Confederation of Catholic Farmers) – a mass organisation that came to rival the socialist-led FNTT.

The countryside became a battleground. Disputes took place at local level about wages and land redistribution. But the pace of change was slow – the new Republic was anxious to avoid too much dislocation, and only 10 per cent of uncultivated arable land was in fact redistributed between 1931 and 1933. This generated a violent reaction as peasants were disappointed – most noticeably in Casas Viejas near Cadiz, where republican police shot 19 peasants. In 1933, internal divisions in the left, together with a right-wing backlash, resulted in the formation of a centre-right **coalition** that reversed the changes. Landowners dominated local tribunals, working-hours legislation was not enforced and confiscated land was returned. Unrest grew in the south. Attempts by the autonomous Catalan government, set up by the new Republic, to redistribute land were foiled by a right-wing reaction that ended self-government in Catalonia.

The splits in the left and the growing power and organisation of the right frustrated land reforms and caused massive resentment. In January 1936, however, the left reunited in the Popular Front, and prospects for rural change improved again. However, this generated even greater fears among the right, and was one of the reasons why the military coup attracted so much support.

Industrial unrest

Despite the establishment of the Republic in 1931, social unrest continued, with the army suppressing CNT strikes. The government arrested and deported anarchist leaders, leading to strikes and local insurrections. There were risings in Zaragoza in 1933 and a major disturbance in 1934 in the Asturias mining area of northern Spain. The communists and anarchists cooperated, and workers attacked police barracks and then took over much of the region. The government sent in colonial troops – the Spanish Foreign Legion and its Moorish soldiers – and the suppression of the revolt was carried out with extreme brutality.

Historical debate:
Most historians agree that the Civil War was not inevitable. However, there is considerable debate over how it might have been prevented. Revisionist historians, such as Stanley Payne, tend to blame the Popular Front (e.g., for its determination to press ahead with significant radical reforms). Other historians, however – such as Helen Graham and Paul Preston – argue that even if the Popular Front had been more moderate, the coup would still have taken place, as the Spanish elites were not prepared to make any concessions as regards reform. Only if the majority of Spaniards had accepted the continuation of massive social and economic inequalities could the civil war have been avoided.

Theory of Knowledge

History and inevitability:
'Historians, like other people, sometimes fall into the rhetorical language and speak of an occurrence as "inevitable", when they mean merely that the conjunction of factors leading one to expect it was overwhelmingly strong ... In practice historians do not assume that events are inevitable before they have taken place. They frequently discuss alternative courses available to the actors in the story ... Nothing in history is inevitable' – E.H. Carr (1892–1982)

Is it justified for historians to discuss whether events are 'inevitable' or is this is an unhistorical concept? Is it helpful to show by considering 'inevitability' that the pressures for an event were very strong and the chances of avoiding it were weak? Or can events always, by the nature of history, be avoided? Is 'inevitability' a 'false friend' in that it seems to be leading to an understanding of causation, but in fact leads to assumptions that because things happened in a certain way, there was no alternative?

End of unit activities

1 In the First World War, there were both short-term triggers and long-term causes. For both wars studied so far, identify the immediate causes and five longer-term causes, using a table similar to the one shown below.

War	Immediate causes	Long-term causes
First World War		
Spanish Civil War		

2 Draw a wall chart showing briefly what all the main political groups in Spain by 1936 stood for. Put the right-wing groups on the right and the left-wing groups on the left.

3 *How justified was the military revolt of 1936?* Hold a class debate based on this question. Prepare for this by each 'side' making cards with a clear line of argument on one side and the justification for it on the other.

4 Discuss the view that 'From 1931 it was inevitable that Spain would experience a civil war.' Factors might include:

   • the long-term divisions in Spanish society

   • the history of civil war

   • the fundamental problems of society and economy.

5 On the other hand, Spain had a Popular Front government without civil war, so without the determined opposition of a few military leaders, perhaps political events might have taken a different turn. Consider this in your discussion.

KEY QUESTIONS

- What were the nature and main practices of the Spanish Civil War?
- What were the main events of the war, and how were they influenced by technology and tactics?
- What was the significance of the mobilisation of human and economic resources, and the home front?
- How important was foreign intervention?

Overview

- The military revolt of 1936 developed into a full-scale civil war in which foreign volunteers and powers also participated. The initial ability of the rebels to take southern Spain was crucial, and although there was a successful republican defence of Madrid, their counterattacks were generally less successful than the assaults made by Franco.

- The divisions on the left, and their failure to win arms and supplies from the Western democracies, together with Franco's ability to use superior manpower and resources in a way that wore down the opposition, led to republican defeat in 1939.

- There is some debate about the relative importance of different reasons for the outcome of the war.

- The war was similar in many respects to the Second World War – particularly in its impact on the civilian population, which endured bombing, evacuation, reprisals, government control and a blurring of the distinction between soldiers and civilians.

- The war also had some effect in terms of social change – for example, on the position of women – but Franco's victory meant that there was reaction rather than revolution, and traditional and repressive rule was established.

- The Republic undertook some changes that could be seen as a Spanish Revolution, but the divisions on the left and the pressure from the nationalists prevented these from coming to fruition.

3.4 What were the nature and main practices of the Spanish Civil War?

The Spanish Civil War was such a bitter conflict between Spaniards that it bore some of the characteristics of total war. Civilians were often seen as legitimate targets for bombing and reprisals, and the entire resources of the Republic were deployed to defeat the revolt. When nationalists conquered regions, they too used all the resources available to them, in a war they perceived could only be won by complete victory or complete defeat. In terms of ideological commitment, the war became a life-and-death struggle for ideals. However, for the foreign countries involved – the USSR, Italy and Germany – the nature of the war was different. Limited resources were employed in a conflict that was not fundamental to their national existence. Foreign intervention meant that more aircraft, tanks and heavy artillery were deployed than would have been the case if the war had been restricted to Spanish forces. However, much of the outcome of the war did not depend on technological advantage, and desperate infantry struggles predominated. The impact of bombing on civilians anticipated that of the Second World War, as did the relatively high casualties and the impossibility of compromise.

3.5 What were the main events and how were they influenced by technology and tactics?

The war began as a military coup planned by a group of generals, including Sanjuro, Quiepo, Goded and Mola. Franco was initially uncertain about the coup, and only joined later, making his way from the Canary Islands to the Spanish Foreign Legion, which had landed in Tetuan, Morocco. Support for the nationalist rebels was focused in the Canary Islands, Spanish Morocco, Galicia, Navarre and parts of rural Castile and Aragon. The map shows the regions held by the two sides in July 1936.

Main events

Popular support kept Madrid and Barcelona loyal to the Republic. The rebel general Goded was killed in Barcelona. When General Sanjuro was killed in a plane crash, three independent nationalist rebel generals were left – Franco, Mola and Quiepo – in charge of only five cities and about a quarter of mainland Spain. Most of the industrial and trading centres were held by the republican government, which also enjoyed the advantage of being the legitimate power. Much of the army was loyal to the Republic, and foreign leaders recognised its authority. Had matters been under control then rebel chances would have been much reduced, but the Popular Front coalition lacked effective discipline over a people in crisis. There were deep divisions in government, and the attacks on monks, nuns and the clergy resulted in 7000 deaths and horrifying violence, increasing moderate and conservative support for the rebels.

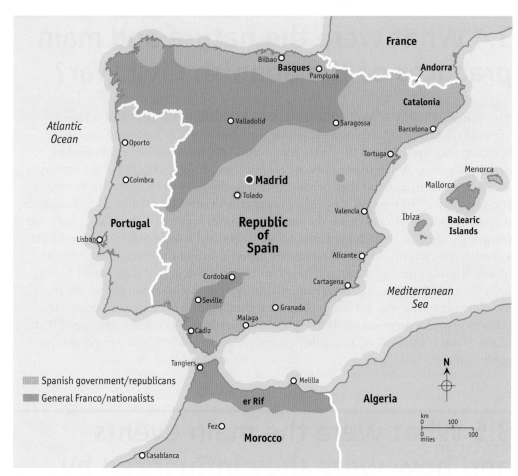

Figure 3.10   A map showing the territory held by the nationalists and the republicans in July 1936

**KEY CONCEPTS
ACTIVITY**

Significance: Find out
some more about the
various republican
militia formed in
the early phase of
the Civil War. Then
write a couple of
paragraphs assessing
their significance,
advantages and
effectiveness as
opposed to regular
army units.

Throughout August and September 1936, Franco brought his Moroccan legion into
Spain with German transport aircraft – one of the key examples of foreign intervention.
Under General Yagüe, nationalist forces took cities and towns in the south. The capture
of Badajoz united two main nationalist forces in Andalucía. Franco then drove towards
Madrid. The republicans had besieged Toledo but could not take its citadel, the Alcazar.
In a famous incident the commander, Colonel Moscado, refused to save his own son,
who had been taken captive, by surrendering, and his son was executed. Franco relieved
Toledo, which had been besieged for 69 days – an event that was of considerable
propaganda value to the nationalists. For their part, the republicans mobilised an
enthusiastic militia.

Franco took eastern Andalucía and Extremadura, but was kept back from Madrid by a
determined defence. The war widened as volunteers arrived from overseas. Italy sent
70 000 regular troops and supplies, and military assistance came to Franco from Portugal
and Germany. A German air force of 100 planes was established at Salamanca. Russia
sent military aid, and international volunteers called the International Brigades were
established.

A nationalist naval victory at Cape Espartel broke the republican blockade of Morocco.
This ensured that men and supplies could cross the Straits of Gibraltar to reinforce the
nationalists.

Sieges, attacks and counterattacks

The major campaign was the siege of Madrid by nationalists, which lasted from 29 October to 23 November 1936. The nationalists had professional troops; the republicans had enthusiastic militia volunteers. A plan to attack the city via the university area was discovered and the republican General Miaja organised the defence. The heroism displayed during this siege passed into Spanish legend. The slogan *No pasarán* ('they shall not pass') recalled the determined French resistance of Verdun in 1916, and the communist leader Dolores Ibárruri, 'La Pasionara', earned renown by her courageous rallying of the troops. The arrival of the International Brigades aided the defence and Madrid survived. A prolonged siege followed. Franco attempted to cut off the city from the north in the Battle of the Coruna Road (December 1936 to January 1937), which ended with 30 000 losses – and a stalemate in the conflict.

In the north, where many areas had initially declared for the rebels, a republican attack was carried out on Vitoria by Basque troops. However, superior air reconnaissance cost them the element of surprise, and better artillery and air support won the day for the nationalists in the Battle of Villareal (30 November to 5 December 1936).

The nationalists had failed to take Madrid but, despite their superior equipment and better-trained soldiers, they faced a formidable task given the regular army units that supported the Republic and the mobilisation of popular militias. Holding central positions and key cities – and having committed support – had helped the Russian revolutionaries survive the attacks of professional armies in the Russian Civil War. However, in Spain, the republicans lacked a clear central authority such as that provided by Lenin and Trotsky, and they were hampered by the difficulty of defending some of the key areas. This was clearly demonstrated when the republican city of Malaga fell to nationalist and Italian forces in February 1937. The consequence was a series of mass executions and a dramatic drop in morale.

Attacks on Madrid continued in February 1937, this time from the Jarama valley in the south. Total losses were more than 45 000. The defenders managed to keep the communication link between Madrid and Valencia open, but the nationalists gained more territory. The International Brigades were once again in the forefront of the fighting. With Italian help, Franco kept the pressure on Madrid with an attack on Guadalajara in March. Well-equipped Italian motorised units were decisive in taking the city, but the advance met bad weather and determined republican counterattacks with air support. The Italians withdrew, leaving behind much of their equipment.

The nationalists renewed their attacks against the Basques in the north in March to June 1937, supported by Italian troops and in the air by the German Condor Legion. Casualties mounted on both sides, but Bilbao – a major port and industrial centre – fell and the terror bombing of Guernica and Durango was effective. In an attempt to take the pressure off the Basques, the republicans attacked at San Ildefonso in May and June, but this only delayed Basque defeat. Another attack to draw nationalist forces from the north was launched in Aragon in June, but superior nationalist artillery destroyed the republicans, and Bilbao could not be saved.

The difficulties of counterattacking had proved greater than holding Madrid, but the republicans continued to attack, this time at Brunette in Estremadura. Making similar mistakes to those of the First World War, the republicans allowed themselves to be drawn into battles for strong defensive points, and they suffered heavy losses. This time republican casualties amounted to 25 000 – more than double those of their opponents.

Fact: From February to November 1916, the French defended the forts at Verdun in eastern France, regardless of the costs. In 1936, their slogan *Ils ne passeront pas* ('they shall not pass') was adopted during the defence of Madrid: *No pasarán*.

Fact: Guernica was the ancient capital of the Basques, who had withstood the advances of the nationalist army since 1936. In April 1937, Guernica was deliberately targeted for aerial bombing. Franco allowed the city to be bombed by the German Condor Legion. A total of 1,654 people were killed and 889 wounded, as air raid defences were minimal.

The Spanish Civil War

Losses of tanks and aircraft were hard to restore, whereas the nationalists could rely on new supplies from their allies.

In the north, the nationalists built on their conquest of the Basque region. Italian help meant that they outnumbered the republicans; Basque troops were disheartened and the republicans at Santander in northern Castile were overwhelmed in August 1937.

The republicans now focused on Aragon, trying to take Saragossa and unite the province, which had been divided by nationalist gains. They failed to take advantage of local successes, however, and once again a dangerous loss of men and tanks resulted (August–September 1937). The republicans had not been able to sustain a successful offensive like that of the nationalists in the north.

In autumn 1937, nationalist forces completed their northern conquests by subduing the Asturias region, although they still faced guerrilla resistance in this republican stronghold. However, many more men were now available for the campaign against Madrid.

To forestall this, the republicans launched an attack at Teruel in December 1937, beginning a hard struggle that lasted until February 1938. Teruel fell, but Franco was determined to retake it, trapping large republican forces in the city. This time total casualties came to more than 100 000. The war had become one of attrition – in some ways similar to the First World War – but the series of failed offensives had weakened the republican side.

Fact: The League of Nations had formed a Non-Intervention Committee in 1937 and banned outside help from reaching the two sides in Spain. Italy and Germany ignored the ban, but Britain and France enforced it (mainly against the Republic, as they did not wish to risk confrontations with Nazi Germany or fascist Italy) and the Republic found it difficult to import war materials. Russia did send supplies, but of poor quality and only erratically.

Franco divides republican territory – a turning point

The results of the failed republican attacks, the erosion of men and war materials and the nationalist northern victories became evident in 1938 when, by concentrating forces against a weakened enemy, Franco was able to drive through Aragon and reach the sea, cutting republican territory in two. This success was aided by Italian artillery and tanks, and the support of the German air force. Only determined resistance by fresh troops prevented the fall of Valencia. This attack was arguably the real turning point of the war.

When a reopening of the French frontier allowed supplies to reach the republican armies, their generals launched yet another offensive over the River Ebro to take Franco's army from the rear. A night attack caught the Moroccan troops of the nationalists by surprise. However, the nationalists stabilised their positions at Gandesa and counterattacked, forcing the republicans back to the Ebro. The attacks lost the republicans 70 000 men and many irreplaceable aircraft, vehicles and supplies. The fighting between July and November 1938 lasted almost as long as the Battle of the Somme during the First World War.

The final push

By the end of 1938, the outcome of the war was no longer in doubt. Nationalist forces swept into Catalonia and took Barcelona, reaching the French frontier by February 1939. In Madrid, a regular army commander on the republican side, Casado, overthrew communist leaders in order to surrender to Franco and gain better terms. A war broke out between the communists and the anarchist troops – this futile in-fighting allowed the nationalists to take Madrid on 28 March 1939, and the war drew to a close.

Franco, the dominant nationalist general since the death of General Mola in 1937, was the new ruler of Spain.

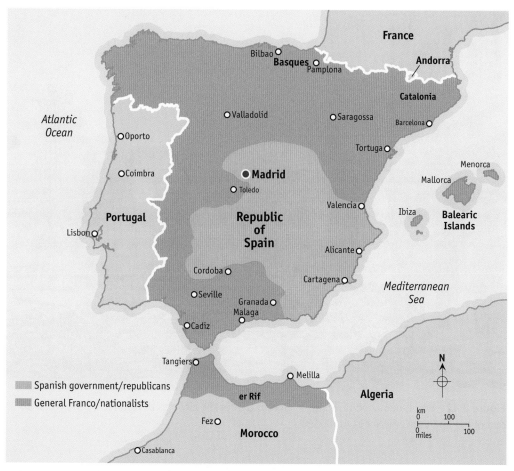

Figure 3.11 A map showing the gains made by the nationalists by February 1939

Technology and tactics

The use of air power had been developed in the First World War, and its potential had been recognised by military theorists. Japan had used air raids as part of its assaults on Manchuria and Chinese cities after 1931. The Spanish air forces were not developed enough to have a decisive effect on the outcome of the war, but Franco did have the assistance of German and Italian aircraft. This gave him an initial advantage, allowing him to move his troops from Morocco in 1936. It also enabled the nationalists to gain air superiority in key campaigns, and to use bombing to terrorise republican-held cities. However, the war could not be decided quickly because neither side achieved permanent air superiority. Individual successes often depended on the ability to deploy aircraft. It was the first war in history in which so many aircraft were used (3000 in all). Franco's successes in Aragon and Catalonia owed a lot to air power, and pointed the way for the use of aircraft in the Second World War and beyond. It continued the total war of the First World War and anticipated the mobilisation of resources and the lack of distinction between solider and civilian in the Second World War. Franco's coordination of aircraft, artillery, tanks and infantry in the Catalonia offensive showed the way forward and anticipated the Blitzkrieg in the Second World War (see Section 4.5). The most important symbol of this total war was the bombing of Guernica, immortalised in **Pablo Picasso**'s painting and vividly demonstrating the devastation inflicted on civilians in 20th-century warfare.

**Pablo Picasso
(1881–1973)**

One of the pioneers of the Cubist movement in art, Picasso is Spain's most famous modern artist. He painted Guernica while living away from Spain, and worked in France for most of his life.

95

Figure 3.12 Bomb-damaged buildings in Guernica after the city was devastated by the worst air raid of the Spanish Civil War in April 1937

KEY CONCEPTS QUESTION

Change and Continuity: In what ways was the fighting in the Spanish Civil War similar to warfare in the First World War? And in what ways was it different?

3.6 What was the significance of the mobilisation of human and economic resources and the home front?

Both sides understood the importance of mobilising human and economic resources, and of propaganda, on the home front and also as a way of securing support and resources from abroad. However, the effects of propaganda and appeals to volunteer was limited on both sides.

Mobilisation of resources

QUESTION

To what extent can the Spanish Civil War be seen as a war in which both sides mobilised all possible resources to achieve victory in the same way as the opposing sides did in the Second World War?

Both had to rely on conscription. In the heavily populated Madrid area, only 10 000 volunteered for the republican side. Both sides relied on professional officers to organise conscription campaigns. Recent research has revealed that more than half of the prisoners taken by the nationalists were induced to change sides and to join their enemies, so problematic was the supply of recruits. In a similar way, both sides had to appropriate economic and financial resources. The republicans had the major share of Spain's assets at the start in terms of industrial regions in the north, the gold and silver resources of the Bank of Spain and the best farm land. They also had more people (60 per cent). The non-intervention treaties signed by more than 30 countries in 1936 made the supply of imported arms difficult, so all resources had to be used. Both sides used taxation, confiscation, sale of assets and both sides resorted to printing money. Neither side was very effective in increasing the yield from taxation, and both sides were limited by Spain's lack of developed industrial capacity for the waging of a modern industrial war. The republican side was most hampered by internal divisions, which made the effective use of resources difficult as separatists resisted control of local assets.

Propaganda

Both sides recognised the importance of propaganda. The republicans set up a ministry of public instruction in September 1938 under Jesus Hernandez, and used Spanish artists to create heroic and encouraging images. In all, more than 2000 posters were designed and produced. The nationalists drew on the experience of the fascist states and urged slogans promoting unity and belief in their leader Franco. Key incidents were used to promote heroic images – the killing of the son of the commander of the Alcazar in Toledo by the republicans, the republican attacks on priests and churches, and even religious statues, which were formally executed by firing squad, were used to rally Catholic Spain. Republicans made much of the bombing of Guernica. Some iconic figures like 'La Pasionara', a vibrant and dedicated communist, **Dolores Ibárruri**, were used for propaganda purposes, touring the front as a symbol of the people's resistance. Revolutionary and counter-revolutionary songs rallied troops and people. Most Spaniards did not fight in the war and it was vital to get their support if possible. However, the effects of propaganda and appeals to volunteer were limited on both sides.

Figure 3.13   Dolores Ibárruri (1895–1989)

She was of Basque origin and became a dedicated communist. She was elected to the parliament in 1936. She became famous for her slogans ('they shall not pass') and her ability to rally crowds with her oratory. She was known as the Passionate Woman (*La Pasionara*). She left Spain in 1939 and was secretary general of the exiled Spanish Communist Party in Russia.

Theory of Knowledge

Visual sources and the historian:
How useful are visual sources to the historian of the 20th century? Are they likely merely to illustrate or should their provenance and value of evidence occupy the historian in the same way, say, that historians of earlier periods pay careful attention to artefacts? Do modern historians pay insufficient attention to visual evidence?

Figure 3.14   This poster was issued by the Junta Delegada de Defensa de Madrid, with the caption ¡Atacad! Soldados de la Republica (Attack! Soldiers of the Republic); it seems more like a Nazi-style poster but it was issued by the republicans, urging the people of Madrid to attack the military rebels

3.7 How significant was foreign intervention?

The Spanish Civil War was international. It involved 30 000 foreign volunteers from 52 countries on the republican side. On the nationalist side were regular forces from Germany, Italy and Russia, who were nominally 'volunteers', together with genuine pro-Franco volunteers from Ireland, Romania and Portugal. However, from 1937 the League of Nations' Non-Intervention Committee banned foreign volunteers. The International Brigades were disbanded by the Spanish Republican government in 1938 to try and gain foreign diplomatic support.

The International Brigades took part in the defence of Madrid in 1936, in the battles of the Jarama River and Guadalajara in 1937, in Teruel and the Ebro offensive in 1938. Initially their arrival was good for morale – it seemed that the world was supporting the Republic. They were incorporated into the Spanish army as a Foreign Legion in 1937. Many had served during the First World War, but despite their fervour, it is doubtful if they were decisive, and they may have turned European governments against the Spanish Republic – many were treated with great suspicion on their return, and some of the more extreme political groups among the volunteers fought among themselves. They brought little equipment, and language problems seriously weakened their military effectiveness.

There was more effective support from foreign governments for the nationalists: the tanks, artillery and machine guns offered by Germany and Italy were more significant than the manpower of the International Brigades. The USSR did send the Republic 800 planes and more than 350 tanks, but these were erratically delivered (they were often lost on the way), and some were outdated. Mexico contributed some more modern planes and $2 million of aid to the Republic.

In the end, the war was won by dogged application of superior manpower and firepower by Franco. By the time of the Ebro offensive in 1938, he had an army of a million men. Five hundred cannon bombarded the republicans with 13 500 shells a day for four months. In this context, the efforts of the International Brigades – their bravery and willingness to endure losses (one in five volunteers died in Spain) – were less significant than the embargo on arms imports imposed by the League of Nations under British and French pressure, or the equipment given by Germany and Italy to the nationalists.

Historical debate:
Historians such as D. Tierney see the nature and extent of foreign intervention as the most significant factor in determining the outcome of the civil war. Others, however – such as E. Solstein and S. Meditz – see republican divisions as being much more decisive.

End of unit activities

1 Look at this table of important events in the war and create a similar one. Consider whether these events show that Franco's leadership (FRANCO), foreign aid (FOR), and/or divisions in the Republican side (DIV) were most significant.

Key event	FRANCO/FOR/DIV
July 1936: Franco's forces cross from Morocco with German and Italian air support	
August 1936: the capture of Badajoz links nationalist forces in the south with those in the north and seals the border with Portugal	
September 1936: the nationalist General Mola's victory at Irun controls much of the northern Spanish coastline	
September 1936: the nationalist navy controls the Straits of Gibraltar	
June 1937: Bilbao falls and the Basque region is conquered by the nationalists	
1937: persistent failures of Republican offensives	
1938: Franco's Aragon Campaign	
1938: the decision by the communist prime minister Juan Negrin, who replaced the Socialist leader Largo Caballero, in conjunction with Stalin to remove the International Brigades	
September 1938: the distraction of Europe by the Munich crisis	
March 1939: the revolt in Madrid and the fall of the city to Franco	

2 Find out about the foreign volunteers who fought for Franco. What impact did the International Brigades have on the Spanish Civil War and has their importance been overrated? What impression do memoirs like George Orwell's *Homage to Catalonia* give? What can films like Ken Loach's *Land and Freedom* tell us about this war?

3 Should the democracies have given more assistance to the Republic? Discuss this question. Britain and France pursued a policy of non-intervention. This has often been criticised as being unfair and part of an attitude of appeasement towards the dictators. What are the arguments for and against this view? To prepare for this, write a clear argument on one side of a card and then find some supporting material for it and put it on the other. Arrange the cards in order of importance to help your speech or your contribution to the debate.

4 Find out about a civil war in Africa in the 20th century. Are there any similarities between it and the war in Spain?

KEY QUESTIONS

- What were the political results of the war?
- What were the main economic and social consequences?
- How did the war affect Spain's position in the world?

Overview

- Spain's population in 1936 was 24 million. By 1938 there were 2 million people in the armies of the contending sides. Of these, half a million died in battle. Many more were wounded and post-war Spain had many severely mutilated inhabitants. There were also 250 000 exiles, many of whom did not return until after Franco's death in 1975. Thousands were homeless and the war destroyed a considerable number of homes and buildings.

- The war caused a great deal of bitterness and a desire for revenge, with concentration camps, reprisals, punishments and executions continuing for years afterwards.

- Politically, Franco established a dictatorship that lasted until his death in 1975, but which had more in common with a military dictatorship based on tradition and support for the Church than with the fascist states who supported him in the 1930s.

- Spain stayed out of the Second World War and was not invaded by the Allies. Following the war, it experienced isolation from Europe. For many in Europe, Spain was an outcast state tainted by repression, a thinly disguised dictatorship and association by its ruler with the failed Nazi and fascist regimes brought down in the Second World War. Only with the Cold War and the US need for allies did it emerge from isolation and begin to shake off its pro-Nazi reputation. These circumstances led Spain into closer relations with the USA, but as a **client state**, receiving large amounts of aid.

- Economically, Spain stagnated until the late 1950s, but then saw economic growth and the development of the modern tourist industry.

- The war ended the social changes and reforms getting underway in the 1930s, and Spain seemed increasingly old-fashioned by the late 1950s. It was only after 1975 that the country modernised socially and politically.

- Franco did look forward near the end of his rule by fixing the succession on the future King Juan Carlos.

3.8 What were the political results of the war?

Client state: A state that gives uncritical allegiance to another state, usually in return for economic or political support.

Figure 3.15 General Francisco Franco in 1936

Dictatorship after 1939

Franco ruled until 1975, but he did not attempt to introduce a fully fledged fascist state. Repression in Spain was greater than that in Mussolini's Italy, but there was little in the way of compensating social policy. The historian Paul Preston has written: 'From 1939 Spain was governed as if it were a country occupied by a victorious foreign army.' There were restricted educational opportunities and expenditure on health and welfare was among the lowest in Europe. The dictatorship was, by and large, backed by the pre-war élites in business, the Catholic Church and the army. The 1938 Labour Charter established syndicates of workers and employees to discuss conditions, but its main policy was to make the right to work fundamental. It also made strikes a crime against the state.

Historical debate:
As well as the Civil War itself being a controversial topic, there is intense debate about the repression Franco unleashed after 1939. Historians such as Paul Preston have pointed out how this continued for at least two decades after the end of the civil war – with little or no condemnation from the Catholic Church. Thousands of men and women were tortured, imprisoned, sent to slave labour camps, or executed, often in secret – several hundred even ended up in Nazi death camps. From the year 2000, Spanish families have been insisting that the authorities take steps to discover the fate of 'disappeared' family members.

Caudillo: Like Hitler's title of 'Führer' or Mussolini's 'Il Duce', Franco's meant leader. There was a 'cult of Franco', but he did not encourage this to the extent of other 20th-century dictators.

Regional self-government had to wait until the post-Franco era: the events of 1939 were a victory for the dominance of the centralised Castilian Spanish-speaking state. There was a façade of constitutional government. The law of the Cortes of 1942 established a parliament, but this was powerless and, like the Cabinet, or Council of State, consisted largely of people appointed by Franco, who reserved the right to rule by decree as the supreme leader or **Caudillo**. A law of 1945 introduced referenda, or direct voting on key issues, but this remained at Franco's discretion. The constitution most resembled that of another military dictator – Napoleon I of France (1799–1814). Like Napoleon, the Franco regime kept a tight hold on regional and local government.

Spain was to be traditional, Catholic and monarchical – Franco was merely a regent and could nominate a royal successor. After his death, the Bourbon monarchy did in fact return by his wish. In place of politics, there was the national movement – a mixture of pre-war Catholic, fascist parties, administrators, and professional and technical experts. Talk was of 'family' rather than class or party.

In 1966, these constitutional arrangements were confirmed, but overt fascist terms were removed. Behind a façade of elections and referenda, the old authoritarian dictatorship continued, supported by the Church and army. Censorship and oppression of opposition continued for 26 years after 1939, but Franco did not establish a totalitarian system – obedience, but not wholehearted commitment, to an ideology or total control of the economy was required. In this respect, the results of the Civil War were very different from those of Russia or China. The fascist Falange had little real influence, especially after most of its key leaders were killed in the Civil War.

There was a reaction against the reforms of the Second Republic: civil marriage and divorce were not permitted; trade unions were prohibited, as were all political parties except the national movement; regional independence and official use of the Basque and Catalan languages were forbidden. Land was returned to the landlords and strikes were punishable as treason.

SOURCE B

With all my heart, I pardon all those who declared themselves my enemies, even if I did not regard them as such. I believe and wish it to be the case that I never had any other enemies than those who were the enemies of Spain.

From the deathbed testament of Franco, 1975. Quoted at www.altafilms.com/las13rosas/des-cargas/FrancosCrimesCrome.pdf.

ACTIVITIES

Compare and contrast the impression of Franco given in Sources B and C.

Which do you find more reliable and why?

What additional knowledge would confirm or challenge Ciano's view in Source C?

SOURCE C

In mid-July 1939 Count Ciano, the foreign minister of fascist Italy, arrived in Barcelona (on a state visit). Having been an enthusiastic advocate of Franco's cause during the war, he was assured of a warm welcome. Among the entertainments ... was a tour of the battlefields. Near one of them, he was shown a group of Republican prisoners working. He noted 'They are not prisoners, they are slaves of war'. He described Franco to a friend, 'That queer fish of a Caudillo (leader) ... surrounded by mountains of files of prisoners condemned to death.'

P. Preston. 1986. The Spanish Civil War. London: Harper, p. 317.

3.9 What were the main economic and social consequences?

Economic consequences

Spain's economy was burdened by economic dislocation of trade and industry and a large war debt owed to Germany and Italy. The loss of labour, of economic expertise, and the diversion of resources to war production took their toll. In 1951, wages were at only 60 per cent of 1936 levels.

Economically, Spain reverted to self-sufficiency as a result of the war; wages were very low but prices rose because of shortages in the 1940s. Unlike other European countries,

Spain could not benefit either from Marshall Aid after 1947 or from the communist bloc's subsidies from the USSR.

Rather, as in the case of post-Mao China, Spain had to relax its controls and self-sufficiency. The USA, eager to sustain an anti-communist regime, encouraged investment and there were relaxations on economic activity. However, as in China, there were no relaxations of the dictatorship. From 1956, Spain's economy began to modernise and there was more contact with other European countries.

It was not until the later 1950s that post-war isolation begin to give way to modernisation. The 1960s were a period of economic growth, greater prosperity and a resurgence of industrial unrest. It was as though Spain had been frozen from the late 1930s, and only after 25 years did there seem continuity with the pre-war period. With the prosperity and the arrival of mass tourism in the 1960s the regime began to relax, permitting greater religious toleration and less stringent censorship. In 1969, Franco named his heir, Prince Juan Carlos de Borbón, giving some hope for a new Spain. Juan Carlos succeeded Franco in 1975, after which there was a return to democratic government. In the 1970s, with Basque terrorism and demands for regional autonomy, the right to strike and political freedom, pressure for change finally began to make its mark.

Figure 3.16 Benidorm in the 1960s

Social consequences

Impact on civilians

The Spanish Civil War had a considerable effect on the civilian population that, as with European civilians in the Second World War, suffered bombing raids and reprisals.

The clergy endured republican violence; teachers, trade unionists and known political activists were likely to be killed by the nationalists. Perhaps 77 000 were executed by the right and 55 000 by the left during the course of the war. The dangers of being taken prisoner or having one's territory occupied must have been more motivating than any poster or political speech, and the desire for revenge and retribution ran high.

The fighting made no distinction between civilians and combatants, and evacuation was a feature of both sides. The republican authorities arranged the evacuation of children. These refugees were sent to many European and South American countries. Some returned after 1939, others stayed with their families, especially those who had been sent to Russia. The nationalist side also arranged evacuations of children, women and the elderly from war zones. Refugee camps were established in Portugal, and some refugees went to Belgium and Italy. Again, this evacuation foreshadowed what became a common occurrence in the Second World War.

War and social change

The war forced both sides to take considerable control over the resources of their territories and their civilian populations. In some republican areas this led to a social revolution, involving the confiscation of landowners' property and the establishment of local communes. Anti-clericalism was widespread and there were concessions to separatism with regional self-government. In nationalist areas, the power of the Church grew, but there was little attempt to put fascist social and economic reforms into practice. As nationalist troops advanced, the social revolution was suppressed – and thousands of captured republicans were systematically executed.

The war did see an increase in the movement for greater rights for women in the Republic. Lucía Sánchez Saornil, secretary general of Spain's version of the Red Cross, joined with Amparo Poch, director of social assistance at the Ministry of Health and Social Assistance, and established in Barcelona what became known as the **Mujeres Libres**, an organisation that fought for women's rights. This was the rallying cry for women all over Spain to join the war effort. Women participated in some of the fighting, and set up hospitals as well as working in factories. There was a greater politicisation of women in the Republic. Against that, war resulted in more widespread prostitution, and resulted in the death of women and children in air raids. Women, too, were political victims, and hundreds were executed. The victory of the nationalists brought an end to emancipation, but the experience of playing a more active part in public affairs, as well as the greater economic, social and sexual freedom they experienced during the war, did lay the basis for long-term change in Spain after the end of Franco's dictatorship.

In conclusion, it is worth considering the consequences of a republican victory for Europe. The initial rebellion was not guaranteed to succeed, and victory was only achieved after a long, gruelling war. Would a republican victory have given Spain a better future or more sustained and continuing violence and repression? Would it have been safer or more dangerous for the Western democracies? Would it have had a major effect on the outcome of the Second World War? Do you think that this sort of 'guesswork' has any value? Should a historian even attempt to think 'counter-factually' and speculate on what might have happened?

Probably the sad truth is that the divisions in Spain by 1936 were so profound that whatever the result, the mixture of social conflict, ideological extremism, regional tensions and a lack of strong democratic tradition would have resulted in a tragic outcome.

Mujeres Libres: Meaning 'Free Women', this organisation did not insist on voting rights or feminism, but worked for greater health care and social rights for women.

KEY CONCEPTS ACTIVITY

Change and Continuity: Draw up a table with two columns: one to be headed '1931–9' and the other 'After 1939'. Then list the ways in which the position and rights of women in Spain altered in those two periods.

Theory of Knowledge

History, emotion and truth: *'The past is never dead. It's not even past'* – William Faulkner (1897–1962)

The Spanish Civil War – at least in part – involved a life-and-death struggle between fascism and its opponents, and seemed to many to be a precursor for the Second World War. Given that Franco's dictatorship only ended in 1975, and that neo-fascist groups are still active in several countries, are historians who write about the civil war able to avoid bias?

3.10 How did the war affect Spain's position in the world?

Franco was favourably inclined to the Axis powers, but despite a meeting with Hitler in 1940, Franco restricted this to allowing German aircraft and submarines the use of Spanish facilities and allowing 'volunteers' – some 18 000 men of the **Blue Division** – to fight in Russia between 1941 and 1943. When the tide turned, Franco was careful to cultivate better relations with the Allies and was 'benevolently neutral' in 1944. This defused Stalin's suggestion that the Allies invade Spain in 1945.

The Cold War led to the USA lifting restrictions on trading with Franco, and offering financial aid in 1950. The 1953 Pact of Madrid made Spain a virtual US ally and more aid flowed in. The reward for not being an enemy to the winning side was considerable US support in the Cold War period, when Franco was seen as a bastion against communism. Thus his dictatorship, like that of the Portuguese dictator Salazar, lived on while those of Hitler and Mussolini did not.

European countries were not willing at first to allow Spain to join NATO or the EC, but a trade agreement in 1970 came close to bringing Spain back into better relations with Europe, apart from Britain, with whom there was a longstanding quarrel over Gibraltar.

> **Blue Division:** These were the 18 000 Spanish volunteers that went to fight for Germany in Russia in 1941. In total, 45 000 Spaniards served with German forces and suffered some 14 000 casualties. They wore red berets at home – the uniform of the 19th-century Carlists. They saw themselves in a tradition of defending Christian values against communism.

End of unit activities

1   What would have been the consequences if Franco had been defeated?

   Historians should not really think counter-factually (i.e., try to think what might have happened as opposed to what did happen), but it has been suggested that:

   • A successful republic would have been heavily dependent on the Soviet Union. The communists had purged their enemies and by the end of the war had managed to install a pro-communist prime minister.

   • A virtual Soviet colony dominating the Mediterranean would have had enormous consequences, not least for France and Britain.

   a   Would these countries have been so ready to go to war with Germany in 1939?

   b   Would Hitler have been seen much more as an anti-communist saviour and would he have avoided a two-front war?

   c   Alternatively, would Franco's defeat have removed pressure from France, allowing it to take action (with or without British support) in alliance with the USSR to oppose Hitler's growing expansionism in Europe?

2   The Spanish Civil War had considerable effects on Spain. Using ICT, create a presentation on why you consider one element to be more important than others. Do you think that the political impact was the greatest? If so, why? Select illustrations to make your talk more interesting.

3   Many people refused to go to Spain for holidays in the 1960s. Given what you know about post-1939 Spain, were they right?

> **KEY CONCEPTS QUESTION**
>
> **Significance:** What do you think was the main reason why, after 1945, the US decided to leave Franco's dictatorship in place – despite his earlier close links with Nazi Germany and fascist Italy – rather than to 'restore democracy' in Spain? Does the case of Franco show that the US was more concerned with 'containing' communism than defending democracy?

End of chapter activities

Paper 1 exam practice

Question

With reference to its origin, purpose and content, analyse the value and
limitations of Source A for a historian studying nationalist aims.   [4 marks]

Skill

Value/limitations of sources.

SOURCE A

There must be liberty and fraternity without the abuse of liberty and tyranny; work for
all; social justice accomplished without rancour or violence, and a fair and progressive
distribution of wealth without destroying or endangering the Spanish economy. Before
this there must be war without mercy on the exploiters of politics, on the deceivers of
the honest worker, on the foreigners and the foreign-orientated people who openly or
deceitfully endeavour to destroy Spain. There must be Fraternity! Liberty! Equality!

*Text prepared by General Franco and broadcast on Radio Tenerife, 18 July 1936. Quoted in
B. Crozier. 1967.* Franco. *London: Eyre and Spottiswood, p. 184.*

Examiner's tips

Utility/reliability questions require you to assess the source – over a range of possible
issues/aspects – and to comment on their value to historians studying a particular event
or period of history. The main areas you need to consider in relation to the source and
the information/view it provides, are:

* origin, purpose and content;
* value and limitations.

Before you write your answer, draw a rough chart or spider diagram to show, where
relevant, these various aspects. Make sure you do this for both sources.

Common mistakes

Do not fall into the trap of writing out what the sources say. Ensure that your
comments are specific. Do not simply say that the source is limited because it leaves
a lot out. Finally, take care to address both sides of origin and purpose. If you only
concentrate on value, with just a passing reference to limitations, you will be unable to
obtain the higher marks.

Remember to make sure you understand what the question is asking.

Simplified mark scheme

Band		Marks
1	Explicit/ developed consideration of **both** origin, purpose and content **and** value and limitations.	3–4
2	Limited consideration/comments on origin, purpose and content **and** value and limitations. **Or** more developed comments on **either** origin, purpose and content **or** value and limitations.	0–2

Student answer

Source A is a declaration, published in 1936 just when the military revolt was beginning, written by someone who was a major leader. While its origin might present both value and limitations, it is not difficult to assess its purpose. It is intended to rally support from as wide a section of the people as possible and to give the impression that this is a crusade for justice and not just a military coup. It refers to justice for the workers and uses language from the French Revolution – 'Liberty, fraternity and equality'. It attempts to draw a distinction between false liberty – presumably the abuses carried out by the anarchists in pursuit of their ideas of freedom and true liberty.

These aspects affect the source's value and point to possible limitations. It certainly provides some valuable 'insider' information about how the aims of the rebels were set out, but it is not reliable. It seems to suggest a concern for the whole population, but the rebels were opposed to the reforms of the Republic for workers and peasants. When it refers to 'War without mercy' it is probably closer to the real aims of Franco, as there were many brutal executions of enemies. There is limited reference here to conservatism, tradition and the intense Catholicism which were also part of nationalist aims.

Examiner's comment

There is good assessment of Source A, referring explicitly to both origin and possible purpose, and to value and limitations. These comments are valid and are clearly linked to the question. The candidate has thus done enough to get into Band 1, and so be awarded three marks.

Activity

Look again at the source, the simplified mark scheme and the student answer. Now try to write a paragraph or two to push the answer up to the top of Band 1 (possibly by saying more about content), and so obtain the full four marks.

Summary activities

- Produce a mind map with a central circle 'The causes of the Spanish Civil War', and then 'branches' for each of the key elements – the army, the rise of the left, religious issues, short-term causes. To do this, use the information from this chapter, and any other resources available to you. Remember to make sure you include all the main events and turning points.
- Prepare revision cards to help you assess the results of the war. On the front of the card, write the key result with a brief explanation. On the back, put in as much supporting detail as you can.

- Make sure you have attempted all the various questions that appear in the margins – many of these are designed to help you understand key events and turning points. There are also questions designed to develop your skills in dealing with Paper 1-type questions, such as comprehension of sources, and assessing sources for their value and limitations for historians. Remember, to do these sorts of questions, you will need to look at a range of aspects, such as origin, nature and possible purpose. Don't forget, even if a source has many limitations, it can still be valuable for a historian.

Paper 2 practice questions

1 Examine the causes and results of the Spanish Civil War.
2 Examine the social and economic effects of the Spanish Civil War.
3 Compare and contrast the reasons for and impact of two of the following: the Spanish Civil War; the Russian Civil War; the Chinese Civil War.
4 Evaluate the reasons for the outcome of the Spanish Civil War.
5 Evaluate the importance of foreign intervention in any two civil wars you have studied.

Further reading

Try reading the relevant chapters/sections of the following books:

Beevor, Antony (2007) *The Battle for Spain*, London: Phoenix.

Brennan, Gerald (1990) *The Spanish Labyrinth*, Cambridge: Cambridge University Press.

Browne, Harry (1996) *Spain's Civil War*, London: Longman.

Carr, Raymond (2001) *Modern Spain*, Oxford: Oxford University Press.

Matthews, James (2013) *Reluctant Winners*, Oxford: Oxford University Press

Preston, Paul (1986) *The Spanish Civil War: Reaction, Revolution and Revenge*, London: Harper.

Preston, Paul (2006) *The Spanish Civil War*. London: Harper.

Romero Salvado, Francis (1999). *Twentieth-Century Spain*, London: Palgrave.

The Second World War

Causes of the Second World War

KEY QUESTIONS

- What were the main long-term causes of the war?
- What were the main short-term causes of the war?
- What were the ideological, political, economic, territorial causes?

Overview

- The term 'Second World War' actually encompasses a number of linked conflicts, and in this respect it is very like the First World War. In Europe, the main struggle from 1939 to 1941 was between Germany, France and Britain, and it focused on the Treaty of Versailles. In September 1939, Germany invaded Poland – in part to recover lands lost in the treaty, but also to gain further Polish territory. Britain could not accept this violation, especially as it had guaranteed Polish independence (if not Polish territory), and both Britain and France declared war in support of Poland. Although factors other than the terms of a treaty were involved, the Versailles settlement is a useful starting point in explaining the war in Europe in 1939.

- The war was initially characterised by a series of attacks by Japan, Germany and Italy to gain territories that the militaristic regimes of these countries thought should be rightfully theirs, and which they claimed for ideological and economic reasons.

- Resistance by the rest of the world, individually and through the collective organisation set up to keep peace – the League of Nations – was weak, both before the outbreak of war and in its initial stages. However, resistance grew and the so-called Allied nations successfully prevented further expansion by the Axis powers by 1943. The Allies then began a large-scale counterattack.

- The resources of the Allies proved to be greater than those of the Axis powers, and they developed a determination that was as strong as that of their enemy. Unprecedented manpower and industrial capacity were employed in the war, and technology became increasingly important, especially in terms of air warfare.

TIMELINE

1915 Japan issues its 21 Demands.

1917 Russian Revolution.

1919–22 Post-war peace settlements.

1922 Mussolini comes to power in Italy.

1923 France occupies the Ruhr.

1929 Wall Street Crash and start of the Great Depression.

1931 Japan invades Manchuria.

1933 Hitler comes to power in Germany.

1935 Mussolini invades Ethiopia.

1936 Germany remilitarises the Rhineland.

1936–9 Spanish Civil War.

1937 War between Japan and China.

1938 Germany annexes Austria; Czech crisis; Munich Conference.

1939 Germany annexes Bohemia and Moravia; Czechoslovakia no longer an independent nation; Nazi–Soviet Pact.

The Second World War

- Civilian casualties were inflicted on an unprecedented scale as states pursued their aims with total commitment. Nazi Germany used the war to fulfil its dream of racial destruction. The Allies pursued a policy of victory at any cost, and demanded unconditional surrender. Increasingly less distinction was made between military and civilian targets. The culmination of this was the use by the US of atomic weapons against Japan in 1945.

- The scale of the war had an unprecedented impact on political, social and economic life. Communism was extended by Mao Zedong's victory in China and by Soviet leader Joseph Stalin's domination of Eastern Europe. This led to an extended period of conflict (the Cold War) that lasted for 45 years. The post-war world faced the possibility of total destruction and continued ideological conflict. The end of European empires and the emergence of two dominant superpowers brought about a totally new balance of power.

Introduction

When studying the First World War, you looked at the causes, practices and effects of a cross-regional war between different states, heavily dependent on industrial power and mass armies controlled by powerful states. This chapter will enable you to compare that war with another total war. When reading this chapter, be aware of the differences and similarities between the two world wars. Remember that you will not be asked to describe events, but rather to use information to support explanations and comparisons.

Like the First World War, the Second World War was a cross-regional war, which brought together a number of linked conflicts. In the Second World War, these conflicts were wider as they included East Asia as well as Europe. Chronologically, the conflicts occurred as follows:

- the first was a war fought between China and Japan from 1937 to 1945;
- in 1939, a European war began between Germany – which, following the Nazi–Soviet Non-Aggression Pact, invaded Poland – and France and Britain, which both declared war on Germany;
- in 1940, Italy joined the war on Germany's side;
- in 1941, Germany invaded Greece, Yugoslavia and Romania, and then Russia;
- in 1941, Japan attacked the possessions of the USA, Britain, the Netherlands and Portugal in Southeast Asia;
- in 1945, Russia declared war on Japan.

From 1941, there was a Grand Alliance between Britain, the USA and the USSR, which also included China. Germany, Italy, Japan and their allies were known as the Axis powers, named after the treaties between Italy, Germany and Japan known as the Rome–Berlin–Tokyo Axis. Their enemies called themselves the United Nations and are more commonly known as the Allies.

The nature of the Second World War

Like the First World War, this was a total war fought between major industrial nations. It was the last of its kind. By 1945, the era of great wars between great economic powers eager to control economic resources at all costs came to an end. Total wars would only result in the mass destruction of cities and, after 1950 – when both the Soviet Union and the USA had atomic weapons – the possible end of the planet.

This was war on a new scale: 61 countries with 1.7 billion people – three-quarters of the world's population – took part. A total of 110 million people were mobilised for military service, more than half of those by three countries: the USSR (22–30 million), Germany (17 million) and the United States (16 million). For the major participants, the largest numbers on duty at any one time were as follows: USSR (12 500 000); US (12 245 000); Germany (10 938 000); British Empire and Commonwealth (8 720 000); Japan (7 193 000); and China (5 000 000).

After the Second World War

Because of the large-scale application of industrial, technological and military force, the Second World War achieved the decisive and lasting victory that its winners hoped for. In modern terms, there was 'regime change' in Germany and Italy. However, the costs and dangers of repeating such a war were high, and since 1945 no major power has engaged in total war on a similar scale for imperialistic or political gain.

Instead of a sustained and destructive conflict for control of Europe, what emerged was a Cold War, in which the USSR and the West built up huge forces they did not dare use. Instead of wars between peoples, there were wars among peoples. In these conflicts, the powers that had developed such massive resources found they could not use them in the same way they had during the war, and were compelled to give way to much less well-equipped forces. Having mass tanks or nuclear bombs could not defeat guerrilla soldiers or force local populations to support the Great Powers' chosen regimes. For example:

- the USA could not achieve a decisive victory in Vietnam despite having superior weapons and technology;
- Israel could not, despite military victories, gain security for itself in the Middle East;
- Afghanistan proved impossible to control by both the post-1945 superpowers, the USSR and the USA.

4.1 What were the main long-term causes of the war?

In many ways, the causes of the Second World War – both long- and short-term – are often seen as being located in Europe. Most notably, attention has been focused on the tensions arising from the First World War – especially those resulting from the peace treaties that ended that war. However, tensions also existed in Asia – some of which pre-dated the First World War – and, in fact, it is possible to argue that the Second World War began in Asia rather than in Europe.

The impact of the Treaty of Versailles

Although the Treaty of Versailles was less harsh to Germany than France had hoped (and much less harsh than the Treaty of Brest-Litovsk which Germany had imposed on Soviet Russia in 1918), it clearly laid the basis for future problems, and is regarded as a major cause of the Second World War. The main issue was that Germany had not

Fact: Vietnam had been a French colony (French Indochina) but was occupied by Japan in 1940. Communist guerrillas fought the Japanese and then successfully resisted the French. In 1954, an international conference divided Vietnam between a communist North and a non-communist South. The US could not defend the South against North Vietnam, despite the superior technology of the forces it used against the communists.

Fact: The new state of Israel was established, out of part of the territory of Palestine, in 1948. It then fought wars against Arab states in 1948–9, 1956, 1967, 1973–4 and 1982. Israel won the wars (taking over the whole of Palestine, along with territories from other Arab states such as Jordan and Syria), but has not achieved lasting security.

been totally defeated and occupied in 1918 (as it was to be in 1945). Its armies had been victorious in Russia and had gained the German people valuable lands in western Russia in March 1918. The attacks on the Western Front in Europe had been some of the most successful of the war before ceasing in the summer of 1918. The German forces in the West were not destroyed in a massive battle and Germany was not invaded. The situation by November 1918 was that, with increasing numbers of US troops pouring in, insufficient supplies and internal unrest, Germany simply felt it was unlikely to win.

The armistice was not surrender, it was merely an agreement to stop fighting, but it was treated as a surrender by the French. Thereafter, the new German government faced so many internal problems, alongside the effects of a severe British naval blockade which left its people short of food, that it had to accept a settlement that would have been more appropriate had German forces been spectacularly defeated, not just pushed back.

Table 4.1 Why the terms and conditions of the peace treaty caused resentment in Germany and helped to bring about another war

Conditions of Germany's surrender in the First World War	Effects and subsequent results of Germany's surrender
Diktat.	The German delegation did not negotiate the terms. They were given the choice of accepting them, but really had no alternative.
The Germans had signed an armistice based on a US proposal of peace terms – the Fourteen Points.	The treaty made it appear that the Germans had unconditionally surrendered and some of the Fourteen Points were not honoured.
The German leaders who signed the armistice and had to accept the peace terms were not the men who had decided on the war.	The treaty blamed Germany for the war and made no allowance for the changes in Germany's government in 1918 when the kaiser abdicated.
Germany was forced to accept a small army of 100 000 men and limitations on warships, submarines and armoured vehicles.	This was humiliating for a nation with a strong military tradition and which had shown pride in establishing a navy. It also meant that Germany would not be able defend itself from possible external enemies in the future.
Germany lost its overseas colonies.	Although never very popular in Germany, all major European states had empires and this was a sign that Germany was inferior.
Germany lost Posen, West Prussia and Upper Silesia to Poland, and East Prussia was separated from the rest of Germany by a corridor of Polish territory. The German city of Danzig was placed under the control of the League of Nations but was dominated by Poland.	Danzig was a major city and the loss of the Polish lands was seen as a national disgrace with an eccentric territorial arrangement in the 'corridor'. Germans found themselves under Polish rule.

Conditions of Germany's surrender in the First World War	Effects and subsequent results of Germany's surrender
There were other territorial losses – Alsace-Lorraine to France; Eupen, Malmedy and Moresnet to Belgium; North Schleswig to Denmark; Memel to Lithuania.	The major change was Alsace-Lorraine, but this had belonged to Germany only since 1870. However, these western areas had economic significance in terms of valuable natural resources.
The Saarland was to be run by the League of Nations and the coal from its mines was to go to France for 15 years, when a vote would be taken and the area would be free to join France or Germany.	Again, this had economic consequences and the period – 15 years – was a long one.
The Rhineland was to be demilitarised to a depth of 50km (30 miles) to prevent any invasion threat to France.	This was a 'heartland' area and the demilitarisation was an insult to German independence.
Germany was blamed for the war and ordered to pay reparations to the victorious powers. These were fixed at £6600 million later in 1921.	It clearly distorted historical events to blame Germany entirely for the war, and the reparations seemed to threaten German economic recovery. The reparations seemed likely to stretch on for years and to be a painful reminder of defeat and humiliation.
Union with Austria was forbidden.	The post-war settlement had made much of creating new nations – such as Poland – but the territorial arrangements left substantial German minorities under foreign rule or, in the case of Austria, forbidden to join with other Germans.

Psychologically, the Treaty of Versailles was a blow to many Germans, and it left the country in a genuine crisis. Germany faced a hostile and well-armed France in the west; it was ringed by a number of 'new' nations in the east, some of which were allied to France. Beyond that lay communist Russia. Before 1914, German statesmen and soldiers spoke of **encirclement,** despite Germany's alliances with Austria and Italy. Now there really was encirclement, with little chance, it seemed, of Germany recovering its pre-war position in central Europe.

The reality of the situation was that no German state would ever be able to accept the consequences of the treaty in the long term. However, the only way to change the terms was by negotiation or by force. Negotiation would be difficult – the French had learned the lessons of 1870 and 1914, and were determined to prevent Germany amassing enough power to invade again. On the other hand, the German leadership could not accept what it saw as encirclement by its enemies. Nor would it endure being kept in a weak and subordinate position indefinitely. Sooner or later, another conflict was sure to emerge.

Marshal Foch of France understood the truth of this. 'It is not a peace,' he famously stated, 'it is an armistice for twenty years.' He knew it would only be a matter of time

Fact: In 1870, Prussia and its confederation in north Germany, together with the independent south German states, invaded France after a dispute about a proposal to place a German king on the Spanish throne. France was defeated. In 1914, Germany invaded France at the start of the First World War as part of the Schlieffen Plan to defeat France before attacking Russia.

Fact: In 1921, the French were determined to make Germany pay reparations (payments for damages). The Germans argued that they could not afford this, so the French sent in troops to the border area of the Ruhr, Germany's largest industrial area. In April 1923, when payments ceased, French and Belgian troops occupied the Ruhr. Germany offered passive resistance and the crisis led to a collapse of the German currency and widespread hardship. There were communist risings and also an attempt by the right-wing Nazi Party to take power.

Encirclement: Many in Germany saw the alliance between France and Russia in the 1890s and the colonial agreements between Britain and France (1904) and Britain and Russia (1907) as resulting in Germany being surrounded (encircled) by enemies.

Figure 4.1 Winston Churchill (1874–1965)

He was Britain's prime minister during the Second World War. He had been enthusiastic for war in 1914 and held important positions during and after the First World War. As chancellor of the Exchequer (finance minister), he wanted to cut spending and urged international peace and arms reduction in the 1920s, but wanted rearmament after 1933 so that Britain could oppose Hitler. He opposed the British policy of appeasement in the 1930s, although he had earlier favoured a conciliatory attitude towards Germany, and indeed had coined the term 'appeasement' – by referring to 'appeasement of European hatreds'.

before Germany recovered enough to challenge the position it had been forced into in 1919. The Germans felt vulnerable for several reasons:

- With a smaller armed force than neighbouring countries, it was potentially at their mercy.
- Like all the European countries, Germany faced a communist Russia, which openly stated its intention to spread revolution. Germany thus needed the means to defend itself.
- Germany was in no position to assist German-speakers in surrounding countries should they be threatened – something that seemed quite likely.
- Germany was also at the mercy of a precarious world economy. It had no overseas empire, like Britain and France, nor did it control the resources of a former empire, like Russia. There was little prospect of being able to gain resources and Germany was therefore economically vulnerable. Reparations also stood in the way of economic recovery.

The failure to pay reparations led to further humiliation in 1923, when French and Belgian troops occupied the Ruhr region of north-west Germany. This incident did little to assuage any German thoughts of revenge. It also aroused the sympathies of Britain to German grievances – Britain was not willing to back France's hard line to keep Germany weak. Instead, Britain began to support a relaxation of the Treaty of Versailles and to promote what **Winston Churchill** called 'appeasement of European hatreds'. This also became popular in France, as the costs of maintaining massive forces to overawe Germany was growing oppressive. In truth, however, the hard line that France originally advocated may have prevented war breaking out.

In 1925, a meeting was held at Locarno in Switzerland, at which Britain and France – in return for German guarantees of Western European boundaries – hinted strongly that they might accept revisions in the east, despite France's alliances with Eastern European countries. However, overturning the majority of the treaty terms and allowing Germany to rise as a great power again would never be acceptable to either France or Britain, so in some ways concessions were more dangerous than rigid enforcement of the treaty.

The League of Nations

The tensions brought about by post-war disputes could have been resolved by the new 'world parliament', created in 1920. The League of Nations' objective was to prevent conflicts escalating into war, as they had in 1914. However, it was clear by 1933 that this was not going to happen. Successful in small disputes, the League showed early on that it had little power to control the aggression of larger powers. When Italy bombarded the Greek island of Corfu in 1923, the League could not act decisively and relied instead on the Conference of Ambassadors. With the USA declining to join and with the USSR a member only between 1934 and 1939, in practice the League depended on Britain and France. They were not prepared to back effective action against Italy, either in 1923 or when the Italian leader Benito Mussolini invaded the African state of Abyssinia in 1935. Aggressor powers simply left the League when criticised, as in the case of Japan in 1933 following attacks on China, or Italy in 1935 after its invasion of Abyssinia. Germany left in 1933. Without its own army or committed support from the major powers, the League was unable to prevent another major war, and the failure to develop an effective international organisation could be seen as a cause of war. Instead of nations being prepared to confront aggression in the name of peace, it became all too easy for them to believe that it was somehow the job of the League of Nations to do this.

Conflict in Asia

The conflict in Asia had its roots in the rise of Japan as a strong regional power in the 1800s. From the mid-19th century, Japan had modernised rapidly and built up its armed forces and industries. There was a strong feeling that the influence of the West had corrupted traditional Japanese culture – that foreign ways were destroying the essence of Japan. In an attempt to reverse this, there was a revival in traditional Shinto culture and emperor-worship, as well as in the study of Japanese **samurai** chivalric codes and stories. However, in order to fully escape the shame of Western domination, Japan needed access to Western technology, which could be used to gain the raw materials to turn Japan into a self-sufficient empire.

However, Japan did not really have enough raw materials to be the great power that its rulers dreamed of. What it did have was immense national pride, based on a belief in Japan's special status as the chosen land of the sun goddess. The Japanese also strongly believed in the superiority of their moral strength and military virtues. When China descended into chaos after a revolution in 1911, which ended the Manchu Qing dynasty, Japan made increasing demands – such as the 21 demands of 1915 – that threatened China's sovereignty.

Despite being allied to the Entente Powers during the First World War, Japan was not awarded the lands and dominant position in China that it wanted in the Treaty of Versailles. Rather than winning control over Shandong province in China, Japan was in fact forced to withdraw from China. It was also only given the right to administer Pacific islands south of the Equator, not absolute ownership of them. In addition, Japan was affronted when a racial equality clause was rejected as a principle of the League of Nations' Charter. As with Italy, Versailles thus became a grievance for Japan, as well as for 'loser' nations in the settlement, such as Germany.

Although nominally a parliamentary state, power in Japan lay with the emperor and his family, the military chiefs and the great industrial concerns. The legacy of the samurai (warrior) tradition meant that the military had enormous prestige and respect in Japan. Throughout the 1920s, a new and more extreme nationalistic officer class emerged and, often ignoring Japan's civilian governments, acted with increasing freedom from control in border regions. The economic situation in Japan led many to believe that national survival depended on Japan gaining access to raw materials, fuel and markets.

The decline in prices for agricultural products had led to considerable hardship in rural areas by the late 1920s and, with the Wall Street Crash and the drop in US trade, many of Japan's industries, such as silk, were hard-hit. Like the German nationalists, Japanese patriots believed that their country could not go on being dependent on Western capitalism, but had to create a self-sufficient empire. They also resented the growing US presence in the Pacific – which they saw as a Japanese 'sphere of influence'.

Activity

Using whatever resources are available to you, carry out some additional research on growing US interests in Asia and the Pacific. Then list at least two ways in which this might have led to resentment and suspicion in Japan.

Samurai: A special class of warriors in pre-1867. They were skilled in martial arts and had to be respected by ordinary people on pain of death. They fought for feudal lords (*daimyu*) and their code of conduct did not permit surrender. They would fight to the death, killing themselves rather than submitting. This code was revived in Japan in the 20th century.

Fact: In 1854, Japan had been forced by the US to end its 200-year long seclusion, to open up two of its ports to US businesses, and to grant the US the status of 'most-favoured nation'. In the following years, Japan was pressured into signing further trade treaties, with US and with other Western nations.

Fact: On 18 January 1915, the Japanese government secretly presented to China a list of 21 grievances, which included demands that Japan be given ascendancy over Manchuria and Shandong, and that China accept so-called 'advisers' from Japan in its government. Although the Versailles Treaty of 1919 granted the Japanese control over former German territories in Shandong, during the Washington Conference of 1921–2, Japan was forced to agree to withdraw its forces in these areas and accept full restoration of sovereignty to China. This could be seen as the origin of the war in the Far East.

4.2 What were the main short-term causes of the war?

By the late 1920s, there was an air of greater optimism across Europe. French and German statesmen seemed to be on good terms; Britain was promoting international cooperation and trade links with Germany; reparations had been agreed and the US had provided loans to help Germany; and the German economy was booming. Two factors ended this period of optimism:

1   The economic crash that occurred in the US in 1929, and the worldwide depression that ensued.
2   The rise to power of an aggressive nationalist regime in Germany, which was determined to end the humiliations of Versailles and to make Germany a major world power again.

Factors after 1929

The crisis in the American stock market in October 1929 led the US to withdraw its loans to Germany. Germany was at the mercy of economic events and its banks began to collapse, taking businesses with them. Unemployment rose rapidly and urban workers and small businesses joined farmers as victims of an unstable international economy. Extremist groups offered drastic solutions – the communists offered a totally controlled economic system and a social revolution. The Nazis stood for a national revival, during which those to blame for Germany's situation would be punished, and a new Germany would emerge that would protect its people from the uncertainties of the world economy. Nazi leader **Adolf Hitler** blamed the Treaty of Versailles for many of Germany's problems – reparations, which had just been renegotiated in the Young Plan, were a particular target, wealthy Jews were another. The **'November Criminals'** who had agreed to an armistice in 1918 had humiliated Germany. The Nazis stated that Germany needed to establish a strong army, to rid itself of its enemies, to find 'living space' (*Lebensraum*) to expand, to take control of resources and to set up a new German racial state at the expense of the inferior Slavs, who so humiliatingly ruled over German minorities.

Figure 4.2 Adolf Hitler (1889–1945)

He was born in Austria, but moved to Munich in 1913. He served in the German army after war broke out the following year. After the war, he joined the extreme right-wing nationalist German Workers' Party (which later became the Nazi Party) and began to formulate his ideological solutions to Germany's post-war problems. After a failed uprising in 1923, Hitler was imprisoned for nine months, during which time he wrote his book *Mein Kampf*. In 1933, he became chancellor and proceeded to set up a dictatorship. His policies contributed to the outbreak of war in 1939. At the end of the war, with Germany's failure assured, Hitler committed suicide.

'November criminals': Hitler called Jews, socialists and 'defeatists' the 'November Criminals'. He blamed them for the 'criminal' decision to accept an armistice in November 1918. Thus all his political enemies were lumped together and blamed for defeat, even though it was the leading generals who took the decision to stop fighting the First World War.

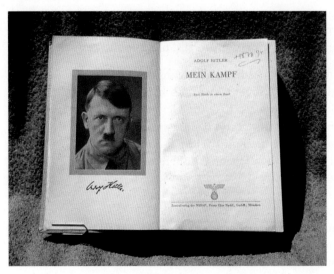

Figure 4.3   Hitler's worldview – Mein Kampf ('My Struggle'), dictated when he was in prison in 1924 and a bestseller in Nazi Germany when it was published in 1925

Hitler's policies as a cause of war

Calls to revise the Treaty of Versailles now became part of a vision for the future in which Germany would be a great power as it was before 1914. This would mean rearmament – a great Germany could not permit fellow Germans to exist under foreign rule or to live under constant threat from France. However, the racial state proposed by Hitler and the Nazis also had a mission to eradicate communism and end the 'conspiracy' of Jews and communists that had taken over Russia in 1917. Communism was another threat that needed to be wiped out, and the reward for the German people would be limitless land on which to settle true German human breeding stock and ensure a Thousand-Year state.

If a fraction of this vision was actually carried out then war would be inevitable. Britain and France might accept some revision of the treaty terms, but not a dominant Germany at the heart of central Europe. Such a circumstance was why Britain had gone to war in 1914. France would never be secure with a German mega-state – it was central to French interests to prevent this. If Hitler's plans were fully executed, Germany would take over all lands populated by German minorities and assault communist Russia. This would challenge the whole settlement of Europe that had been established in 1919.

In 1933, however, it was not clear whether these ideas would really evolve into hard-and-fast policy. French and British statesmen hoped that Hitler would become a 'normal' statesman and that they could negotiate a revision of what seemed to Germany an unjust treaty, while doing what they could to protect their own countries in the event that war did break out. In adopting these policies, together called **appeasement**, they probably precipitated war.

Appeasement as a cause of war

Table 4.2 gives an outline of major events, with their significance as causes of war.

Table 4.2 Major events, with their significance as causes of war

Event	Germany	Other countries
January 1933: Hitler becomes chancellor of Germany.	Germans had given significant support to a leader who offered rearmament and opposition to the Treaty of Versailles, and whose writings included a call for territorial expansion in the east to create a new racial empire.	Britain and France were preoccupied by internal economic problems and there would have been little public support for any attempt to take action. Germany still had only a small army. Britain's navy was powerful and the French army and the new defence lines in the west were strong. France had alliances with Eastern Europe.
1933: Hitler leaves the League of Nations.	Many Germans associated the League with the despised Treaty of Versailles and admired Hitler's independent stance.	Although this was a worrying development, by now British and French statesmen had lost faith in the League and did not see this as a definitive move towards war.

(continued)

Fact: At the end of the First World War, many nationalist groups emerged in Germany, but it was the National Socialists (Nazis) who had become the leading right-wing opposition group by 1930. Hitler spoke passionately against the Treaty of Versailles and for a national revival – ideas that won support among many different social groups. Hitler's paramilitary forces, his brilliant oratory, and the propaganda and organisation of his party led to the Nazis being the largest party by 1932 and Hitler became Germany's chancellor in 1933.

KEY CONCEPTS

Causation and consequences: In what ways did the Great Depression act as a cause of the Second World War? Do you think war would have broken out if the Wall Street Crash had not happened?

Appeasement: There was talk in the 1920s of an appeasement of European hatreds – i.e., ending conflicts by negotiation. In the 1930s, appeasement came to mean the policy led by the British Prime Minister Neville Chamberlain of taking active measures to meet Germany's grievances at the expense of other people in Europe to give Britain the chance to rearm.

Table 4.2 (*continued*)

Event	Germany	Other countries
1934: Hitler signs a ten-year peace pact with Poland and a Nazi takeover in Austria is foiled. Mussolini brings troops to the border as a warning to Germany not to intervene in Austria.	Germany seemed to be showing some restraint.	Britain and France believed that the Italian dictator was putting national interest above support for a fellow right-wing leader to protect the Versailles settlement.
1935: Hitler reintroduces conscription.	This was a turning point in the development of Germany as a revived military power.	Britain and France did not act, although ties with Italy were increased.
1935: The Saar region votes to rejoin Germany.	A show of support for the Nazi regime.	
1935: Italy invades Ethiopia.	Ethiopia appealed to the League of Nations. Germany benefited from the division between Italy and Britain and France.	Public opinion forced the British and French governments to criticise Mussolini, losing his support.
1935: Anglo–German Naval Treaty.	Hitler benefited from a British attempt to control German naval expansion.	Britain undermined the Treaty of Versailles in its own interests to control German battleship expansion to keep it less than Britain's.
March 1936: Germany remilitarises the Rhineland.	This was without negotiation and in violation of the Treaty of Versailles. Hitler saw it as a major gamble and won. Rearmament increased.	Despite having the necessary force to intervene, France did not do so. There was little support in Britain for any action. Arms production increased.
1936: Rome–Berlin Axis.	A limited treaty of friendship between Italy and Germany given maximum publicity; also both countries gave aid to a right-wing military revolt in Spain against the Republican government.	Britain adopted a policy of neutrality in Spain.

Event	Germany	Other countries
March 1938: Germany occupies and annexes Austria.	With Italy now sympathetic, Hitler took advantage of favourable circumstances to insist on a Nazi government in Austria, which called for German annexation.	British Prime Minister Neville Chamberlain hoped to negotiate a major revision of the Treaty of Versailles while 'preparing for the worst' and building up Britain's defences. Neither France nor Britain acted.
Summer 1938: Hitler demands concessions for the 3 million German speakers living in the Sudetenland in Czechoslovakia. There seems a danger of war and German invasion.	The 'Sudeten' Germans were formerly part of the Austrian Empire, not Germany. This was the first attempt to take action on behalf of the wider German-speaking minorities created in the general peace settlement of 1919.	France had an alliance with Czechoslovakia, but Britain did not. Chamberlain was anxious not to be drawn into a war between France and Germany, and attempted to find a peaceful solution.
15 September 1938: Hitler and Chamberlain meet at Berchtesgaden.	Hitler had made threatening speeches but lost the initiative to Chamberlain, who flew to see him at Berchtesgaden. Hitler agreed to a deal, successfully manipulating Britain into taking the lead in satisfying German grievances.	Chamberlain persuaded France and Czechoslovakia to accept a settlement over the Sudetenland Germans and flew back to tell Hitler.
22 September 1938: Hitler rejects the deal at a subsequent meeting at Godesberg, insisting on the immediate secession of the Sudetenland areas.	This was 'brinkmanship' risking war.	Chamberlain reluctantly faced the prospect of war – without any attempt to involve Russia and with no British Expeditionary Force.
30 September 1938: Hitler accepts Italian mediation and, at a conference at Munich, Britain and France accept his terms – the Sudetenland is taken by Germany.	Hitler gained his stated objective and German rearmament continued.	After the relief of Munich, there was an awareness that the long-term problem remained. British rearmament substantially increased.

(continued)

4

The Second World War

Table 4.2 *(continued)*

Event	Germany	Other countries
1939: Europe is now engaged in an arms race. Nazi Germany becomes more radical – there is heightened anti-Semitism and more Nazi control over the armed forces. In March 1939 the rest of Czechoslovakia is taken. Germany establishes a protectorate over Bohemia and Moravia, and Slovakia becomes a right-wing puppet state.	Hitler had established a foreign-policy aim not linked to the Treaty of Versailles by taking over a non-German state. German rearmament was not planned to be completed before 1942 but was now accelerated.	Chamberlain was openly critical of Hitler, and Britain offered Poland a guarantee of independence (not territorial integrity) and began negotiations with Russia. Conscription was introduced to Britain in April.
1939: Germany occupies Memel in Lithuania and there are demands for the Polish Corridor. A diplomatic coup in August gives Hitler a non-aggression pact with the USSR and a secret deal to divide Poland. On 1 September 1939, Germany invades Poland.	Once German forces were committed in Poland there was no real possibility of a Munich-type settlement. The USSR non-aggression pact offered the chance to amass forces against Poland. The planning of the invasion included death squads and the racial war in the east began. There was no significant action by either side on the Western Front.	British attempts to negotiate with the USSR were very limited. Despite rearmament, Britain was in no position to wage an offensive war. Chamberlain may well have hoped for more negotiations, but public opinion and his own cabinet and party would have prevented this. There was a delay after the German invasion, but on 3 September Britain declared war and France followed suit.

Historical debate:
There has been a major historical debate over appeasement. At the time, the future British prime minister, Winston Churchill, criticised it as showing weakness and making war more, not less, likely. In his post-war book *History of the Second World War* he developed an argument against it. Post-war historians agreed, but a post-war revisionist school of history has argued that the prime minister, Neville Chamberlain, had little option except to rearm and buy time by making concessions in the light of British public opinion, the weakness of Britain's economy, its lack of military preparedness and its unreliable allies. This view can be seen, for example, in *Chamberlain and the Lost Peace* by John Charmley.

As Table 4.2 shows, there was little attempt to defend the Treaty of Versailles, deter German rearmament or establish firm alliances to prevent German expansion. Neither was much effort put into developing a British force capable of taking the initiative in case of war, or to stand firm against any aggressive action by Hitler or his allies.

The case against appeasement

Once war began, it was easy to blame the British and French statesmen who had attempted to find a peaceful solution. It seemed obvious that, had firmer action

120

been taken at the outset, the sequence of events that led to the invasion of Poland in 1939 might have been avoided. If France and Britain had forced Germany out of the demilitarised zone in 1936, Hitler would have suffered a humiliating defeat. His generals might have turned against him and public support for his vision might have dwindled. The Rhineland gave the impetus to further rearmament, which could not then logically be stopped by Britain and France. This in turn led to success against Austria. Once Austria had fallen, Czechoslovakia was harder to defend.

Once British and French statesmen began to give in to Hitler's demands, the German leader had no reason to believe they would oppose him in any further action he might take. In Hitler's eyes, appeasement showed that they had scant regard for the treaty obligations or any democratic rights in Eastern Europe. The cheering crowds that met **Neville Chamberlain** and **Édouard Daladier,** the French prime minister, after Munich (1938) confirmed to Hitler that the people of France and Britain were not ready for war, and that longer-term plans to expand might begin more quickly than he had anticipated. It must have been clear that not a lot would be done to protect Czechoslovakia in March 1939. The policy of appeasement might have convinced Hitler that the Polish Guarantee (the British guarantee of Polish independence offered in March 1939) was meaningless and that nothing would be done to stop any invasion of Poland. He was right.

If the case against appeasement outlined above is true, then certainly the policy was a contributing factor to the outbreak of war. Throughout the 1920s, the British and French governments failed to maintain strong enough armed forces to threaten a national revival in Germany. The Locarno Treaty pointed the way to concessions in Eastern Europe. The early withdrawal of Allied troops from the Rhineland in 1930 demonstrated a limited commitment to maintain the 'watch on the Rhine', and anticipated the acceptance of the demilitarisation of 1936. The rundown of British military spending made it difficult for governments to offer any resistance, which in turn encouraged Hitler to risk war.

The alternative view

The case against appeasement, however, is based on later perspectives. Those responsible for the policy played no part in the drawing up of the Versailles Treaty – an agreement considered unfair both within and beyond Germany. Those who endorsed appeasement did not bring about the economic crisis that distracted governments and people from foreign-policy issues and made large-scale defence spending difficult and unpopular. They were facing a global system in which both Russia and the USA were cut off from European politics and unlikely to intervene in any war. They had to deal with a new phenomenon – one-party dictators – and to try to separate the fanaticism of these dictators' internal politics from their foreign policies. It was not as clear then as it later became that the Nazi ideology and Hitler's foreign policy were so closely linked. This element of **ideology** sets the causes of the Second World War apart from those of the First World War and made it difficult for political leaders to make the right decisions.

Evaluation

It is easy to understand why Chamberlain and Daladier acted to appease Hitler, and easy to see that criticisms at the time were not always realistic. However, it is also difficult to consider appeasement a success. Britain and France became embroiled in the war

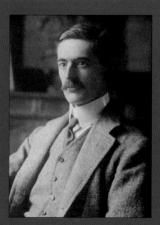

Figure 4.4   Neville Chamberlain (1869–1940)

He was prime minister of Britain from 1937 to 1940, and is one of the most debated political figures of the 20th century. He was a clear and logical thinker, who argued that Britain did not have the resources for war and needed to make concessions to Hitler's demands to regain Germany's lost lands, while building Britain's defences. However, this failed to prevent war and after 1940 it seemed that Chamberlain had been weak and unrealistic.

Édouard Daladier (1884–1970)

He was prime minister of France between 1938 and 1940. He was a moderate reforming politician of the Radical Party. He clearly saw the danger Germany posed. However, he found little support for war among French politicians and generals, and accepted Chamberlain's leadership in making concessions to Germany in which he did not really believe.

4

The Second World War

despite the policy, and appeasement undoubtedly encouraged Hitler to pursue policies that made a general war more likely. He was skilled at exploiting any weakness on the part of his enemies. Also, the fact that Stalin viewed appeasement as hostile towards the USSR made it easier for Hitler to gain a pact with the Soviet leader in 1939, which allowed him to conquer Poland and attack the West without fear of Russian intervention.

Ideology: A deep-rooted set of beliefs that underpin political actions. Hitler believed the German race to be natural masters, whose destiny was to dominate Europe. He believed that it was the right of Germans to have 'living space' at the expense of so-called inferior races, especially the Slavs of Eastern Europe. Hitler believed in setting up a pure-bred racial state by eliminating 'impure' races like the Jews; he believed that the nature of humanity was to struggle so that only the fittest and best survived. Other European statesmen did not realise how deeply infected his policies were by these ideas until it was too late.

QUESTION

To what extent does this cartoon support the alternative view above? What are the value and limitations of this cartoon as evidence for the impact of Munich?

Figure 4.5 'What, no chair for me?' – a cartoon from the London Evening Standard, October 1938 by David Low shows the four statesmen (Hitler, Chamberlain, Daladier and Mussolini) agreeing to grant Germany land from Czechoslovakia; Stalin, the Soviet leader, has been excluded, despite his alliance with France

Short-term factors in Asia

As well as significant developments in Europe, short-term factors in Asia also paved the way for what eventually become a world war. In particular, these involved Japan's reactions to the world economic depression, and its decision to solve its problems by expanding at the expense of its neighbours – mostly notably China – in order to obtain cheap supplies of the agricultural and industrial raw materials it needed.

Manchuria

The most accessible source of these materials was the Chinese province of Manchuria, which was rich in coal, iron ore, bauxite and soya – and also people to buy Japanese products and provide cheap labour. Manchuria was weakly controlled by China's nationalist government and Japan had been negotiating with its warlords. It would be a small step for Japan to take over and control the province. In September 1931, at the height of the economic depression, the local Japanese army in Kwantung staged explosions along the Japanese-owned South Manchuria Railway and used these as a pretext to invade. The authorities in Tokyo could not dishonour their own officers by failing to support such a move, and were thus spared the responsibility for war.

122

Arguably, Japan's road towards the Second World War began with this event in Manchuria. Japan rejected all foreign protests, left the League of Nations, established a Manchurian puppet state, renamed Manchukuo, and waged war in neighbouring Chinese areas.

Figure 4.6 Japanese troops enter Manchuria in 1931

WELL, I HARDLY KNOW WHICH TO TAKE FIRST!

Figure 4.7 'Well, I hardly know which to take first!' A cartoon commenting on the territorial expansion of the US, following its defeat of Spain in 1898

The Japanese had developed a highly disciplined and effective army, and in 1937 a large-scale invasion of China began. Despite the establishment of a single government and the defeat of regional warlords, the Chinese Guomindang (nationalist) government, under the leadership of Jiang Jieshi, faced a large-scale communist threat. The unity shown by the nationalist and communist factions in China was superficial.

Fact: Japanese control of China was an unwelcome prospect for those great powers that had trading interests in China and direct control of some coastal areas. It would also threaten the considerable European and US colonies in Southeast Asia. However, little action could be taken without US leadership, and this was not forthcoming.

Fact: After defeating Spain in the Spanish-American War of 1898, the US effectively took over Spain's former colonies – these included the Philippines in the Pacific. In the same year, the US took over Hawaii and Guam. In the decades that followed, US businesses expanded rapidly in the region, and increasingly came into conflict with Japanese interests. At the same time, the US increased its military – and especially its naval – presence in the region.

QUESTION

What is the message of this cartoon? Which territory depicted in the cartoon would have caused concern to Japanese nationalists?

Fact: The Anti-Comintern Pact was an agreement concluded first between Germany and Japan (25 November 1936) and later between Italy, Germany and Japan (6 November 1937). The pact, sought by Germany, was ostensibly directed against international communism, but was specifically directed against the Soviet Union.

For Japan, China was still a weak and tempting prize that would solve many of its problems in terms of trade and raw materials. However, despite an appalling terror campaign in Nanjing, characterised by total ruthlessness on the part of the Japanese, Japan found itself involved in a protracted and costly campaign that it could not bring to an end. The conflict required ever-increasing supplies of metal, rubber and oil, and was costing vast sums of money. It was also unpopular in Europe and the USA, where newsreels showed the devastating effects of Japanese bombing on Chinese cities.

When fighting broke out in Europe, Japan took the opportunity to occupy French Indochina in 1940 as part of a move to prevent supplies reaching Jiang and to attack China more effectively. This seemed to place Britain's colonies of Singapore, Malaya, Borneo and Hong Kong at risk, as well as the Dutch East Indies, Portuguese Timor and Macao, and the US Philippines. These territories were rich in oil, rubber and rice, and would have been a valuable gain for Japan.

When Hitler invaded Russia in 1941, another prospect emerged for Japan – an invasion of eastern Russia. Despite treaties with Germany and Italy, and the Anti-Comintern Pact of 1939, Japan was under no obligation to assist Germany. However, just as the US strained neutrality by its financial credit and naval support to Britain and its trade with Germany's enemies, it was also putting pressure on Japan. Japanese assets had been frozen, and a virtual embargo had been placed on imports of oil and metal ore to Japan. The US assumed that its naval force in Pearl Harbor, together with its army in the Philippines, would deter any potential Japanese action.

4.3 What were the ideological, political, economic, territorial causes?

As well as the various long- and short-term causes examined above, there were also several other significant factors that contributed to the outbreak of fighting in the period 1937–40. The main ones are explored below.

Ideological causes

The Second World War was the most destructive conflict in history to date. Although it started as a war for the revision of the Treaty of Versailles, and had other causes of a more usual nature (such as the important economic resources in Eastern Europe), as far as Hitler was concerned, these were secondary to his ideological 'dream'.

Nazi ideology

Hitler was not simply a strong national leader who wanted to regain lost territory. He had a distinct political worldview. In many ways, the war was driven by these ideological factors:

- fighting communism;
- dealing with the Jews.

In fact, in Hitler's mind, communism was deeply linked to the 'threat' from the Jews and he often referred to Judeo-Bolshevism.

He saw the mission of the German race (*Volk*) as being to create 'living space' (*Lebensraum*) in Eastern Europe. This could only be done under a strong leader who was inspired by a clear vision. Superior races like the Germans had a duty to enslave lesser races like the Slavs of Poland and Russia who would support a new Thousand-Year state. That state would be racially pure because linked in to expansion was the extermination of the lesser races – the Jews and Roma – who would be the natural enemy of this new world and who would pollute its purity. From the start, the war in Poland was waged with a fanaticism and violence not to be seen in later campaigns in the West. Poland was to be cleared for the racial resettlement and later Russia would be invaded to end the menace of the Jewish-communist state and to give the resources needed to establish a new order. This was a completely new type of warfare. The appeasers had not taken into account the ideological elements in German foreign policy.

The German conquest of Poland in 1939 was the first major development of the Second World War in Europe. The move was partly intended to regain lost territory, but it also had ideological elements, as Germany was expanding its living space at the expense of 'racially inferior' people, some of whom were enslaved (the Poles) and others who were persecuted or killed (the Jews in Poland). Thus the Second World War shifted from being a conflict over the balance of power in Europe and the terms of the Treaty of Versailles at the start, to increasingly being driven by Nazi ideology. The war also encompassed an ideological struggle between Nazism and communism, which reached its fullest form in June 1941, when Hitler was strong enough to attempt an invasion of the USSR. Ultimately, the Second World War had little to do with traditional concerns about the balance of power and diplomacy.

Hitler's invasion of the USSR, 1941

The German invasion of the Soviet Union was thus motivated by several factors:

- In Nazi ideological terms, it would be the final great battle between the 'forces of light', epitomised by the German racial state, against a conspiracy planned in the name of **Judeo-communism** that threatened civilisation.

- In political terms, it would confirm the strength of Nazism and show its superiority as a system over a corrupt communist state.

- In economic terms, it would give Germany access to vast reserves of fuel, food and raw materials. It would provide land for the idealised German peasants and markets for German manufacturers. It would provide the labour that Germany was short of, so that the country would never again be at the mercy of international markets. It would create a closed economic system in which a greater Germany would be economically self-sufficient. Germany could control the population of its new empire and create an ideal economic balance.

- Racially it would mean the extermination of millions of Jews, Roma and Slavs, and the creation of a new 'racially pure' super-state.

All these motives are well-documented, but at their root there may be a simpler reason: Hitler invaded the USSR because he thought he would succeed. In the so-called Winter War of 1939–40, when Russia fought Finland to gain territory north of Leningrad (formerly St Petersburg), Russian troops had initially been outfought and defeated by far smaller Finnish forces. The Finns lost in the end, but Russian casualties were heavy. No one thought that Russia would survive an attack by the expert, battle-hardened German forces. If Russia fell, Britain would not hold out and Germany could threaten Britain's Middle-Eastern oil supplies, as well as India itself – the jewel in Britain's crown.

Judeo-communism: In Nazi propaganda, Jews and communists were linked. The Jews were blamed for the Russian Revolution and communism was portrayed as a Jewish conspiracy to control the world. Karl Marx was a Jew, and there were Jews among the leading Bolsheviks in revolutionary Russia. Stalin, the Russian communist dictator, however, was actually anti-Semitic.

Fact: The German policy of self-sufficiency was based on the idea of not depending on imports or exports. It was thought that Germany had suffered in the Great Depression of 1929–33 because it had been dependent on loans from the USA and on events in the international economy. Hitler wanted Germany to have a permanent source of raw materials and an outlet for its goods in a colonised Eastern Europe.

Figure 4.8 Franklin D. Roosevelt (1882–1945)

He was Democratic president of the USA from 1933 to 1945. He was responsible for the New Deal, which mitigated the problems of the Great Depression. He followed an isolationist foreign policy, but in practice showed sympathy for European democracies. He put trade and financial embargoes on Japan after its occupation of Indochina, and provided Britain with credit and some war supplies in 1940–1.

What characterised Hitler's 1941 invasion of Russia was confidence. There were few in-depth preparations for a long campaign, and there was every expectation that Stalin's USSR would quickly disintegrate. The widespread surrender of the Soviet armies in the first weeks after the invasion seemed to confirm all these expectations. In the wake of the invading German armies came *Einsatzgruppen* – special death squads – to carry the racial war of extermination to the Judeo-Bolsheviks and other minorities like the Roma and Sinti, and Slavs. Communist officials and Jews were particularly targeted, but such huge numbers of Slav civilians were killed that the campaign seemed to be motivated more by murderous ideological urges than merely territorial or economic aims.

Activity

Compare the reasons for the German invasion of Russia in 1941 with the German invasion of France in 1914. Think about the following:

- the German need for security against an enemy;
- economic gains;
- racial and ideological motives.

Do you think the differences outweigh the similarities?

Ideology in Britain and the USA

Britain also needed to motivate its people for what was clearly going to be a long conflict. In the First World War, 'For King and Country' had been a popular rallying cry, and there was a sense that Britain was fighting for high ideals in contrast to German militarism.

As Britain cooperated more with the USA in 1940 and 1941, there seemed a need for a clear ideology, and so the Atlantic Charter was rather hastily drawn up. This was a declaration of common beliefs agreed by Churchill and **Franklin D. Roosevelt** – who endeavoured to establish a good personal relationship with one another – at a meeting at Placentia Bay, off the coast of Newfoundland, on 14 August 1941, even before the USA had joined the war. It was affirmed that all peoples had the right to self-determination and that there should be freedom of trade. This pleased Roosevelt more than Churchill, but it was at least a documented opposition to the ideologies of Nazism and fascism.

QUESTION

In August 1941 the USA was not at war. What do you think were the main reasons why the US eventually became involved in the Second World War?

SOURCE A

The President of the United States of America and the Prime Minister, Mr. Churchill:

… respect the right of all peoples to choose the form of government under which they will live; and they wish to see sovereign rights and self-government restored to those who have been forcibly deprived of them. …

After the final destruction of the Nazi tyranny, they hope to see established a peace which will afford to all nations the means of dwelling in safety within their own boundaries, and which will afford assurance that all the men in all the lands may live out their lives in freedom from fear and want. …

They believe that all of the nations of the world, for realistic as well as spiritual reasons, must come to the abandonment of the use of force.

Extract from the Atlantic Charter, 1941. Quoted at www.nato.int.

Figure 4.9 Winston Churchill (right) and Franklin D. Roosevelt, 1941; Roosevelt's decision to give Britain 50 destroyers in exchange for US military bases on British territory was an indication that he was sympathetic to Britain in 1941

Theory of Knowledge

The historian and 'great men' in history:
'Universal history, the history of what man has accomplished in this world, is at bottom the History of the Great Men who have worked here' – Thomas Carlyle (1795–1881)

To what extent should historians focus on the study of great men like Churchill and Roosevelt when making historical explanations? Was the war brought about by Hitler's overwhelming personal ambition? Was it won by the efforts of great national leaders like Churchill? Did the USA enter the war because of Roosevelt's ideals and policies? Does this oversimplify complex events?

Ideology in Japan

There were also important elements of ideology behind Japan's actions before the start of the war. The revival of Shinto and the belief in the Emperor as a divine presence were both important. More significant, however, was the nationalist belief that it was the 'mission' of Japan to use the methods of the Western 'barbarians' to reassert the purity of the divine homeland.

SOURCE B

From an explanation produced by leading Japanese academics in 1937 at the request of the government explaining National Policy.

The various ideological and social evils of present-day Japan are the result of ignoring the fundamental and running after the trivial. Too much importance is given to the individual and too little to the community. Since the days of the Meiji era so many aspects of US and European culture have been imported too rapidly. Our aim is to create a new Japanese culture with national policy as the basis of the mission of the people.

QUESTION

What is Source B saying about the impact of Western influence in Japan? How far did the 'mission' of the Japanese people influence Japanese foreign policy after 1937?

Political causes

There is certainly a link between ideology and politics, but there were causes of the war that related more to internal and international politics than to ideology. One was the fears for the balance of power. In 1914, Britain was concerned that Germany, if it defeated France and Russia might dominate the continent, which would be a threat to Britain. In 1939 there was equally a fear that Germany, regardless of the nature of the Nazi regime, should not be allowed to become the dominant power in Europe. This was a view shared by the USA.

The balance of power

It has been argued that Britain and the USA could have chosen not to take any action in the face of the rising power of Germany. The populations of both countries had no

Fact: In 1914, Britain feared that Germany would dominate Europe. Britain could not stand by and see France defeated. In 1939, the 'balance of power' was again threatened by Germany.

desire for war, and they were ruled by politicians whose success relied on maintaining public favour. Both countries had large territorial possessions and no ambitions to expand these further. Neither Britain nor the USA had a large army in 1939. However, both nations were concerned about the significant shift that would occur in the balance of power if Germany's own ambitions were realised. It is here that the greatest parallels can be drawn between the two world wars. If Germany dominated the coastline of northern Europe then British security and trade would be threatened, just as it would have been in 1914. A German-dominated continent would affect Britain as a major European trader. It would put Britain at Germany's mercy. It was also not in the US's long-term interests in terms of international politics. Strategically, German naval vessels would dominate ports and bases in the Atlantic, and could pose a considerable danger to US interests. By 1940, the US held the key to Britain's continuing participation in the Second World War. Without US supplies and credit, Britain would not be able to carry on. These circumstances, along with some key decisions taken in 1940 and 1941, caused the European war of 1939 to evolve into a world war. However, politically, the US government could not afford to enter a war when so many Americans were anxious to stay out of European conflicts. Political factors had led British and French governments into the policy of appeasement because there was so much political support for avoiding war. This had brought war closer. Not until Japan attacked America could the US declare war on Japan. It was still not certain that war against Hitler would follow. In the end a political decision led to war as Hitler decided to declare war. His dislike of the democratic US system and his desire to unleash his U-boats on the US overcame more rational foreign policy aims.

Economic and territorial factors

Germany and Japan had both suffered economically from the Wall Street Crash and the Great Depression and in both cases economic hardship had led to nationalism. Both countries needed guaranteed markets and raw materials and both believed that it was the destiny of their peoples to dominate 'inferior' races and use their resources. These economic and nationalist views combined and led to expansionist territorial aims. While the US's security would not be threatened, a German-dominated Europe would result in European markets that were controlled by a closed Nazi economic system at the same time as Far Eastern markets – in which the US had been expanding since the 19th century – would be controlled by a Japanese economic system. This would threaten American trade. British economic interests, too, would be hurt by a German-dominated Europe. Thus economic and territorial factors were closely related as significant causes of the Second World War.

US interests

Isolationism: This is the term used to describe a belief that a country should not involve itself in binding agreements with other countries or in any foreign policy that does not touch its own interests directly. However, although many in the US were keen to avoid becoming involved in European affairs after 1918, US foreign policy in Latin America and the Pacific was far from isolationist.

In the US, there was a considerable public backlash against the country's involvement in the First World War, and **isolationism** became a major element in US foreign policy after 1920. However, total isolationism was not possible: the economic links between the US and Europe were too great. After 1933, Roosevelt was forced to steer an uneasy path. On one hand, he needed to pacify a public that demanded economic recovery and resisted any potential involvement in European quarrels over European ideologies and territorial disputes. On the other hand, he had to consider America's wider economic and strategic interests, which were connected to events in Europe and Asia. The decisions Roosevelt made were a contributing factor in the expansion of the war beyond the boundaries of Europe.

The president had expressed sympathy for the cause of democracy, but the problem was that both France and Britain were imperial powers. Britain's human-rights record in some of its colonies was not much better than that of Hitler in Germany. In addition, Britain and its empire had imposed tariffs on foreign goods in 1932 and showed little interest in trade with the US. Thus, the moral and practical issues were not always clear-cut. When war went badly for Britain in 1940, Roosevelt would not allow himself to be persuaded to intervene, even by Churchill's most ardent pleas. He condemned Germany's invasion of France but took no direct action. He did, however, keep open Britain's credit links and, in return for valuable West Indian bases, gave Britain some old-fashioned destroyers. There was little real generosity here, but the increasing cooperation of the US navy in escorting the convoys as far as Iceland, and the meeting with Churchill at Newfoundland in August 1941, meant that Britain continued to hope for US help. There was also something of an emotional alignment, demonstrated by a joint declaration of principles – the Atlantic Charter. The US's 'neutrality', therefore, was not wholehearted. Despite this, it was not Churchill's pleas, nor a moral obligation to defend France, nor even fear of a Nazi-dominated European economy that officially drew the US into the war. On 11 December 1941, Germany itself declared war on the US.

Japanese interests

By 1941, the Japanese government faced a dilemma. With large forces tied up on its home territory, and with an economy that could not compete with that of the USA, it was in no real position to embark on what might turn out to be a lengthy war. However, US economic pressure – applied since July 1941 – was humiliating and was preventing a successful conclusion to the war in China. With Russia locked in a massive conflict with Germany, with France defeated and Britain distracted by war in the Mediterranean and the struggle against German naval forces in the Atlantic, the time might be favourable for a rapid strike. The Japanese hoped this would help them establish such a strong defence perimeter that its enemies would exhaust themselves trying to break it.

Meanwhile, the 'Greater East Asia Co-Prosperity Zone', as the Japanese misleadingly called it, could be used to supply Japan's forces. In any case, rational calculation was not the only factor. Japan would revenge itself for the violation of its homeland in 1853 (when the US had first tried to force it to 'open up' to US business interests) and the way that the West had seen it as inferior. The emperor's status would be raised and the spirit of Japan would be morally strengthened. Japanese culture would dominate Southeast Asia, and there was a good chance that India would fall, allowing Japan to seize Britain's most prized possession. Australasia might also be won and, in the long term, Japan would never be short of land, resources or markets.

There were obvious economic factors in Japan's decision to increase its expansion into China, which led to conflict with the USA, and also in its decision to attack the US and European colonies that were so rich in resources in order to set up a closed economic system to protect itself against the dangers of economic upheaval and ensure markets and raw materials. The political developments of nationalism and the greater influence of the army and members of the royal family in politics in Japan were key elements as was the economic and political weakness of China, divided by a civil war between communists and nationalists. However, there were important elements of ideology. The revival of Shinto and the belief in the emperor as a divine presence and the mission of Japan to use the methods of the Western 'barbarians' to reassert the purity of the divine homeland were a great motivator. The overwhelming belief in national superiority dominated

QUESTION

To what extent did US policy under Roosevelt give Germany little option other than to declare war?

Fact: Even after Japan's invasion of China in 1937, the US had continued to trade with Japan. However, when Japan decided to place large armed forces in southern Indochina, the US placed an embargo on the sale of all essential supplies – including oil and iron – to Japan; other Western nations, including Britain and the Netherlands, followed suit. The US also froze all Japanese assets in the US. This had a serious impact on Japan, which had to import 80 per cent of its oil requirements.

Fact: India was directly ruled by Britain from 1857, whose kings and queens became emperors of India after 1876. It was the largest of Britain's imperial possessions and was regarded as the most important. Ruling India was a major British 'mission' and India was referred to as the 'jewel' in the British 'crown'. Britain granted India independence in 1947.

The Second World War

the way that the 'Co-Prosperity Zone' worked, not a rational belief in developing economic resources. The political disappointments of 1919 and desire for greater influence were rooted in imperial ideology and desire to pursue a historical mission.

A web of factors

In many ways, there was a complex mixture of motives and factors – common to both Japan and Germany – that characterises many of the causes of the Second World War.

These factors were linked to a belief in the importance of military planning. Hitler did not believe he could lose against Poland, France or Russia. Japan – by 1941 concerned by the build-up of US military forces in the Pacific – was certain that the air attacks on Pearl Harbor would be so devastating that they would buy the necessary time to establish Japanese defences against a counterattack. Japan also believed that its military experience and sheer morale would overcome resistance in the European and US colonies.

In some ways, both Hitler and the Japanese leaders were right, but both plans contained short-term weaknesses and long-term miscalculations. Neither the Germans nor the Japanese had the resources to defeat the countries that became post-war superpowers. Both underestimated the economic strength and fighting ability of their enemies. Hitler's forces failed to capture their vital first objectives, Moscow and Leningrad; Japan failed to destroy the all-important US aircraft carriers at Pearl Harbor. Both began wars that could never be ended by negotiation, and both faced unprecedented mobilisation of human and material resources that, in the end, overwhelmed them.

The Japanese decision for war, 2 July 1941:

Our Empire is determined to establish the Greater Asia Co-prosperity Zone and will by this contribute to world peace.

Our Empire will continue its efforts to effect a settlement of the China incident (i.e. the war in China from 1937) and will seek to establish a solid basis for the security and preservation of the nation. This will involve taking steps to advance south.

The Empire will not be deterred by the possibility of being involved in a war against Great Britain and the United States.

Minutes of Imperial Conference, Tokyo. Quoted in R.J. Overy. 1987. The Origins of the Second World War, London: Longman, p. 114.

Japan, Germany and Italy were all aggrieved and disappointed by the outcome of the First World War. Their states manipulated the mass discontent of the populace and each state had beliefs rooted in military values and the glories of a distant past. All sought territorial gains to solve immediate problems. All took advantage of neighbours they considered weak, but whose strength they underestimated. All thought in terms of using conquered empires to both increase economic power and develop further military strength. Racial pride was an element in calculating that risky attacks would be victorious. All were encouraged by weak initial responses to aggression by more democratic powers, and by a belief that the peoples in those democracies were unwilling to sustain long and costly wars.

QUESTION

How similar were the causes of war in Europe and the Far East?

KEY CONCEPTS ACTIVITY

Significance: Identify the main economic factors, territorial factors, ideological factors and political factors as causes of war in both Europe and the Far East. For each of the factors, write the main elements on cards and then put them in order of importance for both Germany and Japan.

QUESTION

What, according to Source C, are the reasons why Japan went to war?

What are the value and limitations of this source as a reliable guide to Japan's motives?

Table 4.3 General causes of the Second World War – Germany, Italy and Japan

Element	Germany	Italy	Japan
Ideological factors	German nationalism grew after 1871, was a major force before 1914 and was used by Hitler to gain support. Nationalists resented Versailles, looked to a greater Germany that would include all German-speakers, and had strong beliefs in the superiority of German culture. This was an important element in Nazism and also in racialism, which were important elements in bringing about war.	Italian nationalism was slower to emerge after unification, but Mussolini stressed the inheritance of the Roman Empire and played on the disappointments of the peace settlement. The taking of Fiume from Yugoslavia in 1924 was popular and many were impressed by Mussolini making Italy more of a world power. He reversed the national humiliation of 1896, when Italy had been defeated by Ethiopia, in the war of 1935–6. He revived Italian national claims to Nice in 1940.	Japan's internal reforms gave it the means to expand its territory considerably after 1874. Nationalists associated expansion with the greater glory of the emperor-god. There were patriotic associations which set up traditional culture as far superior to Western influences. The expansion of 1941–2 was a culmination of nationalist feeling and territorial ambition. There was a strong element of racial superiority in the way that the war against the supposedly inferior Chinese was portrayed.
Economic and territorial factors	Hitler's Germany depended heavily on the prosperity generated by arms spending. However, this produced inflationary pressure, shortages of materials and the need to pay for expensive imports. The solution was to go to war to acquire materials and to loot other countries to pay for arms and to maintain the standard of living of the German people.	Mussolini's regime faced economic pressures after 1929 but Italy's conquests – Ethiopia 1936, Albania 1939, Nice (South of France) in 1940 and Greece, 1940 – were driven not by the need for greater economic resources as much as for prestige to bolster a regime that had not delivered the economic gains promised.	There were strong economic motives for the conquest of Manchuria in 1931. Japan's shortage of essential military raw materials and the restrictions placed on imports of oil and metal ores by the USA were significant motives for expansion. There was a plan for a Japanese-controlled closed economic system in Southeast Asia – the 'Co-Prosperity Zone' – but in practice the resources of conquered areas were taken by Japan to sustain the war.
Political factors	Hitler needed foreign policy successes for his personal popularity and had a strong political vision of a Thousand Year Reich of pure-bred Aryans dominating Europe. Politically the war was portrayed in 1939 as being against the political restrictions of Versailles and from 1941 as being against the danger of communism.	Mussolini's strong image depended on foreign policy successes. However, much of his prestige derived from being an international statesman who helped to keep the peace – for example, at Munich. The popularity of easy successes following German victories lured him into war in 1940.	Plans for the political development of an independent Asia, freed from colonialism under Japanese protection, were set out, but little was done to implement them. Conquered territories were exploited and oppressed.

The war becomes global

On 7 December 1941, the Japanese attacked the US naval fleet at Pearl Harbor in Hawaii, and four days later the disparate conflicts of the Second World War were linked by Germany's declaration of war on the USA. There has been much debate about this decision. Hitler had no obligation to support the Japanese. Relations between Germany and Japan were not close, and Hitler had not informed the Japanese before invading Russia in June 1941. US indignation against the Japanese attack on Pearl Harbor was intense, but this could have led to pressure on the US government to focus resources on the Pacific and disengage with any potential hostilities with Germany. Instead, Hitler's sudden declaration of war connected the three ongoing conflicts:

- The continuing opposition of Britain to Germany – after the conclusion of the first part of the Second World War in Europe in 1940 – linked the struggle over Versailles and the balance of power to the ideological conflict between Germany and Russia.
- Britain's efforts to cooperate with the USA, and the attacks made by Japan on both British and US colonies in Southeast Asia in December 1941, linked Britain and America to a conflict in the Far East.
- Germany's declaration of war on the USA linked all these conflicts, and turned a series of wars into a world war.

Some have seen Hitler's decision to declare war as a moment of hate-filled madness, some as a gesture to please Japan and to express gratitude for the Japanese attacks that weakened Britain. However, it seems likely that the real reason was that Hitler wanted to put an end to the undeclared war that had been building in the Atlantic between US ships and German U-boats. If Germany and the USA were officially at war, it would allow Hitler's admirals free rein in attacking US shipping, which was supplying Germany's enemies. The result of Hitler's declaration was the formation of a Grand Alliance – Britain, the USA and the USSR (together with China) – against Germany, Italy and Japan.

End of unit activities

1 Look in Chapter 2 for a summary of the causes of the First World War. What are the main similarities and differences?

Think about the four main areas listed in the table below. Copy and complete a similar table. Give each cause a numerical value between 0 and 10, in which 0 means not important and 10 means very important. Give a brief explanation of your judgement.

Cause	Importance for First World War	Importance for Second World War
Ideological factors		
Political factors		
Economic factors		
Territorial factors		

2 Look back at the causes of the First and Second World Wars. Both had long-term causes and short-term causes.

Divide into groups – a short-term group and a long-term group. The long-term group should make cards with the long-term causes of both wars (e.g., the rise of Japan after 1853) and give a brief explanation of why that could be a cause of war. The short-term group should do the same with short-term causes (e.g., the assassination of Archduke Franz Ferdinand).

Now highlight the cards. Red = very important; green = some importance; blue = less important. Spread out the cards. Use them to reach a decision about whether long-term or short-term causes were more important in the First World War and the Second World War.

3 See what you can find about the historian A.J.P. Taylor and his view of the causes of the Second World War. How would you assess his opinion of Hitler's actions?

2 Unit

Practices of the Second World War

TIMELINE

1939 Germany invades Poland.

1940 Germany conquers Norway, Denmark, Holland, Belgium and France.

Winston Churchill becomes prime minister of Britain.

Battle of Britain.

War in North Africa.

1941 Germany conquers Greece, Yugoslavia and Romania.

Germany invades Russia.

Japan attacks American, British, Dutch and Portuguese colonies in the Far East.

1942–3 Turning points of Stalingrad, Midway and El Alamein.

1943 Battle of Kursk invasion of Italy by Allies; Mussolini falls.

1944 D-Day invasion Russian forces enter Eastern Europe.

1945 Battles of Iwo Jima and Okinawa.

First and only use of atomic weapons.

Conferences at Yalta and Potsdam.

Germany and Japan surrender.

KEY QUESTIONS

- What were the main practices of the Second World War?
- What were the main events and how were they influenced by new technology and tactics?
- What was the significance of the mobilisation of human and economic resources and the home front?

Overview

- The Second World War was the greatest of the 20th century's total wars. The First World War had been a prolonged conflict, bringing the total resources of the major participants to bear in a huge exertion of force. When the Second World War came, states, peoples and armies knew that once again war would be unlimited – that it would use every resource available. All industrial and human resources, all modern technology, and the whole power of the state would be applied to ensure a total victory.

- More than any previous conflict, this was a war between peoples and against peoples. The line between soldier and civilian was blurred – the great industrial cities and their factory workers kept the war effort going and so were targets for destruction. Some of the nations involved had grand plans for the annihilation of whole peoples they considered a threat to their existence. Ordinary men, women and children, therefore, became the enemy on an unprecedented scale.

- Modern weaponry grew even more destructive than it had been in the First World War, and huge casualties made a peaceful settlement even more difficult to achieve. In the end, the war was won only with the most enormous application of force against the total population of the enemy – whether or not they served in uniform.

- The state power of the participating countries exerted a control over all aspects of life. War was an all-consuming activity and became a fight for national survival that could not be abandoned until there was no alternative. In Germany's case, this point was reached when enemy forces occupied most of the country and its leader, Adolf Hitler, committed suicide. In Japan's case it came when the most destructive weapon ever used – the atomic bomb – wiped out two major cities, Hiroshima and Nagasaki.

4.4 What were the main practices of the Second World War?

What differentiated the Second World War from the First World War was its general mobility and periods of rapid and decisive movement. Like the First World War, the Second World War depended heavily on industry and the mobilisation of a range of resources by powerful states with a great deal of control over their populations. Technical developments also came to be increasingly important.

Unlike the First World War, however, the development of air warfare and fluid fronts in which tank warfare predominated meant that successful leadership depended on movement, logistics and managerial-type planning. As this type of warfare also depends on civilian workers and a strong industrial base, the home front was just as important as the battlefield. Civilians were seen as essential targets for destruction to prevent war materials reaching the front lines, and to injure the morale and even national existence of the enemy. The racial element in this war meant that ethnic groups were regarded as enemies of the state who should be attacked and killed. This had occurred in the First World War – for example with the Turkish massacre of an estimated 1 million Armenians in 1915 – but not to the same extent. One historian called the Second World War 'The war against the Jews', but in fact persecution included several ethnic minorities during and immediately after the war in many countries.

4.5 What were the main events and how were they influenced by new technology and tactics?

Three main phases

For the purposes of study, the Second World War can be divided into three main phases:

1 *Blitzkrieg* and rapid advances, 1939–42

The initial phases of the war were characterised by rapid attacks, which were far more successful than their equivalents in the First World War. Poland fell within weeks of the German invasion, as did Norway, Denmark, Belgium, the Netherlands and France. In contrast, between 1914 and 1918, sustained heavy fighting prevented decisive conquests. Axis forces quickly conquered the Balkans, and Russian forces overran eastern Poland and the Baltic States. Where Britain was able to attack in North Africa, it also achieved rapid victories over Italian forces – only to face equally swift defeats at the hands of the German Afrika Korps. After June 1941, Germany conquered vast areas of Russia until the onset of winter slowed the advance. Japan achieved quick victories by a series of attacks on US and European colonies from December 1941 to February 1942, and rapid conquest everywhere continued throughout the year. This period became known as the *Blitzkrieg*, or 'lightning war'.

Fact: The Battle of Midway, 4–7 June 1942, occurred when the Japanese hoped to lead the US fleet into a trap by attacking the island of Midway in the Pacific. However, US planes operating from aircraft carriers inflicted great damage on the Japanese fleet. This battle is seen as the turning point of the Pacific War, forcing Japan onto the defensive.

2 Counterattacks from 1942

At the end of 1942, the situation began to reverse. The Allied powers mounted a series of successful counterattacks. Russia began the long drive to expel Germany by a victory at Stalingrad. British forces drove the Germans back at El Alamein in North Africa. The Americans held the Solomon Islands in the Pacific and, after the naval victory at Midway, the US was able to begin the long struggle to recapture lost territory. The British turned the tide of German U-boat success. By 1943, the initiative had passed to the Allies and the Axis powers found themselves on the defensive.

3 The heavy and costly fighting in the later part of the war

The Axis powers realised that victory was growing increasingly remote, but there was little they could do to end the war. The later stages were therefore characterised by costly and extensive campaigns designed to wear down the opposition. Civilian casualties increased and the element of attrition grew. The rapid successes of the German *Blitzkrieg* in Europe and of the Japanese invasion of Malaya and Singapore gave way to a large-scale industrial war. Massive resources were assembled and maximum force applied, regardless of casualties. Technical innovation, including widespread aerial bombing, became a key feature of the closing years of the war, and culminated in the use of atomic weapons.

Theory and practice of *Blitzkrieg* in Europe

The opening campaigns of the Second World War were similar to the closing ones of the First World War. The Germans were anxious to avoid more trench warfare and to build on the experiences of 1918, when they had relied on small groups of storm troops and sudden applications of force rather than extended bombardments involving large battalions. They also learnt lessons from the Allied counterattacks of 1918, in which tanks, artillery, aircraft and infantry were combined to avoid costly frontal attacks and to keep the battlefield moving. *Blitzkrieg* made use of fast-moving tanks and motor vehicles, which pushed as far and as fast as possible into enemy territory. These assaults were supported by air attacks and followed up by infantry, backed up by artillery.

Figure 4.10 Heinz Guderian (1888–1954)

He was the major military theorist of his generation, who advocated armoured thrusts to break enemy lines. He saw the potential of the tank not just to support infantry but as the key weapon of war. This was proved right at first, but when opponents developed large numbers of tanks, the shock value of attacks by armoured vehicles was lost.

Everything was done to create a sense of chaos among the enemy – cities were bombed, refugees attacked, false radio messages sent, rumours of spies encouraged. This rapid movement bewildered the defenders and cut them off from their supply bases. The German Stuka dive-bombers were particularly effective in this kind of warfare, but the essence was maximum application of force at key points, followed by swift drives forward by mechanised troops.

The theory for *Blitzkrieg* had been provided by military writers like Captain Basil Liddell Hart and by the German **Heinz Guderian**, who led an armoured division into Poland.

Poland

Between 1 and 17 September 1939, the Polish armies were encircled by two powerful German and Russian thrusts from north and south. Despite some brave resistance, when Russia invaded eastern Poland on 17 September, Poland was forced to surrender.

This victory seemed to prove the value of *Blitzkrieg* tactics, which deployed highly trained forces capable of acting on their own initiative. Far from being dominated by orders from above, the German army was so well trained that even the middle ranks could take over in an emergency and make decisions about how to react to attacks.

Figure 4.11 The German Stuka dive bomber was effective in creating panic and disruption in initial *Blitzkrieg* attacks in Poland, France and the Low Countries

The commanders set broad objectives, but implementation was flexible, allowing strong points to be abandoned if it was deemed necessary and an overall rapid advance to go ahead without every unit waiting for support or reinforcements. Polish forces were spread over a huge frontier of nearly 3000km (1860 miles), and the Polish high command did not consider the possibility of concentrating its main defence on a smaller area. Although this would have meant giving some ground in the initial attack, it would ultimately have made the Germans' task much more difficult. In addition, the Poles had no effective help from their allies. If Britain and France had come quickly to Poland's aid – as France had in 1914 – then Germany would not have been able to concentrate its forces against the Poles. The success of *Blitzkrieg* was thus largely due to the weakness of Germany's enemies.

France and the Netherlands

Many of the same factors came into play during the German invasions of France and the Low Countries in May 1940. British energies had been focused on an unsuccessful campaign in Norway, at the end of which Norway still fell to the Germans. As a result, the British took little initiative on the Western Front. The French relied on a vast fortification system called the **Maginot Line**, but – fatally – this line did not extend along the Belgian frontier. There was limited cooperation and planning between France and Britain. In the event of an invasion by Germany, British troops were to advance into Belgium. The German plan played on this. A heavy attack at the point where the French and British lines met drove a wedge between them. While the British and French pushed into Belgium, German tanks swept into France. The Germans massed their forces at Sedan and broke through. The Allies had erroneously believed that the Ardennes forest would prevent the Germans using tanks.

While German tanks and dive bombers outfought the French in Belgium, further south, at Sedan, a decisive battle took place. Coordination between the German air force and its dive bombers and rapid attacks by Guderian's tanks met with only weak resistance from the French. The better Allied troops and equipment were tied up in Belgium.

Maginot Line: An extensive static defence system built by France after 1931 along its eastern frontier with Germany. Although impressive, it did not extend along the frontier with Belgium, leaving a weak point that Germany exploited in 1940. The existence of the Maginot Line encouraged a false sense of security in France.

The Second World War

Fact: The advancing German army trapped the British and French armies on the beaches around Dunkirk. Some 330 000 men were caught here and became sitting targets for the Germans. From 26 May 1940, small ships transferred soldiers to larger ones, which carried them back to a port in southern Britain (800 of these legendary 'little ships' were used). Despite attacks from German fighter and bomber planes, Hitler's failure to order a full-scale attack on the troops at Dunkirk was his first fatal mistake of the war. Although the bulk of British equipment was lost, more than 300 000 troops were saved, which allowed Britain to continue the war.

QUESTION

In 1914, Britain and France held back the German advance and forced Germany into a long campaign of attrition in the West. In 1940, the Germans defeated French and British resistance with ease and won a swift victory. What practices of war explain the difference?

- Discuss in class and find as many explanations as possible.
- Write these explanations on sheets of paper and add supporting knowledge.
- Put the sheets of paper into their order of importance.

On 12–14 May 1940, the Germans crossed the River Meuse and forced the French to retreat. The French seemed unable to cope with the speed of the German breakthrough, and a rapid German thrust cut off the British from the French. Refugees clogged the roads and German aircraft caused maximum disruption in areas leading to the battlefield. The attack was halted on 15 May, and this gave British forces enough time to gather at Dunkirk behind a defensive perimeter. From there, they were evacuated but lost considerable amounts of equipment. The French tried to establish lines on the rivers Somme and Aisne, but successful German breakthroughs further south rendered resistance impossible. Paris fell on 14 June 1940, and the defenders of the Maginot Line found themselves attacked from the rear. On 22 June, France signed an armistice.

Unlike in 1914, there was no heroic attempt to hold the line and no establishment of a firm defensive system. In the First World War, the Schlieffen Plan (see Section 2.5) had failed because Belgian and British resistance caused delays in the German advance. This time, Belgium quickly capitulated and British attempts to halt the German advance were weak in comparison to the actions at Mons and Le Câteau in 1914. German forces were not weakened by being deployed in the East. Relations between Germany and Russia were excellent and Germany was receiving large amounts of Russian imports to help it fight France. The German infantry did not tire as it had in 1914 – the tanks and armoured vehicles kept the advance going and made the front fluid. This time it was the British and French who were restricted by a rigid plan of advancing in Belgium, which took them further way from the German breakthrough point at Sedan.

In 1914, the French general Joffre had seen the exposed German flank and attacked at the Marne using flexibility and initiative. This time, despite seriously exposed flanks, there was no brilliant Allied attack. The violence of the air assaults and the rapidity of German movement left the Allies unable to respond except by withdrawal. It was only the fact that Hitler ordered the tanks to halt their advance on 15 May, and the failure of air attacks to destroy the army on the beach at Dunkirk, that prevented a total destruction of the British army.

Was the German success attributable only to *Blitzkrieg*?

Once again, victory depended on expert German planning and the tactical use of air forces, tanks, artillery and infantry, as well as an ill-prepared and weak enemy response. To the Germans it now seemed that *Blitzkrieg* was an unstoppable formula for victory. However, it is important to note that this method was effective because Germany was essentially fighting on one front at a time. In addition to this, Germany's enemies were not on a full wartime footing in 1939 and 1940, and were not cooperating well with each other. Opposing generals also had flawed defensive plans and they lacked the skill and decisiveness of their German counterparts.

It was also true that France, Britain and Poland had been unable to establish firm defensive fronts, and their air forces had not proved effective in supporting ground troops against sudden and concentrated attack. None of the Allied armies or air forces was prepared for offensive campaigns, and so the Germans were able to take the initiative.

Politically, the Allied civilian populations were not committed to war. Unlike the Germans, they had little to gain from war except maintaining the status quo. France had been divided in the 1930s between the political left and right; many in Britain had supported the policy of appeasement and wanted to avoid the high casualty rates of a modern war. Few in Poland had expected war, and the Polish state was not really prepared for an invasion by Germany, nor for the later invasion from the Soviet Union – the Nazi–Soviet Pact of August 1939 had come as a surprise.

Blitzkrieg in Asia

The lesson of successful rapid-movement warfare against an ill-prepared enemy was not lost on Japan. It also had a well-developed plan – influenced by the British attack on the Italian fleet at Taranto Bay in November 1940 – which involved a sudden and forceful assault against its enemy's main naval base at Pearl Harbor, followed by rapid assaults on the European colonies.

Just as France, Britain and Poland had little strategy for resisting Germany, so Britain, the USA, France and the Netherlands had little or no joint strategy for resisting Japan. The homelands of the forces in French Indochina and the Netherlands' Indies had been conquered by Germany in 1940. Britain was fighting a war in North Africa and had to keep substantial forces for home defence. It relied on the naval base at Singapore and the threat of its navy to deter Japan, together with its forces in Malaya and Singapore, which could be reinforced from Australia. These forces were not well-trained or led, nor were they militarily or psychologically prepared for a rapid and unexpected advance. The Japanese dealt with the naval threat by sinking the two great British warships, the *Prince of Wales* and the *Repulse*, which were without air cover and prey to Japanese air attack. With numerically inferior forces, the Japanese landed in Malaya and fought their way through the jungle to Singapore. Just as in France, sudden movement and the appearance of tanks disoriented the British. The great naval guns pointed out to sea were turned round, but by the time they were used the Japanese were threatening Singapore.

Figure 4.12 The key event of the war for the British Empire: Britain surrenders to a smaller force in Singapore

Fact: In the Nazi–Soviet Pact, signed on 23 August 1939, the USSR and Germany agreed not to fight each other and, in secret, to divide Poland between them, with the USSR reclaiming the territory it had been forced to relinquish to Poland in 1921. This pact allowed Hitler to invade Poland without fear of Russian retaliation, and Stalin to occupy the Baltic States and eastern Poland. Stalin was surprised when, without first defeating Britain, Hitler invaded Russia in 1941.

Fact: The Japanese attacked the major US naval base in the Pacific, Pearl Harbor, Hawaii, on 7 December 1941. More than 300 fighters, bombers and torpedo bombers took part, using six aircraft carriers. The most serious casualty was the warship USS *Arizona*, and 1,177 sailors were killed; the *Utah* and the *Oklahoma* never sailed again, but all the other ships damaged in the attack were repaired. The Japanese did not destroy all the fuel installations, nor the US aircraft carriers, which were at sea. Roosevelt called the attack 'infamy' and it provoked a massive demonstration of support among the American people for total victory.

Faced with the prospect of heavy civilian casualties from Japanese bombing and street fighting, the British General Arthur Percival chose to surrender. Australian reinforcements stepped off the ships almost directly into Japanese captivity. Successful amphibious landings led to rapid Japanese occupation of the US Philippines and the Netherlands' East Indies (Java and Sumatra). Japanese forces pushed into Burma and threatened India, and Australia feared an invasion of its northern territories. It was not troop numbers, but the effective use of air power and rapid movement, that was the key to Japanese victories. Given the relative smallness of Japanese forces and the problems of amphibious landings, the victories were by no means certain. What made them possible was a weak response by distracted and poorly prepared European and American enemies.

Why did the war continue?

For all their successes, the Axis powers still made some fatal miscalculations that contributed to their ultimate defeat.

The role of Britain

Germany could not end Britain's participation in the war. Its failure to destroy British forces at Dunkirk left Britain with more than 300 000 soldiers as the nucleus of an army. The German air force lost control of the war in the air during the Battle of Britain, and failure to devote resources to the German navy before 1939 allowed Britain to maintain its domination of the Channel and the North Sea. This made any invasion of the British Isles potentially dangerous. In addition, the emergence of Winston Churchill as prime minister gave Britain a determined leadership. Churchill, hoping for US support, refused to negotiate with Hitler.

Not only did Britain not surrender but it took an active role in attacking Italian forces in North Africa from its base in Egypt. The support of its empire provided Britain with important resources of manpower (240 million people lived in the British Empire), overseas bases and raw materials. Britain remained a dogged opponent and was a central element in anti-German coalitions, and Britain's involvement effectively forced Hitler to fight the war on two fronts for most of its duration.

US aid to Britain

Germany's second miscalculation was also linked to the struggle with Britain. Britain depended not only on US credit but also on North American industries for war supplies. British naval forces escorted merchant convoys, but trade between the US and Britain was vulnerable to German U-boat attacks, just as it had been in the First World War. In March 1941, the Lend-Lease Act was passed by Congress, allowing the president to 'sell, transfer, exchange, lease or lend' war supplies to any nation whose defence was seen as vital to the defence of the USA.

In December 1940, Roosevelt spoke of the USA as the 'arsenal of democracy' and, throughout this year, America had already been gearing its economy towards war production. It became vital for Germany to cut off this line of supply. Incidents involving attacks on US shipping increased and culminated in a U-boat attack on the USS Greer, provoking Roosevelt to issue a 'shoot first' order to US naval vessels in the Atlantic if confronted with German U-boats. The failure to end the war with Britain had involved Germany in a struggle with the USA that ultimately proved disastrous. The miscalculation lay in assuming that US isolationism would prevent America from sustaining Britain.

German setbacks in Eastern Europe

The third miscalculation lay in German policy towards Eastern Europe. The successes against Poland and then Norway, Denmark, the Netherlands, Belgium and France were followed by similar victories in Greece, where a German force helped out an unsuccessful Italian invasion, and Yugoslavia. The Germans, therefore, had every reason to believe that an invasion of Russia – Operation Barbarossa, launched on 22 June 1941 – would be yet another success. Certainly, formidable forces were assembled. The Germans had superiority over Russia in aircraft, tanks and men (4:1 aircraft; 1.6:1 in men; 1.8:1 in artillery; 1.5:1 in tanks). The plans were built around previous successes, and involved three massive concentrations of force:

- in the north, aimed at Leningrad;
- in the centre, aimed at Moscow;
- in the south, pushing towards Kiev and then to the Black Sea.

The principles of concentrated force, rapid mechanised movement, strong air support and encirclement of enemy forces were applied on a much larger scale. Just as in 1939 and 1940, the forces of Germany's enemies were poorly led, taken by surprise, disoriented by ruthless and rapid advance and driven back. An incredible 4.5 million Soviet troops had been lost by the end of 1941. The unpopularity of Russian communist rule in many of the invaded areas was another advantage that the Germans could have exploited, but they were so confident of victory that they failed to do so. Conquered areas like the Ukraine or Belorussia suffered extreme violence, oppression and confiscation of property at the hands of the Germans. Russian armies surrendered and, by December 1941, 90 million Russians found themselves under German rule. Moscow and Leningrad had been bombed, and German forces were stationed in the outlying areas of the cities. However, unlike in France and Poland, the Russian forces managed to stabilise a front line by the end of October.

The Germans blamed bad weather for stopping the advance, but equally significant was the ability of the Russian forces to counterattack and hold their positions. Moscow was defended and the German advance halted. An attack in the Rostov area of the northern sector prevented Germany deploying forces from their northern armies in support of the army group in the centre. Poor weather conditions made German advance difficult as winter set in.

Fact: Operation Barbarossa was named after a medieval German crusading emperor and was the biggest invasion in the history of warfare. It was the culmination of Germany's military preparations since 1933. Four and a half million troops invaded across 2,900km (1,800 miles).

Figure 4.13
German soldiers using horses and carts in the Ukraine during a snowstorm

**Figure 4.14 Joseph
Stalin (1878–1953)**

He started his political career
as a revolutionary in Georgia.
He rose in the Bolshevik Party
to become general secretary
under Lenin. By 1928, he
had defeated his rivals to
become the party leader, and
created a dictatorship. He
forced the Russian peasants
into collective farms and
established a police state,
in which millions of people
were imprisoned or killed. In
1939, Stalin signed a pact
with Hitler, and was surprised
when the Germans invaded
in 1941. He rallied Russia to
heroic resistance and after
1945 imposed his rule on
much of Eastern Europe.

Fact: Ever since Pearl
Harbor, there have been
suggestions – including
from retired US Navy Rear
Admiral Theobald – that the
US government was aware
of the impending attack,
but let it go ahead in order
to persuade the US public
to support involvement in
the war. However, most
historians believe that
this theory has not been
convincingly proved.

Despite huge losses, the Soviets were able to call up increasing numbers of troops to
aid their defence. The halt before Moscow was of enormous significance. During
the First World War, advances had taken armies further from their own supplies and
reinforcements and closer to enemy railheads, where additional reinforcements and
supplies gathered. This had resulted in bitter struggles in which the industries and
transport of the 'home side' blocked advance by the 'invading side'. In the Second
World War, Germany had so far avoided this situation by rapid victories. Now *Blitzkrieg*
failed to deliver – not dramatically, as German forces were still close to their objectives,
but enough for the USSR to recover and bring its considerable industrial and manpower
resources to bear. French leaders had not been prepared for the huge sacrifice of human
life that continued resistance would have meant. **Joseph Stalin** had no such qualms.
The powerful communist state he had developed imposed an iron discipline on its
people. Failure meant death. There was no compromise and no sacrifice was too great.
The Nazi invaders faced a regime as ruthless and determined as their own, and Hitler
underestimated the economic potential and political strength of the USSR. In addition,
Nazi atrocities provoked a genuinely strong nationalist resistance among Soviet citizens.
By the beginning of 1942, German forces were no longer engaged in a rapid advance,
but rather a protracted war of attrition. They also faced war on a number of fronts – the
North African desert against Britain; the war at sea against the British and US navies,
and an air war that placed German civilians and cities on the front line.

Japanese failures in the Pacific

Japan had also miscalculated. The sudden air attack on the US naval base at Pearl
Harbor failed to destroy the US aircraft carriers, which were out at sea. However,
US commanders had failed to take elementary precautions or pay heed to intelligence
reports. Again, weakness helped victory. Despite this, the damage done to US
battleships and destroyers was not a decisive element of success. Most of the ships sunk
were later restored and took part in the war. The war in the Pacific was eventually
dominated by aircraft and so the survival of the main US carriers, *Lexington* and
Enterprise, was more important. The attack killed 2400 people, sank three battleships,
damaged many smaller vessels and destroyed two-thirds of US naval aircraft. This
was achieved with limited Japanese losses (29 aircraft and five midget submarines),
and prevented any US interference with the Japanese invasion of Western colonies.
However, the potential of the world's greatest economy to rebuild and extend its naval
power, and the determination of the US to avenge the 'day of infamy', as Roosevelt
called it, seem to have been underestimated by Japan.

The key element in Pacific warfare – the use of aircraft carriers and air power – gave
the advantage to the US, due to its capacity to produce these weapons by a modern
industrial economy. The defeat of the Japanese navy at the Battle of Midway in June
1942 prevented Japan securing its hoped-for defensive ring and destroyed vital Japanese
carriers. This decisive battle, which halted further expansion, occurred soon after Pearl
Harbor and showed the limited understanding Japan had of US resources and energy.

The high cost of war

In general, Germany underestimated the costs of modern war. Easy and relatively cheap
successes in 1939 and 1940, together with products and loot taken from occupied
countries, seemed to suggest that the Nazi state was delivering victory without the
terrible sacrifices that Germany had faced between 1914 and 1918. However, losses
began to mount on the Eastern Front from October 1941, and the first bombing raids

by the Allies on Germany were signs that Hitler and his people had miscalculated what could be achieved by modern 'scientific' warfare against weak opponents.

Inadequate preparation by Italy

As an ally of Germany, Italy had hoped for swift victories, but reverses in Greece and the need to supply forces for the Russian Front, together with losses in North Africa and the defeats in Ethiopia and Somaliland, had shown this to be an illusion by the start of 1942. Italian preparation for war had been inadequate.

Why did the tide turn in 1942–3?

There were a number of **turning points** in 1942:

- Japan was defeated at the naval Battle of Midway, which stopped further advances.
- The Germans were defeated at El Alamein in North Africa, which led to their withdrawal from Africa. This was the first major British victory of the war.
- In Russia, the Germans were held at the Battle of Stalingrad, which led to a major defeat in February 1943.

The Battle of Stalingrad

One of the most significant turning points of the war was the Battle of Stalingrad. By 1942, the war had turned out to be one of prolonged sieges and assaults on cities – characteristics that made it quite different from the First World War. The battlefields of 1914–18 were in the countryside, and only small towns or villages that happened to be in the way were destroyed; the major cities of Europe suffered little damage. However, in 1942, great sieges took place in Moscow and Leningrad between German and Russian forces, while the Allies used air power to batter German cities – a tactic applied as soon as possible by the Americans to Tokyo and other major Japanese urban centres. The civilian casualty rate increased, while millions were drawn into the Russian campaigns. To break this, the Germans adopted their greatest plan of the war – an attack on the Southern Front that would win them the key city of Stalingrad. This would open up the possibility of a link between German armies in Russia and their forces in North Africa, and consequently enable Germany to take Egypt and the Suez Canal, and control the oil of the Middle East and southern Russia. In the event, the British were able to hold Egypt and the Russians held Stalingrad.

The Russians absorbed casualties that ran into millions and were on a scale unlike anything seen in the First World War, but they were working from their home bases and could pour reinforcements and supplies into the besieged cities. The Germans were working at a considerable distance from their home base and did not have reserves of manpower. Their industries were suffering from Allied bombing and their resources had to be spread to maintain control of their new European empire, to fight in North Africa and to guard against a possible invasion of France. Fatally, they had to rely on allies – Romania and Italy – and the Russians found their weak points. German troops at Stalingrad, weakened by the ice and snow of the Russian winter and unable to receive enough supplies, were encircled by a Russian attack on their weakest point and forced to surrender in February 1943. This was the first time that a German army had failed in this way, and Friedrich Paulus became the first German field marshal to surrender (Hitler promoted him to this rank in order that he should die rather than surrender, but he failed to shoot himself). The German North African army, short of fuel and outnumbered, had already been defeated and forced back at **El Alamein** in October 1942.

Turning points: Historians make a distinction between changes and developments and the more significant turning points – something that decisively and irreversibly changes the course of history.

Fact: Stalingrad was a major industrial city in south-west Russia. If it had fallen, Germany would have been able to pour forces into the Caucasus region and gain vital oil supplies.

Fact: The Suez Canal was the major route from the Mediterranean to the British possessions in India and the Far East. It was considered vital that Germany should not capture the canal and be in a position to stop oil supplies reaching Britain or force all shipping to take the much longer route via South Africa.

Fact: The sheer scale of the war in Russia is hard to comprehend. Russian losses amounted to 8 million troops – the equivalent of the total losses in all countries between 1914 and 1918. More Russians died in the siege of Leningrad than the total of British forces in the whole of the First World War. Russia mobilised 30 million people in the war as a whole.

El Alamein: This was the first major British victory of the war. Under General Montgomery, the British defeated the German Afrika Korps under Rommel, which ended the threat to Egypt and subsequently pushed German forces out of North Africa. It enabled the Allies to invade Sicily and Italy in 1943, and showed that the German army could be defeated.

QUESTION

Why were these turning points more significant than so many of the battles of the First World War, and why did the Axis powers suffer so many reverses in fortune in 1942–3 without the war actually ending?

Against the advice of his generals, Hitler sought to retrieve the situation by a breakthrough in the central part of the Russian Front. In the biggest tank battle in history, the Russians showed that in a great war between two heavily industrialised nations, the one defending and closest to its resources is likely to win. The Battle of Kursk ended the German advance permanently, and initiated the long retreat (6600 tanks took part; the Red Army had 3600 and the Germans 3000). After this, tanks were no longer used for dynamic forward movement. The Russian tanks wore down the German tanks in a brutal war of attrition.

The Far East and North Africa

The Japanese, too, found that dynamic and sudden attack had its limits. They could not conquer New Guinea and were driven back in a bloody and drawn-out encounter with determined US forces in the Solomon Islands, supported by the US navy and air force. Now that the US was on a sustained war footing, the weight of its resistance was far greater than it had been in early 1942.

With the US in support, the British succeeded in forcing the Germans out of North Africa. By 1943, the Allies were ready to begin their counterattack in Italy.

The impossibility of compromise

Why did the war not end at this point? In terms of industrial capacity, the Axis powers could not match their enemies. Germany was no longer fighting an unwilling Britain and France and weak countries in Eastern Europe. It was under threat from Russia and the USA, whose resources were much greater. It had also lost the initiative – *Blitzkrieg* could not be applied to great invading forces. The German populace was under pressure from bombing and the only war aim that seemed likely to succeed was the annihilation of the Jews (the **Holocaust**), which was being undertaken with considerable energy in death camps.

Holocaust: The attempted genocide of European Jews during the Second World War by the Nazis. In all, almost 6 million European Jews were slaughtered, along with almost 5 million others – these included Roma, Sinti, Slavs, gay men and lesbians, and trade unionists, socialists and communists. Genocide is different from mere attacks on people of different races/ nationalities/views, and involves a deliberate attempt to eradicate a particular racial/religious/ethnic group. The first ethnic group to be a victim of genocide in 20th-century Europe was the Armenians, approximately 1.5 million of whom were slaughtered by the Turkish authorities during 1915–22.

Historical debate:
'It seems unreasonable to judge of the measures embraced during one period, by the maxims which prevail in another' – David Hume (1711–76)

While historians such as Daniel Goldhagen and Christopher Browning disagree over the moral responsibility of ordinary German civilians for the

Figure 4.15   Millions of Jews and other enemies of the Third Reich died in camps like Auschwitz, pictured here

Similarities can be seen here with the events of the First World War. With the masses of population mobilised, and with ideological war at the forefront, how could peace be brought about without complete victory or complete defeat? Hitler and his closest circle were essentially adventurers, not statesmen, and they actively sought death and destruction. They were not conventional leaders, and for men like **Joseph Goebbels** the experience of wholesale slaughter was exhilarating. Stalin's Russia was bolstered by ideology, but from the very start he had also believed in victory, expansion, the recovery of lands lost in 1918 and the domination of Eastern Europe. Costs in human life and suffering were not considered any more than they had been in Russia in the 1920s and 1930s. The Allied democracies were pledged to exact unconditional surrender and post-war reconstruction. The violence of the attacks by Japan and Germany had rendered any negotiated settlement unacceptable. Finally, the Japanese ethical code, which despised surrender and regarded death as a noble way of serving its empire, made surrender difficult. Against the whole logic of the situation in 1943, the war not only continued but expanded.

The long final phase

The Allied counterattacks from 1943 onwards were characterised by elements that had not figured prominently in the First World War.

Amphibious landings (seaborne invasions)

First were amphibious landings on an increasingly large scale. The only significant landings in the First World War had occurred at Gallipoli, when Britain attempted to defeat Turkey by landing troops to seize Constantinople. These were not successful in achieving breakthrough. Hitler had not risked landings in Britain in 1940, although airborne landings did defeat British forces in Crete in 1941. However, from 1943, the Allies embarked on a number of seaborne landings following the success of Operation Torch – the US landings in North Africa in 1942. Sicily was invaded and this was followed by a seaborne invasion of Italy and an attempt to speed the occupation of Italy by landings at Anzio, south of Rome. The biggest invasion force in seaborne warfare came on 6 June 1944, with the invasion of Normandy – D-Day.

The US invasion forces had to control the island defences that Japan had set up in the Pacific – **'island hopping'**, for example, by forces of US marines, strongly supported by naval bombardments and air attacks, became a normal method of warfare. In 1945, this culminated in the assaults on Iwo Jima and Okinawa, technically part of the Japanese homeland. There were plans for an amphibious assault on the real homeland, but these were never executed because the use of the atomic bombs ended the war. Amphibious landings depended on a high level of cooperation between the different parts of the Allied forces, considerable logistical organisation, planning and control of the seas and the airspace. They would not have been possible if Germany had developed a stronger navy, or if US naval resources had not overcome the Japanese. Superior Allied resources, ship and aircraft building – in turn dependent on a strong industrial and technical base – made this type of warfare possible.

Air power

The second element of the Allied counterattacks in the closing stages of the war was a much-increased use of air power. Germany and Japan had used air power in support

Holocaust, others – notably David Irving – have questioned the Holocaust as a concept. Holocaust denial is a crime in some countries. Should there be a limit on the conclusions that a historian draws from a study of the past, or should all historical opinions – however wrong they seem to be – be considered with equal respect? Or, given the exposure at the end of the 1990s of Irving's falsification – and even fabrication – of evidence in several of his books, and his links with far-right/neo-Nazi organisations, should he be precluded from the description of 'historian'?

Figure 4.16   Joseph Goebbels (1897–1945)

A fanatical and devoted follower of Hitler, Goebbels masterminded the propaganda that helped the Nazis win power. He became Reich minister of enlightenment – controlling propaganda and the media. He supported the idea of total war and the Holocaust. He and his wife killed their six children and then themselves in May 1945, when it was clear that Germany had lost the war.

Island hopping: This name was given to the series of seaborne attacks on Japanese-held Pacific islands by the USA. The name suggests an easy and playful process, but in fact resistance was strong and casualties were high on both sides.

KEY CONCEPTS ACTIVITY

Change and continuity: Using this chapter, and any other resources available to you, carry out some additional research on how civilians were affected in both world wars. Then draw up a table to show both similarities and differences between the two wars. Finally, write a couple of paragraphs to summarise your findings.

Fact: Water-borne landings of troops had been a feature of many past wars, but had faced considerable problems. The development of landing crafts and the use of air support made amphibious landings a key part of the Second World War and became a major element in the practice of war. This was because the German victories of 1940 enabled them to create a 'European fortress' to keep their US and British enemies out. Similarly the occupation of so much land in the Pacific by Japan entailed a large number of landings by US forces to recapture them. Any invasion of Japan would have to be amphibious. Amphibious landings played a limited role

of land forces, but lacked the resources for sustained engagement with the much larger Anglo–American force. German bombers had inflicted considerable damage on the civilian populations of its enemies. However, Allied bombing of Germany and Japan was on an altogether different scale.

Technically, both bombers and fighters developed rapidly during the war, and the advent of jet aircraft transformed air power. The use of radar made it possible to track air attacks and this played a significant part in the Battle of Britain in 1940. There was a race to improve air technology. Germany developed rockets, but these came too late to be decisive in the outcome of the war and their bases were captured. The most profound technical development – that of atomic weapons – was only possible in an advanced industrial country with the resources available to develop scientific ideas and make them a reality.

In an effort to bring total victory and end the high casualties of infantry warfare, the Allies had few qualms about targeting the cities in enemy countries, and military and civilian targets alike were chosen, often with minimal justification. This bombing certainly had its origins in 1914 and was increasing by 1918, but the scale on which it was executed was entirely new. By 1944 the Germans had developed pilotless rockets, which inflicted considerable damage on Britain. These V1 and V2 weapons anticipated later missile systems and were difficult to stop. The V1s were produced on a large scale – 10 000 were fired, each carrying higher levels of explosives than a conventional bomb. Only the Allied capture of launching sites prevented them having a considerable impact on Britain.

Modern warfare: weapons and techniques

The third feature of the war's closing phase again derived from the later stages of the First World War, when tanks, smaller and more self-contained infantry units and air cover were used. However, the huge use of tanks – for example in the battles of Kursk, Orel and Kharkov in Russia in 1943, and on the Western Front after the invasion of Normandy – was unprecedented.

Figure 4.17   Japanese troops in 1942

The nature of war, in which relatively small infantry units worked in units controlled by efficient radio communications by commanders aware of the overall plan, was also more characteristic of modern warfare than the mass assaults that dominated most of the First World War. Also, this approach was not totally reliant on new technology. The British campaigns against Japan in Burma were particularly characterised by high levels of devolved responsibility. The most spectacular of these were the behind-the-lines guerrilla activities of the so-called Chindits, led by Orde Wingate. But the main advance through Burma in 1944–5, led by General Slim, relied on British mastery of jungle warfare and the ability to work in small units – expertise that had advanced considerably since events in Malaya in 1941.

Determined attacks

The Italian fascist regime under Benito Mussolini fell easily in 1943, but Japan and Germany kept up a remarkably intense resistance, even when it was clear that victory could no longer be achieved. The battle for Berlin between Soviet invaders and German defenders in 1945, for example, was as heavy and determined as any engagement of the war. British forces met relentless resistance to the invasion of western Germany, and casualties in the campaigns that followed D-Day often had a rate as high as the bloodbaths of Passchendaele and the Somme in the First World War. The difference was that the front was mobile and, despite the casualties, progress was being made. Even disastrous setbacks did not stop the inexorable and optimistic progress of the British and Americans. One example of this was the misguided attempt to drop forces by parachute, which would then be joined by a rapid motorised advance to take the Rhine Bridge at Arnhem in the Netherlands. Poor planning and unexpected German resistance defeated Operation Market Garden, as it was known. Another major Allied setback was a German attack in the Ardennes in the winter of 1944, which caught inexperienced US defenders unawares. This showed how formidable the Germans still were, but it could not alter the outcome of the war.

Japanese resistance was equally strong, even when defeat loomed, as evidenced by the struggle for Iwo Jima in 1945. Here, Japanese forces tunnelled into a barren island, allowed the US to land and then fought suicidally, inflicting massive casualties. The use of *kamikaze* (suicide) planes by Japan at the Battle of Okinawa, and the mass suicide of civilians on captured islands, also demonstrated the extent of Japanese resistance. Ironically, this heroism may have made the US all the more willing to use the atomic bombs to prevent equally terrible fighting if Japan itself were invaded.

There were some similarities with the First World War. The slow progress made by Allied forces in the battle for Italy echoed the grim infantry struggles of the First World War. When Mussolini fell, German forces took over the defence of Italy and prepared formidable defensive lines. Despite modern air assaults, there were deadlocked periods of trench warfare, such as the German defence of Monte Cassino. However, the war did not solidify around lines of trenches. Tactics, firepower, the coordination of air, land and sea resources, and the relentless production of war supplies kept up the impetus of Allied attacks, bolstered by the power of the modern state and effective mass propaganda methods – far in advance of anything witnessed in the First World War.

The war at sea and in the air

During the First World War, an effective naval blockade had been imposed on Germany by Britain. In the Second World War, the tables were turned. The vast

in the First World war and the main example, the Allied landings at Gallipoli in 1915, ended in failure. Amphibious operations were costly and not always successful, but resulted in a major change in the war in 1944 with the establishment of another front in Northern France.

Fact: The invasion of Normandy by British and US forces on 6 June 1944, called D-Day, opened up the long-awaited second front in Europe. Operation Overlord saw 175 000 British and American troops land on five beaches (Omaha, Utah, Gold, Sword and Juno), supported by 5,000 ships and Allied air superiority. This was the greatest amphibious operation of the war, and enabled Allied forces to pour into northern France and begin the long struggle to invade Germany.

Fact: A major development in the practice of war was the use of airpower. This had been a feature of the First World War, but the technical developments of aircraft made it far more significant in the Second World War. Firstly, it changed traditional sea warfare. Air attacks could destroy the largest ships without air protection. The decisive battle in the Pacific, Midway in 1942 was decided by aircraft taking off from powerful aircraft carriers. Second, it transformed the home front. Large-scale civilian bombing made cities and towns front line areas of war. In the end, the use of the atomic bomb decided the outcome of the war against Japan, or at least the timing of the Japanese decision to surrender. Third, air support became a key element in land conflict.

4

Fact: Airpower's importance in land conflict can be seen in the key part played by German dive bombers in the *Blitzkrieg* campaigns and later by the close support given by aircraft to ground attacks. The losses of aircraft by both Germany and Japan were key elements in their military failure, although not decisive in themselves. The relative importance of land, air and naval warfare in bringing about the final outcome of the war helps us to understand the nature and outcome of the war.

Fact: German cities with populations of more than 500 000 and the percentage destroyed:

City	% destroyed
Berlin	33
Cologne	61
Dortmund	54
Dresden	59
Düsseldorf	64
Essen	50
Frankfurt	52
Hamburg	75
Leipzig	20
Munich	42

QUESTION

What are the value and limitations of this image for understanding the impact of the atomic bomb on the civilian population of Hiroshima?

swathes of territory that Germany had gained meant that it had plenty of food and supplies. However, Britain was dependent on supplies from its empire and North America, and these were vulnerable to attacks by U-boats. This had been the case in the First World War, but now the submarine menace was even greater given the additional numbers and technical development of the German U-boat fleet. Germany's surface vessels could not rival the great British fleet, but in the Battle of the Atlantic, Germany very nearly cut Britain off from the means to wage war and feed its people. The dangers faced by the British Royal and Merchant Navies in crossing the Atlantic, as well as in sending supplies to Russia, were considerable. However, the use of convoys and the development of effective depth charges and radar detection meant that the German submarine threat had been countered by 1943. Vital to this was the interception of German signals by the British **Ultra** code-breaking machines, which used prototype computing techniques.

The war highlighted the importance of submarine warfare as well as air power. Without air cover, great ships were vulnerable to attack, as the sinking of the *Prince of Wales* and the *Repulse* showed in 1941. The war in the Pacific was fought by aircraft taking off from aircraft carriers – something new in this war. The invasions that the Allies made – of Sicily and Italy, of France in 1944, of the Japanese-held Pacific islands – were made using ships and landing craft, but also with careful coordination of air support.

The end of the war

Germany

By the time of Hitler's suicide and the subsequent surrender of Germany on 8 May 1945, there could be no doubt of the result. There was no repeat of the situation in 1918, when German commanders made a decision that the war could not be won, even though there were substantial numbers of forces intact and no occupation of German territory had taken place. Germany's major cities had been destroyed. British, US and Soviet occupying forces met on the River Elbe. The Russians occupied Berlin and placed the Soviet flag on the Reichstag (the German parliament building). Germany's civilian population faced starvation, as well as retaliation and abuse by Soviet troops. The discovery of the death camps disgraced Germany in the eyes of the civilised world. German minorities suffered persecution and expulsion in Eastern Europe. There could be no doubt about the scale of defeat.

Japan

By the time Japan surrendered on 2 September 1945, its cities too were in ruins, as shown by the statistics in the table opposite. Its armies had been pushed back in all theatres of war (although not completely defeated). However, when Russia finally declared war and occupied Korea, Manchuria and Sakhalin, defeat was inevitable. The bulk of Japan's air force and navy had been destroyed in disastrous engagements in 1944 and 1945, and two hitherto untouched cities – Hiroshima and Nagasaki – had been destroyed by just two bombs in August 1945. The emperor bowed to the inevitable, and made his first broadcast to the nation, informing them that the war had not necessarily gone in a way that was to Japan's advantage. This massive understatement ended the Second World War on 15 August 1945.

Figure 4.18   Hiroshima after the atomic bomb, August 1945

What best explains the defeat of the Axis powers?

Japan and Germany had formidable war machines and their states exerted a powerful hold over the people. Their ideologies were strong and their leaders determined. However, in the long term, they lacked the industrial resources to sustain a lengthy war, and they were vulnerable to attack on two fronts. As in 1914, the failure to win decisive victory in the opening campaigns proved fatal. British resistance provided a key link between the different elements of the war and so Britain played a part out of all proportion to its military contribution or losses. However, at the heart of any explanation for the defeat of the Axis nations must be the resources of the two post-war superpowers. The ability of the USA and the USSR to produce war materials on a scale hitherto unknown in world history, combined with their extensive manpower resources, made the defeat of the Axis powers inevitable.

This is not to discount the role of individual commanders of genius, however – among them **Erwin Rommel**, **Georgy Zhukov** and **Bernard Montgomery**. Nor should the role of military leaders of great organisational ability such as **Dwight D. Eisenhower** and statesmen of heroic determination, such as Churchill and Roosevelt, be forgotten. Indeed, the democratic nature of British and US war-making, with planning and decisions taken by military committees rather than an unstable dictator like Hitler (whose personal military decisions in Russia were disastrous), may have been a significant factor.

Ultra: This was the biggest secret of the war. British code-breakers at Bletchley Park in Britain had used a captured German coding device, the Enigma machine, to break a complex German code, allowing Allied commanders to read German military and naval signals. The chief code-breaker, Alan Turing, virtually developed a computer and made a major contribution to Allied victory. After the war (when same-sex relations were still illegal), Turing was harassed and prosecuted by the authorities for being gay – leading to his apparent suicide in 1954. In 2009, the British government apologised for the way he had been treated and he was pardoned in 2013.

Fact: The Second World War saw armies equipped with more transport and with faster-moving, more powerful tanks than during the First World War. The Battle of Kursk was an outstanding example of the key role of the tank. However, it remains a matter of debate whether new technology alone was decisive or whether the human factors of decision-making, generalship and endurance were the most important. The Japanese advance in 1941–2 owed little to technology and everything to planning and determination. The considerable advantage that the Allies had in terms of equipment did not prevent military disasters and a slow and costly campaign to defeat Germany in 1944–5.

Fact: Operation Market Garden took place on 17 September 1944. The plan was to drop air brigades by parachute to take the Arnhem bridge, and then bring up armoured vehicles and open up a crossing into Germany to end the war more quickly. The parachutists were dispersed. However, there were unexpected German troops in the area and the tanks had to advance along a single-track road vulnerable to enemy attacks and delays. The operation was a serious failure for the Allies.

Fact: Events at Monte Cassino consisted of four major attacks by Allied troops against the German Gustav Line, from 17 January to 18 May 1944. They destroyed one of Europe's most important religious sites, and showed that even with air power and numerical superiority, it was still difficult to take well-defended positions.

Fact: Conventional bombing damage to Japanese cities in the Second World War:

City	% destroyed
City	58
Yokohama	51
Tokyo	99
Toyama	40
Nagoya	35.1
Osaka	50
Nishinomiya	11.9

4.6 What was the significance of the mobilisation of human and economic resources and the home front?

Total war on such a scale needed a high level of commitment from the population and increasing amounts of government control. Even more than in the First World War, the distinction between the home front and the fighting front became blurred. All resources had to be mobilised by the state and the commitment of the populations had to be maintained.

The growth of government power

Even before 1939, the dictators of Italy, Russia and Germany, and the military leaders of Japan, had established considerable control by the use of secret police and restrictions on criticism. The war increased this still further. Any hint of criticism was punished severely and the role of the German Gestapo and the Japanese Kempetai (secret police) was extended to occupied territory. Britain and the USA became more repressive. Censorship was imposed. Potential enemies were imprisoned without trial (German refugees in Britain ended up in camps and Japanese Americans were regarded as enemy aliens, regardless of how long they had been in the USA). Countries used every resource at their disposal – taxes were high, rationing was imposed, conscription both for armed service and for war work was universal. In Britain and the USA, however, normal political life continued – Churchill was criticised in the House of Commons and Roosevelt stood for re-election in 1944.

Economic resources and controls

The experience of the First World War led most combatant nations to introduce controls of resources early on in the war. Arms production and military supplies had to take priority over other production. The numbers in the armed forces and in support organisations had to be increased. Rationing had to be introduced as there was a danger to imports from naval action by the enemy. Scarce gold reserves had to be used for war supplies and not for other imports. Transport was subject to control for movements of troops and armaments. In Britain, drastic action was taken to protect the young from expected bombing by evacuation from cities and industrial areas.

Some countries, like the USSR, already had a very firm control by government over economic resources so this made it easier for them to adapt to wartime requirements and Russia was able to maintain production by wholesale movement of industrial production and make good the heavy losses to the industrial areas of western Russia in 1941–2. This constant flood of equipment from a centrally directed economy was one of the unexpected factors that helped win the war. The Germans had seen Russia as backward and inefficient, its efficiency eroded by communism. However, Stalin utilised not only Russia's considerable human resources but its industrial capacity. Russia endured vast population losses yet still produced large armies.

The entry into war of the USA in December 1941 gave the Allies considerable superiority in terms of the supply of war materials. The US had already been able to supply Britain and Roosevelt had seen it as 'the arsenal of democracy'. After 1941, the spare capacity of the US economy, weakened by years of recession, was taken up once again. Despite fighting both Germany and Japan, the US was able to produce huge amounts of military equipment. This was beyond both the Japanese and the German economies, both of which, unlike the USA, were hit by bombing raids. US shipping and aircraft were replaced far more quickly and although the technology of the Allies was not as strong in many ways as that of Germany, the sheer volume of material produced proved a major element in the eventual outcome of the war.

That is not to say that German economic power was insignificant. Germany had benefited from its conquest earlier in the war. It had not had to rely so much on rationing and had taken considerable amounts of raw materials and equipment from the lands it had conquered. There was also a ready supply of labour, some of it reasonably free, some of it inefficiently used slave labour. Not until 1943 did Germany declare the total war that Britain and Russia had been fighting. Despite losses of factories in increasingly severe bombing, Germany produced the highly effective Tiger tank, feared by the Allies and greatly superior to the mass-produced Sherman tanks of the USA. The Germans were also able to produce the VI flying bomb and the V2 rocket. However, Japan was not able to recover from the very extensive bombing of its industrial areas and the Allies were able to cut its supplies from the conquered lands that had boosted its economic war-making ability in 1942.

In a modern war, economic capacity was extremely important, but its impact on the outcome of the war can be exaggerated. The outcome was determined a lot by the failure of the Japanese and the Germans on one side and the Allies on the other to accept anything less than the 'unconditional surrender' of the other side. Thus the war continued even when victory was clearly impossible. This was not related to economic factors but the extreme nature of the struggle, the ideologies involved and the determination for total victory by both governments and people.

Activity

Find material to support the view that 'Economic factors had a major impact on the outcome of the Second World War'. Do you think that they were the most important reason for the outcome?

Propaganda and the home front

The need to rally opinion was greater in the Second World War than the First, because of the strong ideological element. The development of media between the wars – radio, the greater attendance at cinema, the rise of the 'talkies' (film with sound), even primitive television – also made it necessary for propaganda to be more sophisticated than during the First World War. No longer was propaganda characterised by crude posters and staged films of heroic battles. Germany and the Allies both shared much information with their populations. Goebbels' declaration of total war and the solemn admission of failure at Stalingrad united Germany more than any crude propaganda. Hitler and his people faced defeat heroically. In Britain, no attempt was made to minimise the sacrifices expected and emphasis was placed on pulling together, with the promise of a better post-war world. US propaganda used Hollywood's greatest skills, and offered a vision of a United Nations and future peace. Soviet propaganda made use of traditional patriotism and Russian values, as well as the power of the state

QUESTION

Was victory dependent on technology?

How did overall strategy affect the outcome?

Figure 4.19 Erwin Rommel (1891–1944)

Known as the 'Desert Fox', he was the leader of the German Afrika Korps, which inflicted major defeats on British forces in North Africa, 1941–2. Only lack of resources and the dogged tactics of Montgomery led to his defeat at El Alamein. He was forced to commit suicide due to his involvement in a plot to overthrow Hitler in 1944.

Figure 4.20 Georgy Zhukov (1896–1974)

He was Russia's leading general. He masterminded the defences of Moscow and Stalingrad, and was behind the successful attacks on Berlin in 1945. Stalin was jealous of his popularity and his influence later declined.

Figure 4.21 Bernard Montgomery (1887–1976)

He was Britain's most colourful war leader. The son of a bishop, he was an excellent communicator, and led the successful attack at El Alamein that drove the Germans out of North Africa. He also helped plan the D-Day invasion of France in 1944.

in preventing defeatism and desertion, and deporting potential enemies. Stalin was portrayed as more of a national than a communist hero, and images of the Motherland were used cleverly to portray safer rural districts.

As civilian bombing increased, women and children were victims. Family life was severely affected by the destruction of homes and the evacuation of children from areas likely to be bombed. In Britain this led to millions of children encountering different lifestyles as well as experiencing considerable hardship, both emotional and physical. In badly affected European war zones, some children became feral and out of control. The emotional impact on children of loss on such a scale is incalculable. By the end of the war, boys as young as 12, often recruited from the Hitler Youth, were fighting for Germany on the front lines. Children were also victims of genocide.

Mass destruction

The First World War had witnessed civilian casualties in bombings and in attacks on civilians that arose out of war. However, the Second World War triggered or allowed genocidal fantasies to be made reality and removed restraints on racial hatred. The Japanese atrocities in the war against China did not spare civilians, and occupied territory saw very severe treatment of people considered by the Japanese as inferior. Rape and the murder of women and children were common, especially during the period of the Japanese retreat.

The Nazi regime made a determined attempt to eradicate the entire Jewish population of Europe. Other racial victims included the Roma and Sinti (gypsies) and large numbers of Slavs. Persecution of racial groups considered inferior had been ongoing since 1933, but the war ended any hopes of removing despised races and by 1941 the Nazi leadership had decided on a 'Final Solution' of annihilation. The details were established at a meeting of leading German party members at the Wannsee Conference in early 1942 and endorsed by government officials in Berlin. It has been argued that only the extreme conditions of war made such ambitious mass murder possible.

Reprisals against resistance in Nazi-occupied Europe commonly involved actions against men, women and children. When Russian forces entered Germany, there were tens of thousands of rapes and an onslaught against defenceless civilians. The German and Japanese civilians who died in Allied bombing raids included many thousands of children. In total war, every civilian was seen as a potential asset that should be destroyed to prevent the enemy waging war.

Theory of Knowledge

The historian and moral judgement:
'There is one way in which the historian may reinforce the initial moral judgment and thereby assist the cause of morality in general; and that way lies directly within his province, for it entails merely describing, say, the massacre or the persecution, laying it out in concrete detail, and giving the specification of what it means in actuality' – Herbert Butterfield (1900–79)

Is the question 'Were the Allies right to use atomic weapons against Japan in 1945?' a historical question or a moral question? Should historians seek to explain why rather than to assess whether the action was justified, or is this to escape a key function of looking at the past?

End of unit activities

1 What features most made the Second World War so different from the First World War? Copy and complete the table below (one example has been done for you).

Feature	Explanation
The greater use of air power in coordination with armies.	This made it difficult for defenders to maintain trench warfare. It also helped sudden attacks like *Blitzkrieg*. It disrupted communications and helped amphibious attacks – so D-Day succeeded while the 1915 Gallipoli attacks failed.

2 Prepare a presentation on the Battle of Iwo Jima, showing the experience of both the Japanese and American troops and discussing why there was such determined resistance.

What was the importance of the battle?

Do you think that the US experience on Iwo Jima was a factor in the decision to use atomic weapons? (The 2006 film *Letters from Iwo Jima* directed by Clint Eastwood is a good source to watch and discuss.)

3 Why do you think that trench warfare was so important in the First World War, yet the Second World War was much more mobile?

4 Do some more reading on bombing in the Second World War. Do you think that countries relied on it too much? Draw up a chart showing why bombing could be seen as important and why it could be seen as ineffective.

Figure 4.22 Dwight D. Eisenhower (1890–1969)

From June 1942, 'Ike' was commander of the European theatre, and led the US invasion of North Africa and the Allied landings in Sicily and Italy. He was the overall commander of Operation Overlord and the subsequent campaign that led to Allied victory. Calm, diplomatic and realistic, Eisenhower coped well with the more fiery and temperamental Allied generals under his command.

KEY CONCEPTS QUESTION

Significance: To what extent do you agree with the view that both world wars were won by the side with the most effective leaders? What other factors could have been the most important?

KEY QUESTIONS

- What political and territorial changes resulted from the Second World War?
- What economic and social changes arose from the Second World War?
- What were the successes and failures of peacemaking?

Overview

- The human costs of the war were much higher than in the First World War. Table 4.4 gives some idea of the scale of the tragedy. The statistics, however, do not reveal the traumas of war: the effects of wounds, shock, loss, psychological damage and the impact of homelessness, the vast numbers of refugees, the missing and bereaved. Living with fear and anxiety, whether for oneself or one's family and friends, made an indelible impact on a generation and beyond. Adjusting to peace and normal post-war life was often an intolerable strain, and the true and lasting impact of this extraordinary period of violence is impossible to express in numbers.

- There was not the creation of new states that followed the First World War, but a considerable amount of population movement took place in Europe, as millions of ethnic Germans were driven out of Eastern Europe. Frontiers were altered, as in the case of Poland and Germany, which was divided between the East and the West. As much of Eastern Europe was absorbed into a new Soviet empire, the change was in fact greater than territorial boundaries show.

- In economic terms, the disasters of the inter-war period were avoided and progress was made on both sides of the new 'Iron Curtain' – but not in equal measure. The West experienced an unprecedented degree of prosperity that profoundly changed its societies.

- The social consequences of the war were linked to the economic ones. It proved difficult for many groups to return to the 'normal' pre-war world. The war had generated demands for change that saw different opportunities emerge for women and for racial minorities.

- In terms of international relations, the war resulted in a different type of conflict – the Cold War – and brought about a new and potentially devastating threat – that of nuclear conflict. The shadow of the arms race settled over the world.

- In broader terms, the Western European-centred world gave way to one in which the superpowers held sway and European empires collapsed. International bodies became much more important than they had been in the inter-war period, and political nationalism and racism were discredited.

Table 4.4 The number of deaths by country in the Second World War

Country	Military	Civilian	Total
Soviet Union	8 668 000	16 900 000	25 568 000
China	1 324 000	10 000 000	11 324 000
Germany	3 250 000	3 810 000	7 060 000
Poland	850 000	6 000 000	6 850 000
Japan	1 506 000	300 000	1 806 000
Yugoslavia	300 000	1 400 000	1 700 000
Romania	520 000	465 000	985 000
France	340 000	470 000	810 000
Austria	380 000	145 000	525 000
Italy	330 000	80 000	410 000
Great Britain	326 000	62 000	388 000
USA	295 000		295 000

Total, circa 61 million.

4.7 What political and territorial changes resulted from the Second World War?

Peace conferences and settlements

During the First World War there were few political conferences, and a major peace conference and settlement was agreed after the war. Although the Axis powers did not hold major conferences during the Second World War, the Allies did, and had largely shaped post-war Europe before the conflict ended. The major conferences took place at Yalta and Potsdam in 1945. Germany was divided for more than 40 years and the territorial changes in the East have remained. The Allies created four 'zones of occupation' for France, Britain, the USA and the USSR, with Berlin – in the Soviet Zone – further divided. This unwieldy arrangement was worse than the pre-war **Polish Corridor**, but lasted longer.

As relations between the victorious powers worsened, so the divisions became more distinct. By 1949, West Germany (the German Federal Republic) had emerged as a separate country from the French, British and American zones, and incorporated West

Polish Corridor: The land dividing East Prussia from the rest of Germany was given to Poland in 1919. This was a major grievance. It did not stop a similar situation being created in 1945, with West Berlin being cut off from the western part of Germany by territory dominated by the USSR.

Fact: At the Yalta Conference of 4–11 February 1945, the 'Big Three' – Joseph Stalin, Winston Churchill and Franklin Roosevelt – agreed to a United Nations organisation and to confirm the Atlantic Charter. They also agreed to free elections of governments responsive to the will of the people in liberated countries. The division of Germany was also decided upon; Polish boundaries were established, with lands going to Russia in the East in exchange for lands in the West taken from Germany. The Soviet Union would join the Allies in the war in the Pacific, in return for South Sakhalin and the Kuril Islands.

Fact: At the Potsdam Conference of 17 July to 2 August 1945, and with new leaders present – Clement Attlee for Britain and Harry S. Truman for the US – there was less warmth and more tension. However, Yalta's decisions were confirmed. The conference also established the Council of Foreign Ministers to undertake the necessary preparatory work for the peace settlements. Discussions on the disarmament of Germany agreed that Germany be occupied by a 'Control Council'; Germany was to be de-Nazified. The arrangements about Poland were issued as a declaration.

Berlin, even though it was located deep inside what became East Germany (the German People's Republic). Thus, the defeat of 1945 had a more drastic and long-lasting effect on Germany than that of 1918 in terms of territorial divisions. Austria, too, was divided, but Russia withdrew in 1955 and it regained its independence. Little attempt was made to repeat the nation-building that had characterised the Treaty of Versailles. Where the Russian armies had occupied Eastern Europe, the countries became so-called 'people's democracies', which meant domination by the USSR and one-party communist states. Latvia, Lithuania and Estonia remained Russian republics. Russia gained part of East Prussia. Polish boundaries were pushed westwards, but Poland, like Romania, Bulgaria, Hungary and – from 1948 – Czechoslovakia, became part of a virtual Soviet empire. Albania and Yugoslavia, although communist, did not fall directly under Russian control. Finland and Greece escaped.

Japan lost its pre-war and wartime territorial gains and was occupied by US troops. The emperor was permitted to remain as head of state, but was declared to be human not divine. Korea gained its independence, although it was divided between a communist North and a non-communist South. Manchuria reverted to China after a Russian invasion had stripped it of resources. The USSR took reparations from its conquered enemies; the West did not, and indeed for humanitarian as well as political reasons injected money and supplies into Germany and Japan. In addition, the end of the war in China meant that both the communists and nationalists, united to defeat Japan, could resume the Chinese Civil War that had been raging since 1927 (see Chapter 5). There was no protracted formal post-war peace conference, as the Second World War quickly developed into the Cold War.

Activity

Carry out some research on the 'Percentages Agreement' of 1944. Then list possible reasons why the Soviet Union felt the need for a 'security belt' in Eastern Europe.

4.8 What economic and social changes arose from the Second World War?

Economic change

The financial burden of the war was unprecedented. The US spent an estimated $341 billion, including $50 billion for lend-lease supplies, of which $31 billion went to Britain, $11 billion to the Soviet Union, $5 billion to China and $3 billion to 35 other countries. Germany was next, with $272 billion; followed by the Soviet Union, $192 billion; and then Britain, $120 billion; Italy, $94 billion; and Japan, $56 billion. The Soviet government calculated that the USSR lost 30 per cent of its national wealth, while Nazi thefts and looting were of incalculable amounts in the occupied countries. The full cost to Japan has been estimated at $562 billion.

The short-term damage to Europe and the war zones of Asia was considerably greater than that caused by the war of 1914–18. A much more mobile conflict, together with improvements in air power, meant more widespread destruction. No major city was destroyed in the First World War, but nearly all the major cities of the combatants in the Second World War suffered damage and some, like Warsaw in Poland, were almost totally destroyed.

However, the long-term effects of the wars were very different. The dislocations of world trade and payments caused by the First World War, allied to the long-term decline of heavy industry and the fall in agricultural prices, led to a profound depression in the late 1920s. After 1945, there was a period of intense suffering in Europe, but the USA's willingness to remain engaged with Europe was of vital importance. After 1919, the USA took no responsibility for world peace or prosperity; after 1945 the country was a global superpower and became a major player in helping Western Europe recover economically, and it also took a key role in establishing and supporting the United Nations.

In 1948, Western European economies began to revive. From 1950 onwards, the rate of economic growth increased. The sustained upsurge in the US economy, stimulated by war production, continued into a period of unprecedented growth. US industry was able to exploit a flourishing foreign and domestic market, and make use of cheap power and technological progress. The USA was able to supply key aid to Europe, which in turn sustained US growth.

Economic progress also grew out of wartime experience of government intervention in Europe. Seeing what had been achieved by planned wartime production led to a belief in government intervention to prevent unemployment and depression. Increased spending on social policy stimulated home markets. In France, Jean Monnet, the commissioner of the Plan for the Reconstruction of Key Industries, drew up a comprehensive scheme of modernisation in 1946. West Germany and Italy continued modernisation policies, beginning with greater government controls than in the pre-war era.

Growth in world trade also helped economic recovery. After the war, many European countries had realised the disastrous effects of **tariffs** on inter-European trade. Tariffs and closed economic systems were associated with fascist or extreme nationalist policies, and the US pressed for freer trade – which is associated with the interests of capitalist corporations. Western Europe began to cooperate economically and tried to lower its tariffs. Both the Organisation for European Economic Co-operation (OEEC) and the European Economic Community (EEC) worked hard to reduce tariffs between European states.

The rebuilding necessary after the war, and the demand for primary products, ensured that countries in Asia and Africa did not face the disastrous price drops they had after the First World War. This in turn provided markets for European products. The war had stimulated progress in chemicals and electrical industries. Social changes, too, such as more working women, encouraged the development of new domestic appliances. A developing consumer industry, with its origins in pre-war change, helped to sustain prosperity in the late 1940s and 1950s.

However, probably the greatest economic impact came as a direct result of North America's wartime prosperity. The US distributed large amounts of aid from 1943 onwards, first through the United Nations Relief and Rehabilitation Administration, which distributed 22 million tonnes of supplies to Italy and Eastern Europe by 1948. The International Bank for Reconstruction and Development (later the World Bank)

QUESTION

QUESTION

Why might the US have been more prepared to get involved with Europe in 1945 than it had been in 1918?

Tariffs: Customs duties imposed on imported goods.

KEY CONCEPTS QUESTION

Perspectives: Attempting to evaluate the reasons for and impact of different economic policies is often difficult. Is it possible for historians and economists, with their different political perspectives and beliefs, to make impartial assessments of such issues?

The International Monetary Fund (IMF) was set up in July 1944 with 45 members. It now has more than 180. To stabilise exchange rates, countries contributed to a fund, out of which money could be lent to countries in order to protect their currencies in times of difficulty. It is one of the most important financial legacies of the war. Its headquarters were then – and still are – in Washington, DC, and the US is the dominant member. Today, the IMF (and the World Bank, set up at the same time) tends to insist that countries follow economic policies that are conducive to the construction of a neo-liberal global capitalism. Their structural adjustment programmes usually insist that recipient countries reduce social spending and privatise any publically or socially owned assets (such as railways and other public utilities).

The Marshall Plan was an aid programme proposed by the US secretary of state George Marshall in 1947 and launched in 1948. Half went to Britain, France and West Germany, and it was administered by the Organisation for European Economic Co-operation (16 nations). It was offered to communist Europe but US insistence that public assets should be privatised and capitalist economic policies introduced meant it was blocked by Stalin.

and the **International Monetary Fund** set up in 1944 provided short-term loans for reconstruction and development. Most significant of all was the $12 billion provided to Western Europe through the **Marshall Plan**.

By 1950, the productivity of Western Europe exceeded the pre-1939 average by 25 per cent. In 1952, productivity was twice that of 1938. Intra-European trade revived. By 1952, Europe had not only recovered from its economic distress but was on the point of having the greatest boom in its history. Between 1950 and 1960, the annual rate of growth in the output of goods produced in the West jumped to 3.9 per cent, whereas the rate of growth was about 2.7 per cent between 1870 and 1913. This economic prosperity cushioned the transition of post-war Europe from dictatorship to democracy, and consolidated the Western European unity that had emerged from the war.

Social change

Women

The need for war production and to mobilise the entire population meant that women became an essential part of the war effort. This war involved more women in sustaining the fighting than had been the case in the First World War, but the involvement of women in the war effort was no longer an innovation. Some 22 million women were participating in the production of war materials by 1945. The Nazis had to compromise their ideals of pure womanhood, removed from the world of politics and struggle, and came to depend on women in factories and essential services. Women were also used in the process of industrial death in the concentration camps.

In Britain and the USA, the experience of the First World War was developed, and women worked in factories, on farms, in transport, as well as being recruited into the armed services. Many women learnt to drive and pilot aircraft. With the increasingly 'total' nature of war, they became targets for bombing as much as men. More women served in the armed forces than during the First World War. In Britain, women were conscripted into key areas. In the USA, around 320 000 women served in uniform, although only 16 were killed in action. Some 2000 Polish women fighters were prisoners of war, and more were killed. In areas where there was guerrilla warfare or partisan fighting, it was common for women to play a combatant role and to suffer the consequences of defeat, death or capture. Women were an important element of the Soviet army, as well as being part of the industrial machine. Women were used in guerrilla warfare and in undercover operations in enemy territory. They were also of considerable importance in the Chinese communist armies and in the post-war liberation movements in Asia. Mao Zedong famously declared that 'Women hold up half the sky'. There was little that men did in the war that women did not also do, but on a more limited scale.

Huge advances were made in supporting working women with families – including cheap restaurants and childcare – but these measures did not survive into post-war Britain. In Russia, women were used in mass labour and in the fighting services.

To wage total war, prejudices had to be abandoned, but despite some measurable gains for women – such as gaining the right to vote in France in 1944 – much ground won in the war was lost in the return to peace. However, whether it was the direct experience of war, the expansion of female education, greater labour-saving devices in the home or the wider availability of contraception, there was a distinct change in the role of women between 1939 and 2000, even if a lot of attitudes remain rooted in the past.

There was a tension between the greater independence that the war offered to many women and the desire after 1945 to return to 'normal'. The war had seen more women in the workplace than ever before. Domestic service had declined and the range of jobs undertaken by women increased. Women travelled more – both for work and as part of the war effort. They were financially more independent, more confident in displaying a range of skills, and freer from the demands of home. The growth of the post-war feminist movement and campaigns for equal pay and rights were influenced by wartime experience. However, for some, the war merely added to the burden of looking after their family. The support given in terms of childcare and cheap meals did not often survive the war. The 'baby boom' of the 1950s caused more pressure to look after children, and returning soldiers often took back jobs done by women.

In countries shattered by war and coping with the impact of the vast loss of life, women were burdened with problems of sheer survival rather than being 'liberated' by new challenges. There is a moving memorial in Berlin to the 'rubble women', who cleared millions of tonnes of debris. The greater independence of American women was not shared by many African-Americans, who continued in low-paid or domestic employment. In the West, the post-war prosperity apparent in the 1950s tended to glorify family life at the expense of female independence, and it was not until the 1960s that a **women's movement** emerged in reaction to this, and rediscovered the achievements of wartime women.

In totalitarian states, there was more official equality of reward and status. This was partly ideological – with the belief that oppression of women was equivalent to the oppression of social classes – and partly practical. So many men had died that women were needed to fulfil large-scale economic plans. At the local level, however, there was often more of a gap between the declared goals of sexual equality and centuries of ingrained male domination. The end of Nazi and fascist rule, which brought women into political and community life, may have been a regressive step, as liberal consumer capitalism rested to some extent on women playing the more dependent role as wives, mothers and consumers.

War – the challenge to tradition

Related to changes in the role of women were erosions of traditional attitudes and practices linked to the disruption of war. Class changes were obvious in areas where communism took power and broke the stranglehold of traditional élites. Social change was considerable in non-communist countries, too. In both Britain and Germany there was a rise of a meritocratic middle class and a decline of the aristocracy. Sustained wartime effort needed an efficient and technologically aware leadership. In Germany, the conservative upper class suffered from its attempt to remove Hitler in the **Bomb Plot of 1944**, and from Hitler's impatience with the traditional Prussian military and administrative élite. Defeat in Japan ousted the military aristocracy and imperial cliques. The monarchy was swept away in Italy after the fall of Mussolini. The post-war world was considerably less deferential, and dependence on new technology meant that more highly trained people from all backgrounds were needed.

Family life

Family life had been considerably disrupted by urban bombings, mass conscription and the absence of heads of families for long periods. Traditional morality was undermined by the presence of foreign workers or forces, and the absence of husbands and fathers.

Historical debate: Historians are divided about US motives concerning Marshall Aid. While some argue that it stemmed from a genuine desire to help Europe recover from the devastation of war, others tend to stress how it was mainly intended to aid US companies through a rapid revival of trade – and even to allow the US to dominate Western Europe. It has also been seen as part of US Cold War strategy to 'contain' communism, and to weaken the Soviet Union and its growing influence in Eastern Europe.

Women's movement: Betty Friedan's 1963 book *The Feminine Mystique* is often seen as the trigger for a feminist movement in the USA, and subsequently in Britain and Western Europe, for greater awareness of the need for social, economic, political and sexual equality. It has been compared with parallel movements for civil rights.

Bomb Plot of 1944: In July 1944, some high-ranking German military and civil service conspirators tried to kill Hitler in the Bomb Plot. They hoped to end the war before Germany was destroyed. Many were Junkers (aristocrats). The plot failed, although Hitler was injured by the bomb, which was left under a conference table by Count von Stauffenberg. The Nazis took revenge on the German aristocrats, and some leaders of the plot were hanged using piano wire, and their agonies filmed.

The Second World War

In a situation where sudden death was a daily reality, sexual release ceased to carry pre-war stigmas. This could lead to problems and even tragedies – in Norway, for instance, the children of Norwegian mothers and German fathers were treated badly after the war. French women who had had relations with the occupying forces were treated savagely in the 'liberation'. The hundreds of thousands of German women raped by Soviet forces in Germany in 1945 found it difficult to rebuild a normal family life. Post-war juvenile problems and crime were blamed on wartime disruption, but the social effects in terms of the relationship between men and women, children and adults, employers and workforce may be immeasurable. The widespread increase in cigarette smoking in the war may have been as disastrous to long-term health as aspects of wartime wounds. Conflict on the scale of the Second World War profoundly affected a whole variety of human relations and aspects of everyday life.

Racism and minority rights

The German genocide against the Jews had its origins before the war, but only the war itself permitted mass murder to proceed unchecked by internal or external disapproval, or opposition. In its closed European empire, Nazi Germany fulfilled its racial ambitions. First Jews were killed in **pogroms**, often with the collaboration of hostile local populations. Then Eastern European Jews were forced into ghettoes in several Polish cities. Many died from hunger, and random killings continued.

From 1942, a more systematic extermination campaign was carried out in special death camps, and Jews were gathered from all over occupied Europe. The policy veered between using able-bodied Jewish labour, killing those unable to work, and universal slaughter. As the war turned against Germany, the tempo of killing increased. At the end, the survivors were taken on death marches, so frenzied was the desire to at least win the war against a trapped and helpless people. The revelations of the horrors of the camps when Allied troops overran German-held territory challenged many of the assumptions of Western civilisation. Germany had been at the centre of modern culture, science, technology and scholarship. Yet in a developed, modern country it had been possible for 6 million people to be brutally killed and every type of inhuman cruelty and degradation to take place. The impact of this on the West, on the belief in progress, culture and civilisation, was profound. It challenged any idea that European values were better than others and led to a critical view of racial attitudes in the European empires and in the USA.

In the short term, the end of the war did not end ethnic conflicts – in many European states local minorities were driven out or persecuted, including ethnic Germans, and there were high casualties as revenge was taken. Anti-Semitic acts were still being perpetrated in Germany in the late 1940s, and a poll conducted in 1952 showed that Hitler was still seen by a majority as Germany's greatest leader. Soviet Russia was also on the verge of a major anti-Semitic campaign in the early 1950s.

The lessons of the Second World War did not prevent the emergence of genocide in the world after 1945, but they did lead to the questioning of racialism in some areas. The war led to a greater influx of black workers from the southern states of the USA into northern cities. It gave more black Americans a wider experience of the world as they served in Europe and the Far East. The war led America to reconfirm its commitment to democracy. All this contributed to the growth of **civil rights** after the war. Returning black GIs found pre-war US attitudes to race less tolerable.

Pogrom: A term originating in tsarist Russia for attacks on Jews. Pogroms were often condoned and even initiated by the tsarist authorities. Before 1914, Russia had the worst reputation for anti-Semitism, while Germany was not known for violence against Jews.

Civil rights: These derive from 18th-century theories that everyone has natural rights. Civil rights were defined in the US Declaration of Independence as 'life, liberty and the pursuit of happiness'. They have come to include justice in law, protection from discrimination, individual political freedom – including the rights of individuals and the right to participate in civil society and politics.

A war for freedom abroad had implications for freedom within the US, restricted as it was by segregated education and limited or no voting rights in the southern states. Activists had needed wartime demand for black labour:

- The black trade unionist A. Philip Randolph had threatened a workers' march on Washington in June 1941 to persuade Roosevelt to issue Executive Order 8802, which banned racial discrimination in defence industries and federal offices; the Fair Employment Act that followed made this federal law.
- Randolph's campaign for racial equality in the armed forces led to another significant executive order – 9981 – in July 1948, which banned segregation in the US military. Membership of civil rights organisations increased during the war and greater prosperity in industrial work helped to foster demands for better education and civil rights.

Ideology

Conflicting ideologies had been very important during the war. Extreme nationalist and racist dictatorships had been seen to fail, and democracies had shown themselves able to wage war as ruthlessly and effectively as militaristic states. Communism, in the sense of state-planning and striving for social justice, was also boosted in the eyes of many. Communist parties in Western Europe were associated with resistance to Nazism and fascism, and gained greater support in France and Italy.

In Britain, the 1945 elections gave power to a moderate socialist government, which introduced a significant change in health care – in the form of the National Health Service – and nationalised some major industries. The idea of a welfare state, in which the state took responsibility 'from cradle to grave' for those unable to care for themselves, and attempted to ensure a decent standard of living for all, was influential for 30 years after the war and was a significant consequence of the conflict. Most countries in Western Europe did not return to pre-war, laissez-faire capitalism. In Eastern Europe, communism took over as the dominant political ideology. The Soviet Union's success in uniting its people in the war and in producing masses of war supplies was seen as an inspiration. In Asia, the victory of communist China in 1949 was a major turning point.

Theory of Knowledge

The historian's responsibilities:
'It is the responsibility of intellectuals to speak the truth and to expose lies' – Noam Chomsky (b. 1928)

Is a historian justified in expressing any view about issues such as racism and genocide? How should a historian deal with racist views and should s/he explicitly condemn them? Does the Turkish government have a right to insist that the deaths of Armenians in Turkey in 1915 should not be described as a Holocaust?

4.9 What were the successes and failures of peacemaking?

There was no formal peace conference to resolve all the issues of the war as there had been in 1919, so 'peacemaking' really was the sum total of the developments after the war ended.

The war had been fought in Europe to defend Poland from Germany and in a more general way to defend Europe from territorial aggression. Britain and France had guaranteed Polish independence because of the revulsion against the annexation of Czechoslovakia by Germany in 1938. Continued expansion would threaten any stability in Europe, overturn the balance of power and make Britain and France insecure. In Asia, the war had been fought from Japan's point of view to establish a self-sufficient economic and political empire and from the point of view of its enemies to defend their possessions.

The war had destroyed the Nazi and fascist regimes in Germany and Italy and ended the threat. The peacemaking could not really be made directly with Germany because there was no legitimate government left after the fall of the regime. Thus there was no general peace conference like the Treaty of Versailles. The victorious powers occupied their enemies' territories. Italy, which had overthrown Mussolini in 1943 and then been occupied by Germany, could be seen as a victim and an ally. Japan and Germany were occupied until the Allies decided to restore their independence.

In Europe, the expansion of Russian control over the Eastern European countries (which, with the exception of Czechoslovakia, had been authoritarian dictatorships before 1939) ensured that there was no establishment of democracy. In particular, if the aim of the war had been to ensure Polish independence, then this failed, as Russian-dominated communist governments ruled the country until the fall of communism after 1989. In the Far East, the Allies had fought to restore their control over the lands taken by Japan in 1941–2. Japan was defeated and evacuated the territories, but the European and American possessions were granted independence as it proved too difficult to restore control after the humiliating defeats by Japan.

The outcomes varied of the de facto settlements. Germany was divided and was no longer a threat, but the emergence of the USSR's control of Eastern Europe entailed a long period of costly defence of Europe against a possible Soviet threat. For the USSR, the war ended the threat from Germany and gave it control over most of Eastern Europe and its resources, so the outcome was successful. However, it also led to a long period of hostility with the West involving a massive build-up of arms that was ultimately unsustainable. The outcomes were characterised by successes in ending the instability caused by German, Japanese and Italian ambitions, but failure in establishing a stable international order on the part of any of the participants. Japan's East Asia Prosperity Zone, Germany's Thousand-Year Reich and Italy's dream of a new Roman Empire collapsed. However, the dreams of the Atlantic Charter for a new democratic world were not realised either. Stability did not emerge because of the new Cold War and the resulting build-up of arms. In Asia the emergence of Communist China in 1949 and the end of the European and US Empires caused new problems.

International relations after the war

Not surprisingly, given the global and total nature of the war, international relations after 1945 went through many changes.

The Cold War

Although the **Cold War** originated in pre-war disagreements and ideological conflict, its development in the post-war period was one of the most significant consequences of the Second World War. The US developed a policy of 'containment', pledging to oppose the further spread of communism in the Truman Doctrine of 1947 and backing it up by extensive economic aid to Europe in the Marshall Plan. Stalin coordinated his Eastern European states by creating Comecon, a joint economic system, and Cominform, a way of politically coordinating the communist world. The phrase 'Iron Curtain', used by Churchill in a speech delivered during a visit to the USA in March 1946, came to be seen as a reality, as Western and Eastern Europe became more divided.

Cold War: Tensions between the Soviet Union and the West did not lead to a military conflict but instead to a long period of mutual hostility and a build-up of arms on both sides. This became known as the Cold War – a war of ideas, words, threats, spying and mistrust, but no actual fighting. It finally ended with the collapse of the Soviet Union at the end of 1991.

SOURCE D

It is my duty, however, to place before you certain facts about the present position in Europe.

From Stettin in the Baltic to Trieste in the Adriatic an Iron Curtain has descended across the Continent. Behind that line lie all the capitals of the ancient states of Central and Eastern Europe, Warsaw, Berlin, Prague, Vienna, Budapest, Belgrade, Bucharest and Sofia; all these famous cities and the populations around them lie in what I must call the Soviet sphere, and all are subject, in one form or another, not only to Soviet influence but to a very high and in some cases increasing measure of control from Moscow.

Except in the British Commonwealth and in the United States where communism is in its infancy, the communist parties … constitute a growing challenge and peril to Christian civilisation.

Churchill's 'Iron Curtain' speech, published in his book The Sinews of Peace. *Quoted in M.A. Kishlansky (ed.). 1995.* Sources of World History. *New York: HarperCollins. pp. 298–302.*

QUESTION

What effect was this speech likely to have on relations between Russia and the West?

Why did Churchill use the term 'Christian civilisation' in his speech?

Pre-emptive strike: An attack to 'get in first' and prevent an attack on you by an enemy.

Conventional warfare: This is, non-nuclear war between established armed forces of different countries. This is in comparison with, for example, guerrilla wars fought by states against 'rebel' organisations within a state.

The nuclear age

The development of atomic weapons to defeat Japan and to prevent the millions of casualties that the Allies anticipated if they invaded the Japanese homeland had a most profound effect on the post-war world. Between 1945 and 2000, more than 128 000 nuclear warheads were built. The USSR built 55 000 and America 70 000. The development of nuclear weapons can be seen in the timeline.

With the proliferation of intercontinental ballistic missiles, nuclear submarines and tactical battlefield devices, both the sheer destructive potential of nuclear weapons and the speed and flexibility with which they could be deployed were developed to a considerable extent in the Cold War. Initially the cost and technical sophistication required to build these weapons restricted membership of the 'Nuclear Club', but it was not possible to maintain this control. It was not only Cold War conflicts that saw the danger of nuclear escalation, but also the long-running conflicts in the Middle East and between India and Pakistan.

In 1945, the implications of atomic weapons were not widely grasped, i.e., the long-term effects of radiation or the possibility that civilisation itself might be destroyed. However, with proliferation and greater understanding came widespread anxiety. The post-war generation was profoundly affected by the threat of the bomb (the Campaign for Nuclear Disarmament, CND, was established as early as 1958), especially as international crises brought its deployment uncomfortably close. In 1962, during the Cuban Missile Crisis, the Americans resolutely stood against the USSR having nuclear sites in Cuba. It gave rise to the likelihood of a **pre-emptive strike** that might have led to a full-scale nuclear war. There was, therefore, an increased awareness of how close the world was to destruction.

In the event, atomic weapons were used only in 1945. **Conventional warfare** like that of the Second World War – on a total and unlimited scale between major industrial powers, involving the destruction of resources, cities and peoples – did not recur because it was simply too dangerous to embark on it. The Cold War remained cold, and ended when the pressure to produce new weapons and to sustain huge conventional forces became too much for the USSR by 1989. An arms race, not the actual use of the arms, brought a decisive result.

TIMELINE

Atomic bomb first tested	Country
1945	USA
1949	USSR
1952	UK
1960	France
1964	China
1974	India
Possibly 1979	Israel
1998	Pakistan

The Second World War

Anti-imperialism

Tied to the rise of communism was the decline in the overseas empires of the great powers (see map). There had been nationalist movements before the war, but the war accelerated the end of empires.

The defeats of the Europeans and Americans by Japan in 1940–2 exposed the whole racial myth that Europeans were superior to Asians. The rapid capture of the Southeast Asian colonies was a blow to European prestige. It encouraged greater resistance to British rule in India, from the political 'Quit India' campaign to the creation of the Indian National Army. The latter, led by the former Congress Party politician Subhas Chandra Bose, was allied to Japan during the war.

KEY CONCEPTS ACTIVITY

Causation and consequences: Draw up a table with two columns, labelled 'Reasons' and 'Results'. Then complete this table to show the main reasons for the breakdown of the Grand Alliance, and the main consequences.

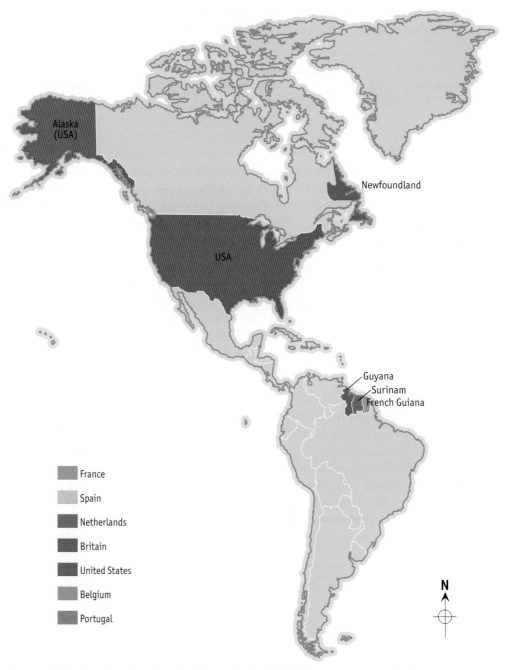

Figure 4.23 Map showing the colonial empires by 1945; it is worth noting that in 1945, many of these countries would have had very different names

The logic of a war against racist doctrines and greedy nationalists taking other people's lands also made the survival of European empires difficult to sustain. The USA was deeply unsympathetic to fighting a war so that Britain could maintain its empire and operate a closed economic system by trading with it and excluding the USA. The costs of maintaining overseas empires was also too great for European countries after the war.

Generally in Britain and Europe there was a shift to the political left. In Britain, the Labour Party was a lot less committed, for example, to maintaining the pre-war empire than its Conservative predecessors had been.

4

The key event in the decline of imperialism was the granting of Indian independence in 1947. Faced with a resurgence of nationalism, an unsympathetic USA, rising defence costs and a programme of social and economic change at home, the British decided to bring forward plans for greater self-government and opt for withdrawal. The short-term results of this rushed decision were disastrous. Hurried demarcations were made between Muslim and Hindu areas to try and avoid conflict between the two major religions. Muslims had called for a separate state since 1917 and were given the somewhat artificial state of Pakistan. The two parts of Pakistan, East and West, were separated by Indian territory. It proved impossible to draw neat boundary lines between the religions and, in the race of refugees to reach Hindu or Muslim areas, there was widespread communal violence. The territories of Jammu and Kashmir were disputed, and the boundaries have never been accepted by Pakistan. In 1971, after a brutal civil war and Indian intervention, East Pakistan broke away to form Bangladesh. Change would probably have come regardless, but the Second World War dictated when and how India and Pakistan were formed.

Fact: In contrast to other independent states in Africa, Rhodesia and South Africa were dominated by white minorities. Under Ian Smith, Rhodesia declared independence from Britain and continued to impose white rule on its black majority until a civil war resulted in the new independent country of Zimbabwe. South Africa imposed official discrimination – Apartheid – from 1948 until it too accepted black majority rule in the 1990s after Nelson Mandela's release from prison. Rhodesian and South African troops had fought against the racist regime of Nazi Germany in the Second World War.

After the British withdrawal from India, it was only a matter of time before the European empires worldwide collapsed (see maps). Britain also withdrew from Palestine in 1948, leaving further religious conflict, this time between the Arabs and the Jewish settlers that Britain had admitted since 1917. Other European countries also found they lacked the resources to maintain colonies. In France's case there was more reluctance to let go because of the humiliation of occupation during the war and a desire to be a great power again. French forces resisted Indochina's demands to break away, but were defeated by the Vietnamese at Dien Bien Phu in 1954. France also resisted independence movements in Algeria, where there were substantial numbers of French white settlers. After a protracted war (1954–61), the colony was lost. Britain was more successful in defeating communist insurgency in Malaya, but did not maintain its Southeast Asian empire in its old form, allowing greater self-government and finally independence. Britain fought hard against 'rebel' nationalists in Africa but by the 1950s it was giving way to what one British leader called 'the wind of change'. White regimes attempted to stem the tide of black nationalism in Rhodesia (Zimbabwe) and South Africa, but the long-term effects of the Second World War made this resistance to change impossible.

Greater unity and international cooperation

In an effort to prevent another major war, France and West Germany followed the lead of Holland, Belgium and the Netherlands, who had agreed on economic integration when the war was still going on and their governments were in exile in 1944. Britain and France signed an economic agreement in 1947, and in 1948 there was a 16-nation OEEC agreement. The key pact came in 1952, with the formation of the European Coal and Steel Community, which developed into the European Economic Community (EEC) of 1958 under the Treaty of Rome, and which was the basis for the European Community (EC). The deadly rivalry between Germany and France that had led to two major wars did not recur after 1945. Economic and political cooperation also developed in Eastern Europe with Comecon (the Council for Mutual Economic Assistance, formed in 1949). Because of the political division of Europe, economic development proceeded in a different and more controlled way in the East, with lower growth rates and less consumer spending, but less of a social divide between rich and poor.

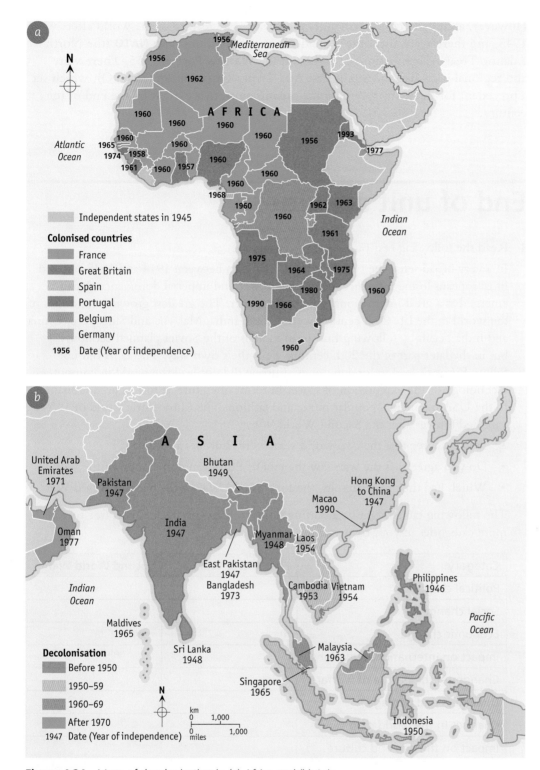

Figure 4.24 Maps of decolonisation in (a) Africa and (b) Asia

The wartime meetings of the Allied statesmen, and the talk of post-war reconstruction and aims, also reflected a new internationalism. The creation of the United Nations (UN) organisation offered hopes of a more effective world body to maintain peace than had been achieved after the First World War.

NATO: This emerged out of a Western European defence pact in 1948, signed by France, the Netherlands, Belgium, Luxemburg and Britain. On 4 April 1949, the USA joined to establish a permanent headquarters in Brussels for a military pact to defend the Western democracies. After 1991, despite promises to the contrary, the US has insisted that NATO membership be extended to former East European satellites – this has caused tensions with post-Soviet Russia.

Warsaw Pact: Russia created a military alliance among its satellite states in Eastern Europe that lasted from 1955 to 1991 and arose in reaction to West Germany joining NATO in 1954. Although dominated by Russia, the armed forces of the Soviet bloc made joint plans to ensure the security of the USSR and its satellite states.

However, although economic cooperation was a key feature of the world after 1945, and there were also large-scale defence organisations with **NATO** (the North Atlantic Treaty Organisation) of 1949 and the **Warsaw Pact** of 1955. There were also regional pacts like the South East Asia Treaty Organisation (SEATO), which set a precedent for the many international organisations that existed by the end of the century.

End of unit activities

1   Read the following text on long-term change.

In a very broad sense the two European civil wars between 1914 and 1945 resulted in Europeans losing influence, economic power and imperial dominance. Japan emerged as a great international economic power. The greatest growth economies of the world in the late 20th century were China, India, Malaysia and Singapore. China and India began by following European models of the Soviet planned economy but in the later part of the 20th century went their own way. The USA did not follow Europe's lead in foreign policy. Europe did not lead the world in computer technology or the exploration of space. In terms of culture, it lost its predominance to the USA in cinema, popular music and fashion. The Eurocentric world of 1939 vanished forever after the Second World War.

*   Do you agree that the two world wars were 'European civil wars'?
*   Do you agree that the wars saw the end of European domination of the world?
*   Which had the greater results, the First World War or the Second World War?

The following table might be a starting point to help you decide. Feel free to add more categories in your own version.

Category	First World War	Second World War
Political changes		
Social change		
Economic change		
Impact on international relations		
Changes in the nature of warfare		
Direct loss and damage		
Changes in the world map		
Impact on the arts and culture		

2   With regard to the long-term consequences of the world wars, consider how you might explain why there were years of economic depression after the First World War, yet the period after the Second World War was characterised by economic growth.

End of chapter activities

Paper 1 exam practice

Question

Compare and contrast what Sources A and B below reveal about the reasons for the German invasion of Poland. [6 marks]

Skill

Cross-referencing

SOURCE A

Danzig is not the main issue or objective. It is a matter of expanding our living space to the east, of making our food supplies secure, and of solving the problem of the Baltic States. To provide sufficient food, you must have sparsely settled areas. This is fertile soil, whose surpluses will be very much increased by German thorough management. There is no question of sparing Poland and the decision remains to attack Poland at the first suitable opportunity. We cannot expect a repetition of Czechoslovakia. Poland will always be on the side of our enemies. Poland has always intended to exploit every opportunity against us.

Hitler speaking to his generals, 23 May 1939. Quoted in A.P. Adamthwaite, 1977. The Making of the Second World War. *London: Allen and Unwin, p. 214.*

SOURCE B

On 4 August 1939 a long-simmering customs dispute between Poland and the Danzig authorities suddenly erupted. A report that the Danzig authorities no longer intended to recognise the Polish customs inspectors reached the Polish government. Any such action, the President of the Danzig Senate was told, would be considered grounds for war. Hitler was infuriated. He ordered an immediate press campaign against Poland. The British consul general in Danzig considered that the Polish government had taken a fatal step. The ultimatum of 4 August had been a terrible mistake and had precipitated the crisis. It had destroyed any hope of a peaceful settlement of German-Polish differences and led to war.

S. Aster. 1973. 1939: The Making of the Second World War. *London: Andre Deutsch, pp. 510 and 623.*

169

Examiner's tips

Cross-referencing questions require you to compare and contrast the information/content/nature of two sources, relating to a particular issue.

Before you write your answer, draw a rough chart or diagram to show the similarities and the differences between the two sources. That way, you should ensure that you address both aspects/elements of the question.

Common mistakes

When asked to compare and contrast two sources, make sure you don't just comment on one of the sources! Such an oversight happens every year – and will lose you four of the six marks available.

Simplified mark scheme

Band		Marks
1	Both sources linked, with detailed references to **both** sources, identifying both similarities **and** differences	6
2	Both sources linked, with detailed references to **both** sources, identifying either similarities **or** differences.	4–5
3	Comments on both sources, but treating each one separately.	3
4	Discusses/comments on just one source.	0–2

Student answer

Sources A and B give quite different reasons for the invasion of Poland. Source A, Hitler's own words, says that Danzig is not the issue, but the diplomat in Source B thinks that the Polish ultimatum about the customs inspectors is the key issue, as it was a fatal step that prevented peaceful negotiations. A is much more concerned with long-term aims of getting Polish land for use for food and resources. This is not taken into account in Source B, which focuses on the short-term issue that infuriated Hitler and was a cause of war. Source B refers to a longstanding hatred of Poland and a belief that the Poles were working against Germany's interest. It is written before 4 August and the dispute over the customs, and shows that Hitler had longstanding plans for war with Poland. It thus disproves the English consul's view that war could have been avoided and that it was Poland's fault. Even if Poland had not provoked Hitler, then Source A shows that there would have been invasion and war because Hitler had plans for 'living space', to dominate the Baltic States and to end Polish hostility. Therefore, there is a more limited and naive view in B that a single incident brought war.

Examiner's comments

There are several clear/precise references to both the sources, and several differences/contrasts are identified. Also, the sources are clearly linked, rather than being dealt with separately. The candidate has thus done enough to get into Band 2, and so be awarded four or five marks. However, as no similarities/comparisons are made, this answer fails to get into Band 1.

Activity

Look again at the two sources, the simplified mark scheme and the student answer. Now try to write a paragraph or two to push the answer up into Band 1, and so obtain the full six marks. You need to consider whether there are any similarities.

Summary activities

- Produce a set of revision cards – to cover (via bullet points) the main causes of the Second World War in both Europe and Asia. To do this, use the information from this chapter, and any other resources available to you. Remember to make sure you include all the main events.

- Create a spider diagram like the one below and fill in the results of war. Don't try and put in too much detail – you can prepare a set of revision cards for that.

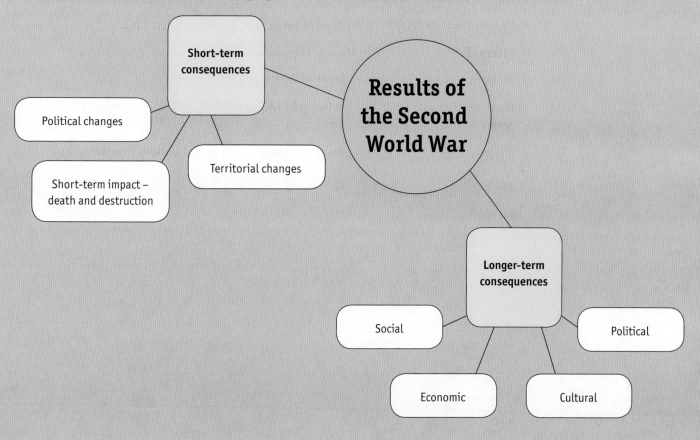

Paper 2 practice questions

1 Compare and contrast the causes of the First and Second World Wars.
2 Examine the main results of either the First or the Second World War.
3 Evaluate the reasons for either the defeat of the Central Powers in the First World War, or of the Axis powers in the Second World War.
4 Examine the role of ideology as a cause of the Second World War.
5 'The use of the air power was the most significant factor in deciding the outcome of the Second World War.' To what extent do you agree with this statement?

Further reading

Try reading the relevant chapters/sections of the following books:

Hobsbawm, Eric (1995) *The Age of Extremes*, London: Abacus.

Judt, Tony (2007) *Postwar: A History of Europe Since 1945*, London: Pimlico.

Keegan, John (1989) *The Second World War*, London: Hutchinson.

Mazower, Mark (2008) *Dark Continent: Europe's Twentieth Century*. London: Penguin.

Nye, Joseph S. (2003) *Understanding International Conflicts: An Introduction to Theory and History*, London: Longman.

Overy, Richard (2009) *1939: Countdown to War*, London: Allen Lane.

Overy, Richard (2009) *The Road to War*, London: Vintage.

Roberts, Andrew (2010) *The Storm of War*, London: Penguin.

Ross, Stewart and MacCarthy-Morrogh, Deirdre (1995) *Causes and Consequences of the Second World War*, London: Evans.

Taylor, A.J.P. (2001) *The Origins of the Second World War*, London: Penguin.

Causes of the Chinese Civil War

TIMELINE

1900 Boxer Rebellion.

1911 Revolution; end of the Qing dynasty.

1912 Chinese Republic established; formation of Guomindang (GMD).

1914 Dictatorship of Yuan Shikai.

1919 Fourth of May Movement established.

1921 Chinese Communist Party (CCP) formed.

1926 Northern Expedition takes place.

1927 Civil War begins between nationalist Guomindang and communists.

1937 Outbreak of war with Japan; civil war hostilities officially suspended.

1945 Civil war recommences.

KEY QUESTIONS

- What were the main long-term causes of the war?
- What were the main short-term causes of the war?
- What were the political, ideological and economic causes of the war?

Overview

- By 1900, China was a weak country, dominated by European powers and defeated by a more modern Japan in 1895. Forces of nationalism and reform existed, but these were blocked by an old-fashioned and restrictive imperial ruling class.

- The revolution of 1911 began a process of change, but in the short term this led to military dictatorship and the disintegration of China into independent provinces dominated by local warlords, including those allied to the nationalist Guomindang (see map).

- Disappointment with the Treaty of Versailles after the First World War, and resentment towards Japan, led to the reforming Fourth of May Movement, and both nationalism and communism emerged as possible agents of change.

- For a while, under Russian influence, these groups worked together and the warlords were brought under control, but in 1928 the nationalists turned on the communists and began a civil war which, while not fought continuously, did not end until 1949.

Introduction

You have now considered three wars of different types, and will have developed your own explanations for and analysis of these conflicts. This chapter discusses another civil war, in a different IB region. You can bring your knowledge of China and Japan in the Second World War to this topic. This chapter will also enable you to compare the

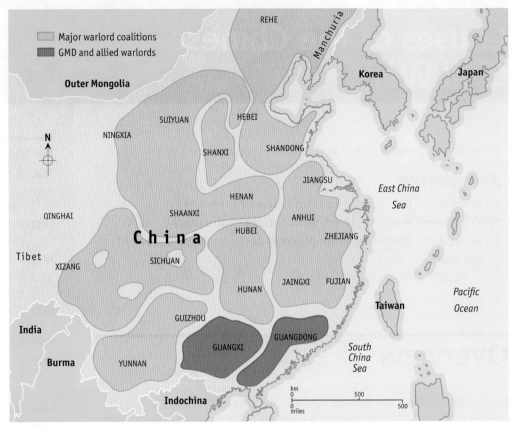

Figure 5.1 This map of China in 1925 reveals the extent of disunity that affected the country after the fall of the last imperial dynasty in 1911

causes, practice and effects of two civil wars. The effects of the Chinese Civil War are still felt, and the scale of the war was different from that in Spain. However, there are similarities in the situations that gave rise to both civil wars and in the way that the conflicts in China and Spain both led to personal dictatorships in those countries.

The Chinese Civil War is unique in the history of 20th century warfare. The first example of this is its duration – 22 years. This represents an epic struggle that dwarfs the battle for Madrid in the Spanish Civil War, for example, or the defence of central Russia by the Bolsheviks in 1918–20. In China, the battlefields were huge, and the retreat of the communists northwards in 1934 – the so-called 'Long March' – has few parallels in the history of modern conflicts. The sheer size of China and the number of people involved in the fighting made this civil conflict on an unprecedented scale. The war was characterised by a struggle between two charismatic figures – the nationalist Jiang Jieshi and the communist Mao Zedong – both of whom were complex and deeply flawed figures with vastly different visions for the future of their country.

Because of the unequal strength of the opposing sides for most of its duration, the Chinese Civil War was characterised by irregular guerrilla warfare. On the occasions when the nationalists were able to engage the communists in more traditional encounters, the nationalists usually won. It was not until late in the war that a more

The modern spelling of Chinese names has mostly been used in this book. Older books may refer to Chiang Kai-Shek and Mao Tse-Tung, but here they are Jiang Jieshi and Mao Zedong.

conventional form of attack was possible for the communists. So the Chinese Civil War was distinctive, and Mao's strategy was adopted by other communist leaders, including Fidel Castro in Cuba and Ho Chi Minh in Vietnam. Whether victory came from the success of guerrilla warfare or the weakness of the enemy will be discussed later in the chapter.

The death toll on both sides was considerable. The war did not affect every part of China, but in those regions where fighting did occur, the damage was significant. This situation was made worse by the Japanese invasions. The political effects of the communist victory also took their toll on human lives. As in Spain, repression continued after the war as the communists redistributed land. Attacks on wealthier peasants and landowners accounted for millions of deaths. In the cities, destructive purges against opponents of communism were carried out. Economic experimentation led to widespread famine in 1958, and this was followed by more political upheaval – and more deaths. The Chinese invasion and occupation of Tibet – ongoing today – brings the total deaths arising from the war and its consequences to a possible 44 million or higher.

Mao's victory also meant that two of the largest countries in the world – China and the USSR – were under communist control. This heightened fears in many other countries, notably the USA, about the spread of communism.

5.1 What were the main long-term causes of the war?

Developments, 1900–18

China had been under increasingly weak imperial rule by the Manchu Qing dynasty. The Manchu rulers established power over the native Han Chinese in the 17th century, and retained control until 1911. The Manchu imposed their will by force; the hairstyle they forced Chinese men to adopt – shaving the front of their heads and putting their hair into a queue (a long ponytail) – was a mark of submission.

In the 19th century, China came increasingly under European control, and its traditional society and underdeveloped economy could not compete with the West. Unlike neighbouring Japan, China had not modernised after the mid-century and paid the price by being defeated in a war against Japan in 1894–5.

China's weaknesses had been exploited by European powers anxious to profit from Chinese trade. When a rebellion broke out against this foreign influence in 1900, China was humiliated by a joint European military action to put down the so-called **Boxer Rebellion**. China's economy and system of government had been stagnant for decades, and an attempt by the ruling class of the Qing dynasty to introduce reforms after 1900 came too late.

There were various points of contention in China. A minority saw the need for a Western-style constitutional government and modernisation. There was considerable discontent in the army and in some provinces. China had a long history of rural unrest

Fact: Fidel Castro led a revolution in Cuba against the dictatorship of Fulgencio Batista from 1956 to 1959. He ruled Cuba from that time until 2008.

Fact: Ho Chi Minh was the leader of the Vietnamese communists and, after 1954, the ruler of communist North Vietnam who led attempts to unify the country. He died in 1969. Vietnam was reunited in 1975.

Fact: The Sino–Japanese War of 1894–5 was fought over Korea and resulted in the Japanese occupation of Manchuria, Korea and Taiwan, as well as a huge indemnity payment from China to Japan. Japan was forced to relinquish some of its gains to foreign powers, but annexed Korea in 1910. Chinese weaknesses were exposed, and European powers took advantage to gain ports.

Boxer Rebellion: Anti-Christian and anti-foreign groups called the 'Harmonious Fists' (hence Boxer) emerged after 1898. The Boxers were initially suppressed by the government, but in 1900 they attacked Western missions in northern China. The Boxers besieged foreign embassies in Beijing for 55 days before being suppressed by an international relief force. China had to pay compensation and once again its weakness was revealed.

and peasant riots, and some landowners and traders became discontented with the obvious weakness of the monarchy. In 1911, splits in the ruling class, and especially among elements of the army, led to a revolution and subsequently the Manchus were removed from power. This revolution, originating in Sichuan, saw regional risings against the regime. It was not a great popular uprising, nor was it led by a well-organised party like the Russian Revolution was in 1917. It was more to do with a culmination of discontent among various groups, and the failure of traditional élites in army and government to support the regime.

The revolution led to the end of the Qing dynasty and the formation of a republic in 1912. The revolution's most prominent theoretical reformer, Sun Yat-Sen, became the first president of China. However, real power rested with the dominant army commander, Yuan Shikai, who moved to create a military dictatorship by 1914 and proclaimed himself emperor in 1916.

By that time, China had disintegrated into regional regimes dominated by local army commanders – the so-called warlords. The party that aimed for unification with some sort of democratic constitutional republic was called the **Guomindang (GMD)**. It took as its models the Western constitutional states and Japan, which had a parliamentary system based on that of Germany. Sun Yat-Sen was its leader and inspiration.

> **Guomindang (GMD):** A political party set up in China by Sun Yat-Sen in 1912. In 1924, Sun announced that the GMD was based on Three Principles – national freedom, democratic government and the people's welfare. The GMD was then reorganised with a Leninist structure. After Sun's death in 1925, Jiang Jieshi assumed leadership and the GMD became more right-wing. Following his defeat by the Chinese Communist Party (CCP) in 1949, Jiang established a GMD regime in Taiwan. Older textbooks refer to the GMD as the Kuomintang.

Figure 5.2 Guomindang leader Sun Yat-Sen (centre) in 1912

Sun Yat Sen had been educated in the West, and had become a revolutionary. In the wake of China's defeat by Japan in 1895, Sun led a failed revolution, after which he was forced into exile. He developed a programme that aimed to overthrow the Qing dynasty – which he saw as alien – and to establish a democratic republic and pursue social revolution to create more equality in landholding and wealth. Sun borrowed both from constitutional ideas in the West and from socialism.

In 1905, Sun created the Chinese United League. This was a forerunner of the Chinese Nationalist Party – the Guomindang – which was established in 1912 to bring together the various reforming groups in China. Sun accepted that a period of military dictatorship might have to precede a full constitutional democracy. However, he and his party were faced with the consequences of this sooner than expected. In 1913, Yuan Shikai ordered the assassination of one the GMD's leading members. Sun attempted a second revolution, but this was suppressed, and in November 1912 the party was banned and Sun had to flee. He remained in exile in Japan until 1917, and made little headway in uniting nationalist groups as China became deeply divided between the warlords. It was the Fourth of May Movement that offered opportunities for reforming groups, and this movement inspired Sun to re-form the GMD in 1920. After Sun's death in 1925, **Jiang Jieshi** emerged as the leader of the GMD and one of the key figures in the Chinese Civil War.

The Fourth of May Movement

The announcement of the peace terms that ended the First World War was the spark for a massive protest movement in China in 1919, which became known as the Fourth of May Movement. Although China had fought on the side of the Allies, it did not regain the rights to Shandong province, which Germany had taken. Instead, Shandong was given to Japan.

Figure 5.3   Jiang Jieshi (1887–1975)

He was the son of a wine merchant. He became a professional soldier and trained in Japan. Jieshi supported reform and took part in the 1911 revolution, capturing Shanghai. He was a protégé of Sun Yat-Sen, who sent him to Moscow for political training. Jiang was also the commander of the influential Huangpu Military Academy. Jiang led the Northern Expedition of 1926 and turned against the communists. He became the leading figure in the Guomindang government and led Chinese forces against both the Japanese and the communists. He launched the traditionalist New Life Movement in 1934. With US support, Jieshi hoped to defeat the communists after 1945 but was himself defeated and fled to Taiwan, where he established an alternative Republic of China.

Figure 5.4   Protests in the Fourth of May Movement, 1919

This seemed to confirm China's weakness and subordination to foreign powers. Demonstrations were held in the streets, and intellectuals and reformers realised that China must undergo radical change to break away from its old way of life: **Confucianism**, regional divisions, weak central government, low economic growth and a largely rural economy. The answer, it was believed, lay in adopting the social ideologies and structures of the West. Some in China turned to Marxism; the GMD turned to national unity and democracy.

Confucianism: Confucius (551–479 BCE) was the most renowned Chinese philosopher. He taught that humans should aim for personal improvement and moral perfection through both individual endeavour and good communal living. He urged respect for authority in both the state and family, filial piety and courteous manners.

> **SOURCE A**
>
> The Modern Civilisation of the West is built on the foundation of the search for human happiness. It has increased the enjoyment of material life, but can also satisfy the spiritual needs of mankind. It has ended the religion of superstition and established rational belief. It has ended outdated belief in Divine Power and established a humanistic religion.
>
> *Hu Shi (a reforming intellectual). 1919. 'Our Attitude Towards Modern Western Civilisation'. Quoted at http://afe.easia.columbia.edu/ps/cup/ hushi_western_civ.pdf.*

ACTIVITY

Why is Source A an important source?

What does it tell us about changing attitudes in China after the First World War?

Which groups would have been influenced by this sort of writing?

KEY CONCEPTS QUESTION

Causation: Why was China so unstable before 1927?

5.2 What were the main short-term causes of the war?

The 1926 Northern Expedition

Sun Yat-Sen wanted to overthrow the independent warlords in the north of China. When he died in 1925, the nationalist GMD party was divided into left and right wings. Wang Jingwei was the leftist leader and Hu Hanmin led the right. The real power, however, lay with Jiang Jieshi who, as superintendent of the Huangpu Military Academy, was in near complete control of the armed forces. With this military strength, the Guomindang confirmed its power in the southern provinces of Guangdong and Guangxi.

By 1926, the nationalists had been able to establish a rival government to that of the warlords, who had a loose coalition based in Beijing. Jiang Jieshi and his army decided to lead an expedition in alliance with the right and left wings of the GMD – as well as the communists – against the warlords in the north. Russia offered supplies and military advisers. The campaign against three warlords (Wu Peifu, Sun Chuanfang and Zhang Zuolin), as well as independent factions, was a success, but the GMD coalition grew increasingly divided.

Jiang was largely responsible for the divisions within the coalition. Although he had been sent to Moscow by Sun Yat-Sen for political training, he became increasingly suspicious of the communists. Jiang was not as Western-orientated as others in the GMD, and by 1927 he had turned decisively to the right. These ideas subsequently emerged as the New Life Movement, based not so much on the Western values of the Fourth of May Movement, but on Confucianism – order, cleanliness, simplicity, hard work, obedience and honour. In other words, military values.

By the end of 1926, Jiang's 260 000-strong army had conquered half a million square miles and 170 million people. The speed and success of this advance, together with Jiang's own views, brought about some fateful events.

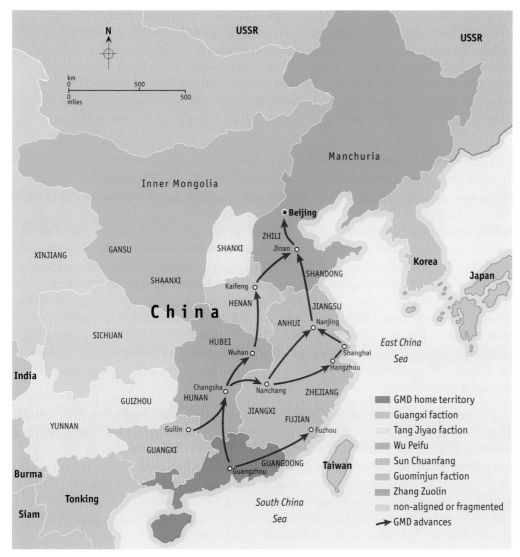

Figure 5.5 Map of the Northern Expedition, 1926–7

Jiang Jieshi's attack on the communists

In Jiang's eyes, the communists represented an alien philosophy. Like many in the GMD, Jiang saw the traditional Chinese values of hard-working families linked to modern capitalism as the key to:

- progress in general;
- building up a strong army to resist the warlords;
- ensuring that China would not be dominated by Japan or the stronger Western European powers and the USA, which enjoyed trade and investment with China and virtually controlled key ports.

A peasant and working-class China would not deliver this progress, and would challenge Jiang and the landowners, as well as the army officers and the financial and industrial élites who were supporting the nationalist movement.

Fact: Originally there were 33 treaty ports (key ports) in which European powers had concessions and their own self-government in China. A major city like Shanghai had three different foreign areas outside Chinese control. These were established at a time when the Chinese were unable to withstand foreign pressure, and their continuance was a major source of national shame.

Although the war between the GMD and the CCP was not constant from 1927 to its end in 1949 – and was affected by events of the Second World War (notably the struggle between Japan and China for control of Asia) – it was intense. Before 1937, the communists fought a desperate struggle to avoid destruction. After 1945, they gradually gained support and were able to defeat the GMD and drive Jiang to Taiwan (Formosa), where he formed an alternative government. Although this was recognised by, and received support from, the Western powers, in reality China became a communist republic in 1949.

The Shanghai Massacre of 1927

In April 1927, Jiang turned on the communists in Shanghai and began a civil war that lasted until 1949. Jiang wanted to move on Shanghai and to control the city. He needed the support of the powerful underworld organisation called the Green Gang, which was opposed to communist influence in the trade unions in the city. Jiang allied himself to its leader, and also to a powerful business and financial family in the city, the Sungs, by marrying Sung Meiling. The first signs of what Jiang planned were seen in the execution of communists on the way to Shanghai. As he approached the city, Jiang ordered the suppression of a communist strike that had in fact been organised in his support, in the mistaken belief that he was still an ally of the left. The Green Gang boss, 'Big Ears Du', was allowed by the GMD commanders to attack the communists in a purge. On 11 April, the labour leader Wang Shouhua was killed, and on 12 April between 5 000 and 10 000 communists were killed. This event became known as the Shanghai Massacre.

The terror spread – men, women and children were beheaded, broken on the rack, left to die in cages, buried alive or shot. The communists responded with a large-scale rural revolt in Hunan, the Autumn Harvest Uprising, which failed at the cost of 300 000 lives. **Zhou Enlai** led a revolt in the Jiangxi capital, Nanchang, which was crushed. The Soviet leader Joseph Stalin encouraged an uprising in Guangzhou in December 1927, which led to some of the worst atrocities. Around 5700 people were killed, and there were reports of communists having their hearts eaten and their heads pickled in brine. By the end of 1927, some 37 000 communists had been killed.

Zhou Enlai (1898–1976)

He was a student political activist and was arrested for protests about Japanese goods after the Fourth of May agitations. He lived abroad and became a communist in 1922. He worked with the GMD from 1925 at the Huangpu Military Academy, and took part in expeditions against the warlords. He organised a communist rising in 1928 but escaped and later joined the Jiangxi Soviet, a state established by Mao Zedong. He was an associate of Mao, and became the first premier of communist China in 1949 and later foreign minister.

Figure 5.6 The policy of decapitation proved to be a powerful antidote to strike fever in Shanghai; this picture shows the 'Execution Patrol' which consisted of a dozen soldiers with fixed bayonets and the headsman with a bard blade

The extreme brutality of the Shanghai Massacre prevented any easy revival of the alliance between the GMD and the CCP. Jiang's dominance was firmly established by 1928, when he was recalled after opposition to his repression had temporarily led to his removal. This meant that the nationalists, now established at Nanjing as the government of China, had an implacable anti-communist as their leader – one who was also closely associated with paramilitary gangster groups and their financial and business interests. Jiang also had a distinct political and moral philosophy that was opposed to communism as compared to the original more generally leftist view of **Sun's Three Principles**. However, Jiang was not able to crush the communists completely, so his actions in April 1927 led not to outright victory but to a prolonged civil war.

The communists' survival and resistance – the first phase of the war up to 1937

There are a number of reasons why the communists were able to survive and begin to fight back.

- The organisation of the communists into small units gave them the flexibility to survive persecution and meant that key leaders were not killed.

- The ideals of communism were powerful and gave strength to the opponents of Jiang Jieshi. The violence of the repression offered little hope of compromise, instead encouraging desperate and continuing resistance.

- Jiang was opposed by the leftist wing of the GMD in 1927–8 and went into retirement. When he returned in 1928, Jiang was rarely able to deploy his full forces and attention to defeating the communists. He was faced with the need to defeat the warlords as well as the communists. From 1931, his nationalist government also had to deal with a Japanese invasion.

- The sheer size of China and the rapid movement of the fleeing communists were a problem for Jiang. The communists were able to establish strongholds in remote areas. More than a dozen rural bases were set up between 1928 and 1934 in isolated areas with poor communications. This hindered the movement of conventional forces but favoured fast-moving, flexible, small groups of guerrillas. Here, the CCP attracted support from wandering gangs, former warlord troops and GMD deserters. The first of these guerrilla groups, called E-yu-wan, was set up by 200 partisans in the mountains of southern Hubei. From a base in west Hubei, military leader He Long developed his force from 20 men to a 20000-strong army, winning over peasants with land reforms and by establishing a flourishing local economy. Mao led 1500 men from Changsha to a base in the Jiangxi Mountains, linking up with men from Nanchang and with former members of the Northern Expedition. By 1930, the bases had 65000 men and were even able to launch attacks on nationalist-held cities. By 1931, the **Jiangxi Soviet** covered 26000 square kilometres (10000 square miles) based on the town of Ruijin.

- The communists' discipline and willingness to accept loss of life were also factors in their success. To confirm his power in Jiangxi, Mao savagely attacked would-be opponents, whom he accused of collaboration with the GMD. His men castrated these enemies of communism and sliced off the breasts of their wives. The death toll ran into tens of thousands. This total ruthlessness enabled the CCP to survive.

- The communists also offered the local peasant population reforms and hope for the future. Increasingly, Mao came to see the peasants as the key to successful revolution.

Sun's Three Principles: Nationalism, democracy and the people's welfare.

KEY CONCEPTS ACTIVITY

Significance: Carry out some additional research on the Shanghai Massacre. Then write a couple of paragraphs to explain the importance of this event for the Chinese Civil War.

Jiangxi Soviet: The name given to the independent, peasant-based government in the Jiangxi province of south-eastern China. It was established in 1931 by Mao Zedong and the communists, whose headquarters lay in the city of Ruijin.

One war or two wars – a lull in hostilities, 1937–45

The Chinese Civil War between the communists and nationalists started in 1927. Fighting continued up to and throughout the large-scale Japanese invasion of China in 1937, which was resisted by both communists and nationalists. Hostilities ceased – officially at least – between the end of 1937 until 1945: despite internal clashes, the priority was to defeat Japan. Once that had been achieved, the wartime truce and cooperation quickly fell apart

Why the civil war resumed, 1945–9

The war had taken a considerable toll on nationalist troops involved in pitched battles with the Japanese. The final phase of the war saw rapid development – the declaration of war on Japan by Russia and the Russian occupation of Manchuria, as well as the dropping of two atomic bombs on Japan by the USA. The USA tried to negotiate a coalition between nationalists and communists, but too much bitterness remained, and both sides hoped to take advantage of recent events. Jiang wanted to use his numerical superiority of almost 4:1 and to gain US aid for a final conflict. By 1945, Mao had assembled an army of 900 000 with additional militia forces of 2 million. The CCP had 1 121 000 members and ruled more than 95 million people. Even while negotiations were taking place, Jiang was attacking CCP forces. When the communist attacked in Manchuria in 1946, the war entered its final phase.

The ideological divide between the nationalists and communists had become too great for any real compromise. For Jiang, the communists had always been a bigger threat to traditional values than the Japanese. The communists, however, believed that the rule of the peasants and workers was inevitable, and abhorred the idea of a peacetime collaboration with Jiang's capitalist forces. The victory of communist Russia over Nazi Germany in 1945 was a major boost to communism in Asia. The war had given Mao and the communists great prestige and reputation, as well as allowing the growth of a large army. The intense hardships and bitter fighting since 1927, however, meant that it would have been virtually impossible to bring the two sides to any lasting peace.

> ### QUESTION
>
> What long- and short-term reasons led to the resumption of war. Which do you think were the most important?

> ### Borodin (1884–1951)
>
> Borodin's real name was Mikhail Gruzenberg. He was a Russian communist who had lived in the USA before the Russian Revolution of 1917, and so he was seen as a foreign-policy agent. He advised Sun Yat-Sen and arranged for arms to be sent to the Guomindang, which he believed to be a better ally for the USSR than the Chinese communists. Borodin was arrested in 1928 and returned to Russia, where he was later arrested as a foreign agent. He died in a labour camp.

5.3 What were the political, ideological and economic causes of the war?

Political and ideological causes

The growth of nationalism and communism

The upsurge of enthusiasm for Western-based reforms led both the GMD and the small Chinese Communist Party (CCP) to look to the example of Russia. There were key parallels between Russia and China:

- Both China and Russia had been ruled by autocratic emperors who claimed divine right.
- Both rulers had been overthrown by revolution.

- Both countries were large and relatively backward, both economically and socially.
- Both countries needed new ideas.

In Russia, it could be seen that the forces of reform had defeated their enemies. During the Russian Civil War, Lenin's communists had defeated the monarchist generals and thrown out the Western forces that had tried to intervene. Like China, Russia had lost lands as a result of the Versailles treaty. In Russia, there were experiments in popular democracy and social justice. It was natural, therefore, that when China's revolutionary groups were offered Russian aid and advice, they accepted. The Soviet adviser **Borodin** helped the GMD to organise its party along Soviet lines, and Russia also advised the small CCP to cooperate with the larger revolutionary group.

From 1923, a common front was established between the GMD and the communists with the aims of bringing unity to China, defeating the regional warlords and establishing Western-based reforms. As with many reforming groups, there were divisions within the GMD regarding how to go about reform. Some believed that a form of socialism offered the best chance of success. Others saw nationalism and a restoration of Chinese power and values as the key. The 1924 GMD conference adopted the three principles of Sun Yat-Sen:

- *Minzu* (nationalism)
- *Minquan* (democracy)
- *Minsheng* (people's welfare – the right for people to earn a living).

The growth of the Chinese Communist Party to 1927

Marxism had very little influence in China until the Russian Revolution. The 1911 revolution in China opened the way to different ideas, but the influential 1915 journal *New Youth*, which introduced all sorts of new theories, made little reference to Marxism. However, the Russian Revolution of 1917, which occurred in a predominantly rural neighbouring country, made Chinese political radicals more aware of Marxism. This, combined with the wave of radicalism associated with the Fourth of May Movement, led some to see socialism as a way of modernising and reforming China.

Interest in communism grew rapidly after the disillusion many felt at the terms of the Treaty of Versailles. At first this interest grew up among groups of intellectuals like Chen Duxiu, Li Dazhao and the young **Mao Zedong** at Beijing University. Marx's *Communist Manifesto* was published in a Chinese translation in 1920. Later the same year, *New Youth* magazine became Marxist. Chen Duxiu, a key figure in the Fourth of May Movement, was the main influence in encouraging Marxism. A member of a wealthy family and a university teacher, Chen had originally been a supporter of democracy, and this led him to a belief in economic equality and Christian socialism. However, he converted to Marxism in 1920.

Unlike Lenin, Chen favoured a mass party and he adapted Lenin's ideas to apply Marxism to a vast agrarian country (China had little industry and orthodox Marxism saw industrial workers as the key revolutionary group). Chen met with Russian communists, and in August 1920 the first **Chinese Communist Party (CCP)** was formed in Shanghai. There were publications, a youth league and a training centre. Groups were formed in Beijing, Changsha (by Mao Zedong) and other cities. Originally the party included

Figure 5.7   Mao Zedong (1893–1976)

He was born in Shaoshan, in Hunan, into a wealthy peasant family. He trained as a teacher and took a post as a librarian at Beijing University, where he also became an early member of the Chinese Communist Party. He worked as a communist organiser in Shanghai and organised peasant resistance in Changsha. He deviated from the party line by his belief in the peasantry as a basis for power. Mao rose to prominence during early uprisings and then in the Long March. He was effectively the leader of the communists after 1935 and proclaimed the People's Republic of China in 1949.

Chinese Communist Party (CCP): The CCP was founded in China by Mao Zedong, Chen Duxiu and Li Dazhao. Its membership grew steadily throughout the 1920s, and eventually founded the People's Republic of China, which is still in power today.

Comintern: This was an
association of nationalist
communist parties. Two
attempts had been made
to set up a permanent
organisation of socialists.
These had been called
'Internationals'. The Third
Communist International
of 1919 was formed to link
communist movements
throughout the world and
to encourage revolution.
It was dominated by the
Russian communists.

different socialist ideologies, but Chen soon turned against the anarchists and founded
the official party, based on Leninist ideas, in July 1921. He received aid from the
Russian-dominated organisation **Comintern**.

Figure 5.8 The young Mao Zedong

Historical debate:
Several historians – such
as Michael Dillon – see the
actions of the CCP during
the second half of the
1920s as being distorted
by the power struggle that
was taking place in the
Soviet Union, between the
supporters of Stalin and
Trotsky, following Lenin's
death in 1924. Certainly the
China policies associated
with Stalin help explain
CCP failures during this
period. In addition, they
led to increasing tensions
between the Soviet Union
and leaders of the CCP that,
in the 1960s, led to an open
breach between the USSR
and Communist China.

The influence of the Comintern representative was strong, but the party was committed
to working-class agitation and attempted to organise strikes – with little success. The
relatively small numbers and inexperience of the CCP members meant that in industrial
areas like Shanghai the party had little impact. After 1923, the CCP was also committed
to a Moscow-led association with the GMD, as this group was seen as the most likely
vehicle for revolution.

The CCP was still only 1000 strong in January 1924. It grew to 3000 by
October 1925 and to 58000 by April 1927. It had made some headway in
organisation, but it only grew by its association with the GMD. Its leaders tended to
be divided, and there was still no consensus about the role of the peasants.
The alliance with the GMD in the Northern Expedition of 1926 was a turning
point, giving the CCP prominence. The CCP had allies, particularly in the more
radical wing of the GMD, and it achieved influence through its organisation of
industrial workers and through peasant unrest in support of the campaign against
the warlords. Jiang Jieshi, the leader of the GMD, came to see the CCP as a threat to
his own party.

In a short time, the CCP had gone from being a small collection of academics studying
Marxist ideas to a participant in national political life, with a developed organisation.
In 1927, however, it still lacked widespread support among both peasants and workers,
and its military force was weak. Participation in the Northern Expedition brought the
CCP to the fore and led to attacks against it. These attacks brought about the Chinese
Civil War.

Economic causes

The basis of the communist ideology was a Marxist belief in the need to change ownership of the means of production. Thus economic change lay at the heart of the conflict. The communist aim was to change society by redistribution of wealth, ending the power of the landlords and capitalists and creating a new form of social democracy where the workers would dominate the means of production and therefore the state, led by their 'vanguard', the communists. In traditional Marxism, the key element was the industrial workers. In Mao's adaptation, the key was the peasants, as China's industrial development had not created a large class of industrial workers.

Figure 5.9 Modern and ancient farming methods in 1922; rapid change was taking place

Thus peasant economic hardship and discontent was the key to gaining support for the revolution. There were considerable economic grievances, as the GMD had not done much to improve poor conditions in workshops and factories. Wages were often low and the use of child labour common. The GMD was seen to favour the middle classes and industrial and commercial interests and to do little that might increase labour costs. Although conditions varied, there was a substantial amount of peasant hardship and resentment about the power and influence of landlords and the shortage of land. Famines in rural areas often met with little attempt to offer relief. As well as the long-term problems and the desire for land reform, there were immediate economic causes. The poorly paid nationalist armies often robbed and despoiled rural areas in a way that the communists, as a matter of deliberate policy did not. The problems of inflation were also intense in the period after 1945 and US aid did not always reach its destination because of the corruption of officials. Thus the communists gained more support as a party that promised reform as well as one that offered fundamental economic change and equality.

Theory of Knowledge

The role of the individual in history:

'The very fact that all history rests upon antitheses, contrasts, struggles and wars, explains the decisive influence of certain men in definite occasions' – Antonio Labriola, philosopher (1843–1904)

The historiography of modern China is dominated by studies of Mao Zedong with, now, a considerable body of revisionist writing questioning his character and impact. Can complex events be understood by biographies, or do biographies by their very nature distort explanations and give excessive weight to elements in the lives of 'great men'? Is the struggle for China best seen in terms of the personalities and policies of its dominant rivals, Mao and Jiang?

Figure 5.10 Starving Chinese peasants during the civil war

End of unit activities

1 Design a poster showing what the communists offered the people of China by the 1930s. Then use this to make a presentation to the class on the differences between nationalist and communist hopes for their country.

2 Give a presentation on the reasons for the outbreak of civil war, making a distinction between long- and short-term causes and using appropriate illustrations. Think about what you are going to present as the most important factor.

3 Put a line across the classroom. Explain the reasons why the communists survived and the war carried on so long after 1927 on cards, then arrange the cards on the line in order of importance. Ask classmates to change the order if they want – but they must give reasons for their decisions.

4 Was it inevitable that war should start again in 1945? Find out more about why talks broke down between the two sides despite US mediation.

KEY QUESTIONS

- What were the nature and main practices of the Chinese Civil War?
- What were the main events of the war and how were they influenced by technology and tactics?
- What was the significance of the mobilisation of human and economic resources and the home front?
- How significant was foreign intervention?

Overview

- The attacks on the communists nearly succeeded in crushing the movement, but enough members survived to defend relatively small areas and to use the sheer size of China to avoid being overwhelmed by the nationalists' greatly superior numbers and equipment.

- Despite the Japanese invasion of China in 1937, the nationalists still saw the communists as their biggest threat. However, an uneasy truce was agreed.

- After the defeat of Japan, the civil war resumed. The communists had increased their support during the war, and there was little chance of working together with the nationalists after bitter warfare between the two sides.

- In the renewal of the Civil War after 1945, the balance swung to the communists because of the failures of the nationalists to deal effectively with problems or to win mass support. The military tactics of the communists in avoiding pitched battles proved successful until they were strong enough to defeat the nationalists in more open conflict.

5.4 What were the nature and main practices of the Chinese Civil War?

The nature of the Chinese Civil War is hard to categorise because it went on for so long and changed its character during different phases. Initially, the war was a struggle by a minority party to survive an onslaught from the army of the established government of China. The army had successfully imposed its power over warlords, and its leaders saw the attack on the communists as an extension of this. To the extent that Jiang and his generals aimed to eradicate communism, and had little concern for civilian casualties or any sense of restraint, the Chinese Civil War also had elements of total war. However, the amount of force deployed by the communists was so limited that it cannot be seen as a normal 'war'.

As the communists who survived past 1935 gathered more resources and formed their own strongholds, the struggle became more like a war between two distinct armed forces with established domestic bases. However, resources were very unbalanced, with air power, heavy artillery and numbers of men being heavily weighted to the nationalist side. It became clear that irregular warfare in remote regions was more advantageous to smaller, well-motivated and flexible groups than to regular conscript armies, however well-equipped they might be. This pattern recurred after 1945, in Vietnam, for example. It is still the case in Afghanistan.

The situation changed after the defeat of Japan in 1945 and the acquisition of greater supplies of weapons by the communists. They were not able to field large-scale conventional forces until relatively late in the war. Even then, foreign aid favoured the acquisition of greater air resources by the nationalists. The war was total in the sense that it was clear after the negotiations of 1945 that neither side could accept a compromise of power-sharing. What resources each side had were fully deployed, but the nature of the fighting was relatively mobile and victory could not be achieved by heavy bombing of civilian areas. Resources were less important than skilled manoeuvre, but gradually the balance of numbers of men swung to the communist side. The nationalists had failed

Figure 5.11 A group of communist Chinese male and female guerrillas on parade with their spears in the 1930s

to mobilise support in the same way that the communists had. The lesson of the world wars was that it was essential for the whole population to be emotionally and physically engaged if total victory was to be achieved. With propaganda and skilled political appeals, the communists achieved this to a greater extent, and used their resources to greater effect. As was the case in many 20th-century wars, military tactics alone were not enough. Neither was foreign intervention, especially as the USA realised that no amount of aid would give the nationalists victory over a well-organised and increasingly popular communist movement.

5.5 What were the main events of the war and how were they influenced by technology and tactics?

Main events

The Encirclement Campaigns

From 1930 to 1934, Jiang launched five major campaigns against the communist areas. He intended to surround the Jiangxi Soviet and use the superior troop numbers and equipment at his disposal. In bringing the war to the communists, however, the nationalists were further from their own bases, while the communists had the home-ground advantage. Also, the communist strategy was to keep their forces mobile and exploit gaps in the nationalists' line of attack, avoiding full engagements and using guerrilla tactics to move behind enemy lines. This, and the fact that Jiang was distracted by the Japanese invasion of Manchuria in September 1931, led to a series of failures by the nationalists. In the first and second Encirclement Campaigns, the communists were able to maintain their position, but the third campaign, although a success, was more costly.

By the fourth and fifth campaigns, the situation had changed. The communists moved to more determined frontal assaults on nationalist positions, which were strengthened by the building of **blockhouses**. These were much stronger than any communist defences, and gave the advancing troops firm defensive bases from which to probe communist positions. They also enabled the nationalists to weaken the communist forces and gave the conscript soldiers of the nationalists more confidence.

However, of even greater significance was the sheer weight of numbers. By amassing not only GMD troops but also forces from the warlords, Jiang brought nearly a million men into the field – numbers approximating to the Schlieffen Plan in the First World War (see Section 2.5) and far in excess of any fighting in Spain. In September 1933, the fifth campaign began, with strictly controlled offensives establishing a front line, building blockhouses and only advancing gradually once communist counterattacks had spent themselves. In December 1933, the communists were tempted to a full open field attack on the second phase of the GMD advance, which had fewer men and poorer equipment. In April 1934, numerically superior nationalist

Fact: Manchuria was a key area of China because of its coal, bauxite and soya, and its large population. Japan occupied Manchuria in 1894 but was denied control in 1895. Japan then gained control of Port Arthur and the main railway in 1905, and overran the province again in 1931 after staging explosions on the railway and laming China. This began the long struggle between China and Japan that intensified with the Japanese invasion of 1937.

Blockhouses: Solidly constructed forts built in a chain to prevent communists escaping from the encircling nationalist forces.

forces took the communist stronghold of Guanchang. By now the five campaigns had cost the communists more men than they could replace – even if the first four had been communist victories, the war of attrition was working in Jiang's favour. By then, Jiang was receiving military aid and advice from Nazi Germany. In September, fearing a final assault that would destroy them, the communists decided to abandon the Jiangxi area.

It had taken four years of war to subdue the communist enclaves. However, total victory depended on annihilation of the Red Army – after violence on such a large scale since 1927, there was little chance of any negotiated settlement. Final victory was foiled by the communists once again using manoeuvre and movement successfully and retreating into China's huge hinterland.

The Long March

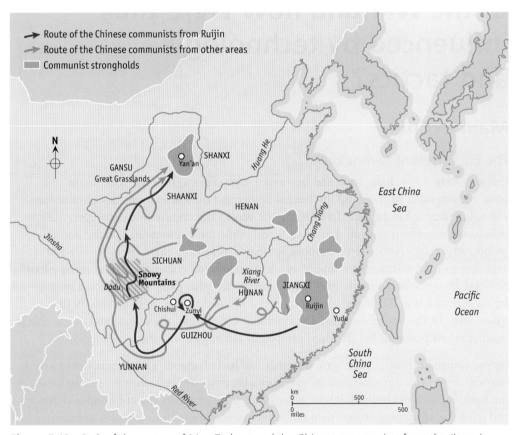

Figure 5.12 Path of the escape of Mao Zedong and the Chinese communists from the Jiangxi Soviet – the Long March, 1934–5

The Long March has become the most celebrated part of the Chinese Civil War. It refers to the withdrawal of Mao Zedong and the First (or Central) Red Army from Yudu in Jiangxi to Yan'an in Shaanxi. In this phase, the Long March lasted from 16 October 1934 to 19 October 1935. However, the withdrawal also included two other forces retreating under pressure from the Guomindang: the Second Red Army and the Fourth Red Army. The retreat was not complete until 22 October 1936, when the three forces linked up in Shaanxi.

The breakout began in October 1934, and consisted of 86 000 people and considerable amounts of weaponry and equipment, including typewriters and printing presses. The column stretched 97km (60 miles). It found a gap in the nationalist line and crossed the Xiang River, with some heavy losses.

The local warlord in Guizhou allowed the column to pass through a corridor some 48km (30 miles) wide. Guizhou province was difficult territory to cross. By the time the Reds had crossed the Xiang and suffered the hardships of the journey they were down to 30 000 people.

The final destination had not been decided – the original plan was to go north to join with forces under He Long, but Jiang had 250 000 men ready to prevent this. Mao argued at the Tongdao Conference for a move west. Mao's leadership was established when the column took Zunyi after an advance of 322km (200 miles). At a council, Mao's leadership was accepted by Zhou Enlai and Peng Dehuai. The old leaders, Otto Braun and Bo Gu, were ousted; Mao and **Zhu De** were now in charge of the campaign.

The region could not support the Red forces, so it was decided to move north and to cross the Chang Jiang (Yangtze) River. However, the approach to the Chang Jiang was dominated by the town of Chishui, which was strongly defended, and Mao faced an attack from the rear. He seriously underestimated the strength of this force and failed to defeat it.

Mao was forced to cross the Red River and drive into Yunnan, but then unexpectedly turned back into Guizhou. His movements confused the nationalists, and Mao was able to cross the Jinsha River. He did not attempt to cross the Chang Jiang and join with the larger Fourth Army of Zhang Guotao. Lin Biao, one of Mao's leading commanders, questioned the wisdom of this. Despite later myths, there were in fact several disagreements about Mao's leadership, and not all of the Long March was as heroic as it was later portrayed.

The crossing of the suspension bridge over the Dadu River was portrayed as a superhuman feat, with brave volunteers crossing a partly destroyed bridge in a race to take it from its defenders. In fact, the communists had superior machine guns that pinned down poorly armed warlord troops.

Mao then faced a small range of high mountains, called the Snowy Mountains. He could have taken a route to the west of this range, which would have followed a caravan route, but this would have taken him through a region populated by potentially hostile Tibetans. He could also have chosen a route to the east of the range, but that might have exposed the Red Army to attack by Jiang's forces. Instead, Mao chose to take a route through the Snowy Mountains that involved crossing a pass with an altitude of 4270m (14 000ft). It was a heroic passage. On the far side of the Snowy Mountains, Mao's First Army was met by a contingent of Zhang's Fourth Red Army.

Mao and Zhang agreed to move north, combining their armies closer to Russian territory, hoping they could receive supplies from Outer Mongolia. This involved crossing the boggy area between the Huang He (Yellow River) and the Chang Jiang

Figure 5.13 Zhu De (1886–1976)

He was the son of a landowner who became a fervent nationalist. From 1916, he was a warlord but joined the communists in 1922. He was a leader of the Long March and was later influential in developing guerrilla warfare. He led the Red Army after 1945. Zhu was disgraced during the Cultural Revolution but returned to high office in 1971. He is one of the most significant military leaders of the 20th century.

called the Great Grasslands – a deserted area of deadly marsh and swamp 3000m (10 000ft) above sea level. Hundreds of people died of cold and exhaustion in the single week it took to traverse the Great Grasslands.

It became clear that Zhang wanted to stop heading north, and was even prepared to arrest Mao. Mao, therefore, extricated his forces and headed north, while Zhang's forces moved south.

The last major obstacle to getting to the northern Gansu province was the Lazikou Pass, a narrow pass heavily defended by nationalist blockhouses. Mao used mountaineers to move above the defences and attacked them with grenades. On 21 September 1935, Mao reached Hadapu in Gansu, where he learned of a communist enclave in Shaanxi. It was there that he and his surviving 6000 followers made their final destination.

Figure 5.14   The Long March (for some) – Mao and his troops on the way to Shaanxi in 1935

SOURCE B

Mao did not want to go to Sichuan, to do so would mean joining up with Zhang Guodao, a veteran communist with a much stronger force of 80,000. Once they joined up with this powerful force, there would be no hope [of Mao being in power]…

The Red army for two months circled in an ever decreasing area; it had fought gratuitous battles at horrendous cost. Mao had not only brought disaster on the army under him, he was placing Zhang's army in jeopardy waiting for him in Sichuan. Huge losses were due to him jockeying for personal power.

J. Chang and J. Halliday. 2007. Mao: The Unknown Story. *London: Vintage, pp. 173 and 180.*

SOURCE C

The most important thing was that the Party had survived. And in the process of surviving the party and the Red Army had come into face-to-face contact with ordinary Chinese peasants and in many cases had impressed them. As Mao declared, the Long March had sowed the seeds of Revolution:

'It is a manifesto, a propaganda force, a seeding machine. It has proclaimed to the world that the Red Army is an army of heroes. It has announced to some 200 million people … that the Red Army is their only route to liberation.'

S. Breslin. 1998. Mao. London: Longman, p. 32.

QUESTION

Which of Sources B and C gives the more favourable view of Mao?

What evidence would support the view in Source B, and what might challenge it?

How far was the Long March a triumph for Mao's leadership?

Success of the Long March for the communists

The Long March established a heroic image of the communists that lasted for many years, and it gave them a base in Shaanxi that Jiang was unable to take. However, at the end of 1935, the communists were still a long way from victory, and the events of the Long March had revealed deep divisions, especially between Mao and Zhang.

In the event, external factors saved the communists. Jiang wanted to exterminate communist forces in Yan'an, but to do so he needed the support of local warlord troops. These were commanded by Zhang Xueliang, who was more concerned about the threat from Japan. In December 1936, Jiang flew north to prepare for what he hoped would be a final battle against the communists, but he was kidnapped by Zhang and forced into a united front against the Japanese. Communist forces were equipped by the nationalists in an 8th Route Army to fight the Japanese. The massive Japanese invasion in 1937 after the Marco Polo Bridge incident relieved the pressure on the communists, and the Chinese Civil War merged into a larger conflict.

However, even the war that Jiang fought against the Japanese did not prevent further attacks on the communists. He stated: 'Communism is a disease of the heart; the Japanese a disease of the skin.' In the autumn of 1940 there were clashes between the communist Fourth Army and nationalist troops. Jiang ordered the communists to leave Anhui province, but while the 9000-strong communist force was retreating, the nationalists ambushed them, and thousands were killed. It was clear that once the war against Japan was over, battle between the factions within China would resume.

Fact: Between 1932 and 1937, the Japanese had occupied most of the area to the north of Beijing. The boundary was a famous bridge – the Marco Polo Bridge. In June 1937, the Japanese began military manoeuvres near the bridge and, on 7 June, firing broke out between Chinese sentries and the Japanese (the Marco Polo Bridge incident). This fighting led to a larger battle in July and to a full-scale Japanese invasion of China.

KEY CONCEPTS ACTIVITY

Significance: Make a two-column table, showing the main factors that made the Long March so important for Mao on one side and for the CCP on the other.

The war after 1945

By autumn 1946, nationalist forces held the major cities in Manchuria and, although they had not driven the communists from central China and Shandong, they had forced them into defending themselves against much larger numbers. At this stage Jiang was receiving aid and support from the USA. Mao lacked air power and tanks, and the US was confident of a nationalist victory in China.

Despite this, the nationalist government faced severe internal problems – inflation was rising and, even among the propertied classes and business élites, support was dwindling. Everything depended on military success, but nationalist attacks proved indecisive. The pressure was increased at the start of 1947 by attacks on lines of communication between the separate communist areas. The communists responded with **strategic retreats** and

Strategic retreats: When an army withdraws to positions that are easier to defend, or regroups so as to be able to attack more effectively.

mobile attacks to catch the nationalists off-guard. Lin Biao effectively divided his forces, kept them mobile and continued attacks in Manchuria. Strategic misjudgements and the desire to concentrate their forces led the nationalists to lose half their territory in Manchuria and considerable war supplies by the end of 1947. Morale was dropping (see Source C).

QUESTION

What are the value and limitations of Source D for gaining an understanding the result of the war?

SOURCE D

The US consul in Shenyang wrote in May 1947:

There is good evidence that apathy, resentment and defeatism are spreading fast in nationalist ranks. The communists have ever mounting numerical superiority by using native [Manchurian] recruits, aid from underground units and volunteers from Korea. The nationalists are fighting far from home, the communists for native soil.

D. Wilson. 1991. China's Revolutionary War. London: *Weidenfeld & Nicholson, p. 150.*

Jiang failed to see the dangers of large forces being cut off in Manchuria and did not pull out. In Shandong, flexible communist tactics, surprise attacks and the use of guerrillas behind the lines hindered a major nationalist advance on the city of Linyi. When the city fell, the communist general, Chen Yi, withdrew to avoid a decisive battle – it was a hollow victory. This was followed by a surprise attack by Chen on the withdrawing forces, which prevented the nationalists from taking Shandong.

There was a huge concentration of forces against the famous Shaanxi base, but Mao did not regard territory as worth defending for its own sake – there was no Chinese Battle of Verdun (see Section 2.5). Instead, Mao began another Long March and headed north, again using China's distances as a weapon: 'Our policy is to keep the enemy on the run, to tire him out, to reduce his food supply and then look for the opportunity to destroy him.'

By autumn 1947, the communist general Lin Biao had 300 000 well-equipped soldiers in Manchuria. The communists had seized Japanese equipment and weapons as well as supplies from the nationalists. The nationalists were penned up in the cities, and the communist guerrillas had cut rail links between them. Jiang poured resources into defending the major city Changchun.

The nationalists had overextended their lines and weakened their forces by focusing on the defence of Manchuria. In August 1947, the communists began their counterattacks, retaking Shaanxi.

By 1948, the communists had the upper hand, and Jiang's forces were dangerously spread out, attempting to wage war in too many areas. Although the communists were still outnumbered, it was apparent that they had become the stronger and better-motivated force.

The first half of 1948 saw the communists consolidate their successes in northern China and Manchuria, increasingly bottling up nationalist forces in cities. However, in May 1948 there was an important turning point – the Battle of Kaifeng in Henan. This was the first major open-order battle by the communists. The city fell to them in June. Jiang brought up forces to retake Kaifeng and a conventional battle took place outside the city from late June to early July 1948. Although the communists retreated, nationalist losses were high, and they had failed to defeat the communists. Defeats and desertions had reduced the nationalist numerical superiority. The war was now being taken into GMD territory. The attack on Jinan was the beginning of the end in September 1948.

The nationalist-held cities in Manchuria fell in autumn 1948, and Lin Biao destroyed a nationalist army by brilliant rapid manoeuvres at Jinzhou. The autumn losses amounted to 400 000 – men whom Jiang could not easily replace.

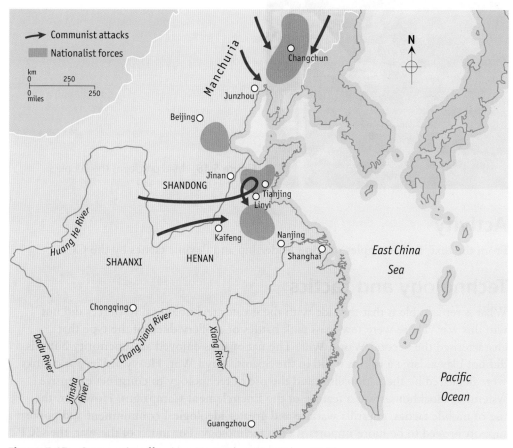

Figure 5.15   Communist offensives, September–November 1948

The fight was now for control of southern China. Some 600 000 men faced each other for the decisive battle, with the communists mobilising 2 million peasants to help supply and support their army.

The scale of the Battle of Huaihai – the largest fought in China in the 20th century – makes it one of the great encounters in world history. It should be as famous as Gettysburg, Waterloo, the Somme or D-Day. The communist commander Chen Yi might be compared to Napoleon for his skill in encircling and destroying the nationalist forces. The battle stretched across four provinces, lasted 65 days and resulted in 600 000 nationalist losses.

The balance of numbers now lay with the communists – 1.6 million to the nationalists' 1.5 million. The nationalists still held some key cities, but it was only a matter of time before these fell. In January 1949, Tianjin was taken; half a million men surrendered at Beijing. Nanjing and Shanghai fell in May, Chongqing in September and Guangzhou in October. On 1 October 1949, Mao Zedong proclaimed the People's Republic of China in Beijing.

Figure 5.16 Mao proclaims the People's Republic of China, 1949

Activity

From the text, find examples of good leadership and flexible tactics by the CCP.

Technology and tactics

What is remarkable is that the side with the greater technological resources did not win this war. There were few mass tank battles or artillery duels of the type that characterised the Second World War. The nationalists enjoyed air superiority but this did not play as large a role as it did in the Spanish Civil War. Heavy artillery and tanks were deployed by the nationalists, and the use of technology to construct extensive systems of blockhouses was a feature of the Encirclement Campaigns. However, the use of mobile tactics, guerrilla warfare and greater ideological commitment and popular support proved to be more important than technology. For much of the war, the CCP could not mount conventional battles, and this determined how the war was fought.

Mao dominated strategy after 1945

SOURCE E

Mao on war, 1947:

Strive to annihilate the enemy in mobile warfare, but at the same time pay attention to tactics of positional attack for seizing enemy strongholds and cities. In the matter of siege operations, resolutely seize all the weakly defended enemy positions or cities. In the case of an enemy position or city defended with medium strength, seize it when the opportunity arises and circumstances permit. In the case of a strongly defended enemy position, take it only when the conditions are ripe.

Quoted in D. Wilson. 1991. China's Revolutionary War. London, UK. Weidenfeld & Nicholson. p. 157.

The decisive element in the war was the change made by the communists from a largely defensive strategy to a sustained offensive through nationalist territory. The fact that the conflict was largely conducted away from the nationalists' bases of support had been difficult for them. Mao's armies did not have the same problem. Increasingly, the population was sympathetic to the communists in a way that they had not been to the nationalists. Mao's flexible tactics found gaps in the nationalist defences: they avoided strong points, they had more popular support and their forces battled with a sense of purpose lacking in the larger nationalist forces, many of whom were unwilling conscripts.

Activity

Look at Source E. Using information from this chapter, write a couple of paragraphs to show whether you agree or disagree with the argument that Mao followed this policy.

Guerrilla warfare – a major feature of the Chinese Civil War

What made the Chinese Civil War so different in nature from the war in Spain was the need for the communists to avoid pitched battles, because for much of the war they lacked sufficient troop numbers and equipment. In Spain, the republican assaults of 1937, for example, would not have been possible for the communists in China for most of the campaign. They were forced to rely on movement, on reaching remote areas difficult to attack, on winning over the civilian population and on guerrilla warfare. Guerrilla forces avoid major battles where superior enemy equipment and numbers can be decisive. The enemy is harried by small groups, forced to divert troops to deal with sudden attacks. Large numbers of troops operating together are avoided for fear of a decisive loss. Local knowledge is used to find enemy weak points and to maintain the initiative. The enemy is put on the defensive and made to feel vulnerable to sudden small-scale attacks. Guerrilla warfare was often associated with anti-colonial campaigns and was effective against armies that had technological superiority but were fighting away from their support bases.

Guerrilla warfare was often met by fierce reprisals against civilians suspected of sheltering guerrilla forces – perhaps 2 million Chinese people were killed by nationalist forces during the war. Guerrilla warfare relies on considerable commitment from its soldiers, who usually worked in smaller units than the mass armies of the First World War, for example. It was used against the Japanese and also against the nationalists. Both these forces relied on strong equipment – air power and artillery – but against both, the communists used China's sheer size to draw out the nationalists and make them vulnerable to attacks from the rear.

Much of the communists' success lay in their ability to establish bases in remote areas. Their counteroffensives depended on flexible tactics, dividing forces and penetrating enemy weak points. This could only have been done by well-motivated forces capable of acting independently. The mass armies of the GMD were not well-enough trained, motivated or led to conduct this type of warfare. By the late 1940s, it was not unusual for GMD conscripts to be tied together to prevent them deserting. Poorly paid, they often existed at the expense of the peasants, whereas communist forces were scrupulous about not living off the land without payment to or consent from the peasantry. Thus, military and political tactics were joined – flexible and responsible tactics led not only to military success but also to growing support among the peasantry, and more recruits.

It is true that the Chinese communists gained equipment abandoned by the Japanese in Manchuria. However, although a factor, this was probably not decisive in what was a relatively 'low-tech' war.

KEY CONCEPTS QUESTION

Causation and consequences: Why did the communists use guerrilla warfare rather than fight big battles? What were the main military and political results of their guerrilla campaigns?

5.6 What was the significance of the mobilisation of human and economic resources and the home front?

Mobilisation of resources

The much larger forces of the GMD depended heavily on conscription and coercion. One of the weaknesses of the army led by Jiang Jieshi was the poor pay, the harsh conditions and low levels of concern for morale. The resources of China were not put on a total war footing and there was dependence on foreign aid, particularly from the USA, which was not always well used. The resort to printing money and heavy borrowing caused inflation and fuelled discontent.

The communists were able to make use of captured Japanese resources but did not have access to a major industrial base and their manpower was less than the nationalists until the later stages of the war. The policy of not looting or stealing peasant resources was a well-considered one and although the communists did have to live off the land, they tried to do so with a degree of consent from local populations and to offer payment where possible.

Propaganda

The importance of persuasion and popular support led to a propaganda war that was eventually won by the communists. Propaganda continued to be a major feature of China after 1949. The Long March offered the chance to show the communists as heroic and self-sacrificing. The war fought between the communists and the Japanese offered the chance to portray Mao Zedong as a true patriot. Similar themes emerged after 1945, when propaganda branded Jiang as being dominated by the United States and working for foreign commercial interests. Much was made of Mao's writings and a cult of Mao developed, depicting him as an infallible war leader, a supporter of women (see Source F) and a hope for peasant justice and freedom. In addition to this, the Red Army developed an image as being not only heroic in battle but also fair to the inhabitants of the lands it occupied, and democratic and cooperative in nature.

The Guomindang failed to produce such clear propaganda messages – partly because as the ruling party it was blamed for post-war problems, and partly because the image it created had less appeal to the key element, the peasants. As communist victories increased after 1948, propaganda encouraged a wave of support that led the CCP to have more numerous forces than the nationalists for the first time.

Women

'Women hold up half the sky' was one of Mao's most famous statements. His personal life did not bear out his concern for women, but in official party programmes sexual equality was of great importance. Women did play a role in the war effort – although only 35 went on the Long March and none in her own right but rather as the partners of male participants. Nevertheless, as in the other wars covered in this book, war did create considerable opportunities for women. Nationalists, too, aimed to modernise traditional oppressive attitudes towards women, and campaigned against foot binding after 1911. Jiang's wife, **Sung Meiling**, was powerful in her own right. However, Mao's official policy took equality further.

SOURCE F

Under capitalism, the female half of the human race suffers under a double yoke. The working woman and peasant woman are oppressed by capital; but in addition to that, even in the most democratic of bourgeois republics, they are, firstly, in an inferior position because the law denies them equality with men, and secondly, and this is most important, they are 'in domestic slavery,' they are 'domestic slaves,' crushed by the most petty, most menial, most arduous, and most stultifying work of the kitchen, and by isolated domestic, family economy in general.

Mao Zedong on women. 1927. Quoted at http://sfr-21.org/mao-women.html.

SOURCE G

In order to build a great socialist society it is of the utmost importance to arouse the broad masses of women to join in productive activity. Men and women must receive equal pay for equal work in production. Genuine equality between the sexes can only be realised in the process of the socialist transformation of society as a whole.

Mao Zedong. 1955. Introductory note to 'Women Have Gone to the Labor Front', in The Socialist Upsurge in China's Countryside, Vol. I. Quoted at www.marxists.org.

Women did contribute to the war effort, and much was made of those who suffered. The case of Liu Hulan, a local communist leader who was forced to watch her comrades beheaded by GMD forces in 1947 before she was executed herself, was made famous by propaganda – but does show women taking an active and heroic role.

Figure 5.17   Sung Meiling (1898–2003)

She married Jiang Jieshi in 1927 and took a leading role in politics, founding the New Life Movement – the ideological heart of the Guomindang. She was active in the ruling council of the party, and when the war with Japan started she was an effective ambassador. She took the US by storm during a visit in 1943, addressing both Houses of Congress – a rare honour for a woman at the time. She was an effective 'first lady' of Taiwan after 1949.

Historical debate:
The commitment of Mao and the CCP to equality for women has been criticised. Ding Ling, for instance, accused them of applying double-standards and maintaining an essentially male-dominated system; whilst Xiufen Lu has claimed that the CCP exaggerated the extent of the subordination of women in pre-revolutionary China in order to make their post-1949 reforms seem more impressive.

Figure 5.18   A statue in honour of Liu Hulan, showing her as a communist heroine

Theory of Knowledge

The historian and social history:
'The general effect of the new social history has been to enlarge the map of historical knowledge and legitimate major new areas of scholarly inquiry – as for example the study of house-holds and kinship; the history of popular culture; the fate of the outcast and the oppressed' – Marxist historian Raphael Samuel (1934–96)

To what extent should school history syllabuses focus on gender issues with a distinct aim of increasing awareness of inequalities and the struggle for progress, even if it is at the expense of the consideration of political, economic and diplomatic history? Does a historian have any responsibility to use the past to highlight particular social issues? Or should a historian merely focus on what he or she considers to be the most important aspects of the period/country studied? Have women 'disappeared from history' too much because historians have chosen not to focus on their role and importance? Is 'history' (the study of the past) too narrow given the huge range of human activities in past 'history'?

Fact: Post-war problems – the most significant of which was rampant inflation – included disrupted trade and industrial production, and many Chinese felt that the government was still dominated by foreign powers.

5.7 How significant was foreign intervention?

There was remarkably little outside interference in the Chinese Civil War when compared to that in Spain. The Japanese invasion had a major effect on the civil war, forcing the nationalists to abandon their relentless attacks on the communists, as well as earning them huge prestige as the group who had waged war on the Japanese by using the power of the people. Such a reputation was not entirely justified, as the communists played a far smaller part than the nationalists in the ultimate defeat of the Japanese.

Throughout the Second World War the USA had considered China a significant ally, and between 1945 and 1947 the US made great efforts to bring the two sides together. The US secretary of state, George Marshall, went in person to try and negotiate a peace and bring about a democratic China. The USA airlifted Jiang's forces to northern China in 1945, and gave considerable sums of money, supplies and equipment. However, it did not offer direct military assistance or even, after 1948, much in the way of economic aid. Relations between nationalists and communists during the war had not been good and there was little confidence in Jiang's corrupt and unpopular regime. The US was more concerned with events in Europe during the emergence of the Cold War.

On the other side, Soviet leader Joseph Stalin did little for the communists, perhaps hoping for a stalemate and the chance to mediate, or perhaps never quite giving up his previous support for the GMD or his mistrust of Chinese communism. Also, Russia faced severe challenges of its own in rebuilding after the Second World War and in absorbing its new empire in Eastern Europe.

Thus, the critical phase of the struggle (1945–9) was fought, to a larger extent than had been the case in Spain, by the people alone.

End of unit activities

1   Produce a timeline to show the main events of the Chinese Civil War. Mark the key turning points in red.

2   Why did the communists win the war? Put all the different reasons you can think of on separate cards. On the back, write some explanations and examples. Arrange the cards in order of importance. Have you put military reasons or political reasons first?

3   Was the war lost by the nationalists or won by the communists? Discuss this question in small groups.

4   Using the table below, compare the strengths and weaknesses with those of the civil war in Spain. In each war, was the strength of the winning side more important or less important than the weakness of the losing side?

Communist strengths	Nationalist weaknesses
Support from peasants	Stole from and exploited peasants
Good morale of troops	Conscripts treated badly
Strategy of mobility and avoiding pitched battles	Concentrated forces, refused to withdraw from Manchuria
Able to attack effectively	Attacks failed
Good generals	Lacked effective leadership
Took over Japanese supplies in Manchuria and used them well	Had strong air power but could not use it
Reputation for fair dealing	Suffered from inflation and corruption

QUESTION

Why did the Chinese Civil War last so long?

Does Mao deserve his reputation as the 'architect of victory'?

5   How useful is Source H in estimating the importance of US aid in the outcome of the Chinese Civil War?

SOURCE H

Since 1945, the United States Government has authorised aid to nationalist China in the form of grants and credits totaling approximately 2 billion dollars, an amount proportionately greater than the United States has provided to any nation of Western Europe since the end of the war. In addition, the United States Government has sold the Chinese Government large quantities of military and civilian war surplus property with a total procurement cost of over 1 billion dollars, for which the agreed realisation to the United States was 232 million dollars. A large proportion of the military supplies furnished to the Chinese armies by the United States since V-J Day has, however, fallen into the hands of the Chinese Communists through the military ineptitude of the nationalist leaders, their defections and surrenders, and the absence among their forces of the will to fight.

A realistic appraisal of conditions in China, past and present, leads to the conclusion that the only alternative open to the United States was full-scale intervention on behalf of a Government which had lost the confidence of its own troops and its own people. This would have been condemned by the American people.

Extract from a speech given by US secretary of state Dean Acheson in 1949.

6   Carry out further research on the critical view of Mao in the biography *Mao: The Unknown Story* by Jung Chang and Jon Halliday (Vintage Books, 2007). Do you think this view is justified?

7   Find out more about Jiang Jieshi. Discuss how far he was to blame for the failure of the Guomindang by 1949.

Effects of the Chinese Civil War

KEY QUESTIONS

- What were the political results of the war?
- What were the main economic and social consequences?
- How did the war affect China's position in the world?

Overview

- The establishment of a communist regime in such a large area had a profound effect on both China and the world.

- The cost in terms of loss of life and damage to property was significant. There was tremendous damage in areas where the fighting was heavy. The political effects, too, had a terrible impact in terms of loss of life – for example, the programme of land distribution, with its attacks on richer peasants and landowners, led to millions of deaths, while vast numbers perished in the famine caused by the economic policies of 1958. The Chinese invasion of Tibet and the consequent repression there were the cause of many more deaths. More than 44 million people are estimated to have died as a result of the war and its consequences.

- Despite the extent of the loss of life in the war and the dislocation of China's trade and economy, China launched a series of major initiatives to increase its economic strength – major land redistribution, a Five-Year Plan and then the most ambitious policy, the Great Leap Forward.

- Mao's personal dictatorship became the main characteristic of post-1949 China. His determination to ensure a constant state of revolutionary activity culminated in the Cultural Revolution of 1966.

- China remained relatively isolated for many years after the Civil War. Relations with the USSR were not strong. A border war with India caused lasting animosity with Asia's other potential superpower. The USA and the West were distrustful after the Korean War and relations did not begin to improve until US President Richard Nixon made a historic visit to China in 1972.

- China only began to modernise its economic policies after Mao's death in 1976.

- The CCP has maintained a monopoly of political power in China since its victory over the GMD in 1949.

5.8 What were the political results of the war?

Revolution and dictatorship

The immediate political consequence of the war was that China was divided. The nationalists under Jiang Jieshi's leadership withdrew to Taiwan (Formosa) and proclaimed the Republic of China. For many years this was recognised by the West as 'China', as opposed to Mao's People's Republic on the mainland. Taiwan remains a source of tension in China to this day.

Like the communist regime in Russia, the regime that emerged in mainland China after 1949 owed much to the experiences of war. The war had brought Mao Zedong to prominence. His strategies had been proved to be more realistic than those of the nationalists, and he had transformed the traditional emphasis of communism on urban workers to a reliance on peasant support. The China that materialised after 1949 was strongly influenced by Mao himself. To support this, there was a high level of repression and China developed into a police state. By the 1960s, a cult of Mao had developed that was so strong that he has been seen as a 'Red Emperor'. Parallels can be drawn here with the successful general Yuan Shikai, who proclaimed himself emperor in 1916. For all the communist ideals and propaganda, at heart China became a dictatorship.

After Mao's death, the role of individual leaders was reduced, but the political monopoly of the Chinese Communist Party remained. Political conformity is still a priority, and opportunities for legitimate opposition remain limited. The transformation of Spain after Franco has some parallels with China, but only economically. There was no comparable development of a real constitutional democracy such as the one that emerged in Spain after 1975. Mao's successors did not aspire to his semi-imperial status, but neither did they move real power away from the party they headed.

> **QUESTION**
> Did a majority of the Chinese people benefit from the communist victory?

5.9 What were the main economic and social consequences?

Economic consequences

The changes in the countryside may have been one of the greatest developments in the history of China – if not the world – given the numbers involved. The redistribution of land to the peasants under the guidance of the CCP was a massive economic revolution. However, as a Marxist, Mao could not merely create a peasant China. In order to defend itself, the country needed an industrial base and so, in 1953, **Five-Year Plans** on the Soviet model were introduced.

The logic of this was that China's main resource – agricultural produce – needed to be controlled. So, like their Russian counterparts in the 1930s, peasants were persuaded

> **Five-Year Plans:** From 1928, the USSR had driven its economy forward by implementing Five-Year Plans. Collectivised farming supported the construction of massive industries and new towns. The impetus came from the state and the economy was state-run. China needed more industry and began its own plans for rapid development in 1953.

Historical debate:
Some historians – as well as Mao himself – have seen Mao as the CCP leader who was the first to see the importance of an alliance with China's peasantry in the revolutionary struggle. However, as pointed out by Michael Dillon, the first CCP leader to argue for a CCP-peasantry alliance was Peng Pai, who put this idea forward in the early 1920s.

Collectives: A form of agriculture in which individual plots are joined to make a large unit of farmland cultivated by the peasants jointly with state guidance. Decisions are taken communally.

Economic liberalisation: Mao's China was dominated by the Soviet model of state planning and state control. Even if this was adapted in the Great Leap Forward, the state still directed the economy. After 1976, this control was relaxed and greater stress was placed on economic growth, setting up private businesses and encouraging overseas investment and trade. This was not accompanied by a parallel political liberalisation.

KEY CONCEPTS QUESTION

Perspectives:
What are the main advantages and the main disadvantages of economic 'liberalisation'? Should social benefits be considered more important than an unrestricted market economy?

to form **collectives**. By the mid-1950s, China was a planned economy. However, the results were not entirely satisfactory in terms of production. The solution was one of the greatest economic experiments ever undertaken in world history – the Great Leap Forward (1958). This involved:

- new economic units – communes – to link agricultural and industrial production;
- massive schemes to expand agricultural production, using China's greatest resource – labour;
- an increase in steel production, to outstrip all other countries by the use not only of traditional heavy industry, but also of backyard furnaces.

Mao intended that the same selfless spirit and cooperation that had won the war would transform China's economy. There would also be a new society, with less distinction between town and country, and the model would be different from the one that existed in the USSR. The idealism and energy of the Civil War period would be rekindled and Mao would again show his wisdom and leadership.

For all his grand plans, however, Mao failed. The disruption to all aspects of the economy and the millions of deaths caused by resulting famines ravaged China. Its economic growth was retarded, not advanced, and the poor-quality steel so back-breakingly produced was worthless. China's economic growth had to wait for the post-1976 liberalisation. However, that growth has made China the greatest power in the region and is a long-term consequence of the Civil War.

Social consequences

War and social change

There was real social reform after 1949 and destruction of the power of the landowners – conducted in a brutal and murderous way. For the first time, there was wholesale land reform. Gradually the old élites were swept away. Finance and industry were nationalised. The old governing classes were replaced. There was a major change in mass education and a resulting rise in literacy. A new ruling class emerged, linked to the Chinese Communist Party.

The social change was ongoing. Feeling that in Russia the communists had established a new ruling class, Mao challenged this through the Cultural Revolution – a massive purge of the party and of authority in the 1960s. There were attempts, too, to reduce the distinction between urban and rural culture by bringing urban élites into the countryside. The authority of the old was challenged in the 1960s by using the radicalism of the young – schoolchildren and students – to challenge their teachers and revert to the enthusiasm of the early years of communism.

Since Mao's death, traditional values have become more apparent – there has been a revival of Confucianism and of family values as opposed to the veneration of the state that was widely promoted after 1949. **Economic liberalisation** has allowed the rise of business entrepreneurs and increased the gap between rich and poor.

The Revolution and the role of women

By the late 20th century, women made up nearly 40 per cent of China's workforce and a similar proportion of secondary-school students. One in five of the members of China's parliament was a woman – a higher proportion than in most parliaments in Western Europe. This is not to say the war brought about complete equality, or that

Mao's stated policies were either what he believed in or what was put into practice. However, guerrilla warfare does depend on wide participation by the people, and part of communism's appeal was social and sexual modernisation. In China before the Revolution women suffered from discrimination and were often kept under tight control within the family unit, dominated by husbands and their in-laws. The Revolution brought improvements in that bigamy was outlawed and women could no longer be sold. Forced marriages and keeping women as concubines were discouraged. Those women who had been forced into marriages were given the right to divorce. New laws gave women equal legal and educational rights. The communist regime wanted to weaken traditional family ties, which were often oppressive to women and strengthen loyalty to community and state which required greater equality. As Mao said, 'Women hold up half the sky'. Women had opportunities for responsibility within the party that had been rare before. However, despite propaganda and educational campaigns, it was not easy for centuries of tradition to be swept away with regards to women. Old attitudes persisted despite the enthusiasm of many party activists for greater equality for women.

Figure 5.19   Women were encouraged to pursue education

Theory of Knowledge

The historian and consequences:
'The law of unintended consequences, often cited but rarely defined, is that actions of people – and especially of government – always have effects that are unanticipated or unintended' – Rob Norton

How far should a historian go in linking a major event like the Chinese Civil War to 'consequences'? Is there a risk of falling into a pattern summed up by the Latin tag 'Post hoc, ergo propter hoc' – i.e., 'after this, therefore because of this'. How far does the experience of a protracted Civil War still colour the attitude of Chinese leaders today, and how far is it the more recent circumstances of China that determines policy?

KEY CONCEPTS ACTIVITY

Change and continuity: Produce a table that shows what changed and what remained the same in China after the Civil War.

5.10 How did the war affect China's position in the world?

The impact on the Cold War

There was already considerable tension between 'communism' and 'the free world' in Europe. The USA was committed to a policy of containment, and there had been confrontation with the USSR in Germany. When the communists won victory in China, the USA feared a worldwide communist threat. One result of this was a determination in the West to defend Asia against communism, and so the Cold War spread. The Korean War (1950–3) and the long struggle in Vietnam were the long-term results of US fears that there would be a **'domino effect'**, with communism spreading

Domino effect: The belief that if one country became communist then this would have a knock-on effect on its neighbours, which would also become communist, just like knocking down a row of dominos.

Fact: After Japan's defeat in 1945, Korea was divided between a communist North under Russian influence and a non-communist South, which received aid and support from the USA. In 1950, the North invaded the South and swept through the country. The United Nations (UN) came to South Korea's aid and drove back northern troops. The main UN contingent came from the USA. China sent 'volunteers', escalating the conflict, but the fighting ended when the two sides came near to occupying the original starting lines. A ceasefire was agreed in 1953, but there has never been an official end to the war.

Fact: President Nixon had been known for his anti-communist views and his support for bombing in Vietnam. His visit to Mao was imaginative and historic, although undoubtedly made with an eye to headlines as well as international peace. The visit ended a long period of hostility between the US government and China, and paved the way for changes after 1976. The visit is brilliantly portrayed in John Adams' opera *Nixon in China*.

Naxalites: A group of Maoist supporters who originated in West Bengal and are active in 20 Indian states. They have perhaps 20,000–50 000 supporters engaged in a guerrilla war against the Indian government.

to Asian countries beyond China. Not until the 1970s was there a normalisation of US relations with communist China. Until President Nixon visited Beijing in 1972, an undeclared Cold War existed between the West and China.

For years after the Civil War, therefore, China experienced hostility and isolation, and had to maintain a large defence force out of fear of Western aggression. China faced a US defensive perimeter, based in Japan, and considerable US forces in the Pacific, which were seen as a threat.

China and Russia

There was no Russo–Chinese communist bloc. Mao's first visit to Stalin was not a success and relations between the two main communist countries were strained. The rise of a strong power on Russia's border was more of a concern than a cause for celebration, and Chinese communism went in a different direction to that of the USSR.

China and Asia

China's neighbours

The emergence of a new, more centralised and powerful China was a major challenge for its neighbours, especially India, with whom China had outstanding border disputes. China's occupation of Tibet in 1950 showed that historic claims were to be pursued. In 1962, war broke out between India and China over border areas. Clashes have continued to the present day, causing much insecurity in India.

East Asia

Mao's success was seen as a victory for the ordinary people of Asia and as a blow to imperialism in the form of Jiang's Western-style regime. This view had a profound effect on the development of communist parties in Asia. It can be linked to North Korea's attempts to unify the country by attacks on South Korea in 1950–3. The Chinese Civil War also inspired the Vietnamese communists under Ho Chi Minh, as well as communist movements in Laos and Cambodia. It led to a civil war in Malaya. There were Maoist-inspired conflicts in the Philippines and Indonesia, and communism began to gain a foothold in India, with the Maoist **Naxalites**. As recently as April 2010, Maoist guerrillas in India were responsible for acts of resistance against Indian forces.

Mao's victory also led the USA to rely increasingly on Japan as an anti-communist ally, boosting US aid and support there. It led to the USA bolstering anti-communist regimes in Asia in order not to repeat the 'mistake' of 1947–9, when the US failed to offer Jiang sufficient support to defeat the communists.

China's international image

Characterised by its heroic Long March, and the feeling that the communists occupied the moral high ground, the Chinese Civil War was a considerable influence on the development of leftist sentiment worldwide. Communist regimes and parties in Africa looked to China as an inspiration, as did South American communists, particularly in Bolivia. Traditional communism, with its support from industrial workers, had less relevance than the purely peasant-based Chinese communism.

End of unit activities

1   Look at the poster below.

    •   How is Mao being shown here?

    •   What is the purpose of this source?

    •   From your own knowledge, does Mao deserve to be seen in this way?

人 间 正 道 是 沧 桑

Figure 5.20   This poster of 1970 shows the cult of Mao, extolling the benefits of the Cultural Revolution

2   Which conflict had the greater effects: the Chinese Civil War or the Spanish Civil War? Think about the categories shown in the table below and complete one similar to this to help you make a decision.

Category	Spain	China
Direct effects in terms of casualties and destruction		
Political results for the people of the country		
Political results for the wider world		
Social change		
Economic change		
Ideological change		
Change in the way in which war is conducted		

End of chapter activities

Paper 1 exam practice

Question

What message is conveyed by Source A below about the chances of the nationalists to defeat the communists? [2 marks]

Skill

Comprehension of a source

SOURCE A

To achieve the objective of reducing the Chinese Communists to a completely negligible factor it would be necessary for the USA to take over the Chinese government. It is unlikely that any amount of US military or economic aid could make the present Chinese government capable of establishing control throughout all China. It has lost the confidence of the people as reflected in the refusal of soldiers to fight and the refusal of the people to co-operate in economic reforms.

US secretary of state George Marshall, in a secret memo to President Truman, October 1948.

Examiner's tips

Comprehension questions are the most straightforward questions you will face in Paper 1 – they simply require you to understand the message presented by a source and to extract one or two relevant points that relate to the particular question and show/ explain your understanding.

As only two marks are available for this question, make sure you don't waste valuable exam time that should be spent on the higher-scoring questions by writing a long answer here. All that's needed are a couple of short sentences, giving the necessary information to show you've understood the main message of the source. Basically, try to give an overall view of the source, along with a couple of pieces of information to illustrate your points.

Common mistakes

When asked to show your comprehension/understanding of a particular source, make sure you don't just paraphrase the source (or copy out a few sentences from it). Give a couple of sentences that briefly point out the view/message of the source.

Simplified mark scheme

For each point/item of relevant/correct understanding/information identified, award one mark – up to a maximum of two marks.

Student answer

The message of Source A is that the US has lost faith in the nationalists because they thought they could not win the Civil War.

Examiner's comments

The candidate has selected one relevant and explicit piece of information from the source – this is enough to gain one mark. However, as no other reason/information has been identified, this candidate fails to gain the other mark available for the question.

Activity

Look again at the source and the student answer above. Now try to identify one other piece of information from the source, and so obtain the other mark available for this question. Look carefully at exactly why Marshall thought the nationalists were failing.

Summary activities

- Look back through this chapter and write briefly about each of the elements in points 1 and 2 shown in the spider diagram below.
- Make a chart of the outcomes of the wars listed in point 3, using the information from this chapter and any other materials available.

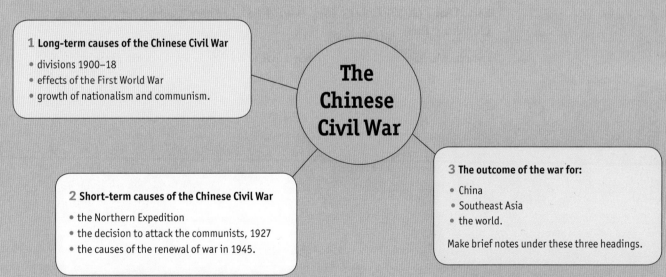

1 Long-term causes of the Chinese Civil War
- divisions 1900–18
- effects of the First World War
- growth of nationalism and communism.

The Chinese Civil War

2 Short-term causes of the Chinese Civil War
- the Northern Expedition
- the decision to attack the communists, 1927
- the causes of the renewal of war in 1945.

3 The outcome of the war for:
- China
- Southeast Asia
- the world.

Make brief notes under these three headings.

Paper 2 practice questions

1 Examine the causes of the Chinese Civil War.
2 Compare and contrast the causes and results of any two civil wars (each must be from a different region).
3 Evaluate the main economic and social results of the Chinese Civil War.
4 'Women in China achieved far more benefits after 1949 than Spanish women did after 1939.' To what extent do you agree with this statement?
5 Examine the impact of foreign intervention on either the Chinese Civil War or the Spanish Civil War.

Further reading

Try reading the relevant chapters/sections of the following books:

Chang, Jung and Halliday, Jon (2007) *Mao: The Unknown Story*, London: Vintage.

Fenby, Jonathan (2005) *Generalissimo, Chiang Kai-Shek*, London: Free Press.

Fenby, Jonathan (2009) *The Penguin History of Modern China*, London: Penguin.

Gray, Jack (1990) *Rebellions and Revolutions*, Oxford: Oxford University Press.

Hsü, Immanuel (1999) *The Rise of Modern China*, New York: Norton.

Lary, Diana (2015) *China's Civil War: A Social History*, Cambridge: Cambridge University Press

Lynch, Michael (2010) *The Chinese Civil War, 1945–49*, Oxford: Osprey.

Causes of the Iran–Iraq War

KEY QUESTIONS

- What were the main long-term causes of tension between Iran and Iraq?
- What were the short-term causes of the Iran–Iraq War?

Overview

- There was a long tradition of hostility between the areas that constitute modern-day Iran and Iraq.

- The religious divide between Shi'a and Sunnis was particularly important in causing tension and hostility, particularly as many Shi'a lived in modern Iraq, but were ruled over by a Sunni-dominated government.

- The rise to power of the Ba'th party, and its leader Saddam Hussein, in Iraq, and the Islamic revolution in Iran, which brought about the downfall of the shah and the emergence of Ayatollah Khomeini served only to increase tensions as Iran looked to spread its version of Islam to neighbouring states.

- The two powers vied with each other to dominate the region, and the turmoil that followed the revolution in Iran provided Iraq with an opportunity to stake its claim for regional dominance.

- Control of the Shatt al-'Arab waterway that separated the two countries was vital to their economies as it was the major route for imports and exports, particularly of oil. It was of particular importance to Iraq who had a very limited coastline and number of ports.

- The threat from Iran to Iraq increased following the revolution as propaganda encouraged Shi'a in Iraq to rise against the government and assassination attempts were made against ministers, but ultimately Iran wanted to bring about the overthrow of Saddam Hussein.

- Border skirmishes along the Shatt al-'Arab waterway developed into full-scale war in September 1980.

TIMELINE

1937 Dispute over Shatt al-'Arab waterway resolved.

1955 Baghdad Pact.

1958 Iraqi army overthrows the monarchy.

1968 Ba'thists seize power in Iraq.

1975 **March:** Algiers Agreement.

1978 **September:** Camp David Agreement between Egypt and Israel.

1979 **26 January:** Shah Mohammed Reza Pahlavi flees Iran.

February: Ayatollah Khomeini returns to Tehran from exile.

1 April: Islamic republic of Iran declared.

June: Iran encourages Iraqis to rise against the state.

16 July: Saddam Hussein becomes president of Iraq.

1980 **8 March:** Iran withdraws its ambassador from Iraq.

1 April: Iran attempts to assassinate the Iraqi deputy premier, Tariq Aziz.

15 April: Attempt to assassinate Iraq's minister of information.

May–August: Border clashes increase.

17 September: Iraq abrogates 1975 Algiers Agreement, claims full sovereignty over Shatt al-'Arab waterway.

23 September: Iraq invades Iran.

Introduction

This unit deals with the events surrounding the conflict between Iran and Iraq, which lasted from 1980 to 1988. It begins with an examination of the causes of the war, then considers the nature of the conflict and concludes by examining the impact of the war on the two countries.

This unit considers the long- and short-term causes of the conflict between Iran and Iraq, placing the war in the context of the two nations' political developments following the seizure of power by Saddam Hussein in Iraq and the Iranian revolution and the long-term struggles between the two countries. It will consider the extent to which the conflict was the result of the long-term tensions or whether it was the result of political and economic developments that followed the events of early 1979 in Iran. Finally, the war will be placed in the context of contemporary international political factors.

Fertile Crescent: This is the crescent-shaped area that contains some of the earliest civilisations and today includes significant parts of Iraq, Iran, Turkey, Syria, Lebanon, Jordan, Palestine and Egypt. The area flourished because of the water supplies, provided by the Tigris, Euphrates and Nile, and the agricultural resources. It contained the ancient civilisations of Mesopotamia, Assyria and Phoenicia.

Achaemenid Empire: The name used to describe the first Persian Empire, which was based in Western Iran and stretched, at its height, from the Balkans and Egypt to the Indus. It is estimated that it ruled over some 50 million people.

Babylonian Empire: The ancient kingdom of Babylon was centred around central and south Mesopotamia, modern-day Iraq, and lasted for some 2000 years.

Sassanid Empire: This was the last Iranian empire before the rise of Islam. Named after the Sassanid dynasty, it ruled from 224 to 651 CE and was the major power in the area along with the Byzantine Empire.

6.1 What were the main long-term causes of tension between Iran and Iraq?

Although the Iran–Iraq War did not begin until 23 September 1980, some have seen it as simply the continuation of a struggle that can be traced back thousands of years as Arabs and Persians attempted to dominate the Gulf (previously known as the Persian or Arabian Gulf) and the **Fertile Crescent**. Rivalry has been seen to extend back to pre-Islamic days and the struggles between the **Achaemenid** and **Babylonian** empires or to the 7th century and the Arab-Muslim destruction of the **Sassanid Empire** and the conversion of most Persians to Islam.

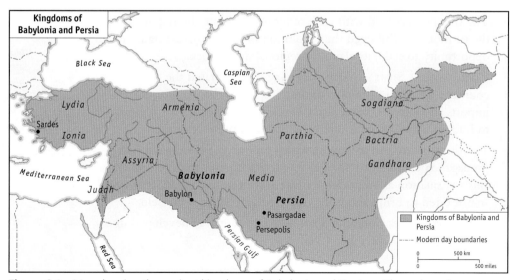

Figure 6.1 Map showing the ancient kingdoms of Babylonia and Persia, with modern-day boundaries superimposed

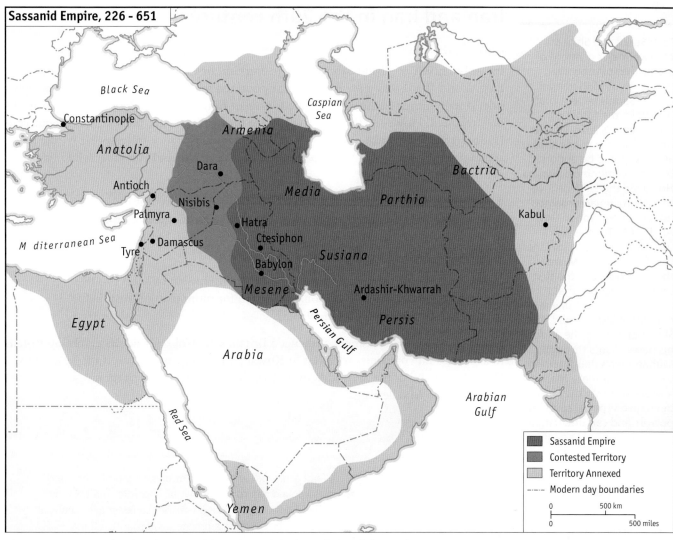

Figure 6.2   A map showing the Sassanid Empire and the boundaries of the modern states

Sunni–Shi'i struggle

There have also been some historians who have seen the struggle as religious between Sunni and Shi'i Islam. The Arabs are predominantly Sunni, while the Iranians were converted in the 16th century to Shi'ism. The Sunnis emphasise the Koran and religious law, while the Shi'a were a minority faction in Islam and trace their origins back to Ali ibn Abi Talib, who was the Prophet **Muhammad**'s cousin and son-in-law. The situation was made more complex because definitive borders did not exist between the Ottoman and Safavid empires, which controlled the area of modern-day Iran and Iraq in the 19th century. This meant that there were many Arabs of Iranian descent and many Shi'a in Iraq and these problems were made more difficult by the existence of many Shi'i shrines in Iraq.

Although these issues might explain why there were deep-seated differences between the two, there were also lengthy periods of peace, particularly in the twentieth century.

Muhammad is viewed as the last of the law-bearing prophets. He preached in Mecca from around 620 CE, urging the people to worship one god, but he was persecuted and fled with some followers to Medina. He established both political and religious authority there. By the time of his death in 632, Muhammad had been able to bring the tribes of Arabia under one religion.

213

6

Iran and Iraq in the 20th century

Iraq 1918–1970s

Iraq – but not Iran – had been part of the Turkish, or Ottoman Empire, when the First World War broke out. When Turkey entered the First World War on Germany's side, Britain promised the Arabs of the Ottoman Empire independence after the war, if they revolted. However, these promises were broken and, after the war, the League of Nations awarded mandates that 'authorised' Britain and France to temporarily rule these areas until they were 'able to stand alone'. Britain got Iraq and Palestine, while France got Syria and Lebanon.

The Arabs were outraged and, in 1920, serious revolts broke out in both Iraq and Syria. These were ruthlessly suppressed, but nationalist dissatisfaction continued in the region. Britain agreed to Iraq's independence in 1930, but retained considerable influence.

In response, the British invited Faisal, son of Sharif Hussein of Mecca to be king of Iraq and lead the government. The monarchy lasted for more than 35 years before it was overthrown by an army coup in 1958.

However, the US increasingly challenged Britain's control – for instance, forcing Britain to allow US oil companies to invest in Kuwait, a British protectorate at the head of the Gulf. By the end of the Second World War, the US had acquired a massive economic interest in the Middle East.

SOURCE A

[Britain's control of the area was not achieved] without the strong disapproval of the US State Department, which acted as spokesman for American oil interests. The US may have withdrawn politically from the Middle East … but it was not liquidating its financial and commercial interests … Eventually, by reaching a private agreement with the British owners of the Turkish Petroleum Company, two American companies – Standard Oil … and [what later became] Mobil Oil – jointly obtained an equal share with the two British companies and the French company in the Iraq Petroleum Company. Iraqi ministers had very little say in any of these proceedings.

P. Mansfield. 1978. The Arabs. Harmondsworth: Penguin, p. 233.

Although the period saw much economic growth, it was the large landowners who gained, while the majority of the population remained landless peasants. This caused widespread discontent.

There was also anger that the Iraqi Petroleum Company was British-dominated and in 1952 they were persuaded to share their profits with the Iraqi government. The people also disliked being tied to the West through the **Baghdad Pact** and this was ended after the army coup.

At the same time the **Ba'th party**, which was Sunni-dominated, gained support in Iraq, calling for Arab unity and the ending of foreign interference in the country. Their growing support enabled them to seize power in 1968. Although the party was Sunni-dominated, they initially brought Shi'a into the government in a show

Fact: Sunni and Shi'a are the two major divisions of Islam. The split followed the death of Muhammad in 632. Sunnis believe that Abu Bakr, the father of Muhammad's wife, was his rightful successor and that leaders should be endorsed by the community, or *Umma*. However, the Shi'a believe that Muhammad ordained his cousin and son-in-law, Ali ibn Abi Talib as his successor. Sunnis follow the first four caliphs, whereas the Shi'a discount the first three and believe that Ali is the second most divine man after Muhammad. The Shi'a believe that he and his descendants through Muhammad's daughters are the only legitimate Islamic leaders and that they have been given special spiritual powers and can understand and interpret the meaning and teachings of Islam.

KEY CONCEPTS ACTIVITY

Causation and Consequence: Explain why and how long-term causes helped to create tensions between Iran and Iraq.

Baghdad Pact: Initially formed by Britain, it included Iraq, Iran, Pakistan and Turkey. The US joined in 1958, and it became known as the Central Treaty Organisation. It was disbanded in 1979.

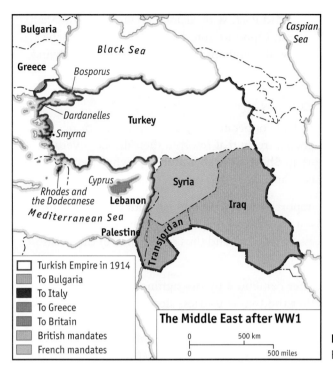

Ba'th party: The term 'Ba'th' means rebirth of Arab power. The Iraqi Ba'th party was based on a mixture of Arab nationalism and socialism, and had originally been part of the pan-Arab socialist Ba'th party, founded in Syria in 1952. This latter party had spread its influence to a number of Arab states, particularly in Iraq. The party wanted Arab unity, but in Iraq they gained support largely because they wanted the government to take a strong stand against foreign interference. Iraq's Ba'th party was at first quite small – in 1958, it had fewer than 1000 members.

Figure 6.3 Map of the Middle East after the First World War

of unity. However, the government – and particularly positions of high office – was dominated by Sunnis. The new government spent large sums of money on defence and the army and, in 1972, nationalised the oil industry. The rise in oil prices from the early 1970s allowed them to carry out many improvements in social conditions, particularly education, where children were indoctrinated in the views of the Ba'th party.

Iran 1918–1970s

Iran was ruled by a monarch, known as a **shah**. Although the country was independent, the oil fields in the south were controlled by a British company, who paid the shah for the right to operate them. At the end of the Second World War, many Iranians wanted their government to take control of the oil fields, or at least get half of the profits. The campaign was led by Mohammed Mossadeq, and in 1951 the shah was forced to appoint him prime minister. The Iranian parliament passed a law that nationalised the oil industry and put Iran in charge. The British retaliated by withdrawing its workforce, persuading other nations not to buy Iranian oil and blockading its ports. Iranian income fell, but Mossadeq was popular because he had stood up to the West. However, Britain and America, worried about Soviet influence and its threat in the area pressured the shah to dismiss Mossadeq, which finally happened in 1953, and the Iranian parliament was also closed down.

With the fall of Mossadeq, the shah moved closer to the United States, but he also introduced reforms to diminish the economic inequality in the country. He took some land away from the wealthiest and redistributed it, improved the position of women and developed education, using the profits from the oil industry. Despite these improvements, there was still a huge gap between the rich and the poor and many became angered by the country's dependence on the non-Muslim West. There was

Shah: The name used to describe the ruler of Iran, the equivalent of king, emperor, tsar or kaiser.

215

Mullah: The name used to describe some Islamic clergy who are experts in Islamic theology and law.

Shatt al-'Arab waterway: The waterway marks the boundary between Iran and Iraq. This waterway was particularly important to Iraq as most of its exports went along it and because Iraq has such a short coastline and the waterway provides its only exit to the Gulf.

Gulf: The Gulf is often referred to as either the Persian Gulf or the Arabian Gulf – countries having a coastline on the Gulf are known as the Gulf states. The most important are Iraq, Iran (known as Persia until 1935), Saudi Arabia and Kuwait. By the early 20th century, it was known that Iran and Iraq were oil-rich areas – and Britain quickly took steps to control this oil.

Fact: After the 1972 Soviet–Iraqi Treaty of Friendship and Co-operation, the shah could portray his disputes with Iraq as part of Cold War rivalry in the region. This gained further support from the US, which encouraged him to give aid to the Kurdish Democratic Party.

dislike of Iran's membership of the Baghdad Pact, with many Iranians seeing the shah as nothing more than a pawn of the West. Opposition to his regime was led by the Shi'a religious leaders within the country, the **mullahs**, who criticised the wealth and corruption of the regime.

Iran–Iraq relations in the 20th century

In the 1920s and 1930s the two states had cooperated to put down ethnic risings in their two countries and, in 1937, signed a treaty that resolved their dispute over the strategically and economically important **Shatt al-'Arab waterway**, which separates Iran from Iraq at the head of the **Gulf** (see map).

This area of water was particularly important to Iraq as Iran has a long Gulf coastline of 2000km (1250 miles), while Iraq has a coastline of only 40km (25 miles). The waterway also provided Iraq with its only access to the Gulf and thus any change in the position would severely impact on Iraq.

This peaceful co-existence was further cemented by the signing of the Baghdad Pact in 1955, which brought together the two countries, along with Britain, Turkey and Pakistan in a pro-Western defence alliance. This was important because with the development of the Cold War after 1945 and the significant oil reserves in the area, the West was keen to maintain its influence, protect its oil supplies and keep the Russians out. However, this cooperation began to break down in the 1960s.

The shah of Iran thus began to develop a closer relationship with the United States of America and this led Iraq to look to the USSR for support. Moreover, with rising revenues from oil, the shah looked to develop Iran's position as the leading power in the region and develop its role as 'the guardian of the Gulf'. It also ended its agreement with Iraq over the Shatt al-'Arab waterway, by which the frontier had been fixed at the lower watermark on the eastern side of the river, giving Iraq control over most of the waterway. The agreement had also stipulated that ships sailing in the Shatt had to have Iraqi pilots and fly the Iraqi flag.

The new Ba'thist regime, which had come to power in Iraq in 1968, worried the shah of Iran. One issue was a dispute about the Iranian province of Khuzestan, which had an Arab majority – some of whom wanted to join with Iraq.

In 1969, taking advantage of Iraq's relative military weakness, the shah abandoned the Iran–Iraq Frontier Treaty of 1937, and reopened the question of the Iran–Iraq borders – especially over the Shatt al-'Arab. He also began to give significant aid to Iraqi Kurds.

Both the shah and the US were concerned about Iraq's relationship with the Soviet Union; and, after Britain withdrew its forces from the Gulf region in November 1971, both wanted Iran to be the dominant power in the Persian Gulf. As a first step, Iran occupied some disputed 'Arab islands' in the Gulf.

The historical legacy of the 20th century

Although there had been conflicts in the past, there must have been specific factors that resulted in the outbreak of war in September. There were a number of factors that had

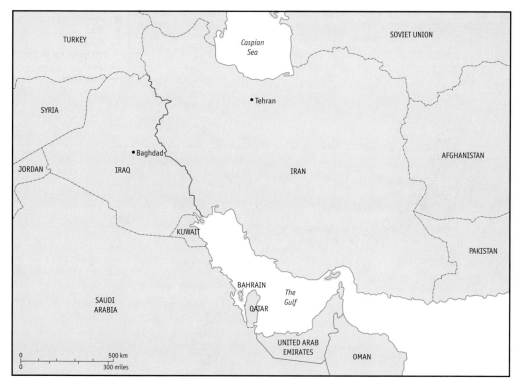

Figure 6.4 The modern-day boundaries between Iraq and Iran

surfaced in the years immediately preceding the outbreak of hostilities in September 1980 and these included:

- border disputes, particularly over the Shatt al-'Arab waterway;
- conflict with the Kurdish people;
- rivalry over leadership within the region;
- protection of their own interests; particularly oil;
- interference in each other's internal affairs.

The impact of Iran ending the agreement was put to the test as Iran refused to pay tolls and require its vessels to fly the Iraqi flag. Iraq responded by threatening to prevent Iran from using the waterway, but in April 1969 an Iranian merchant ship went through the waterway, escorted by a naval vessel and was not stopped. However, it led to a rise in tensions and soon both countries had deployed forces along the river.

The Iranians also increased the political temperature by supplying the Kurds in Iraq with military equipment. This was a major concern for Iraq as much of its oil and food came from the Kurdish area and if it were lost it would render Iraq unviable. The resulting conflict with Iran in the winter of 1973–4 brought Iraq close to collapse and forced Iraq to seek a compromise, which was reached with the Algiers Agreement in March 1975.

Fact: Kurdish people are an Iranian – not Arabic – ethnic group, with their own language. The original region of Kurdistan covers parts of present-day Iraq, Turkey, Iran and Syria. Although they are Sunnis, their desire for an independent Kurdistan has brought them into conflict with Iraqi and Turkish governments over many years. In 1946, the Kurdish Democratic Party (KDP) was set up to campaign for Kurdish autonomy. From 1961 to 1970, a First Kurdish–Iraqi War was fought over this issue. Saddam promised concessions that led to a ceasefire, with the KDP keeping their Peshmerga ('those who face death') armed forces intact – these have existed since the 1920s, and use guerrilla tactics; women form part of these military forces. During the early 1970s, the KDP received support from both Iran and the US. However, the US did not support an independent Kurdistan, but only wanted the KDP to help weaken Iraq when it had good relations with the USSR. The Kurds are the largest ethnic group in the world not to have their own state.

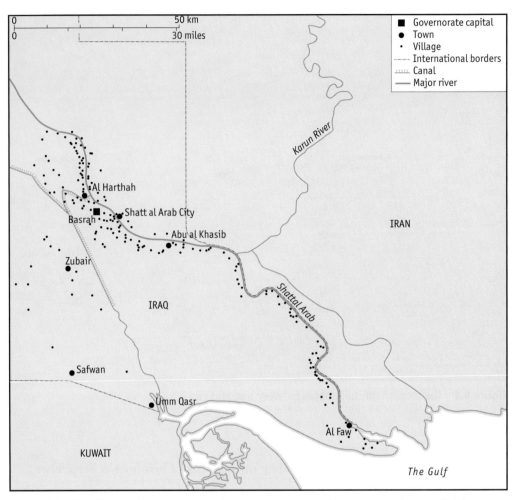

Figure 6.5 The Shatt al-'Arab waterway that separates Iraq and Iran was particularly vital for Iraqi oil exports given its short coastline

The agreement resulted in the Iraqis making numerous concessions:

- Iraq renounced claims to the Iranian province of Khuzestan.
- The boundary of the Shatt al-'Arab waterway was redrawn along the deep waterline, which meant that Iran controlled half of it.

Iraq was in no position to challenge the agreement, but instead the government looked to consolidate its authority at home and defeat the Kurds and rebuild its armed forces.

The importance of the waterway to Iraq's economy remained as Saddam Hussein made clear just before the invasion of Iran:

SOURCE B

The frequent and blatant Iranian violations of Iraqi sovereignty have rendered the 1975 Algiers Agreement null and void. This river must have its Iraqi-Arab identity restored as it was throughout history in name and in reality with all the disposal rights emanating from full sovereignty over the river.

Saddam Hussein speaking to the Iraqi parliament, 17 September 1980.

QUESTIONS
Why was the Shatt al-'Arab waterway and its control so important to Iraq?

Figure 6.6 The shah leaves Iran for medical treatment, never to return

Figure 6.7 Saddam Hussein (1937–2006)

He was born into a landless family near Tikrit. He attended school in Baghdad and was involved in opposition activity. At the age of 20 he joined the Ba'th party, becoming the assistant general secretary of the party in 1966. He played an important role in reforming the party and gained a place on the Revolutionary Command Council. He used his position on that to gradually get his rivals dismissed. In 1968, following a coup, Saddam became deputy president of Iraq; in 1979, he became president. He was one of the signatories of the Algiers Accord in 1975, which may have encouraged his hatred of Iran. His rule was often brutal – although, until 1990, he was supported by the US. After the 2003 invasion of Iraq, he was captured and put on trial; in 2006, he was hanged.

6.2 What were the short-term causes of the Iran–Iraq war?

Nature of the leaderships

Two events were of particular significance in bringing the countries to the brink of war. The first was in Iraq where **Saddam Hussein** became president, following a coup in July 1979. He had been the government minister responsible for extending control over the army and secret police, which he had achieved by increased spending, indoctrination programmes, purges, imprisonment and even execution for disloyalty. The regime had also increased persecution throughout society, targeting opponents or potential opponents, such as the Kurds and Shi'a. Therefore, by the time Saddam Hussein became president, terror and repression had become normalised as part of Iraqi life.

Within a month of his coup, several hundred had been executed – including about 500 senior Ba'thist members. Saddam's coup in 1979 was welcomed by the West, because of his hostility to the communists. In fact, evidence released after the death of **Richard Helms**, former director of the CIA, suggests that Saddam may have been a CIA 'asset' as early as 1959.

The second development was in Iran, where opposition to the shah, led by Muslim religious leaders had continued to grow. The leading opponent was the exiled Ayatollah

Richard Helms (1913–2002):

At the time of the 1963 coup in Iraq, Helms was the CIA's deputy director for plans, responsible for covert actions – and had been involved in plans to overthrow or assassinate Castro after the failed CIA-backed Bay of Pigs invasion of Cuba in 1961. In 1966, he became director of the CIA, first under Johnson and then under Nixon, helping to encourage the 1973 military coup against Allende in Chile. From 1973 to 1977, he was US ambassador to Iran.

Martial law: This when a country or area is ruled by military government and ordinary laws are suspended.

Fact: The Algiers Agreement angered Kurdish leaders who, in 1973, had met Al Haig (the White House chief of staff) and Richard Helms (CIA director) in Washington, who had promised help. The CIA – and Israel – had initially sent 'advisers' into northern Iraq to help them.

Khomeini, who having spent time in both Turkey and Iraq, was now in France, from where his speeches and writings were smuggled into Iran. In 1978 there were widespread strikes and protests against the shah, which called on him to abdicate. The government responded by using force, often killing demonstrators, which served only to increase the protests. In September 1978, the situation had deteriorated to such an extent that the government was forced to introduce **martial law**, but the demonstration that followed saw more than 500 killed. By the end of the year, some troops were refusing to fire on protestors and there was growing sympathy and support for the demonstrators and Khomeini, despite the shah's advisers assuring him he was still popular. The turning point came in January 1979 when the shah left Iran for medical treatment for cancer. He never returned and Khomeini returned from exile and declared an Islamic revolution. Thus the two countries underwent profound political changes at around the same time, the consequences of which pulled the countries into conflict.

Activity

Carry out some research on the shah of Iran and then use this information to write an obituary of him. You can decide whether you support or oppose him, and should comment on the significance of his period in office and not just write all you can find out.

Saddam Hussein and the problems of Iraq

Saddam Hussein acquired complete power in Iraq in July 1979. He faced a number of problems within Iraq, the first was the growing unrest among Shi'a and Kurds within the country, for which he blamed Iran and accused them of encouraging it. The problem of the Kurds – who lived in northern Iraq and constituted more than 15 per cent of Iraq's population – was made worse by the fact that they straddled the borders of both Iraq and Iran. They had lost much of their self-government since the Ba'thists came to power and their leaders had been exiled, imprisoned or even killed, but with support from Iran they were still a serious problem.

In May 1971, Saddam had revealed that Kurdish autonomy would be limited. Military clashes occurred in 1972, with the US providing aid to the Kurdish Democratic Party (KDP). In March 1974, Saddam's regime had forcibly 'resettled' many Kurdish families in Arab villages in southern Iraq and, by the summer of 1974, the Second Kurdish–Iraqi War began.

However, the US then worried that Iranian support for the Kurds might lead to war between the two states. So, without informing the KDP, the US set up talks between Iran and Iraq, resulting in the Algiers Agreement of March 1975.

In return for the US ending their support of the Kurds, Saddam accepted Iran's demands concerning the border in the Shatt al-'Arab waterway.

SOURCE C

Within days [of the Algiers Agreement] Iran had withdrawn all military assistance and had closed the border. Barzani's forces, heavily reliant on Iranian support, could not resist the renewed Iraqi offensives and the revolt collapsed within weeks.

C. Tripp. 2007. A History of Iraq, *Cambridge: Cambridge University Press, pp. 204–5.*

Most KDP forces then went into exile in Iran; however, thousands of Peshmerga accepted an Iraqi amnesty and surrendered, so ending the war. However, after the start of the Iran–Iraq War in 1980, Iraqi Kurds established new bases in Iranian Kurdistan.

The Shi'a presented an even greater threat as they made up the majority of the population and were dominant in the south and centre of the country. The government, meanwhile, was becoming increasingly reliant on the Sunnis – who formed only 20 per cent of Iraq's Muslims – of the north, which alienated much of the population. In fact, the main tensions between the two sects were socio-economic and political, rather than religious. Politically, the Sunni favoured Arab nationalism; while the Shi'a were less sympathetic, with many initially attracted by communism. When, after 1968, the Ba'thist regime had begun tackling the problems of poverty in the south, this had gained Saddam some support. However, this had alarmed Shi'i religious leaders who then established al-Da'wa, a clandestine organisation calling for a new Islamic order.

SOURCE D

[A]s the bulk of the population lived in the rural South, and as the overwhelming majority of these rural-dwellers were Shi'is, the Shi'i accounted for the majority of the rural poor. In addition, as the Shi'i inhabitants of the southern provinces began to migrate to Baghdad in increasing numbers, they also came to constitute the majority of the urban poor that grew up around Baghdad and other cities after the Second World War.

M. Farouk-Sluglett and P. Sluglett. 2003. Iraq Since 1958: From Revolution to Dictatorship, London: I.B. Tauris, pp. 190–1.

Once again Iran, as a Shi'i-dominated state, exploited this and played on Shi'i fears that the **secularist** Ba'thist regime was threatening their existence. Protests within Iraq in 1974–5 were the start of a wider movement, and by 1977 the government had sealed off the Shi'i shrine at Karbala, which led to further protests at another Shi'i site of Najaf. Although the scale of the protests shocked the government and led some members to call for a more lenient approach, it was the hard-line and repressive approach of Saddam Hussein that triumphed. Trials followed and five Shi'i **ulema** and three activists were executed.

Secularist: A non-religious or spiritual party, a secular regime is one that is not based on religious ideals.

Ulema: A group of Muslim scholars who have specialist knowledge of Islamic theology and sacred law.

However, realising that repression alone would not work and that the Shi'a made up the majority of the population, some concessions were made, with economic concessions offered to Shi'a living in the south. They were also allowed to join the Ba'th party, although they were prevented from obtaining high-ranking posts. It has been argued that these concessions prevented large-scale unrest, which could have threatened the existence of the regime. Second, there was the humiliation that followed the Algiers Agreement of 1975 and the desire for revenge against Iran, particularly as Iraq believed that they had been behind much of the unrest.

The third development that impacted on Iraq was the surprise announcement of a peace agreement between Israel and Egypt. This agreement worried Iraq, as they feared that they might be the next target for Israel. In response to this new challenge, Iraq approached Syria to suggest they should be united to resist the Israeli threat. A summit was held in Baghdad to discuss the problem, but hopes of an agreement were shattered

Fact: Stalin ruled the USSR after the death of Lenin in 1924. During the 1930s he used a series of 'show trials' in which people confessed to crimes that they had supposedly committed against the state and Stalin. In most instances they were innocent, but in the trials they acknowledged their guilt, which appeared to justify Stalin's brutal rule and treatment of opponents.

ACTIVITY

Construct a spider diagram to show the problems that Iraq faced in the period between Saddam coming to power and the outbreak of war. By each point, comment on the importance of the problem.

CIA: This is the USA's Central Intelligence Agency, which grew out of the Office of Strategic Services (OSS), the US secret service during World War II.

Abd al-Karim Qasim (1914–63)

He was an Iraqi general, interested in social and welfare reform. He was not a strong pan-Arabic nationalist – this eventually led to disagreements with Ba'th party nationalists. His policies often conflicted with the interests of the US and of Western oil companies.

by developments in Iran. The overthrow of the shah divided Iraq and Syria, with the latter recognising the new leadership in Iran, while Iraq saw it as a further threat to their security.

Despite these challenges and because of the nature of Iraqi government, Saddam was able to consolidate his hold on power. Having become president in 1979, he immediately set out to consolidate and increase his power. As an admirer of Stalin's use of terror and show trials, Saddam soon discovered that there was a conspiracy against both him and the state. Those suspected of involvement were arrested and the tribunal that carried out the trial was made up of his closest allies. Unsurprisingly, those accused were found guilty and 21 of them, all of whom had been his rivals, were executed. But this was not the end, as trade unions, the army, local and regional government and student bodies were also purged. At the same time, Saddam also set out to increase his popularity by increasing the salaries of judges, civil servants, the army, police and intelligence service.

Saddam had been able to assume absolute control because of the lack of tradition of constitutional government in Iraq. In 1958, a coup by army officers, led by **Abd al-Karim Qasim** had overthrown the Iraqi monarchy. This new Iraqi republic appeared to have broad popular support – and its social reforms included giving greater freedom for women. However, Qasim's limited support for Arab nationalism and his foreign policy (which included withdrawal from the pro-Western Baghdad Pact and the establishment of trade links with the Soviet Union) led Ba'thist leaders to plot his overthrow.

The US and British governments were also worried about Qasim's foreign policies. These included territorial claims against Iran – especially regarding the Khuzestan region and the Shatt al-'Arab waterway between Iraq and Iran – and threats to invade Kuwait.

In addition, Western governments and oil companies opposed Qasim's attempts to control the export of Iraqi oil and his role in establishing the Organization of the Petroleum Exporting Countries (OPEC) to reduce Western control of Arab oil.

As early as February 1960, the **CIA** had begun to plan Qasim's assassination, and to encourage Iraqis opposed to Qasim to take action. By 1962, the Ba'th party had grown – and their plot against Qasim gained US and British support. The US assistant military attaché in Baghdad, William Lakeland, helped coordinate the plotters, in return for their promise to destroy the Iraqi Communist Party.

In February 1963, Qasim was overthrown, and shot after a short trial. About 5000 Iraqis died in the fighting and the aftermath – most of them communists, hunted down by the Ba'thist secret police from lists compiled by the CIA. About 10 000 were imprisoned, many of whom were tortured.

SOURCE E

We really had the t's crossed on what was happening [in the Iraqi coup] … We regarded it as a great victory.

Comments made by James Critchfield, head of the CIA in the Middle East in 1963 – the CIA apparently saw the 1963 Iraqi coup as their 'favourite' coup.

A power struggle within the Ba'th party in November 1963 led to several important Ba'thists, including Saddam, being imprisoned. However, in July 1968, another

Ba'thist coup resulted in Saddam becoming deputy president and taking charge of all security forces. Once again, it appears the CIA helped encourage and coordinate this coup.

Moreover, these events also show that ruthlessness was not unusual and that the apparatus to establish a dictatorship was already in place as the party and the secret service were accustomed to such methods and actions.

The overthrow of the shah and the Iranian revolution

It was the return of **Ayatollah Khomeini** that changed the situation in the region. His return led to the shah's prime minister fleeing and ultimately the army declaring its support for the revolution. On his return, Khomeini opposed the provisional government that had been established in Iran following the departure of the shah and promised 'I shall kick their teeth in. I appoint the government.' He appointed his own interim prime minister, Mehdi Bazargan and demanded that since 'I have appointed him, he must be obeyed', any disobedience to him was a 'revolt against God'. Support for Khomeini grew and the provisional government collapsed so that on 30 and 31 March 1979, a referendum to replace the monarchy with an Islamic republic was passed with 98 per cent voting in favour.

In exile, Khomeini had criticised the wealth and corruption of the shah's regime, along with banks that had close ties to Western companies and the film industry, which it was claimed showed un-Islamic, foreign films. Within Iran there was support for Khomeini, as the shah's secret police, which had an increasingly tight hold on society, were very unpopular. His criticism of the old regime while in exile had been decisive and he

Fact: Kuwait had been a British protectorate from 1914 but, in 1961, it became independent. However, many Iraqis saw it as part of Iraq, separated off by Britain in the interests of foreign oil companies, such as the US-British Kuwait Oil Company.

Fact: King Hussein of Jordan, who had close links with the CIA, later confirmed that names of communists from the Iraqi Communist Party to be seized and executed were relayed to the plotters by a CIA radio station in Kuwait.

QUESTION

In what ways did domestic developments in Iraq encourage Saddam Hussein to pursue an aggressive policy towards Iran?

Figure 6.8 Crowds celebrate the return of Ayatollah Khomeini in March 1979

Ayatollah Khomeini (1902–89):

Born Ruhollah Khomeini in 1902, his father was murdered while he was still an infant. He spent his youth studying for a religious career and became an expert in Islamic law. In 1941 he published a book attacking secularism. He was exiled for criticising the shah's regime and its pro-Western policy in 1964 but then spent time in Iraq, where he denounced the Iranian regime. Following the Algiers Accord he was able to transmit his message to Iran via the increasing number of pilgrims who were now allowed to visit the Shi'i sites in Iraq. Eventually he went to France and it was from there that he would return in 1979.

Theory of Knowledge

History and the individual: Ayatollah Khomeini's return to Iran was crucial in the development of the revolution in Iran. However, it can be difficult for historians to separate key personalities from the events that occurred around them. Benjamin Disraeli, the 19th-century British prime minister said: *'There is properly no history, only biography.'* How far does your study of history support this view?

Sectarian: A member of a religious group or sect. Iran hoped to encourage the Shi'a in Iraq to rise up and overthrow the other Islamic sect in the country, the Sunnis.

created an image of himself as the moral antithesis of the shah. He won support, not just for his religious views, but for bread-and-butter or economic reasons. Despite the increasing prosperity of the last years of the shah, there were still large numbers who lived in poverty.

Although Khomeini was challenged by other groups, such as communists and more Western-style liberal groups, it was the Islamic Republican Party that dominated parliament and gained key positions in the government. Khomeini was not prime minister or president, but he held supreme power as 'supreme leader' of Shi'i Iran. His accession to power destroyed any jubilation that Iraq might have felt at the flight of the shah as it brought into power a man who wanted to spread the Islamic revolution and provided a leader for the Shi'a, not just in Iran, but also potentially in Iraq. The return of Khomeini may also have meant the collapse of a major military rival for Iraq on its eastern borders, but it also brought in a regime that wanted to spread a new revolutionary doctrine that would threaten the stability of Iraq with its support for the majority Shi'a group within the country.

Spread of the Islamic revolution

The new regime had been able to seize power and overthrow one of the most powerful military regimes in the region. They had been able to defeat a secret police and armed force of some 400 000 men at a time when widespread economic growth ought to have meant that there was support for the shah and his government, suggesting that there was something in Khomeini's message that struck a chord and won mass support.

The new regime claimed to support oppressed people and soon stated that it was their duty to 'liberate' other such groups throughout the world. They condemned the 'corrupt' governments of states such as Saudi Arabia and the Gulf states, but they also attacked what they called the atheist or non-Muslim government of Iraq, and believed that it was their duty to export their beliefs to other states, which was a direct challenge to the government in Baghdad. Moreover, they also looked to rouse the Shi'a of Iraq in support of these claims and therefore unleash **sectarian** violence in the country in order to liberate it from Sunni rule. The Iranian government also gave its support to the Shi'a al-Da'wa movement in Iraq, which had been set up in 1969 to fight for the Shi'a against what it saw as Sunni tyranny. The shah's government had agreed not to support the movement as part of the deal when the 1975 Algiers Accord had been signed, but by giving their support to the movement they had abrogated the agreement.

Ayatollah Khomeini may not have been president or prime minister of Iran, but he had the ultimate say in government and the making of laws. Khomeini argued that it was the duty of all Muslims to bring about an Islamic revolution in politics and end injustice and corruption. Soon new laws based on the Koran were passed, education was purged of its un-Islamic elements, women were forced to cover their heads and Western cultural influences, such as films and pop music, were banned. More worrying was the terror that followed, first with the trial and execution of many former supporters of the shah. This was not simply a call to establish an other-worldly state, but a practical programme to bring about an Islamic state. Khomeini called for the imposition of divine or Sharia law, which was above secular law. The establishment of a **theocratic state** was a serious concern for all neighbouring states, particularly as Khomeini had been able to overthrow a powerful military state and was now advocating world revolution, as was seen by his call on 11 February 1979, when he stated: 'We will export our revolution to the four corners of the world because our revolution is Islamic; and the struggle will continue until the cry of "there is no God but Allah and Muhammad is his Prophet" prevails throughout the world.'

Although many feared the new Islamic state, it also won much support among Muslims for standing up to the West and attacking the former ally of the shah, the United States. Following the US decision to allow the shah into the country for medical treatment, Iranian students stormed the US embassy in Tehran and took 50 staff hostages.

When Khomeini's new regime began calling for Islamic revolutions in Iraq and across the Muslim world, relations between Iraq and Iran worsened. The US then decided to support Saddam's regime and encourage a war against Iran.

Developments in the Middle East and the Gulf particularly concerned the US and the West as, after 1945, their economies became increasingly dependent on Middle Eastern oil. However, unconditional US support for Israel led some Arab states to reduce their ties with the US and the West. This declining influence in the region worried the US. When, in February 1979, the shah of Iran's dictatorship was overthrown by a mass uprising, the US 'lost' a strategically important client-state in the Gulf. Earlier, in April 1978, in Afghanistan, a military coup had ousted the king and established a left-wing government. The US decided to back fundamentalist Islamist guerrilla groups opposed to the new Afghan government; when the Soviet Union sent in troops to support the Afghan government, in December 1979, US concerns increased.

In January 1980, US President Carter issued the 'Carter Doctrine', claiming that Soviet intervention in Afghanistan threatened US interests in the Gulf – and stating that the US would use military force to protect its national interests there.

SOURCE F

The region which is now threatened by Soviet troops in Afghanistan is of great strategic importance: It contains more than two-thirds of the world's exportable oil … This situation … demands collective efforts to meet this new threat to security in the Persian Gulf and in Southwest Asia … And it demands consultation and close cooperation with countries in the area which might be threatened …

Let our position be absolutely clear: An attempt by any outside force to gain control of the Persian Gulf region will be regarded as an assault on the vital interests of the United States of America, and such an assault will be repelled by any means necessary, including military force.

Extracts from the Carter Doctrine, issued on 23 January 1980.

The Carter Doctrine showed how important the US viewed developments in the Gulf.

Although Iran's actions may have won support among many in the Muslim world, they worried Iraq, as Saddam's regime was seen by Iran as the next target for the Islamic revolution. The new Islamic Iranian state disliked the secular and nationalist nature of Saddam's Iraq, which was thus opposed to any pan-Islamic movement. The new Iran also objected to the exclusion of Shi'a from positions of power and the repression of the Iraqi Shi'a, leading to Khomeini accusing them of being atheist. Iran also supported the struggle of Iraq's Kurds; and pro-Iranian groups soon began carrying out sabotage in Iraq.

This was soon followed by one of Khomeini's broadcasts to the Shi'a in Iraq, where he instructed them to 'Wake up and topple this corrupt regime in your Islamic country

Theocratic state: A system of government where a priest or religious leader rules the country. In Iran this was the ayatollah, the most senior Islamic scholar and expert in interpreting the Koran.

QUESTION

Explain why Khomeini's call to export revolution concerned neighbouring states.

Fact: The Koran or Quran is the central religious text of Islam, which Muslims believe to be the revelation of God. Muslims believe that it was revealed by God, to Muhammad, by the angel Gabriel over a number of years, starting in 609 and concluding in 632. They believe that the Koran is the most important miracle of Muhammad and proof of his prophethood – it is viewed as the only revealed book that has been protected from corruption.

Fact: Yet, during this war against Iran, the US also sold arms secretly – and illegally – to Iran, in order to fund support of the Contras in Nicaragua.

Fact: As the US and the West saw Afghanistan as being within the Soviet Union's 'sphere of influence', the US was not initially concerned by these developments. However, Afghanistan bordered on Iran.

6

QUESTION

To what extent does this cartoon illustrate the comments made in Source F on p. 225?

Figure 6.9 A cartoon commenting on the importance of Middle Eastern oil, and the tensions in the region

before it is too late'. Thus the new regime in Tehran was directly challenging Saddam Hussein's government.

Assassinations of Ba'thist party members by Iran and attempts to overthrow Saddam

Khomeini soon made good his commitment to spread the Islamic revolution. Initially the threat to Iraq did not appear great, but widespread riots in the Shi'i towns of the oil-rich Saudi province of Hasa in November 1979 and February 1980 were an indication of what was to come. This was followed by unrest in Bahrain, while Kuwait saw terrorist attacks. The encouragement given to Shi'a elsewhere was because of the situation in Iraq, composed of 60 per cent Shi'a, and the revolution's desire to inspire them to rise up. Moreover, Iran wanted to encourage unrest in Iraq because the latter was the most powerful Arab state in the Gulf and was therefore the main threat to Iran's desire for regional hegemony as was seen by the comment of an Iranian leader: 'We have taken the path of true Islam and our aim in defeating Saddam Hussein lies in the fact that we consider him the main obstacle to the advance of Islam in the region.'

Public attacks on the Iraqi regime started in June 1979 as the revolutionary regime in Tehran encouraged the Shi'a in Iraq to rise up and overthrow the secular state. Iran also began to try and destabilise the country by resuming the supply of arms to Kurds in the north of Iraq and giving aid to underground Shi'a terrorist groups in the country. This culminated in attacks on leading Iraqi officials. On 1 April 1980, there was a failed attempt to assassinate Tariq Aziz, the deputy prime minister, and two weeks later the minister for information was also attacked. That month saw some 20 Iraqi officials killed by bombs from the underground Shi'a movement. These actions deeply worried Saddam Hussein, who was concerned by stories of Iranian plots to overthrow him, and this would play a significant role in his decision to take action against Iran. Although there had been disputes with the shah, who had opposed Iraqi interests, he had not sought to remove the Ba'th regime and was willing to accept peaceful co-existence, once he had achieved his objectives. However the new regime was very different, motivated by an uncompromising ideology and a pursuit of ambitions that were completely unacceptable to Iraq: the overthrow of its regime. Saddam Hussein's decision to launch a pre-emptive strike against Iran was made for a number of reasons, as the historian Rob Johnson explains:

SOURCE G

The failure of the pro Shah forces and the Americans [to rescue the hostages] prompted Saddam to make more effort to deal with Iran himself. The main calculation was that acting sooner rather than later was to be preferred. Saddam and his elite believed Iran was weak. The Iranian army seemed to be suffering from low morale as it endured a series of purges. There were reports of shortages of vital military equipment, stores and fuel. There was news of conflicts between the president and the ulema. Unemployment was rising, and there were shortages of consumer goods that might herald unrest. The professional middle class were disaffected. Iran had angered the Gulf monarchies with its revolutionary rhetoric, and it faced an imminent economic embargo from the West.

Rob Johnson. The Iran–Iraq War, Basingstoke: Palgrave Macmillan, p. 42.

QUESTION
Using the information in this section, what information is there that either supports or challenges the view of Rob Johnson?

Activity

Construct a spider diagram to show the problems that the Iranian revolution created for Iraq. Beside each problem, comment on how serious the threat to Iraq was.

Border disputes

The most obvious border dispute between the two countries was the longstanding argument about the border between the two states in the south. Iraq was virtually a landlocked country and its access to the sea was very narrow, yet was vital for trade and particularly the export of its most valuable resource, oil. Iran, on the other hand, had a long coastline and a significant number of ports through which it could export oil. Iraq was therefore keen to seize complete control of the Shatt al-'Arab waterway so that it had a secure outlet to the sea for its exports. Iraq might also have been hoping to be able to claim part of south-west Iran, Khuzestan, which was rich in oil. Possession of the Khuzestan coastline would increase Iraq's wealth, given the number of oilfields, and improve the strategic position of Iraq and its control of the Gulf. Saddam Hussein may also have believed that he could get the support of Iranian tribesmen and the Khuzestan 'Arabs' in the region, who would see the Iraqi's as liberators. This success might also spark other counter-revolutionary movements in Iran, which would prevent Iranian action and tie down its forces, preventing them from acting against Iraq. Success would also improve Iraqi standing in the Arab world and help it to replace Egypt as the leading Arab power.

Initially border disputes involved both governments aiding subversive groups within the other states and this resulted in a **proxy war** as both sides avoided full-scale conflict, but

Proxy war: A war that has been encouraged by major powers, but in which they do not fight, but get other groups to fight on their behalf.

used tribesmen and opponents of the regimes to topple their opponents. However, from May 1980 border disputes gradually escalated and by August they had become quite heavy and involved the use of tanks, artillery and even air strikes. These actions and the attempted assassinations served only to increase the pressure on the Iraqi government to take action. By 2 September 1980 there was fighting at Qasr-e Shirin and Iran then shelled Khanaqin and Mandali. Although there are still disagreements as to who had started the firing, it soon escalated. On 6 September, Iraq threatened to seize the Zain al-Qaws area, which it claimed it had been awarded by the Algiers Accord, and this led to the shelling by Iran of more border settlements. These increasing tensions made it very likely that full-scale war would break out and the escalation of the border disputes suggests that both sides were prepared for it.

Internal situation in Iran

In November 1979, Iranian students had seized the American embassy and held 50 American staff hostages. The result was a threat by the West to boycott trade with Iran, which would only add to the chaos facing its economy since the fall of the shah. There were also concerns in Iraq that the US might try and reach a deal with Iran for the release of the hostages, which would lead to an improvement in relations. This would make it harder for Iraq to attack, which therefore encouraged them to launch a pre-emptive strike. However, this was not the approach the US took, and on 24 and 25 April 1980, an attempt was made to rescue the hostages. This was also supposed to be the signal for the anti-Khomeini groups within Iran – who had been receiving support from Iraq and the army – to stage a coup. However, the rescue attempt was aborted and although the army attempted coups in both May and July, they failed on both occasions. The opposition also lost an alternative focus of leadership when the former shah died on 27 July. These events served to convince Saddam Hussein that he would have to deal with Iran alone.

Figure 6.10   Iranian students storm the US embassy in November 1979

This option was further bolstered by the weak hold on power that the new regime had. Iraq believed that over time the Iranian government would be able to strengthen its control and consolidate its power; therefore a pre-emptive strike would be in Iraq's best interests, particularly if this could be carried out before the demoralised army, which had been defeated in the revolution, was able to recover. The army had also been weakened by a series of purges and there were reports of a shortage of equipment and fuel. Many ordinary people in Iran were suffering, with rising unemployment and a growing shortage of consumer goods. Moreover, many of the middle class were dissatisfied with the new regime, which was doing little for them. In addition, the new Iranian regime had lost the support of the US, which had been Iran's main arms-supplier, while the vast expansion of Iraq's armed forces, financed by increased oil revenues, and the end of serious conflict in Kurdistan led Saddam to expect a quick victory.

Not only was there evidence of discontent within Iran, but the revolutionary government had also angered many of the Gulf states with its anti-monarchy rhetoric. It had also lost any chance of Soviet support as unrest in Iran had unleashed disturbances in Afghanistan. Relations with the Soviet Union were made worse by Soviet intervention in Afghanistan in December 1979, which was condemned by Iran as an attack on fellow Muslims. Therefore, not only was there disquiet at home, but Iran had angered much of the communist bloc and was therefore internationally isolated, which strengthened Saddam Hussein's position.

Strengthening of Iraqi regime

Although there were many arguments in favour of an Iraqi pre-emptive strike, there were also arguments against it. Iraq's economic position had improved dramatically. The world price of oil had risen due to a boom in 1979 and 1980, and revenues from oil exports had risen from $1 billion in 1972 to $21 billion in 1979, then $26 billion in 1980 and averaging some $33 billion per year in the months leading up to war. As a result, construction projects and improvements to Iraq's infrastructure were quickly moving ahead and living conditions were therefore improving. A war could jeopardise this.

On the other hand, the increase in revenues meant that Iraq could afford a war. The country also enjoyed good relations with the other Gulf states and, in August 1980, Saddam Hussein toured many of them to discuss the military option against Iran. He also discovered, from former Iranian leaders, that the country was in disarray, with disagreements among the leadership.

A war, particularly if successful, would also improve Iraq's position strategically and economically if the Shatt al-'Arab waterway were taken, while the possibility of gaining the oil fields in south-west Iran was also tempting. This would undoubtedly help to secure Saddam's position within Iraq and improve his standing in the Arab world. As Iran was temporarily weak, it was the ideal opportunity to reduce it and become the dominant power in the region. Moreover, the threat Iran posed to the status quo in the Gulf and to the oil interests of the West meant that he had support.

Given, therefore, the relentless attacks coming from Iran on both Saddam personally and on Iraq, Saddam Hussein was being driven towards the view that the only way to deal with the problem was militarily. Not only were there gains to be made, but Saddam was becoming increasingly fearful of Shi'a militancy within Iraq and the threat it posed to his position if they joined the Iranian revolution. His political position also encouraged a military solution. He controlled most offices of state, which meant that he determined policy.

> **QUESTION**
>
> In what ways was the new regime in Tehran a threat to stability in the region and to the interests of the USA?

It was ultimately the border disputes along the Shatt al-'Arab waterway, which turned wars of words and proxy wars into full-scale conflict. Iraq accused Iran of breaking the Algiers Agreement and demanded Iran evacuate the area. They then moved to 'liberate' these areas, which was completed by 10 September. On 14 September, the Iranian acting chief of staff announced that his country no longer abided by the Algiers Agreement, and on 17 September Iraq responded similarly, dramatically tearing up copies of the agreement. Iraq announced that it now believed it had full sovereignty over the waterway, which Iran disputed, and fighting followed. On 20 September, Iran mobilised its reserves and, on 22 September, Iraqi forces crossed the border into Khuzestan; while several of Iran's military airfields were attacked by Iraqi jets.

Activity

Imagine you are a speech writer for Saddam Hussein. Write a speech that he might have made to the Iraqi people justifying the decision to launch the attack on Iran.

End of unit activities

1 Copy and then complete the chart below to evaluate the reasons for the outbreak of the Iran–Iraq War in 1980. For each cause award a mark out of six to show how important you think the cause was: the higher the mark, the more important the cause. In the final column, explain why you gave it the mark.

Factor	Explanation of the role	Mark out of six for importance	Explanation of importance of factor
Saddam Hussein's rise to power			
The Iranian revolution			
Long-term tensions			
Religious struggle between Sunnis and Shi'a			
Border disputes between the countries			
Control of the Shatt al-'Arab waterway			

Write a paragraph explaining which was the most important factor and why

2 Explain how the Iraqi foreign minister would justify his country's decision to attack Iran.

TIMELINE

1980 **23 September:** Iraqi forces invade Iran.

25–6 October: Iraq fires missiles at Dezful.

30 November: Iran attacks Iraq's nuclear research centre.

1981 **5–11 January:** Iran launches counteroffensive.

7 June: Israel destroys Iraq's nuclear reactor at Osiraq.

1982 **10 April:** Syria closes oil pipeline to Iraq.

13 July–2 August: Operation Ramadan; major Iranian offensive to capture Basra.

1983 **2 November:** Iraq warns merchant vessels to avoid 'war zone' in the Gulf.

1984 **February:** Tanker War begins.

1985 **22 March–8 April:** Second war of the cities.

August–December: Iraqi air campaign against Kharg Island.

1986 **12 August:** Long-range missile attack by Iraq on Iran's oil terminal on Sirri Island.

1987 **January–April:** Third and Fourth war of the cities.

April–May: Kuwait re-registers tankers under USA flag and leases ships from USSR to stop attacks.

4 September: Iran fires missiles at Kuwait.

September–October: USA attacks Iranian mine-laying vessels and patrol boats; Iraq attacks Kuwaiti oil terminal.

1988 **January:** Iran attacks oil tankers.

March–April: Fifth war of the cities.

March: Iraq gasses Kurdish town of Halabja.

3 July: USA shoots down Iranian passenger plane, mistaken for a fighter.

20 August: Ceasefire starts.

24 August: Peace talks start in Geneva.

KEY QUESTIONS

- What was the nature of the war?
- What were the main events of the war?
- How important was technology in determining the outcome?
- How important was foreign involvement?
- How important was the home front?

Overview

- Iraq invaded Iran in September 1980 and initially met little resistance, which led many to think that it would be a short war. However, it lasted for longer than either the First or Second World Wars, largely because of the nature of the Iranian government, which was unwilling to make peace.

- Neither Iran nor Iraq was able to invade far into the other country and therefore much of the fighting took place around the borders, particularly near the Shatt al-'Arab waterway.

- Although Iraq had superior fire-power, and was supported by weaponry from both the West and the USSR, Iran had a larger population and was able to send in large numbers of soldiers who were willing to die for their cause.

- The nature of fighting became very similar to the First World War, with trenches being dug along the borders, the only difference being that these trenches were dug in sand not mud.

- Unable to penetrate far into enemy territory, both sides launched missile attacks against enemy cities and their civilians, known as the 'war of the cities', which brought terror, misery and death to civilians

- Attacks on oil installations and shipping were made to disrupt the economies of the countries and this drew in other nations, particularly the USA, which ultimately led to a ceasefire.

Introduction

This unit considers the nature of the war between Iran and Iraq. It examines the main events of the war and the pattern of the fighting between the two states. Consideration is given to the type of fighting that occurred, particularly the heavy reliance on infantry, and how the stalemate between the two nations encouraged the use of a range of methods, most notably attacks on civilians and the use of a range of chemical weapons. The importance of foreign support, particularly for Iraq, is considered and its discussion is linked to the ending of the war in 1988. In considering the reasons why the war ended, there is also some discussion of the impact of the war on civilians.

6.3 What was the nature of the war?

- Initially Iraq made advances into Iraq, but within a year they had been driven back to their borders.
- From 1981 to the start of 1985 it was the Iranians who launched offensives, but their gains were limited despite their numerical superiority, largely the result of using very young boys to fight.
- Neither side was able to advance far into the other country and eventually a virtual stalemate developed and a system of trench warfare followed.
- Unable to advance, Iraq launched a series of missile attacks against Iranian cities. Large numbers of civilians were killed in the 'wars of the cities'.
- Both sides pursued economic warfare and tried to disrupt the enemies' export of oil by attacking installations and then attacking shipping.
- Gas attacks were launched by the Iraqis against Kurdish settlements, which killed thousands of inhabitants.
- US involvement resulted in the sinking of a number of Iranian ships, the shooting down of an Iranian civilian aircraft that had been mistaken for a fighter and attacks on Iranian oil platforms.
- Both Iraq and Iran also attacked Kuwaiti installations.

SOURCE H

They chant 'Allahu Akbar' and they keep coming, and we keep shooting, sweeping our 50 millimetre machine guns around like sickles. My men are eighteen, nineteen, just a few years older than these kids. I've seen them crying, and at times the officers have had to kick them back to their guns. Once we had Iranian kids on bikes cycling towards us, and my men all started laughing, and then these kids started lobbing their hand grenades and we stopped laughing and started shooting.

An Iraqi officer describes the advance of Iranian boy soldiers and the nature of the fighting. Quoted in Efraim Karsh. 2009. The Iran–Iraq War, 1980–1988. London: Osprey, p. 62.

QUESTION

What can we learn from Source H about those involved in the fighting?

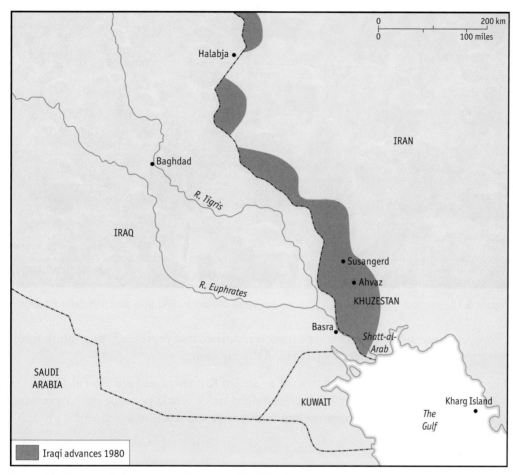

Figure 6.11 Map showing the main areas of fighting in the war

6.4 What were the main events of the war?

The Iraqi ground invasion

Instead of a quick victory for Iraq, it became an eight-year war – and a considerable drain on both countries. During the first year, Iraq had the upper hand but in 1982, Iran counterattacked and was able to drive Iraqi forces from almost all the territory taken during 1980–1. Soon, Iraq was spending $15 billion a year on the war, forcing it to borrow heavily from Saudi Arabia, Kuwait and other Gulf states.

The Iraqi ground invasion began on 22 September 1980 and was focused on Khuzestan. The aim was to separate the important Shatt al-'Arab waterway from the rest of Iran and provide Iraq with security along its southern border. At first they encountered little resistance, in part because of the lack of coordination between the military and the **Pasdaran**. Also, many of the Iranian forces were in the hinterlands or the north of the country, near the border with the Soviet Union. The Pasdaran fought with great bravery and casualties among the Iraqi forces, particularly in urban areas were high.

Pasdaran: These were the Iranian Revolutionary Guards. They had been established by the mullahs who regarded the regular army as the forces of the shah and therefore did not trust them, fearing they would lead a counter-revolution and overthrow the state.

233

Figure 6.12   A military parade in Iran with the Pasdaran demonstrating their zeal and determination

However, it was not the fierceness of Iranian resistance that prevented the country from being overrun, but the limited objectives of the invasion.

The territorial aim did not extend beyond an area of Khuzestan and the Shatt al-'Arab waterway. Saddam Hussein hoped that this limited attack would persuade the government in Iran to stop its attempts to remove him from power and reach an agreement.

Figure 6.13   Saddam Hussein just before he launched the war against Iran

Even if the Iraqis wanted to advance further, it would have been very difficult because of the nature of the terrain around the waterway, which was very marshy and would create logistical problems. The Iranians took advantage of this and flooded areas to halt the advance. Within a week of the invasion, Saddam halted the advance and announced that he was willing to negotiate, but this was rejected. However, the offer gave the Iranians time to reorganise. Moreover, it did not force Khomeini into adopting a more moderate approach, but encouraged the government to consolidate its own position and ended the conflict within the government, further strengthening the regime.

The Iranians responded by attacking Basra, destroying oil terminals near Fao and even launching air attacks against Baghdad. This caused Saddam to relaunch the attack, but by this time the Iranians were better prepared and after the fall of Khorramshahr on 24 October the war became static, so that on 7 December Saddam announced that Iraq had reverted to a defensive strategy and would not attempt to advance any further.

Stalemate

The war remained generally static for some eight months, although there were some exceptions. The most significant of these was an Iranian advance that led to one of the largest tank battles of the war, in which Iran lost some 250 tanks, either destroyed or captured, and Iraq 50. However, for much of the period, both sides used the time to reorganise, this was particularly true for Iran, which improved its defences and adopted an intensive training programme. It also overcame the communication problem between the military and the Pasdaran with the establishment of the Supreme Defence Council to run the war.

Iranian advances

The Iranians were able to go on the offensive in 1981, with the result that they drove the Iraqi forces out of Iran. This began in May 1981, when they drove Iraqi forces from the city of Susangerd, but more significant was the battle for Abadan, where after three days of heavy fighting, the Iraqis were forced to withdraw. These defeats led to a decline in Iraqi morale and this encouraged Iran to launch further offensives. Operation Jerusalem Way was launched in November, which saw the successful use of the **'human wave' tactics**.

As one Iranian reported:

'Human wave' tactics: Iran, with its much larger population, could send in large numbers or waves of new recruits who had been inspired by the revolutionary fervour of the new government. It was hoped that their zeal and the sheer weight of numbers would be sufficient to bring about victory.

QUESTION

What can we learn from Source I about the nature of the Iranian regime?

SOURCE I

Religious slogans are posted everywhere, and sometimes reinforcements arrive cheerfully carrying their own coffins as a sign of willingness to be martyred.

Quoted in Michael Scott Baumann. 2009. Crisis in the Middle East: Israel and the Arab States 1945–2007. *London: Hodder, p. 121.*

This type of warfare would later dominate the battlefield. Iranian advances led Baghdad to sue for peace, but these offers were rejected. Instead Iran launched a series of offensives, starting with Operation Undeniable Victory in March 1982 and involved more than 100 000 troops on each side. The assault began with a surprise night attack, but was soon followed by 'human wave' assaults, which quickly followed one after the other. Iran was able to maintain the momentum and – inspired and even led by mullahs – they made rapid gains so that two Iraqi divisions were destroyed, 20 000 prisoners taken and 400 tanks captured.

In April–May 1982, Iran retook Khorramshahr. Iraqi strongholds in Khuzestan were overrun using guerrilla tactics. Saddam responded by withdrawing from Iranian territory and deploying forces along the border to try and prevent an invasion.

The invasion of Iraq

Saddam Hussein used the Israeli invasion of Lebanon on 6 June 1982 as the reason for the withdrawal and offered to cease fighting so that both sides could send their forces to help the Palestinians. However, Iran – in light of their recent successes – rejected the offer and reiterated their desire to overthrow the Iraqi regime. This was followed by an invasion of Iraq, launched towards Basra, on July 13.

The Iraqi forces were well dug-in, and the number of soldiers had been increased. They resisted five consecutive attacks of 'human waves', numbering more than 100 000. Iran even sent in soldiers to mine fields without minesweeping equipment. Meanwhile, Iraq also resorted to the use of gas, albeit non-lethal tear gas. The deadlock resulted in divisions within the Iranian regime, with moderates arguing that it was wasting resources both human and economic.

Although the hardliners won the argument and attacks were launched in the direction of Baghdad in the autumn of 1982 little was achieved. The other major development during this period was the development of the **Basij**.

During 1983, Iran launched five offensives, all of which were repulsed with heavy losses. The nature of the attacks did not change: large-scale frontal attacks but without proper artillery or air support.

In 1984 Iraq announced that it would attack Iranian cities if the latter continued their acts of aggression. When, on 7 February 1984, Iran launched an attack on the northern front, Iraq had little choice but to start what became known as 'first war of the cities'. This lasted until 22 February but failed to prevent a major Iranian assault, involving some 500 000 men. The first attack, Operation Dawn, attempted to cut the Baghdad to Basra road. Iran gained some high ground about 15 miles from the road. The second attack launched towards Basra appeared as if it might break through as the Iranians crossed the supposedly impenetrable marshland and captured Majnun Island. However, the advance was finally stopped, but through the use of mustard gas and Sarin nerve gas.

Basij: This was a youth volunteer paramilitary organisation set up in 1979 by Ayatollah Khomeini. They were encouraged to fight in the war, often being given benefits in return. They took their orders from the Iranian Revolutionary Guard and were completely loyal to Khomeini. They often consisted of boys aged between 12 and 18 who signed admission forms, which were known as 'Passports to Paradise' before being given limited basic training and sent to the front, where many died.

QUESTION

Why was Iran unwilling to agree to end the fighting?

Activity

Use an atlas to plot on an outline map of Iran and Iraq the places mentioned in this section that witnessed fighting during the war. You could separate those that were attacked in the 'wars of the cities' from those involved in ground fighting.

Foreign intervention

The Iranian advances worried many and resulted in international support for the Iraqi government. The Soviet Union resumed its supply of arms to Iraq, while Egypt, Spain and Brazil also supplied materials. Perhaps most surprisingly, the USA started supplying Iraq with arms. In contrast, Iran was largely devoid of support – although with some from North Korea, Syria and Libya – and was running out of the materials built up under the shah. Some supplies also came in 1985 from Britain, China, Taiwan, Argentina, South Africa, Pakistan, Switzerland and, most surprisingly, Israel, but there was never sufficient.

The result was that the Iranian army became a virtual infantry force, which had serious repercussions for the nature of the war. The Iranians were unable to attain the 3:1 superiority needed for a breakthrough, and their lack of armour and artillery meant that they were unable to get through Iraqi lines, leading to further stalemate.

These developments also allowed Iraq to launch its first major offensive since 1980, which took place in January 1985. Iran responded with another attack towards Basra in March 1985, this time using conventional warfare rather than waves. This brought some success; not only were Iraqi casualties higher, but part of the road between Baghdad and Basra was taken and for a while it appeared Iraq might be cut in two. This resulted in Iraq using chemical weapons, including tabun and cyanide, and also launching large-scale missile attacks against 30 Iranian settlements. Iran responded and thus the second war of the cities began. This type of warfare became more common as ground assaults failed. Missile attacks were launched against civilian and industrial areas and on 15 August, Iraq attacked the oil installation at Kharg Island. Although the damage was limited, it worried Iran who responded not just by attacking towns, but also stopping shipping in the Straits of Hormuz, regardless of the cargo.

The importance of foreign intervention is made explicit in the extract below taken from *The Iran–Iraq War,* written by Rob Johnson.

SOURCE J

Foreign influence played a significant role in the conduct and outcome of the Iran–Iraq war. At the very least, foreign supplies of weapons and munitions to Iraq, the favoured recipient of external support, helped to blunt the power of Iranian land offensives. Iran, by contrast, experienced a slow decline in the quantity and quality of its arsenal. But the supply of weaponry and its uneven distribution also shaped the nature of the war, with Iraq relying on armour and airpower as force multipliers, while Iran was compelled to rely on the moral power of its manpower and the offensive. Foreign intervention, particularly that of the US navy, made the tilt of the US towards Iraq in the late 1980s more than a diplomatic gesture, and may even have been a key factor in the outcome.

Rob Johnson. 2011. The Iran–Iraq War. Basingstoke: Palgrave Macmillan, p. 180.

QUESTION

What according to Source J was the result of foreign intervention?

The battle for Fao

The battle for the Fao peninsula was a turning point in the war. Iran was able to breakthrough Iraqi defences at a number of points and take the peninsula and hold it despite Iraqi attempts to recapture it. Exploiting Iraq's determination to hold Basra, the attack took the peninsula in 24 hours. Iran was aided by bad weather, which prevented the Iraqis using air and artillery power to repulse the assault.

Although Iraq launched a massive counterattack using chemical weapons, they were unable to retake Fao, even though 10 000 Iraqis and 30 000 Iranians were killed. This encouraged a further Iranian offensive towards Kuwait, which was finally halted. However, the success of the Iranians resulted in pressure being put on Syria to rein in Iran. Moreover, Saddam Hussein's prestige had suffered. Iran was increasingly confident of being able to deal a 'final blow' to the Baghdad regime and turned down offers of peace.

As Iraq was unable to persuade Iran to make any concessions, a large-scale aerial campaign was again launched, but this time not just against civilian targets. The Kharg Island oil complex was attacked, and also the oil terminal on Sirri Island, which was 240km (150 miles) north of the Straits of Hormuz, a clear sign that Iraq had the capability to reach any target.

The war of the tankers

Iraq also increased its attacks on civilian shipping. The tanker war had initially started in 1984, although there had been attacks on each other's shipping before. The hope was that the attacks would result in Iran taking drastic action and closing the Straits of Hormuz. This would cut Western oil supplies and force them to intervene. Iran had threatened action if their shipping was stopped and the USA had also stated that it was determined to keep the Gulf open and had sent a task force to the area.

From February 1984, attacks began around Kharg Island, but Iran's response was limited, aware of the consequences. This response limited Western action and it was not until 1987, when Iraq intensified its campaign, that Iran increased its response and intimidated Kuwait. This resulted in the US offering to escort Kuwaiti ships through the Gulf and by the end of 1987, this had grown so that Iran faced a multinational armada of nearly 50 warships. This allowed Iraq to increase its attacks on Iran-bound shipping and hit their economy.

Iraqi recovery

Iran was also unable to make progress on the ground, but in April 1986, Khomeini issued a fatwa ordering victory by 21 March 1987. In response, a major offensive was launched near Basra, but again it failed. Another followed in January 1987 and although it crossed the waterway, it failed to breakthrough. Saddam was also under pressure from his generals and faced a virtual mutiny as they demanded the right to run the war as they wanted.

Having held the Iranian onslaught in early 1987, Iraq went onto the offensive using chemical weapons.

The Iranian offensive appeared to have ground to a halt as economic conditions deteriorated at home and war-weariness set in. This was further reinforced by another war of the cities, launched by Iraq in February 1988. This resulted in more than 200 surface-to-air missiles being launched and numerous air raids. Iran was unable to respond as it lacked volunteers for a ground offensive.

The change in circumstances was made clear in April 1988 when Fao was recaptured and Iran was driven out from near Basra. By July, Iraq was able to threaten invasion

Fact: Chemical weapons were used against the Kurds to prevent them from collaborating with the Iranians, with the most notable in March 1988 at Halabja, where 5000 were killed and some 10 000 injured. However, with the West supporting Iraq, there was little initial condemnation.

unless Iran withdrew from Kurdistan, which it did. Faced also by the desire to avoid a confrontation with the USA, Iran changed policy and the shooting down of an Iranian passenger plane by the USA in July 1988 allowed Iran the opportunity to avoid the impression of a comprehensive defeat and accept a ceasefire.

6.5 How important was technology in determining the outcome?

Although much of the war, particularly Iranian ground attacks, was more similar to the type of fighting associated with the First World War, there was some significant use of technology, particularly by Iraq in the latter stages of the war. The missile attacks on Iranian cities and on shipping helped to bring about the ceasefire of 1988 as they increased the already considerable suffering of Iranian citizens, as well as causing concern that other powers would intervene on an even larger scale to protect their interests – and oil supplies – in the region.

Trench warfare

From 1984, it increasingly became a war of attrition, with extensive trench networks and costly offensives designed to achieve a breakthrough. The US stepped up its military sales to Iraq – worth more than $1.5 billion – indicating the USA's determination to weaken Iran, and ensure Iraq was not defeated. Yet Iranian forces continued to launch massive offensives.

After the initial Iraqi incursions into Iran, Iraq spent much of the conflict on the defensive and preventing the fall of its second city, Basra. Much of this fighting took the form of trench warfare as Iraqi forces dug in on or near the border. Iraq was severely outnumbered by Iran's population and this was one reason that Iraq remained on the defensive for much of the war. This involved a large number of static lines aimed at bleeding Iran both in terms of manpower and resources. Faced with large human wave attacks, Iraq was able to withdraw to lines deeper within their own country and suck Iranian forces in. Once this had happened, they could then be attacked by air and artillery and driven back across the border, often having sustained heavy casualties. This tactic favoured Iraq as they were fighting close to their own bases, from which their forces could be readily supplied, which helped to maintain morale. However, it did little to break the stalemate and some have seen the war gradually resembling the First World War, but with sand replacing mud. It was hard for the Iranian forces to break through decisively as not only could Iraqi forces keep withdrawing to defensive lines further back, but Iranian forces were a long way from their supply lines and materials had to travel across mountain ranges to reach the front, slowing down any possible advance.

Human wave assaults

The use of the 'human wave' assault was adopted by the Iranians for a number of reasons. They lacked heavy weapons and artillery, but outnumbered Iraqi manpower considerably and with the revolutionary and religious zeal present in Iran following the revolution, it was possible to find, at least at the start of the war, sufficient volunteers to launch these attacks. The attack usually had three elements:

- The poorly trained Basij launched the first attack against the weakest part of the Iraqi lines, often using people to clear minefields.
- The Revolutionary Guards would follow up and break Iraqi lines.
- Mechanised forces would go through the breach to surround and defeat the enemy.

The concept of human wave assaults is similar to mass infantry attacks across a wide front, but in this instance it often continued regardless of the number of men lost. Once a weak point had been located in the Iraqi defences, more men would be poured into this. Unlike the mass attacks of the First World War, Iran did vary their tactics at times, attacking by night and using the element of surprise, deception and infiltration.

No matter how these attacks are described, they were very costly in terms of human lives, particularly for Iran, as many of the men were poorly trained and relied on their enthusiasm and zeal for success. Despite this, when they were combined with infiltration and surprise, they did bring Iran a number of victories, particularly as Iraq had often dug in their tanks and infantry to static positions, meaning that entire divisions could be surrounded. However, although this approach did bring some success, these assaults were often not supported by heavy armour and were therefore limited in the gains made. This was made worse by a lack of coordination between the army and the Revolutionary Guards.

Chemical warfare

Theory of Knowledge

The philosopher Bertrand Russell once wrote: '*I find myself incapable of believing that all that is wrong with wanton cruelty is that I don't like it.*' The use of chemical weapons raises questions of morality. When writing the history of a period, should historians just offer explanations, or should they also make moral judgements?

ACTIVITY

Use the internet to carry out research into the use of chemical warfare during the Iran–Iraq war. Why do you think it was used? What was the impact?

Chemical warfare had been used in the First World War, so it might be argued that this was not a new technical development. Moreover some of the chemical attacks used gases similar to those used in that conflict. The deployment of chemical weapons escalated as the war progressed and the type of material used more virulent as Iraq became more desperate. At first it was simply tear gas, but its success in repelling an Iranian human wave assault in 1982 served only to encourage the further use of chemical weapons.

The use of mustard gas and Sarin nerve gas were effective in halting the Iranian advance towards Basra in 1984 and was repeated in 1985, but this time included the use of tabun and cyanide. However, chemical weapons failed to have a decisive impact in the Iraqi attempt to retake Fao in 1986. In 1987, chemical weapons played a significant role in helping to drive Iranian forces from Iraq. Their use became more extensive as the generals gained more power in the conduct of the war and showed less reluctance to use this method of fighting.

However, it was not just the Iranian forces that suffered chemical attacks. In 1987 and 1988 the Kurds were subjected to a brutal chemical campaign as punishment for supporting Iranian forces. These attacks involved the use of mustard gas, cyanide and tabun nerve gas, which had a devastating impact against an unprotected civilian population.

These attacks were particularly effective. Stocks of protective clothing were limited and many Iranian troops refused to shave off their beards before wearing gas masks. In some ways, the best response of Iran was its use of these attacks as propaganda against

Figure 6.14 The aftermath of the Iraqi attack on Halabja

the Iraqi regime, particularly after taking television crews into Halabja. However, even here the impact was limited, as many powers were prepared to support Iraq, almost regardless of the methods they used, because they saw it as a bulwark against the spread of fundamentalist Islam. Therefore, it would be fair to conclude that chemical warfare played a significant role in protecting Iraqi territory from attack and substantially increasing the number of Iranian casualties.

Wars of the cities

Throughout the war, both sides launched air attacks against the other, and Iraq in particular attacked border and other major cities. It had the advantage of a rebuilt air force, largely from the help of the Soviet Union and this gave it an advantage over Iran, which due to sanctions and a lack of spare parts had curtailed its air operations.

During the course of the war there were five so-called 'wars of the cities' – with the first launched in February 1984 – that may have killed as many as 1200 civilians. One major reason for Iraq initially launching these attacks was because while every major city within Iraq was within easy range of Iranian aircraft, the two major Iranian centres of Tehran and Qom were at the extreme limits of Iraqi aircraft. The attacks on Iranian cities began as attacks on economic centres, but the limited accuracy of the missiles meant that there was little distinction between economic and population centres. However, by early 1984, as the war progressed and Iraq was unable to launch ground offensives, attacks were specifically launched against centres of population. These simply led to reprisals from Iran and ultimately resulted in United Nations (UN) mediation, which brought a temporary halt to these attacks. The early 'wars' were designed to force Iran to the negotiating table as Iraq was under increasing pressure from Iranian ground attacks, but they had little success.

> **QUESTION**
> Why did the use of chemical warfare intensify as the war progressed?

> **QUESTION**
> Why do you think there were so many 'wars against the cities'? What was their aim?

Figure 6.15 Missile attacks on Iranian and Iraqi cities often hit civilian targets and, by the end of the war, had an impact on civilian morale

Iraq then attacked economic targets in Iran – especially its oil industry. Iran retaliated by attacking Iraqi oil facilities and ships trading with Iraq – including those of Gulf states loaning funds to Iraq. If the early wars of the cities had little impact on the outcome, that was certainly not the case with the fifth war of the cities, launched by Iraq at the end of February 1988. According to Efraim Karsh, it was this that ultimately broke Iranian morale and forced them to accept a ceasefire. The missile attack resulted in a mass exodus from Tehran, which paralysed the regime and shattered national morale.

Tanker warfare

The tanker war started when Iraq attacked the oil terminal and tankers at Kharg Island. The aim was to force Iran to take drastic measures, close the Straits of Hormuz and therefore force Western powers, particularly the USA, to intervene to protect their oil supplies. The Iranians were aware of the consequences of any action and were more cautious in their response than Iraq had either expected or hoped for.

The arrival of 180 exocets from France allowed Iraq to intensify its attacks against shipping. The attacks on Kharg did have an impact on the Iranian economy, but were not enough to force it to negotiate. This was, at least in part, because Iraq lacked the means to impose a complete blockade on the movement of Iranian oil. Moreover, the glut of oil supplies meant that these actions had little impact on the world's oil markets. Iran attacked Saudi tankers in the hope that they would use their leverage with Iraq, but this policy ended when two Saudi planes brought down two Iranian planes.

The Iranian navy attempted to blockade Iraq and attacked shipping with ship-to-ship missiles, while speedboats were also used to attack tankers. It was an attack by Iranian

Historical debate:
According to Efraim Karsh, in *The Iran–Iraq War, 1980–1988*, 'the road from there to the total collapse of the military's fighting spirit was short'. However, according to Williamson Murray and Kevin Woods, writing in *The Iran–Iraq War: A Military and Strategic History*, these attacks on cities did not achieve their goals. Despite this verdict, it can be argued that the missile attacks on Iranian cities allowed Iraq to strike blows at the enemy, particularly at the time when it was unable to launch ground offensives and could therefore be used by the government to show that it was responding to Iranian offensives, which would help to maintain morale at home.

Figure 6.16   The fast boats used by the Iranians to attack shipping

speedboats on Kuwaiti shipping that led to the latter petitioning foreign powers on
1 November 1986 to help protect its shipping.

It was this that ultimately brought in the USSR and the USA, with the former offering
to charter tankers and the USA offering protection to foreign tankers reflagged and
flying the US flag. The result, according to Martin Navias and E. Hooton writing in
Tanker Wars was:

SOURCE K

Although Saddam Hussein made many mistakes, his decision to attack merchant shipping
proved extremely perceptive. The Iraqi strategy of striking merchant vessels to bring
indirect pressure upon the Iranian war effort, as well as emphasizing the international
aspect of the war, was fully vindicated, for Baghdad was able to manipulate such attacks for
[its] political aims.

Quoted in Williamson Murray and Kevin M. Woods. 2014. The Iran–Iraq War. *Cambridge:
Cambridge University Press, p. 332.*

QUESTION

Why did the attacks
on tankers encourage
the intervention of
foreign powers?

The protection given to tankers trading with Iraq – but not with Iran – did have an
impact and undermined further the already suffering Iranian economy and by bringing
in foreign powers ultimately brought greater pressure for a ceasefire.

Activity

Research the different methods of fighting that were used during the war. From the
internet put together an illustrated PowerPoint presentation of the different methods,
with a commentary as to the significance of each method.

Fact: The US had for some time been backing such Islamist fundamentalist groups in Afghanistan, in their fight against Soviet forces supporting the Afghan government.

Fact: Iraq had been developing chemical weapons, and biological weapons, since the early 1970s – often with materials and expertise purchased from various Western firms. In March 1986, the US was the only country to vote against a UN Security Council statement expressing 'profound concern' at Iraq's use of chemical weapons, and calling it a violation of the Geneva Protocol of 1925.

Fact: However, when the war began to go badly for Iraq in 1982, the USSR resumed its arms shipments to Iraq, as it feared an Iranian victory would destabilise the Middle East and, in particular, have an unsettling effect on its Central Asian republics, where the population was overwhelmingly Islamic. Thus Iraq was helped by both the USSR and the West for most of the war.

6.6 How important was foreign involvement?

Foreign involvement was important for a number of reasons. First, Western powers and other Arab states feared the spread of Islamist fundamentalism.

Consequently, although Saddam's invasion violated international law, the US and other Western states backed Iraq. This continued despite evidence of Iraqi use of chemical weapons against Iran, and its brutal campaign against Iraqi Kurds.

In addition, foreign support certainly played a significant role in the length of the war. Most importantly, foreign involvement ensured the survival of Iraq when it was under pressure from Iranian attacks from the end of 1981 to 1986, by providing the heavy weaponry and missiles Iraq needed. Foreign involvement, most notably that of the USA also helped bring an end to the war through the possibility of direct involvement against Iran in order to protect their oil supplies.

Iran received little foreign help, with the exception of Syria, who supported them because of their rivalry with Iraq. They closed the Iraqi pipeline, which ran through their country to the Mediterranean, and in return received free oil from Iran. However, in terms of military support, Iran received very little. As a consequence, parts that were needed to keep aircraft serviceable were not available and this limited the use Iran could make of air power. Moreover, they lacked the military hardware that Iraq possessed and had a limited number of missiles and heavy artillery available, encouraging their use of 'human wave' assaults. Although there were some states that did supply arms, largely to boost their own arms trade, this was never of the same magnitude as that received by Iraq. Even in 1985–6 when the USA supplied Iran with arms in return for the release of US hostages in Lebanon, this was never on the scale of those supplied to Iraq and when this was exposed (Irangate) it actually drove the USA to increase their efforts to support Iraq and contain the war.

Iraq also received support from other Arab states. This was largely because there were concerns that Iranian forces might liberate the Shi'a in Iraq and, more worryingly, spread their revolutionary Islam, to which the other states were strongly opposed. The war also intensified the Shi'a–Sunni division and reignited the old Arab Persian divide. As a result, Saudi Arabia and some of the other smaller Gulf states, such as Kuwait and Bahrain, along with Egypt and Jordan supplied Iraq with both money and arms. Jordan also provided Iraq with a port, Aqaba, through which it could export goods when access to the Gulf was cut off by Iran.

Western powers and the USSR also provided aid to Iraq. When the war began, the USSR suspended arms sales to Iraq as it was also trying to improve its relations with Iran, with which it shared a common border. This led Iraq to establish closer ties with the West – especially with the USA. On 20 December 1983, Donald Rumsfeld, special envoy to US President Reagan, met Saddam in Baghdad and presented him with a present from Reagan.

On 24 March 1984, Rumsfeld returned to Iraq – on that same day, it was reported in the UN that Iraq had used mustard gas, laced with a nerve agent, against Iranian forces.

Unlike Iran, Iraq was able to get the parts it needed to maintain its air force and this allowed it to maintain air superiority throughout the war. This was crucial for Iraqi

Figure 6.17 A photo from television footage of Donald Rumsfeld, left, shaking hands with Saddam, on a visit to Iraq, in December 1983. The Iran–Iraq War had been going for three years by then

morale at home when they were unable to launch ground offensives. These attacks were also made possible by the supply of Western missiles, which were used in the 'wars of the cities' and did much to damage Iranian morale. Of the Western powers, it was not just the USA that provided aid, but also France and Germany.

Western powers were worried by the possibility of Iranian success and once the Iranian counterattack appeared to have a chance of success and an advance on Baghdad, Western involvement increased. As with the Gulf states, the thought of Iran controlling the region terrified the USA, as they might then be able to control world oil prices given the large amount of supplies they would control. It might also lead to the collapse of other pro-Western states in the region, which would be a threat to security. As a result, the USA provided Iraq with satellite information about the movement of Iranian troops. They also provided Iraq with the materials that were later used to produce the chemical weapons and, just like the Arab states, turned a blind eye when they were used, putting their own interests first. The USSR also resumed arms supplies to Iraq, perhaps fearful of France becoming too influential and taking over the USSR's traditional role as the main supporter of Iraq, but they also feared the spread of revolutionary Islam to its own regions, having witnessed first-hand the problems it could cause in Afghanistan.

However, perhaps the most important contribution of foreign involvement in the outcome of the war was involvement in the 'tanker wars'. Much of the war was focused on the Gulf, through which the oil of both Iraq and Iran was exported. Although Iraq had air superiority, the Iranian navy was much stronger. The Iranians were able to cut off the Iraqi access to the Gulf through the Shatt al-'Arab waterway and thus prevent exports through the Gulf. It was this that ultimately brought the USA in and led to the possibility of a direct conflict between Iran and the USA. Saddam Hussein certainly did all he could to encourage this conflict, but for much of the war Iran did not respond to the provocations.

However, by 1987, with Iranian ground offensives having failed and subject to attack on its shipping and oil installations, Iran was under greater pressure and did attack foreign vessels. This brought the USA to the Gulf in order to offer protection to Iraqi shipping and to reflag and protect Kuwaiti tankers. The USA – along with Britain and France – sent ships to stop Iran's 'tanker war'. There were several clashes between USA and Iranian naval forces during 1987. The USA captured and destroyed Iranian mine-laying vessels and sank patrol boats, further limiting Iran's ability to conduct war. By 1988, the USA had destroyed most of Iran's navy. The combined effects of Iraq's attacks on its oil industry,

Fact: In July 1988, a US warship – in Iranian waters – shot down an Iranian passenger airliner, killing almost 300 civilians. They had apparently mistaken it for a fighter plane.

and the USA's increasing involvement in the Gulf on Iraq's side, eventually forced Iran, in August 1988, to accept the terms of a UN ceasefire. By then, one estimate is that more than 500 000 Iraqi and Iranian troops, as well as civilians, had died in this war.

It was not just the military contribution of the USA that was important in bringing about an end to the war, but its pursuit of a dual strategy. Not only did the USA protect shipping, but it also engineered the passing of UN Security Council Resolution 598 of July 1987, which called for an end to the conflict, and then followed this with the 'second resolution', which called for a UN enforced arms embargo on Iran for its failure to abide by Resolution 598. Iran had always rejected offers of a ceasefire, but given the military pressures and domestic disquiet and declining morale, they were under increased pressure and now faced the prospect of a direct war with the USA. However, any acceptance of a peace deal would defeat Iran's determination to remove the Baghdad regime and spread its version of Islam. Ultimately it was the shooting down by the USA of a civilian Iranian plane on 3 July 1988 that provided Iran with a way out of the conundrum. As Karsh has argued: 'It provided the moral cover of martyrdom and suffering in the face of an unjust superior force that allowed the regime to camouflage the comprehensive defeat of its imperial vision.'

It allowed the regime, after much recrimination, to agree to a ceasefire and on 17 July a letter was sent to the UN secretary-general accepting the proposal. It could be argued that with their economy in ruins and a lack of martyrs willing to fight they had little choice, but the prospect of a full-scale war with the USA may have been the most important reason for their agreement.

KEY CONCEPTS QUESTION

Significance: In what ways was foreign involvement important to the outcome of the war?

6.7 How important was the home front?

In many ways it could be argued that it was the longevity of the war and its impact on the home front that ultimately led to the ceasefire in 1988. Initially Iran had used the war to strengthen the position of the revolutionary government. A policy of **'total war'** was followed from the very outset as the government attempted to mobilise the whole nation in pursuit of **'jihad'**. Workers had a day's pay deducted each month to help pay for the war and there were mass campaigns to persuade people to donate food and money. Non-essential imports were also stopped. These campaigns were initially quite popular, as shown by the number of volunteers, but this did not last. Internal opposition grew during the war, reflected in the decline of volunteers to fight, particularly once stories of the massacres that accompanied the wave assaults began to circulate. This was also accompanied by a collapsing economy and a decline in living standards, with one in two unemployed by 1987. Morale plunged even further when the government appeared unable to prevent the missile attacks on cities and this played a major role in the decision to accept the ceasefire in 1988.

Total war: A war in which all the resources of a state are used; this includes economic power, civilian forces and propaganda as well as military force. It is also unrestricted in terms of the weapons used and the targets hit, often disregarding the usual laws of war.

Jihad: An Arabic word that means 'struggle'. It usually means a struggle to remove an external threat to Muslim lands, but can also be used to describe an internal struggle and even a personal struggle against sin.

The desire of the Iranian government for a vicious and continuous war to overthrow the government in Iraq lost its appeal, despite such sentiments and it appears that the government in Tehran had stretched to the limits Iran's willingness for suffering.

In Iraq, the situation was somewhat different. Even through the period of Iranian advances and the long stalemate, the **guns and butter** policy ensured that the impact of the war was scarcely felt by the civilian population. Development plans that had started before the war continued and the finances from the expanded budget were used for civilian imports, which prevented commodity shortages. Daily life appeared to be unaffected as the blackouts that were imposed at the start of the conflict were soon withdrawn once the majority of the Iranian air force had been disabled or destroyed. This policy did much to eliminate potential domestic opposition and care was also taken to cultivate the support of Shi'a, who it was feared might support Iran. The regime ensured that the high standard of living of the officer corps was improved further, while bereaved families earned a free car, plot of land and an interest-free loan to build a house. All of these policies did much to retain support and while it was impossible to deny the large number of casualties, the population was generally shielded from the impact of the war and morale was maintained.

However, the invasion by Iran did result in guns and butter policy being abandoned as foreign reserves collapsed and the government was forced to cut back on non-essential spending. Despite this, Saddam was able to mobilise Iraqi society and with the threat to the homeland now real, the government was able to rally the nation. They portrayed the nation as defending the Arab world against the fundamentalist Persians. He was also able to win financial and logistical support from the Saudis and Kuwait, which allowed Iraq to weather the economic challenges it faced. This was in contrast to Iran and therefore, despite brutal attacks on opponents at home, allowed the regime to survive as it sheltered most of its inhabitants from the effects of the war.

End of unit activities

1 The following activity is designed to help you evaluate the reasons why the war lasted so long. Copy and complete the chart below to help you reach a judgement as to the relative importance of the reasons why the war lasted from 1980 to 1988. In the third column award a mark out of six for the importance of the factor in causing the war to last so long: the higher the mark, the more important the factor. In the final column explain why you have given the mark.

Factor	Explanation of how it contributed to the length of the war	Mark/6	Explanation for mark
Foreign support			
Religious zeal			
The geography of the region			
Attitudes of the governments			
Trench warfare			
The technology available to the two sides			

Guns and butter: The concept of guns and butter was first used in Nazi Germany to highlight the economic choice between rearmament (guns) and consumer goods (butter). However, the Iraqi government hoped to be able to pursue both so that even though large amounts were spent on weaponry, there was not disquiet within the country because of a shortage of goods.

QUESTION

Which had the greater impact on the outcome of the war: foreign involvement or the impact of the war on the home front? Explain your choice.

KEY CONCEPTS ACTIVITY

Significance: Draw up a chart to show the role of foreign powers in the war. How important a role did foreign powers play in:

- the length of the war
- the nature of the war
- the outcome of the war?

The Iran–Iraq War

Now write an essay plan to answer the question 'Assess the reasons why the Iran–Iraq War lasted so long.'

2 In order to assess the importance of the different methods of warfare in the outcome of the war, complete the following chart:

Method of fighting/ conducting the war	Impact on the war	Mark/6	Explanation of importance
Trench warfare			
Human wave assault			
Chemical warfare			
War against the cities			
Tanker warfare			

TIMELINE

1988 **17 July:** Iran implicitly accepts ceasefire by agreeing to UN Resolution 598.

20 July: Khomeini's acceptance of ceasefire broadcast on Tehran radio.

20 August: Ceasefire starts.

24 August: Peace talks start in Geneva.

1989 **3 June:** Death of Ayatollah Khomeini.

Akbar Hashemi Rafsanjani becomes president of Iran.

1990 **August:** Iraq invades Kuwait.

1991 **January–March:** First Gulf War.

KEY QUESTIONS

- What agreements were made to end the war?
- What territorial changes did the war bring about?
- What was the impact of the war on the social, religious and cultural situation?
- What were the political repercussions of the war?
- How serious was the economic impact of the war?

Overview

- The war was ended by a ceasefire, but attempts to bring about a lasting peace have been difficult, despite Iraq finally evacuating Iranian territory and giving up its claims to the whole of the Shatt al-'Arab waterway.

- Despite almost eight years of fighting, neither side made territorial gains, although the consequences of the war may have been a direct cause of Iraq's invasion of Kuwait.

- The people on both sides suffered a decline in their standards of living because of the amount of money spent on military equipment. Moreover, rising unemployment also added to the lowering of living standards.

- It was the Kurdish population of Northern Iraq who suffered the most as a consequence of the war. Saddam Hussein saw them as traitors for supporting Iran and unleashed a brutal chemical war against them.

- Although the Iranian revolution did not spread, the ending of the war did not see a significant change in internal policy or the lessening of radicalism within the country.

- The failure to gain outright victory did initially weaken the position of Saddam Hussein. The invasion of Kuwait may have been an attempt by Saddam Hussein to regain popularity.

- Both states suffered severe economic consequences. Iraq had serious debts and sought to improve its economic position by invading the oil-rich territory of Kuwait.

Introduction

This unit will examine the impact of the war on both Iran and Iraq. Although there were no territorial changes, it did impact on the home front. This unit will consider the repercussions of the war on the political, social, economic and cultural position of the two states. It will also consider how those developments resulted in further conflicts developing in the region, leading ultimately to the First Gulf War.

6.8 What agreements were made to end the war?

On 17 July 1988, Iran finally sent a letter to the UN secretary-general accepting a ceasefire. Iran declared: 'We have decided to declare officially that the Islamic Republic of Iran – because of the importance it attaches to the saving of lives of human beings and the establishment of justice and regional and international peace and security – accepts UN Resolution 598.'

However, the acceptance of a ceasefire made little impact on Iraq. In the letter agreeing to the ceasefire, Iran had demanded that Iraq accept full responsibility for starting the war, which was a traditional Iranian demand. With Iran in a weak position, Saddam Hussein had no intention of agreeing to the demand and rejected the acceptance of the ceasefire as being too ambiguous. He demanded that Iran's acceptance was endorsed by Khomeini and to show that they were serious in their demands, a series of air-raids were launched the next day. These attacks simply brought retaliatory action from Iran but, lacking the necessary air power, Khomeini was forced to face reality and publicly announce his acceptance. Despite this, he could still not bring himself to make the announcement and it was read out by an announcer and stated:

SOURCE L

Happy are those who have departed through martyrdom. Unhappy am I that I still survive. Taking this decision is more deadly than drinking from a poisoned chalice. I submitted myself to Allah's will and took this drink for his satisfaction. To me it would have been more bearable to accept death and martyrdom [but I was forced to accept the advice of] all the high-ranking military experts. Accepting the [UN] Resolution does not mean that the question of war has been solved. By declaring this decision, we have blunted the propaganda weapon of the world devourers against us. But one cannot forecast this course of events indefinitely.

Quoted in Efraim Karsh. 2009. The Iran–Iraq War, 1980–1988. London: Osprey, p. 79.

This speech only succeeded in forcing Saddam Hussein to demand the immediate start of peace talks in advance of a ceasefire. The Iraqi deputy prime minister, **Tariq Aziz**, stated that Iraq considered the war still to be ongoing until Iran made clear its intentions about other aspects of the Resolution, particularly over prisoners-of-war, of which there were some 70 000 Iraqis. As a result, three weeks of arguments followed and this was accompanied by a series of military clashes, with Iraq looking to take more land and prisoners to improve its negotiating position.

Pressure from the UN and international powers was put on Iraq to agree to the ceasefire. Meanwhile, because of their weak position, Iran, which had previously

Figure 6.18 Tariq Aziz (1936–2015)

He was a close adviser of Saddam Hussein, holding the office of foreign minister and deputy prime minister. He had known Saddam since the 1950s, when they had both been members of the banned Ba'th party. He often represented Iraq at international meetings. He was held prisoner following the Iraqi defeat in 2003, and in 2010 he was sentenced to death, but the president refused to sign the warrant and therefore he remained in custody until dying of a heart attack in June 2015.

QUESTION

What can we learn from Source L about Khomeini's attitude to the ending of the war? Why did he have this attitude?

rejected any talks of peace, now became its most vocal supporter and blamed Iraq for delays. As a result of these pressures Iraq announced a willingness to agree to a ceasefire on 6 August.

The result was that on 8 August the UN declared a ceasefire from 20 August and on 24 August, representatives of Iran and Iraq were to meet under UN auspices to start peace talks. Meanwhile a UN observer group was set up to monitor the ceasefire. As a result of sheer exhaustion, the two sides had been forced to talk and agree to the situation that existed in September 1980. Despite this agreement, however, neither side genuinely saw this as the end of hostilities. As a result, both sides looked to rebuild their forces and rebuild their economies and infrastructure in readiness for the outbreak of another conflict.

The peace talks achieved little, although they continued for the next two years. Iraq insisted on full control of the Shatt al-'Arab waterway, threatening to dig a canal between Basra and Umm Qasr if this was not met. Iran, on the other hand, demanded that Iraq fully comply with the Algiers Agreement of 1975. The result was deadlock and even prisoners were not returned. Therefore, although the fighting had been brought to an end, the problems between the two states were not resolved.

The growing likelihood of Iraq becoming involved in a war with Western powers, meant it became concerned that Iran would mend its relations with the West in order to also attack Iraq. Therefore, soon after the invasion of Kuwait, Baghdad wrote to Iran recognising Iranian rights over the eastern half of the Shatt al-'Arab waterway, which was a return to the situation before the war had started and that Iraq had repudiated a decade earlier. Saddam Hussein also agreed to accept Iran's demands and withdraw Iraq's military from the disputed border area. As a result, a peace agreement was signed, this finalised the terms of the UN resolution, restored diplomatic relations and resulted in the withdrawal of Iraqi troops from the border region during 1990 and 1991. This was then followed by the release of most prisoners of war, resulting in Iran calling it 'the greatest victory in the history of the Islamic Republic of Iran'.

Activity

Research the two Gulf Wars. What has the impact of the wars been on Iraq? How have they changed the balance of power in the area?

6.9 What territorial changes did the war bring about?

The section above has shown that the war itself brought about no territorial changes as the position of September 1980 was confirmed. Most historians agree that it was a territorial stalemate. However, it could be argued that Iraq won as they had stopped Iran's territorial ambitions and persuaded Iran to accept a ceasefire. There are some analysts who have challenged this view and suggested that Iran won because they drove Iraq from their territory, stopped a militarily superior force, prevented Iraq from taking territory and forced Iraq to give up its ambitions for the Shatt al-'Arab waterway.

QUESTION

What reasons were there for Iraq to want to end the war?

Theory of Knowledge

History and hindsight: Historians know that the First Gulf War did not bring about the downfall of Saddam Hussein or protect either the Kurds or Shi'a. They have the benefit of hindsight when writing about the war and its aftermath. How might this affect their interpretation of events? Does it make their task more difficult? What are the advantages and disadvantages of hindsight for the historian?

Fact: Iraq had not recognised Kuwait and had always claimed it needed it as an outlet to the sea, while there were also strong links between Basra and Kuwait. In the 1960s, Iraq had claimed supreme power over it, although in 1963 they recognised its independence but this did not stop tensions. After the Iran–Iraq War and with Saddam's power at home weakened and growing discontent, Iraq invaded in August 1990. A force of 300,000 crossed into Kuwait and took control within three days. The UN condemned the invasion and imposed sanctions, but this had no impact and ultimately led to the First Gulf War in January 1991, when a multinational force, led by the USA, drove Iraq out.

Figure 6.19 At the end of the war there were no clear winners, the border had scarcely moved, yet the loss of life and damage to property was high

Fact: The First Gulf War lasted from January to March 1991 and resulted in the liberation of Kuwait from Iraqi forces. The coalition included Arab states, such as Saudi Arabia, Egypt and Syria, as well as the USA and Britain. The war began with an air assault, which lasted five weeks. Saddam still refused to surrender, firing missiles against Israel in the hope of splitting the coalition, but Israel did not retaliate and the coalition remained intact. The ground attack began in February and Iraq was driven out, but they set fire to Kuwaiti oil-wells.

However, the impact of the war on Iraq, particularly the destabilising effects, did lead to attempts to strengthen the regime and divert attention from domestic issues; this was ultimately one of the major reasons that led to the invasion and overrunning of Kuwait in August 1990. Without intervention from other states, in the First Gulf War of January–March 1991 there would have been a major shift in territorial boundaries as Kuwait would have been absorbed into Iraq.

6.10 What was the impact of the war on the social, religious and cultural situation?

The amount of money that Iraq spent on military equipment, even with the loans it received from other Arab states, meant that less was spent on hospitals and schools. As a result, life expectancy declined and infant mortality rose. This, coupled with the declining living standards and rising unemployment was the recipe for internal unrest. Although the Iraqi regime used terror to control its people, there were still strikes and riots. Most disconcerting for the regime was that some of the unrest was coordinated in the country's mosques. This was a problem for the government as they were beyond the control of Saddam Hussein's police and the army. They could not and would not dare attack mosques as it would simply increase opposition from all Muslims.

The most serious consequences of the war were for the Kurdish population of Iraq. The Kurdish fighters had often been in communication with their Iranian counterparts and planned their attacks to coincide with Iranian offensives.

As a result, the Kurds were able to gain control over large areas of North Iraq. It was therefore not surprising that Saddam Hussein saw them as disloyal, attacking their own country when it was facing a grave crisis. In the early summer of 1988 there were already discussions among the Iraqi leadership about revenge and Saddam Hussein made his intentions clear:

SOURCE M

To all the Kurds [who] are contending that we are afraid to discuss or tackle this issue; our message is that we are willing to discuss the subject of capitalism, communism, Kurds, and so forth or any other subject that they want to discuss. That will teach them a painful lesson; so next time before they think to raise the issue against us they will think twice as they remember the pain that they have suffered in this lesson. We will ask all parties or countries that are for Kurdish self-rule or for improving the current self-rule status to attend these discussions. Ha. Ha. Ha. Our Kurdish elements that are involved in sabotage will be killed this time and if they return a second time they will be killed again until we are rid of them forever.

Quoted in Williamson Murray and Kevin M Woods. 2014. The Iran–Iraq War: A Military and Strategic History. *Cambridge: Cambridge University Press, p. 333.*

QUESTION

Why did the Iran–Iraq War allow Saddam Hussein to attack the Kurds?

Figure 6.21   Ali Hassan al-Majid 'Chemical Ali' (1941–2010)

Ali Hassan al-Majid was a cousin of Saddam Hussein. He was known as 'Chemical Ali' because of his role in the chemical attacks against the Kurds in the north of the country and the Shi'a in the south. He was defence minister, interior minister and chief of the intelligence services. He was captured in 2003 and charged with war crimes, sentenced to death in 2007 and finally hanged in 2010.

Figure 6.20   Photographs of the victims of the notorious Iraqi chemical attack on the town of Halabja

He appointed his cousin, known by the nickname, **'Chemical Ali'** to oversee the operation. Even before the war had ended there had been attacks by the Iraqi regime on them, with a scorched-earth policy launched from February 1988. Villages in guerrilla-controlled areas were destroyed, and all inhabitants – including women and children – were killed. Chemical weapons were used more routinely, the most notorious being the chemical weapons dropped on the town of Halabja, which resulted in the immediate death of some 5000 and possibly a further 12 000 as a consequence. This took place in March 1988, after Iranians had helped Kurds capture the town.

Fact: The attack on Halabja is held by some to be one of the worst war crimes since 1945. Iraqi forces used helicopter gunships – supplied, since 1984, by Reagan's administration in the US – to drop chemical weapons on Halabja and other Kurdish villages.

SOURCE N

Dead bodies – human and animal – littered the streets, huddled in doorways, slumped over steering-wheels of their cars. Survivors stumbled around, laughing hysterically, before collapsing. Those who had been directly exposed to the gas found that their symptoms worsened as the night wore on. Many children died along the way and were abandoned where they fell.

D. McDowell. 2004. A Modern History of the Kurds. *Quoted in Michael Scott Baumann. 2009.* Crisis in the Middle East: Israel and the Arab States 1945–2007. *London: Hodder, p. 127.*

QUESTION

Explain what the 'Kurdish problem' was.

After the ceasefire between Iran and Iraq, Saddam Hussein saw the opportunity to solve 'the Kurdish problem' and set out to depopulate much of the north and destroy the nationalist movement. The full force of the Iraqi army was turned on the Kurds – by the end of August 1988, most organised resistance was over and all Kurdish regions were back in Iraqi hands. By January 1989, the regime could argue that its campaign had been a success. Helicopters had been used to destroy virtually all living things, but ground troops were also sent in and they targeted Kurdish men and boys aged between 15 and 50, rounding them up and shooting them before pushing them into pre-dug graves.

There were calls from within the regime for some easing of the atrocities, even from Saddam Hussein, but this was the response from 'Chemical Ali':

QUESTION

Explain what 'Chemical Ali' is saying in Source O. What was the purpose of his comments?

SOURCE O

So we started to show these senior commanders [army commanders who were objecting to some aspects of the murderous campaign] on TV that [the saboteurs] had surrendered. Am I supposed to keep them in good shape? What am I supposed to do with them, these goats? Then a message reaches me from the great man, the father [Saddam], saying take good care of the families of the saboteurs and this and that. The general command brings it to me. I put his message to my head. But take good care of them? No, I will bury them with bulldozers. Then, they ask me for the names of all the prisoners in order to publish them. I said, 'Weren't you satisfied by what you saw on television and read in the newspaper? Where am I supposed to put all this enormous number of people? I started to distribute them among the governates. I had to send bulldozers hither and thither.

Quoted in Williamson Murray and Kevin M. Woods. 2014. The Iran–Iraq War: A Military and Strategic History, *Cambridge: Cambridge University Press, pp. 333–4.*

It is estimated that somewhere between 150 000 and 200 000 Kurds were killed, with several towns and up to 90 per cent of all villages destroyed. Some were able to flee the region to Turkey, but those who were left and could not flee were often deported to the south of the country, where they often died in appalling conditions. In order to try and protect the Kurds the Americans and British, after the First Gulf war, imposed a **no-fly zone** to provide the Kurds with a safe haven in the north and prevent Saddam Hussein from regaining the land.

No-fly zone: This was an area, initially in the north of Iraq, but later extended to the Shi'i south, over which Iraqi planes were prevented from flying. This was to stop Saddam Hussein launching air-borne attacks against the Kurds.

The Iranian economy had already started to decline with the Revolution, but the war made the situation worse. As a result living standards fell dramatically, leaving the country to be described by the British journalists John Bulloch and Harvey Morris as a 'dour and joyless place [that] seemed to have nothing to offer but endless war'. The situation was made worse as Iran was unable to borrow and this meant that they had to finance the war from oil revenues, with the result that there were fewer available for the country's infrastructure. As a result, the Iranian health care system, similar to that of Iraq, was also put under pressure. Nearly 400 000 Iranians received injuries that needed long-term treatment and between 1980 and 2012 it is estimated that more than 200 000 Iranians died due to war injuries. Moreover, nearly 150 000 children were orphaned as a result.

6.11 What were the political repercussions of the war?

The impact on the Iranian revolution

At the start of the war, the Iranian government's aim had been to topple the regime in Baghdad, but it had failed to achieve this and bring about the spread of radical Islamic fundamentalism in the region. It was therefore forced to abandon its plans for a regional Islamic revolution. However, the war also failed to undermine the regime in Tehran, but by ending the war the revolution was protected. Although Iran would no longer shape the Gulf region along Islamic lines, it had established the vision of 'Islam in one country'.

There were some signs of more moderate forces emerging in the country and a tempering of the revolutionary zeal. However, this did not seem apparent from the reaction to the death of Khomeini in 1989, even after nearly eight years of war and the large number of casualties, he was still revered within the country. He had stood up to Western powers after years of humiliation and it was therefore not surprising that an estimated 12 million people turned out in the streets of Tehran for his funeral, suggesting that the Republic and its ideals still maintained widespread support.

Figure 6.22 Millions turn out for the funeral of Ayatollah Khomeini, suggesting that his popularity in Iran was still strong

The death of Khomeini brought **Akbar Hashemi Rafsanjani** to power as president, having previously been chairman of the Iranian parliament during the war. Despite his attempts to curb the power of the ultra-conservatives, who had dominated Iranian politics during the war, he failed to do so and the Revolutionary Guards were able to consolidate their position, which was further enhanced under Ali Khamenei, who had taken over as supreme leader after the death of Khomeini. Therefore, hopes of political liberalisation did not materialise, even if there was some economic liberalisation.

Iran also embarked on a successful campaign to restore its international position. It was able to regain the support of the USSR, who saw it as a counterbalance to the increased US presence in the area. Relations with France were restored in June 1988 and then with Canada and Britain. In November 1988, the West German foreign minister visited the country. However, these improvements were tempered in February 1989 when the Ayatollah Khomeini announced a **fatwa** against **Salman Rushdie** for writing allegedly blasphemous pieces in his novel *The Satanic Verses*. But despite this, there were still some moderate voices in Iran who offered a solution to the crisis, suggesting that Iran wanted to restore some degree of relationship with the West.

Akbar Hashemi Rafsanjani (b. 1934)

He was president of Iran from 1989 to 1997. During the war he was commander in chief and then chairman of the parliament. As a pragmatist and centrist, in terms of politics, he helped to bring about a moderate approach by Iran in international affairs and also encouraged the development of the free market, supporting the privatisation of state-owned industries. He thus encouraged reconstruction after the war, but these initiatives were not always successful. Although he was popular among the upper and middle classes, he failed to win support among the rural and urban working class. His economic reforms brought them little benefit.

Fatwa: A ruling in Islamic law on an issue; in this instance that Salman Rushdie's writings were blasphemous and, in this instance, that the author should be put to death.

Salman Rushdie (b. 1947) is a British-Indian novelist. It was his fourth novel, *The Satanic Verses*, published in 1988, which brought him notoriety. It provoked protest from many Muslims, because of what was seen to be an irreverent depiction of Muhammad, and led to death threats and a fatwa. He was placed under police protection, but since 2000 has lived in the USA.

The impact on Saddam Hussein and Iraq

In the same way that Khomeini had promised Iran victory, so had Saddam Hussein promised his people victory. Although he had avoided being brought down by the regime in Tehran, his failure to deliver a crushing military victory meant that his own position was vulnerable, not from another regime but from his own people.

Within Iraq, there had been opposition to the war; while the economic problems caused by the war meant Saddam had to break promises about better living standards. The demobilisation of 1.5 million soldiers – most of whom were Shi'i Muslims – increased the potential for internal opposition. More seriously, the officer corps had shown signs of unrest. With the war over, Saddam began to demote or promote officers to increase his support in the armed forces. Several senior officers met with fatal 'accidents' or were placed under house arrest.

Saddam therefore needed to improve the standard of living of his people and provide both peace and prosperity, particularly as he faced a series of riots and strikes. However, in spite of this need, most spending went on rebuilding and developing weapons. Saddam Hussein had to try and maintain the support of his army as many within it felt cheated of victory against Iran, and there were some who in private were blaming Saddam Hussein for it.

His position within Iraq had been weakened and this was reflected in the number of plots against him in late 1988 and early 1989 – but all were uncovered by the authorities and numerous officers were executed for conspiracy in these plans. He even took action against those within his own family, leading him to rule even more repressively.

All of these factors meant that there was a need to divert attention from the growing crisis in the country, and this encouraged Saddam's aims in relation to Kuwait, which would divert the army and provide a supply of oil and wealth that would help to solve Iraq's internal problems.

Saddam Hussein did use the 'victory' to claim that it signified the arrival of another great power in the Middle East. Many in the Arab world, and even in the West, believed him, unaware of the damage that the war had wrought on Iraq and its economy. They accepted his claim that his troops, now battle-hardened, were highly effective and this led some to question the wisdom of taking on the regime following its invasion of Kuwait, believing that the West would be facing 'the reincarnation of the Waffen-SS', failing to realise that Iraq had only triumphed in 1988 because it could spend more on equipping its forces at the end of the war than Iran, largely because of loans and not because its forces were that much superior.

The impact on the region

Although the war had seen most of the Arab states distance themselves from Tehran, the apparent ending of the threat of the spread of fundamentalist Islam brought about a change in attitudes of many nearby states. A significant number, including Kuwait and Bahrain restored relations, while even Saudi Arabia stopped its propaganda attacks against the Iranian government. However, two nations did lose out, Turkey and Syria. Turkey had made significant economic gains during the war through trade and had also benefited from its strategic position in the region as Western powers sought alternative support after the loss of Iran following the revolution there. Syria had been Iran's staunchest ally during the war, and Saddam Hussein was not prepared to forget this and

Fact: There had also been plots in 1981 and in 1982, by officers who disagreed with Saddam's running of the Iran–Iraq War. There is some evidence that the CIA passed on the names of the 1982 plotters to Saddam, who then executed almost 300 of them.

therefore began to aid Syria's enemies, most notably in Lebanon by providing support to the Christian **Maronites**, who had previously been Israel's closest allies. There had also been a lessening of the hard-line attitude of Arab states towards Israel during the war and this appeared to continue afterwards as Iran was still perceived as a greater threat to the region than Israel. However, the region also recognised that it needed Egypt, who had been expelled from the **Arab League** in 1979 for making peace with Israel. Soon after the war started Iraq, the country that had hosted the meeting of the League that had expelled Egypt, was asking for military support. By the end of the war, Egypt had regained its position at the head of the Arab world and was welcomed back into the League at Casablanca in May 1989

Western attitudes to Saddam Hussein after 1988

Since the 1950s, the Middle East had been a key Cold War area. However, the growing economic and political problems of the Soviet Union in the 1980s meant it increasingly sought cooperation with the West and, at the same time, began to reduce its links to states such as Iraq and Syria. The US was thus able to intervene in the Middle East more strongly from the late 1980s.

SOURCE P

Access to Persian Gulf oil and the security of key friendly states in the area are vital to US national security… Normal relations between the United States and Iraq would serve our longer-term interest and promote stability in both the Gulf and the Middle East… [The US should] propose economic and political incentives for Iraq to moderate its behaviour and increase our influence within Iraq.

Part of a National Security Directive 26 issued by US President George Bush in October 1989.

After 1988, the need for reconstruction in Iraq provided good business opportunities for US firms. Although Saddam was ruthless, he was no longer a Soviet client – consequently, the US was at first prepared to ignore his efforts to acquire more sophisticated weaponry.

However, in the US, **Neo-Cons** were coming to play an increasing role in US administrations, arguing for firm foreign policy and military interventions to further global US interests.

6.12 How serious was the economic impact of the war?

Both nations suffered huge destruction, while the financial loss for each country was believed to have exceeded $500 billion. It must be remembered that the war had lasted more than seven years and was one of the most destructive wars since the Second World War. The war had ravaged both countries' economies. While the war continued, economic development was prevented and oil exports – which were the mainstay of both nations' economies – were disrupted.

Maronites: A Christian sect, linked to the Roman Catholic Church. They were of Syrian origin but most live in Lebanon and are opposed to the rule of the Assad family in Syria.

Arab League: The Arab League was established in 1945 and consists of Arab states from around North Africa, the Horn of Africa and Arabia. Its aim is to protect the independence and sovereignty of Arab states and ensure closer cooperation and collaboration between them.

Neo-Cons: This is an abbreviation of 'Neo-Conservatives', and refers to a group of politicians, similar to the earlier 'New Right'. Leading 'Neo-Cons' increasingly came to hold important positions under both George Bush and, especially later under his son, George W. Bush. Shortly after the Gulf War of 1991, many leading Neo-Cons began to call for the US to take military action to remove Saddam from power.

QUESTION

Which of the two nations, Iraq or Iran, suffered the most from the war? Explain your answer.

Iraq's economy suffered severe damage. More than 200 000 were killed and probably another 400 000 wounded, but even those who were not killed or injured were affected by damage to both the health and education systems. This was particularly important for a nation with a population of just 17 million. As the war progressed, ever-increasing amounts of money were spent on weapons, with the result that a nation that began the war with $35 billion in reserve accumulated debts of some $80 billion, approximately twice the size of its gross national product (GNP). Despite Saddam's claims of victory, the war left Iraq with a war-damaged infrastructure – Western estimates put the reconstruction costs at $230 billion.

This can be put into perspective by considering that revenue from oil had dropped to just $13 billion, which did not even cover expenditure. Some 10 million shells had landed in the oil fields around Basra, which limited Iraq's oil production. The war thus turned Iraq from a rich and prosperous country into a physically damaged and very indebted country – mainly to Kuwait and Saudi Arabia. Both these states had opposed the new Iranian regime and had thus been happy to lend Iraq money.

This created further problems for Iraq as foreign states were unwilling to lend any further money, which made it very difficult for the country to rebuild. Initially, Saddam hoped to fund reconstruction from oil revenues but, in 1988, world oil prices fell. As a result, oil revenues were $11 billion – only half that of 1980. By 1990, more than 50 per cent of this went on debt repayments. Consequently, Saddam tried – unsuccessfully – to persuade OPEC to restrict oil production in order to increase prices. As a result, many in the oil industry lost their jobs and added to a growing list of unemployed. Iraq also accused Kuwait of 'slant drilling' and therefore stealing Iraqi oil, which was a further reason for its invasion in 1990, but that would simply make the financial situation worse.

Figure 6.23 A graph showing the decline in oil production, crucial for the economy of the two nations, during the war

The regime actually needed a further $10 billion per year just to cover its expenditure and balance its deficit. Moreover, the size of the Iraqi armed forces added to the problems, costing the Treasury even more money. In an attempt to deal with this, there was a partial demobilisation in 1989, but the economy was unable to absorb the large number who were now added to the labour market.

The war had cost Iraq close to $5000 billion and this would spur Saddam Hussein on to further action in the Gulf to try and recover its losses. The result was that, by February 1990, Saddam Hussein was asking for a complete moratorium on war loans and the immediate loan of a further $30 billion. At the same time he also warned the states: 'Let the Gulf regimes know that if they will not give this money to me, I will know how to get it' – an early warning of the potential seizure of Kuwait.

Iranian losses were estimated to be 500 000, but with a population of some 55 million it was better able to sustain its losses than Iraq. There was now an urgent need to rebuild a significant number of urban areas that had been badly damaged by Iraqi missiles. The end of the war also led to a debate in government circles about the role of the private sector in the reconstruction of the country. It was the pragmatic approach that ultimately triumphed, although it has not been plain sailing and the more doctrinaire among the Iranian government have been able to limit Western aid. Moreover, attempts at reconstruction have not always been successful, economic reforms have not always reached the rural or war zones, which needed the most aid and this created opposition.

Activity

Construct two spider diagrams to show the impact of the war on Iran and Iraq. Organise the material according to themes, such as political, social, economic.

End of unit activity

1 Using the information in this section, complete the balance sheet to help you assess the impact of the war on Iraq and Iran.

Factor	Iran		Iraq	
	Positive	Negative	Positive	Negative
Economic				
Political				
Social				
Population				
Religious				
Financial				
Infrastructure				
Strategic position				

Which of the two nations suffered the most? Explain your answer.

2 In what ways did the war strengthen or weaken the Iranian or Iraqi governments? You might it helpful to construct a chart to summarise this.

Iran		Iraq	
Strengthen	Weaken	Strengthen	Weaken

3 Consider the following two views about the impact of the Iran–Iraq War.

View A: The Iran–Iraq War did little to strengthen the position of Saddam Hussein. All that had changed was that the threat was now from his own people, rather than Iran.

View B: The Iran–Iraq War strengthened the position of Saddam Hussein both at home and throughout the region because Arab states feared a Shi'i Islamic revolution.

Using the information in this chapter, find examples and evidence to support each of the statements. Using this evidence, write a paragraph explaining which of the views about the impact of the war on Iraq you think is most valid and why.

End of chapter activities

Paper 1 exam practice

Question

With reference to its origin, purpose and content, analyse the value and limitations of Source A below for historians studying the impact of the Iran–Iraq War on the Kurds.

[4 marks]

Skill

Value and limitations (reliability/utility) of a source.

> **SOURCE A**
>
> *A reporter comments on the aftermath of the attack on Halabja*
>
> Dead bodies – human and animal – littered the streets, huddled in doorways, slumped over steering-wheels of their cars. Survivors stumbled around, laughing hysterically, before collapsing. Those who had been directly exposed to the gas found that their symptoms worsened as the night wore on. Many children died along the way and were abandoned where they fell.
>
> *D. McDowell. 2004.* A Modern History of the Kurds. *Quoted in Michael Scott Baumann. 2009.* Crisis in the Middle East: Israel and the Arab States 1945–2007. *London: Hodder, p. 127.*

Before you start

Value and limitations (utility/reliability) questions require you to assess a source over a range of possible issues – and try to comment on their value to historians studying a particular event or period of history. You need to consider both the origin, purpose and content, and also the value and limitations, of the source. You should link these in your answer, showing how origin/purpose/content relate to value/limitations.

Before you attempt this question, refer to Chapter 7 for advice on how to tackle these questions, and a simplified mark scheme.

Student answer

Source A is a primary source – a report from a journalist who had visited the region. His purpose was to inform people of what he saw after the attack, but it is just his personal recollections and may be limited by what he actually saw and what he was allowed to see. Therefore, although he was present after the attack, he may not have seen the whole picture, he may also make it more dramatic than it really was. It is the reporter's personal view of the aftermath. It is useful in showing how the Kurds in Halabja suffered – although he provides no specific numbers to allow us to gauge the scale of the attack and its numerical impact. As they are the personal recollections of one journalist, this may limit the accuracy and therefore value of the source, although we know that the attack did kill many and it was one of the episodes for which Saddam Hussein was later put on trial.

Examiner comment

This is quite a thorough answer that deals with most of the issues that are required – origin, purpose, value and limitations. It is better at dealing with some aspects than others, largely ignoring the issue of the content of the source. The analysis of the value could be more fully developed and the organisation of the material could be better structured. However, the answer shows some awareness of the source as evidence for the historian, and this would gain credit, but it would not reach the top as it fails to deal thoroughly with the issue of content. The answer is also well-balanced. The answer would therefore be awarded three out of four marks.

Activity

Look again at the question, the student answer above and the examiner comments. Now try to write an answer that would be awarded full marks.

Summary activity

Having considered the causes of the war, the reasons it lasted so long and the impact of the war, you are now in a position to reach a judgement as to whether the war was a 'pointless and costly failure' for both countries.

In the column under 'Aim', look back to the first unit and consider what the aims of Iran and Iraq were when they went to war. In the second and third columns for each country, use Units 2 and 3 to find evidence that they either achieved or did not achieve the aim.

In order to help you reach a judgement, complete the table below:

Iran			Iraq		
Aim	Evidence it was achieved	Evidence it was not achieved	Aim	Evidence it was achieved	Evidence it was not achieved

Use the evidence in the table to write a paragraph for each country summarising whether the war was 'a pointless and costly failure.'

Paper 2 practice questions

1 Examine the role of religious divisions in the outbreak of the Iran–Iraq War in 1980.

2 Evaluate the reasons why Iraq declared war on Iran in 1980.

3 Examine the reasons why it proved impossible for either side to make large-scale territorial gains during the Iran–Iraq War.

4 Evaluate the role and importance of technology in the outcome of the war.

5 'The most important results of the Iran–Iraq War were economic.' To what extent do you agree with this statement?

6 'Iraq gained more from the Iran–Iraq War than Iran.' To what extent do you agree with this statement?

Further reading

Abdulghani, Jasim (1984) *Iraq and Iran: The Years of Crisis*, Baltimore, MD: Johns Hopkins University Press.

Grumman, S.R. (1982) *The Iran–Iraq War: Islam Embattled*, New York: Praeger.

Johnson, Rob (2011) *The Iran–Iraq War*, Basingstoke: Palgrave Macmillan.

Karsh, Efraim (1987) *The Iran–Iraq War: A Military Analysis*, London: International Institute for Strategic Studies.

Karsh, Efraim (2009) *The Iran–Iraq War, 1980–1988*, London: Osprey.

Murray, Williamson and Woods, Kevin M. (2014) *The Iran–Iraq War: A Military and Strategic History*, Cambridge: Cambridge University Press.

Pelletiere, Stephen (1992) *The Iran–Iraq War: Chaos in a Vacuum*, New York: Praeger.

Introduction

You have now completed your study of the main aspects and events of 20th-century wars using World History Topic 11: The Causes and Effects of 20th-Century Wars. In the previous chapters, you have had practice at answering some of the types of source-based questions you will have to deal with in Paper 1. In this chapter, you will gain experience of dealing with:

- the longer Paper 1 question, which requires you to use both sources and your own knowledge to write a mini-essay;
- the essay questions you will meet in Paper 2.

Exam skills needed for IB History

This book is designed primarily to prepare both Standard and Higher Level students for the Paper 2 topic World History Topic 11: The Causes and Effects of 20th-Century Wars. However, by providing the necessary historical knowledge and understanding, as well as an awareness of the key historical debates and perspectives, it will also help you prepare for Paper 1. The skills you need for answering both Paper 1 and Paper 2 exam questions are explained in the following pages.

In order to analyse and evaluate sources as historical evidence, you will need to ask the following 'W' questions of historical sources:

- **Who** produced it? Were they in a position to know?
- **What** type of source is it? What is its nature – is it a primary or secondary source?
- **Where** and **when** was it produced? What was happening at the time?
- **Why** was it produced? Was its purpose to inform or to persuade? Is it an accurate attempt to record facts, or is it an example of propaganda?
- **Who** was the intended audience – decision-makers, or the general public?

The example below shows you how to find the information related to the 'W' questions. You will need this information in order to evaluate sources for their value and limitations.

Paper 1 exam practice

Paper 1 skills

This section of the book is designed to give you the skills and understanding to tackle Paper 1 questions. These are based on the comprehension, critical analysis and evaluation of different types of historical sources as evidence, along with the use of appropriate historical contextual knowledge.

For example, you will need to test sources for value and limitations (i.e., their reliability and utility, especially in view of their **origin**, **purpose** and **content**) – a skill essential for historians. A range of sources has been provided, including extracts from official documents, tables of statistics, memoirs and speeches, as well as visual sources such as photographs and cartoons.

> ### SOURCE A
>
> Strive to annihilate the enemy in mobile warfare, but at the same time pay attention to tactics of positional attack for seizing enemy strongholds and cities. In the matter of siege operations, resolutely seize all the weakly defended enemy positions or cities. In the case of an enemy position or city defended with medium strength, seize it when the opportunity arises and circumstances permit. In the case of a strongly defended enemy position, take it only when the conditions are ripe.
>
> Extract from an **essay** by **Mao Zedong** on war, **May 1947**, to **guide** his forces. Quoted in D. Wilson. 1991. China's Revolutionary War. London: Weidenfield and Nicolson, p. 157.

Remember: a source doesn't have to be primary to be useful. Remember, too, that content isn't the only aspect to have possible value. The context, the person who produced it, and so on, can be important in offering an insight. Finally, when in the exam room, use the information provided by the Chief Examiner about the four sources, as it can give some useful clues to help you construct a good answer.

This approach will help you become familiar with interpreting, understanding, analysing and evaluating different types of historical sources. It will also aid you in synthesising critical analysis of sources with historical knowledge when constructing an explanation or analysis of some aspect or development of the past. Remember – for Paper 1, as for Paper 2, you need to acquire, select and deploy relevant historical knowledge to explain causes and consequences, continuity and change. You also need to develop and show (where relevant) an awareness of historical debates, and different perspectives and interpretations.

Paper 1 questions will thus involve examining sources in the light of:

- their origin, purpose and content;
- their value and limitations.

The value and limitations of sources to historians will be based on the origin, purpose and content aspects. For example, a source might be useful because it is primary – the

Origin: The 'who, what, when and where?' questions.

Purpose: This means 'reasons, what the writer/creator was trying to achieve, who the intended audience was'.

Content: This is the information or explanation(s) provided by the source.

essay WHAT? (type of source)

Mao Zedong WHO? (produced it)

May 1947 WHEN? (date/time of production)

guide WHY? (possible purpose)

his forces WHO? (intended audience)

event depicted was witnessed by the person producing it. But was the person in a position to know? Is the view an untypical view of the event? What is its nature – is it a private diary entry (therefore possibly more likely to be true), or is it a speech or piece of propaganda intended to persuade? Even if the value of a source is limited by such aspects, it can still have value – for example, as evidence of the types of propaganda put out at the time. Similarly, a secondary – or even a tertiary – source can have more value than some primary sources; for instance, because the writer might be writing at a time when new evidence has become available.

Paper 1 contains four types of question. The first three of these are:

1 Comprehension/understanding of a source. Some will have two marks, others three marks. For such questions, write only a short answer, making two or three points – save your longer answers for the questions carrying the higher marks.

2 Assessing the value and limitations of one source (four marks). Here you need to assess the source over a range of aspects, **and** comment on the source's relative value to historians studying a particular aspect of history. Remember to deal with all of the aspects required: origin, purpose, content, value and limitations.

3 Cross-referencing/comparing or contrasting two sources (six marks). Try to write an integrated comparison. For example, comment on how the two sources deal with one aspect; then compare/contrast the sources on another aspect. This will usually score more highly than answers that deal with the sources separately. Try to avoid simply describing each source in turn – there needs to be explicit comparison/ contrast.

These three types of question are covered in the chapters above. The other, longer, type of Paper 1 question is dealt with below.

Paper 1: judgement questions

The fourth type of Paper 1 is a judgement question. Judgement questions are a synthesis of source evaluation and own knowledge.

Examiner's tips

- This fourth type of Paper 1 question requires you to produce a mini-essay – with a clear/relevant argument – to address the question/statement given in the question. You should try to develop and present an argument and/or come to a balanced judgement by analysing and using these **four** sources **and** your own knowledge.

- Before you write your answer to this kind of question, you may find it useful to draw a rough chart to note what the sources show in relation to the question. This will also make sure you refer to all or at least most of the sources. Note, however, that some sources may hint at more than one factor/ result. When using your own knowledge, make sure it is relevant to the question.

- Look carefully at the simplified mark scheme below. This will help you focus on what you need to do to reach the top bands and so score the higher marks.

Common mistakes

When answering Paper 1 argument/judgement questions, make sure you do not just deal with sources **or** own knowledge. Every year, some candidates (even good ones!) do this, and so limit themselves to – at best – only five out of the nine marks available.

As with the other types of Paper 1 questions, a simplified mark scheme is provided to help you target the most important skills that examiners are looking for.

Simplified mark scheme

Band		Marks
1	**Consistently focused** on the question. **Developed and balanced** analysis, with precise use of **BOTH** sources **AND** relevant/accurate own knowledge. Sources and own knowledge are **used consistently and effectively together**, to support argument/judgement.	8–9
2	**Mostly** focused on the question. **Developed analysis**, with relevant use of **BOTH** sources **AND** some detailed own knowledge. But sources and own knowledge not always **combined** to support analysis/judgement.	6–7
3	**Some focus** on the question. **Some analysis**, using some of the sources **OR** some relevant/accurate own knowledge.	4–5
4	**No/limited focus** on the question. **Limited/generalised** comments on sources **AND/OR** some limited/inaccurate/irrelevant own knowledge.	0–3

Student answers

The student answers below have brief examiner's comments in the margins, as well as a longer overall comment at the end. Those parts of the answers that make use of the sources are highlighted in green. Those parts that deploy relevant own knowledge are highlighted in red. In this way, you should find it easier to follow why particular bands and marks were – or were not – awarded.

Question 1

Using Sources A, B, C and D, **and** your own knowledge, evaluate the reasons for the outbreak of the Iran–Iraq War in 1980. [9 marks]

SOURCE A

We have taken the path of true Islam and our aim in defeating Saddam Hussein lies in the fact that we consider him the main obstacle to the advance of Islam in the region.

Hujjat al-Islam Sadeq Khalkhali, a member of the Iranian leadership speaking in 1979.

SOURCE B

The frequent and blatant Iranian violations of Iraqi sovereignty have rendered the 1975 Algiers Agreement null and void. This river must have its Iraqi-Arab identity restored as it was throughout history in name and in reality with all the disposal rights emanating from full sovereignty over the river.

Saddam Hussein speaking to the Iraqi parliament, 17 September 1980.

SOURCE C

The failure of the pro Shah forces and the Americans [to rescue the hostages] prompted Saddam [Hussein] to make more effort to deal with Iran himself. The main calculation was that acting sooner rather than later was to be preferred. Saddam and his elite believed Iran was weak. The Iranian army seemed to be suffering from low morale as it endured a series of purges. There were reports of shortages of vital military equipment, stores and fuel. There was news of conflicts between the president and the ulema. Unemployment was rising, and there were shortages of consumer goods that might herald unrest. The professional middle class were disaffected. Iran had angered the Gulf monarchies with its revolutionary rhetoric, and it faced an imminent economic embargo from the West.

Rob Johnson. The Iran–Iraq War. *Basingstoke: Palgrave Macmillan, p. 42.*

SOURCE D

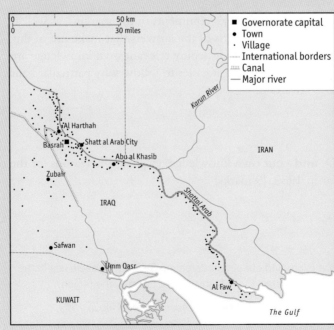

Figure 6.5 The Shatt al-'Arab waterway that separates Iraq and Iran was particularly vital for Iraqi oil exports given its short coastline

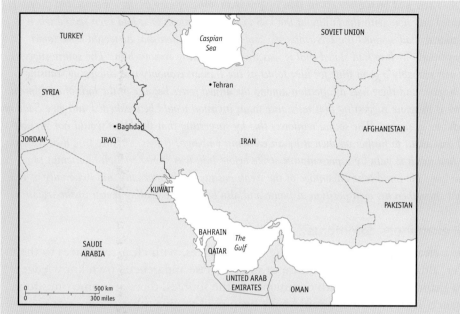

Figure 6.4 The modern-day boundaries between Iraq and Iran

The first map shows the Shatt al-'Arab waterway which separates Iran from Iraq and was used to carry oil supplies into the Gulf and the second map shows the coastline of Iraq.

Student answer

There are a number of reasons why the war between Iran and Iraq broke out in 1980, and some of these are shown by the four sources. One reason is shown by Source A, which shows Iran believed that Iraq was the main obstacle to the spreading of the Islamic revolution in the region. The source is about the need to remove Saddam Hussein in order to spread the Islamic revolution as Iran believed that Iraq was a prime target for the spread of the Islamic revolution as it had a completely secular government and growing religious opposition. It also had a large Shi'i population who were excluded from the top jobs in government, with Khomeini accusing the Baghdad regime of being atheist and corrupt. Source A shows the determination of the new regime in Tehran to spread its form of Islam within the region, but as the source states, that was dependent upon removing the regime in Iraq, which began with Iran's involvement in the assassination of some leading members of the Baathist party in 1980.

Sources B and D suggest that the importance of the Shatt al-'Arab waterway played a crucial role in the outbreak of the war, there was an ongoing dispute about the border in the south and the sources suggest that it came to a head in 1980. Source B suggests that the agreement reached with Iran over control of the waterway, the Algiers Agreement, in 1975 had broken down. Source D shows clearly why control of the waterway was vital to Iraq as it shows that Iraq's access to the sea was very narrow, while Iran had a long coastline. This meant that Iran had several ports through which it could export its oil, while Iraq wanted to gain complete control of the waterway, hence why its invasion focused on the adjoining region of Khuzestan. It might also be argued that Saddam Hussein hoped to be able to claim part of south-west Iran, which was rich in oil, to bolster the Iraqi economy.

Source C argues that there were a number of reasons that prompted the Iraqi invasion. It suggests that Saddam felt he had to act following the failure of pro-shah movements in Iran and the failure

EXAMINER'S COMMENT

This is a good, well-focused, start, with a clear argument – Source A is examined, with a clear link to the question, along with some relevant own knowledge. Although not specifically identifying individual sources, the candidate has flagged up their intention to use the other three sources.

EXAMINER'S COMMENT

Sources B and D and are clearly referred to and used, showing good understanding of the importance of the waterway, and there is some own knowledge about the narrowness of Iraq's access to the sea. In addition, there are comments about the longstanding tensions over the waterway, which had only been resolved through the Algiers Agreement in 1975.

7

EXAMINER'S COMMENT

As before, Source C is clearly used, and there is the hint of a link to Source A. There is also some relevant own knowledge. However, the student has not really made an attempt to evaluate the relative importance of the reasons mentioned in the sources. Nor are any other reasons – not mentioned by the sources – examined.

of the US. There had been attempts in Iran by pro-shah army officers to stage a coup, but they had been defeated and now with the failure of the US to free its hostages who had been seized when Iranian students had stormed the US embassy, Saddam Hussein felt that he would have to act alone, particularly as Iran had stated that it was their intention to remove him. The source suggests that this was probably a good time for him to act as the Iranian economy was collapsing, causing internal disquiet and there was disaffection among the armed forces because of the lack of equipment. The source is therefore suggesting that resistance to an invasion would be weakened and give Saddam the best chance of success. The source reinforces this by suggesting that the West would not support Iran and was about to further weaken it by an economic embargo. It was certainly true that Saddam Hussein had much to gain by a pre-emptive strike before Iran was strong enough to attempt to overthrow him. He could take advantage of the weak position both internally and externally of Iran and would strengthen his own position at home and also become the leading power in the region.

Overall examiner's comments

There is a clear argument, and good use of the sources, with clear references to them. However, although there is a mixture of some precise and general own knowledge, which is mainly integrated with comments on the sources, there are some omissions. For instance, own knowledge could have been used to give other reasons not touched on by the sources – such as the support that Iran was giving to the Shi'a in Iraq. Additionally, something could have been said about the growing control of the Iranian government over the population and its ability to spread anti-Saddam Hussein propaganda into Iraq. Also, there is no real attempt to assess the relative importance of these factors. Hence, this answer fails to get into Band 1 – but this is a reasonably sound Band 2 answer and so probably scores six marks out of the nine available.

Activity

Look again at all the sources, the simplified mark scheme, and the student answer above. Now try to write a few paragraphs to push the answer up into Band 1, and so obtain the full nine marks. As well as using all/most of the sources, and some precise own knowledge, try to integrate the sources with your own knowledge, rather than dealing with sources and own knowledge separately. And don't lose sight of the need to use the sources and your own knowledge to explain which reason you think was most important.

Question 2

Using Sources A, B, C and D, **and** your own knowledge, evaluate the reasons for the victory of the communists in the Chinese Civil War. [9 marks]

SOURCE A

There is good evidence that apathy, resentment and defeatism are spreading fast in nationalist ranks. The communists have ever mounting numerical superiority by using native (Manchurian) recruits, aid from underground units and volunteers from Korea. The nationalists are fighting far from home, the communists for native soil.

Extract from a report by the US consul in Shenyang to the US State Department, May 1947. Quoted in D. Wilson. 1991. China's Revolutionary War. London: Weidenfield and Nicolson, p. 150.

SOURCE B

Strive to annihilate the enemy in mobile warfare, but at the same time pay attention to tactics of positional attack for seizing enemy strongholds and cities. In the matter of siege operations, resolutely seize all the weakly defended enemy positions or cities. In the case of an enemy position or city defended with medium strength, seize it when the opportunity arises and circumstances permit. In the case of a strongly defended enemy position, take it only when the conditions are ripe.

Extract from an essay by Mao Zedong on war, May 1947, to guide his forces. Quoted in D. Wilson. 1991. China's Revolutionary War. *London: Weidenfield and Nicolson, p. 157.*

SOURCE C

Chiang Kai-chek [Jiang Jieshi] was personally honest and well-meaning, [but] he was hemmed in by the untrustworthiness of provincial leaders, the intrigues of his headquarters and the widespread communist influence. In 1947 the communist armies faced nationalist superiority in men and materials of two and half to one. After less than a year of fighting, they had reversed the proportion. The nationalist armies voted with their feet.

J. Gray. 1990. Rebellions and Revolutions: China from the 1800s to the 1980s. *Oxford: Oxford University Press, p. 286.*

SOURCE D

A Chinese poster of about 1950, which reads:

The central people's government constitutes the only legitimate government of all the people of the People's Republic of China. The poster shows a Parade on the occasion of the proclamation of the People's Republic of China on Tian'anmen Square in Beijing, 1 October 1949. Mao stands above, fifth from the right, with members of his first government.

The communists won the Civil War partly as a result of their own strengths and partly as a result of the weaknesses of the nationalists. These four sources deal with both these aspects. First, Source A shows that, in the view of the US consul, the nationalist troops in Manchuria were resentful and defeatist in the face of growing communist strength. Manchuria was a key area in the Civil War, and Jiang Jieshi had got US help in getting his troops there, and this was at the recommencement of Civil War, when the nationalists had better equipment and more men. The US was helping Jiang, so the US consul might have been expected to see his troops favourably, but even he sees that they were weak.

Source C relates to the same sort of explanation: nationalist weakness. Jiang was a weak leader and he faced disunity in his forces. Although he had more men and supplies, he could not keep his forces together and there were widespread desertions, as the source says, the troops voted with their feet. Source C shows the reasons Jiang was dependent on corrupt warlords and financial interests, such as the Sung family in Shanghai. Also, as Source C says, his military leadership was flawed, and he lost the confidence of the US leader. His men were tied to him not by loyalty and a common cause as with the communists but by fear of ferocious discipline in the nationalist forces. Also his planning and his intelligence let him down. His larger forces were no match for Mao's skilled guerrilla tactics and in the end the communists managed to get enough forces to tackle the nationalists in regular warfare and to defeat them. Jiang had thrown away his advantage.

Finally, Sources B and D show communist strengths. In Source B, Mao is suggesting mobile warfare and taking weakly defended enemy positions. Source D confirms that this was successful and popular and shows the successful communist troops in a victory parade and also that the communists produced colourful propaganda. The production of accessible and striking propaganda was part of the political effectiveness of the CCP in appealing to people who could not read. In the Long March, he showed he knew how to lead and good treatment of the peasants meant that more people joined his forces. Mao avoided putting his numerically weaker forces at risk during the fighting after 1946 and relied on avoiding strongly defended points and keeping mobile. Jiang could not meet this type of warfare any more than he had been able to do in the 1930s. In addition, Jiang's forces plundered the countryside and Mao's remained disciplined and did not abuse or rob the peasants. The enthusiasm shown in Source D was widespread because of the unpopularity of Jiang's armies.

So, in conclusion, these four sources touch on all the main reasons why the communists won.

Overall examiner's comments

There is good use of the sources, with clear references to them. However, although there is some own knowledge, which is mainly integrated with comments on the sources, own knowledge could have been used to give other factors not mentioned by the sources. Also, while explaining the sources, there are few explicit explanations as to why these issues were really decisive. Hence this answer fails to get into Band 1. This is a reasonably sound Band 2 answer and so probably scores six marks out of the nine available.

Paper 2 exam practice

Paper 2 skills and questions

For Paper 2, you have to answer two essay questions from two **different** topics from the 12 options offered. Very often, you will be asked to comment on two states from two different IB regions of the world. Although each question has a specific mark scheme, you

EXAMINER'S COMMENT

This is a good, well-focused start that identifies a key area of discussion. It deals clearly with Source A and uses some of the candidate's own knowledge, and notices the origin of the source.

EXAMINER'S COMMENT

The sources (A, C and D) are again clearly referred to and used, showing good understanding, and there is own knowledge. There is also a comment at the end that hints at why the communists won.

EXAMINER'S COMMENT

As before, Sources B and D are clearly used and, in this case, linked. There is also some relevant own knowledge. But there are no explicit explanations/ comments on how these policies led to victory and the Long March is not explained.

can get a good general idea of what examiners are looking for in order to be able to put answers into the higher bands from the 'generic' mark scheme. In particular, you will need to acquire reasonably precise historical knowledge in order to address issues such as cause and effect, or change and continuity, and to learn how to explain historical developments in a clear, coherent, well-supported and relevant way. You will also need to understand and be able to refer to aspects relating to historical debates and interpretations.

Key Concepts

Remember – when answering essay questions, you will often need to consider aspects of one or more of the six Key Concepts. These are:

- Change
- Continuity
- Causation
- Consequence
- Significance
- Perspectives.

Make sure you read the questions carefully, and select your questions wisely. It is a good idea to produce a rough plan of **each** of the essays you intend to attempt, **before** you start to write your answers. That way, you will soon know whether you have enough own knowledge to answer them adequately.

Remember, too, to keep your answers relevant and focused on the question. For example, don't go outside the dates mentioned in the question, or answer on individuals/states different from the ones identified in the question. Don't just describe the events or developments – sometimes, students just focus on one key word or individual, and then write down all they know about it. Instead, select your own knowledge carefully, and pin the relevant information to the key features raised by the question. Also, if the question asks for 'causes/reasons' and 'consequences/results', or two different countries/leaders, make sure you deal with **all** the parts of the question. Otherwise, you will limit yourself to half marks at best.

Examiner's tips

For Paper 2 answers, examiners are looking for clear/precise analysis, and a balanced argument, linked to the question, with the use of good, precise and relevant own knowledge. In order to obtain the highest marks, you should be able to refer, where appropriate, to historical debate and/or different historical perspectives/interpretations, or historians' knowledge, making sure it is both relevant to the question **and** integrated into your answer.

Common mistakes

- When answering Paper 2 questions, try to avoid simply describing what happened. A detailed narrative, with no explicit attempts to link the knowledge to the question, will only get you half marks at most.
- If the question asks you to select examples from **two** different regions, make sure you don't choose two states from the same region. Every year, some candidates do this, and so limit themselves to – at best – only eight out of the 15 marks available.

Exam practice

Simplified mark scheme

Band		Marks
1	Consistently **clear** understanding of and **focus on the question**, with **all main aspects addressed**. Answer is **fully analytical**, balanced and **well-structured/organised**. Own knowledge is detailed, accurate and relevant, with events placed in their historical context. There is developed critical analysis, and **sound understanding** of historical concepts. Examples used are relevant, and used effectively to support analysis/evaluation. The answer also integrates **evaluation** of different historical debates/perspectives. All/almost all of the main points are substantiated, and the answer reaches a **clear/reasoned consistent judgement/conclusion**.	13–15
2	**Clear understanding** of the question, and most of its **main aspects** are addressed. Answer is **mostly well-structured and developed**, though, with some repetition/lack of clarity in places. Supporting own knowledge is **mostly relevant/accurate**, and events are placed in their historical context. The answer is **mainly analytical**, with relevant examples used to support critical analysis/evaluation. There is **some understanding/evaluation** of historical concepts and debates/perspectives. Most of the main points are substantiated, and the answer offers a consistent conclusion.	10–12
3	Demands of the question are understood – but **some aspects not fully developed/addressed**. Mostly relevant/accurate supporting own knowledge, and events generally placed in their historical context. Some **attempts at analysis/evaluation but these are limited/not sustained/inconsistent**.	7–9
4	**Some understanding** of the question. **Some relevant own knowledge**, with **some factors identified** – but with **limited explanation**. **Some attempts at analysis**, but answer lacks clarity/coherence, and is **mainly description/narrative**.	4–6
5	**Limited understanding** of/focus on the question. **Short/generalised answer**, with **very little accurate/relevant own knowledge**. Some **unsupported assertions**, with **no real analysis**.	0–3

Student answers

Those parts of the student answers that follow will have brief examiner's comments in the margins, as well as a longer overall comment at the end. Those parts of student answers that are particularly strong and well-focused will be highlighted in red. Errors/confusions/loss of focus will be highlighted in blue. In this way, you should find it easier to follow why marks were – or were not – awarded.

Question 1

In what ways did the causes of the Second World War differ from the causes of the First World War? [15 marks]

Skill

Analysis/argument/evaluation.

Examiner's tip

Look carefully at the wording of this question, which asks about the causes of the wars. The focus is on the Second World War and the key word is 'differ'. All aspects of the questions will need to be addressed if high marks are to be achieved. And remember – don't just describe what happened. What's needed is explicit comparison, analysis and explanation, with some precise supporting own knowledge.

Student answer

Although there were some similarities between the causes of the wars and Germany was at the heart of both, nevertheless, there were many differences in why these wars broke out. The causes of the Second World War were rooted in the settlement that followed the First World War. This was a big difference. Also, the war, especially as it developed, was wider than the First World War as Japan played a much bigger part in bringing about a world war. In addition, ideology and big political ideas played a much more important role in causing the Second World War than the First. It could be argued that accidental circumstances arising from an unexpected incident brought about the First World War, but the Second World War was widely expected to break out and did not need a 'spark' like the assassination of Archduke Franz Ferdinand.

The peace treaties of 1919 left many powers discontented. Germany had lost valuable border lands, its colonies and was blamed for the war. This caused major resentment and led to the rise of Adolf Hitler and the Nazis. Before the First World War, Germany had not faced any humiliation, but had been a growing power. Germany did not launch a war for revenge or because its people resented an unpopular treaty. In 1914, unlike 1939, there were no German minorities in other countries that the German state wanted to get into Germany. This was the case in 1939 when Hitler wanted to win back German lands given to Poland in the Treaty of Versailles. Italy, too, was disappointed with its gains in 1919 and this was a reason for it to join Germany. Japan was resentful of the Treaty of Versailles and wanted to expand. This was not true in 1914, so the situation was very different.

Japan was much more important in bringing about the Second World War than it had been in causing the First World War. True, its defeat of Russia in 1904–5 helped to turn Russian attention towards the Balkans, but the war in the Far East was much less important in 1914 than it was in the Second World War. The First World War encouraged Japan to want to expand into China, and in 1931 the first major aggression of the inter-war years began when Japan invaded Chinese Manchuria. When Japan invaded China on a larger scale in 1937, it was clear that Britain and the USA were going to do little to stop wars of conquest. However, it was Japan's attack on the USA and the European colonies in 1941 that really made the Second World War a world war and led to heavy fighting in the Pacific. This is in major contrast to the First World War, where Japan played little part in starting the conflict and only exploited it to take German Pacific colonies.

The First World War was fought by empires, and the political ideas of the Austrian, Russian and German emperors were much the same. None of them really wanted to share power and they disliked democracy. They wanted greater power and security for their empires, but not necessarily to dominate Europe.

EXAMINER'S COMMENT

This is a clear and well-focused introduction, showing a good grasp of the key requirements of the question. There is already a lot of comparison and the candidate can use these points to develop explanation and further comparison.

EXAMINER'S COMMENT

There is accurate supporting own knowledge explicitly linked to the comparison – the thrust is towards the Second World War, but that is also the thrust of the question.

EXAMINER'S COMMENT

There is more accurate supporting own knowledge, clearly focused on comparison. Again, the balance is towards the Second World War.

EXAMINER'S COMMENT

This is a strong section which is comparative, analytical and deals with different historical views, mentioning Fischer. The balance is good between the two wars.

EXAMINER'S COMMENT

This section does make comparisons but is a bit more variable in terms of explanation, but the point is made that there was no sudden immediate cause in 1939.

The Second World War was fought by powers that had more expansionist aims and fought for different principles and so was very different from the First World War. Hitler wanted 'Lebensraum' for his pure Aryan Germans to farm and breed, and dreamed of taking over the whole of Eastern Europe to provide slave labour for his 'Thousand-Year Reich'. This was a great ambition that few think that Germany had before 1914. There is a view, held by the historian Fritz Fischer, that the kaiser's Germany was just as expansionist as that of Hitler. However, there is no general agreement that this was true. Belgium was invaded in 1914 just as a means of getting to France, but Poland was invaded in 1939 to expand the German racial state. Germany in 1914 was proud of its nation and the kaiser thought that Germany was superior, but this was more national pride than racial ideology and, despite the theories of historians like Fischer, there is more difference than similarity between the causes of the wars. Similarly, the fascist ideas of expansion held by Mussolini were very different from pre-1914 Italian governments, and the nationalist ideas of Japanese military leaders were much more developed than those of Japanese governments before 1914, who merely wanted to expand into China – not to create the Co-Prosperity Zone and assert Japanese culture over Southeast Asia and beyond, to Australasia.

Given the longstanding resentments, the rise of nationalist regimes and the weaknesses shown by the Western powers, not only in the Far East, but to German expansion in Europe and Italian expansion in Africa, there was a general expectation of war, so there was no sudden incident like the assassination of Archduke Franz Ferdinand in 1914 to spark the war. There had been fighting in Asia since 1937; Hitler made no secret of his desire for expansion. Communism and fascism had been at war in Spain from 1936. It was expected that Hitler would go to war with Poland. Although war had been expected before 1914, there were greater hopes for peace after the settlement of the Balkan Wars without an international war, so the June crisis in 1914 was unexpected and the assassination could be seen as a major short-term cause. The invasions of Poland in 1939 and Russia in 1941 were linked to clearly stated Nazi aims.

Thus, in terms of ideological rivalry, resentment about peace treaties, the role of Japan and the way that war came about, the causes of the wars were different. Alliances were less important in 1939 than in 1914: Italy did not join the war in 1939 despite its pact with Hitler. Both involved issues of the balance of power and at the heart of both, at least in Europe, was a disagreement about Germany's position. However, there were more differences than similarities in the causes of the wars.

Overall examiner's comments

This is a good, well-focused and analytical answer, with some precise and accurate own knowledge to support the points made. The answer is thus good enough to be awarded the mark at the very top of Band 1. The answer is well organised, offers consistent comparison and is aware of some historical interpretation and attempts to evaluate this.

Activity

Look again at the simplified mark scheme and the student answer above. Now try to write an even better answer, with a stronger conclusion (the point about alliances is a little rushed) and to consider other points – perhaps appeasement as a cause of war.

Question 2

Compare and contrast the practice of two civil wars, each from a different region. [15 marks]

Skill

Analysis/argument/evaluation.

Examiner's tip

Look carefully at the wording of this question, which asks for both contrast and comparison. Note the wars must be from different regions and must be civil wars. Don't just write the story of both wars, but think about their nature and how they were fought.

Student answer

The civil wars in China after 1927 and Spain (1936–9) were characterised by very different forms of warfare for most of the time, although there was some similarity in the more conventional fighting in the later stages of the Chinese Civil War. Both wars were fought bitterly and with cruelty. In addition, both wars were fought until one side gained outright victory and control of the country and both wars had foreign intervention.

The characteristic element of the Chinese Civil War was, until 1947–8, that the nationalist side had much larger forces and more equipment than the communist side. Jiang Jieshi was a professional soldier and his government was able to use not only conscript troops raised by the Chinese state, but the armies of warlords with whom he allied. When the CCP met them in conventional battles, they were defeated. In the Spanish Civil War, the official government was the left-wing Republicans and the 'rebels' were not communists, but elements of the professional Spanish army based in Morocco. The leaders of the nationalists in Spain were, like Jiang, military commanders. The sides, however, were much more equally based in Spain. In China, the communists were a minority, but the last elections in Spain before the civil war had shown roughly equal support for the left and the right. In China, a large army attempted to crush a minority political movement. In Spain an element of the army attempted to crush a lawfully elected left-wing government. In both countries, however, the nationalist Right had military advantages because in Spain Franco gained the assistance of the German aircraft and large-scale forces from Italy.

The wars lasted very different periods of time. The Chinese Civil War went on in the period 1927 to 1949, although not continuously. In Spain, the war was shorter and foreign intervention drove the two sides further apart – with the right fearful of Russian and international volunteer aid and the left seeing Hitler and Mussolini wanting to make Spain a fascist state. In China, foreign intervention, in the form of large-scale Japanese invasion to take advantage of the divisions, brought greater unity, but this was not sustained. The Spanish war was shorter because the situation was different – as the Republican attacks failed and key areas were lost, there was little alternative to surrender. In China, because distances were so much greater, decisive defeat was more difficult for the nationalists and so the war lasted longer.

In China, the CCP was able to survive in remote areas which the nationalists found difficult to get to. First was the Jiangxi Soviet, but even when that could not hold out, the communists were able to retreat by the Long March in 1934 to the north and establish themselves in the mountains in the Shaanxi Soviet in Hunan. This remarkable event has no parallel in Spain, where the losing Republicans could not withdraw and establish a defence in some remote area.

China's distances and Mao's skills in leading his army in unexpected directions made it hard for Jiang to find and destroy his enemy. The communists were prepared to put up with heavy losses and hardships on the march to survive. Jiang's conventional forces did not move so quickly and flexibly. The sheer size and geography of China, compared to that of Spain, was a factor in making the ways in which the wars were fought very different.

Mao and his forces relied on guerrilla warfare, which was less significant in Spain. Time was on Mao's side. He was helped by a very strong ideology that believed in victory. Although the

EXAMINER'S COMMENT

This is a focused start – the choices are from different regions and the candidate doesn't tell the story but makes some comparison about the nature of the wars. It is rather general, but acceptable for an introduction.

EXAMINER'S COMMENT

This keep the comparison going – it is mainly about the balance of forces, but the explanation is clear and there is some support. The candidate has not just written about one war, but has remembered the question and made contrasts and comparisons.

EXAMINER'S COMMENT

Although still somewhat general, the points are clearly made and the comparison of the impact of foreign countries is thoughtful.

Exam practice

communists had been defeated in the third and fourth expeditions sent against them in 1933 because they attempted tactics that were too ambitious, Mao believed in patience and won in the end.

Air power and superior forces were important in both wars. The successful nationalist campaigns against Aragon and in the north were helped by air support. When Jiang was able to use air support against the communists he was successful, as in the campaigns against Jiangxi in 1933–4. The German and Italian air power was a major reason for nationalist success. It was less important after 1934 in China: the later stages of the Civil War saw few mass battles in which the CCP met the nationalists in open-order conflict. Morale was a key factor in China. In Spain morale remained high on both sides, but the divisions among the Republicans weakened it. Both sides, however, were fighting for ideals and this strengthened their resistance, making the campaigns of 1937 hard-fought. Military failures rather than a failure of belief were the main reason for Republican surrender. However, in China morale became a key issue in the failure of the nationalists. US observers saw at first-hand the lack of commitment of many of the nationalist troops, who were poorly paid and supplied and had little to fight for. The fighting spirit of the communists, however, remained high. The endurance shown in the Long March indicates that high morale was a crucial feature.

The wars were similar in that both were civil wars that divided the people. Both involved professional soldiers leading forces against left-wing opponents, and both involved foreign support. Both wars involved many civilian casualties and in both there was little mercy for prisoners and bitter fighting. However, the length and nature of the wars differed because of geographical features and the greater emphasis on guerrilla warfare in China.

Overall examiner's comments

This is a good, well-focused and analytical answer, with some precise and accurate own knowledge to support the points made. The answer is thus good enough to be awarded a mark towards the top of Band 2 – probably about 11–12 marks. To reach Band 1, there needed to have been some more support and an awareness of different historical interpretations about the quality of leadership and why the wars took the form they did.

Activity

Look again at the simplified mark scheme and the student answer above.
Now write your own answer and try to push it into the top band, using the following tips:

*   Write about the actual campaigning, especially in China after 1946.
*   Where there is a section predominantly on one country, write more points both comparing and contrasting.
*   Look at different possible explanations of whether Mao or Franco was a better leader.

Question 3

To what extent did technological developments ensure victory in 20th-century wars? [15 marks]

Skill

Analysis/argument/evaluation.

EXAMINER'S COMMENT

So far the comparisons have been well sustained, but the candidate has been tempted to write mainly about Mao in China in this section (see blue text on previous page). Mao's leadership has been challenged and the candidate takes rather an uncritical view. There is analysis, but the question could be better addressed here.

EXAMINER'S COMMENT

There is some effective use of knowledge here. The comparisons are well made and valid. There is support for the importance of morale and the writing is generally analytical.

EXAMINER'S COMMENT

The conclusion sums up concisely.

Examiner's tip

Look carefully at the wording of this question. The crucial element is 'to what extent', which needs a judgement about the relative importance of technology. The focus has to be on technology, but not alone – it has to be weighed against other factors, such as morale, leadership, planning, supplies and support from the home front. It is easy to become too descriptive, so be sure to link information to the title – and remember the words 'to ensure victory'.

Student answer

There were many important technological developments that made the wars in the 20th century very different and helped countries to win. The First World War broke out in 1914 when the archduke was killed and everyone expected it to be over very quickly, but there was a lot of technology, which made casualties high and was important for the war. The new technology of the trenches meant that men fought in mud and faced bad conditions, like rats. There were machine guns and artillery guns as well, which meant that many people were killed in big attacks. Some major battles in this war were the Battle of the Somme and the Battle of Verdun, where thousands of people were killed but little land was taken.

Technology developed during this war and two big changes, tanks and the use of planes, were also important in the Second World War. After the First World War, things could not be the same, as too many people had been killed in the trenches, so tanks were developed to protect the troops and break the enemy lines. This was a major development in technology, as were planes which allowed the enemy to be seen from the air and stopped surprise attacks. Planes were also used for bombing, but these bombs were not very destructive.

In the Second World War there were bigger and better tanks and planes and more bombing. There were big tank battles in Russia which were important and the Germans used new technology in their Blitzkrieg. The tanks meant that the war after 1939 was much faster, with no trenches like the First World War. There was also more technology used in war in the air, with radar and bigger bombings. This was very important when the atom bombs called 'big boy' and 'little boy' were dropped on Japan in 1945. *These bombs killed millions and started a new type of atomic warfare that changed warfare and brought the Second World War to an end, so were more important than any of the new technology in the First World War. What ended the First World War was the war of attrition, but what ended the Second World War was much more involved with new technology such as bombing and especially the atomic bomb and better aircraft.*

After the Second World War there was a big arms race with more nuclear weapons produced. There was MAD (More Actual Destruction) so people feared the destruction of the planet, which meant that the big weapons were not used to bring about victories. In many wars, technology did not bring victory as in the Second World War. In Vietnam for instance, the USA had napalm and bombers but lost to the North Vietcong who had older weapons. In China in the Civil War, Mao had fewer tanks and planes than his enemies but still won. *Sometimes it was morale and belief in a cause that was more important than weapons. The Chinese communists were able to win the civil war by guerrilla warfare, which did not have much technology but surprised the enemy and was effective in not having big battles. This was important in many other wars, for example Vietnam and Korea, and shows that technology is not everything.*

In wars after the Second World War, it was not always technology that was important. Sometimes it was more how well-motivated the fighters were. For example, in Algeria, which defeated France, and Vietnam, which defeated America. The people really believed in their cause and that was more important than weapons. But when big powers fought and had industries and more planes and guns, it was more important that these were better in technology.

EXAMINER'S COMMENT

Instead of looking at the theme of technology and comparing it with other elements, the candidate has written about a particular war, and the focus on technology is not good. There are references to some weapons, but the trenches themselves are not really 'technology' and there is some quite generalised writing.

EXAMINER'S COMMENT

The candidate does make some comparison and links the technology of the atom bombs to victory in 1945, but the writing is clumsy and generalised. Important points are not developed.

EXAMINER'S COMMENT

The candidate is trying hard to answer the question but there is some error (Mutually Assured Destruction is misremembered and Korea is mistakenly seen as a guerrilla war). There is some description about China rather than a real analysis of the importance of factors such as leadership, morale and organisation.

Exam practice

Overall examiner's comments

This is a rather muddled answer, with some confusion/unclear explanation. There are some inaccuracies/vagueness, but also some relevant own knowledge and some attempts to focus on the question. The approach is mainly narrative, although the conclusion attempts to pull it all together. The answer is probably just about on the borderline between the top of Band 4 and the bottom of Band 3, i.e., about six or seven marks. To go higher into Band 3, a clearer understanding of the technology and its importance would be needed, along with more accurate and precise information, and – ideally – a more sustained and supported analytical approach.

Activity

There is an argument offered here that technology was not as important after the Second World War, and some examples are given. The problem is that the answer is not always accurate and is quite generalised. The candidate needs to think much more about different elements and how the answer could be organised, and then needs to build up knowledge so that the points made are better supported. Write your own answer, and try to push it into a higher band by bearing these points in mind.

Index

281

Acknowledgements

Cover: Alex Robinson/Getty Images Fig. 1.2 AFP/Getty Images; Fig. 1.3 Hulton Archive/Getty Images; Fig 2.2 Library of Congress; Fig 2.5 Hulton Archive/Getty Images; Fig 2.6 Bettmann/Getty Images; Fig. 2.7 Hulton Archive/Getty Images; Fig. 2.8 Popperfoto/Getty Images; Fig. 2.10 General Photographic Agency/Getty Images Fig. 2.11 Library of Congress; Fig. 2.12 Hulton Archive/Getty Images; Fig. 2.13 Hulton Archive/Getty Images; Fig. 2.14 akg-images/Alamy Stock Photo Fig. 2.15 Library of Congress; Fig. 2.16 Illustrated LondonNews/Getty Images Fig. 2.17 Wikimedia; Fig. 2.18 Library of Congress; Fig. 2.19 Hulton Archive/Getty Images; Fig. 2.20 Heritage Images/Getty Images; Fig. 2.21 UniversalImagesGroup/Getty Images; Fig. 2.24 Underwood Archives/Getty Images; Fig. 2.25 The British Cartoon Archives; Fig. 2.26 Wallace Kirkland/Getty Images; Fig. 3.1 Popperfoto/Getty Images; Fig. 3.2 Roger Viollet/Topfoto; Fig. 3.3 Apic/Getty Images Fig. 3.5 Imagno/Getty Images Fig. 3.6 The Granger Collection/Topfoto; Fig. 3.7 Keystone-France/Getty Images; Fig. 3.8 Everett Collection Historical/Alamy Stock Photo; Fig. 3.9 Library of Congress; Fig. 3.12 SSPL/Getty Images; Fig. 3.13 TASS/Getty Images; Fig. 3.14 Fotosearch/Getty Images; Fig. 3.15 Hulton Archive/Getty Images; Fig. 3.16 Popperfoto/Getty Images; Fig. 4.1 Library of Congress; Fig. 4.2 Print Collector/GettyImages; Fig. 4.3 Roger Viollet/GettyImages Fig. 4.4 Archive Pics/Alamy Stock Photo Fig. 4.5 Associated Newspapers Ltd./Solo Syndication/The British Cartoon Archives; Fig. 4.6 Hulton Archive/Getty Images; Fig. 4.7 Granger, NYC./Alamy Stock Photo Fig. 4.8 Library of Congress; Fig. 4.9 HultonArchive/Getty Images; Fig. 4.10 ullsteinbild/Getty Images; Fig. 4.11 Roger Viollet/Getty Images; Fig. 4.12 Popperfoto/Getty Images; Fig. 4.13 HultonArchive/Getty Images; Fig. 4.14 ullsteinbild/Getty Images; Fig. 4.15 ullsteinbild/Getty Images; Fig. 4.16 Hulton Archive/Getty Images; Fig. 4.17 Keystone/Getty Images; Fig. 4.18 Popperfoto/Getty Images; Fig. 4.19 Bettmann/Getty Images; Fig. 4.20 Keystone/Getty Images; Fig. 4.21 David Cole/Alamy Stock Photo; Fig. 4.22 Library of Congress; Fig. 5.2 Hulton Archive/Getty Images; Fig. 5.3 Imagno/Getty Images; Fig. 5.4 Sovfoto/Getty images; Fig. 5.6 Popperfoto/Getty Images; Fig. 5.7 UniversalImagesGroup/Getty Images; Fig. 5.8 RDA/Getty Images; Fig. 5.9 Bettmann/Getty Images; Fig. 5.10 Bob Bryant/Getty Images; Fig. 5.11 Hulton Archive/Getty Images; Fig. 5.13 Sovfoto/Getty Images; Fig. 5.14 AFP Photography, LLC/Getty Images; Fig. 5.16 AFP/Getty Images; Fig. 5.17 Bachrach/Getty Images; Fig. 5.18 Unknown; Fig. 5.19 Universal History Archive/Getty Images; Fig. 5.20 Heritage Image Partnership Ltd/Alamy Stock Photo; Fig. 6.6 AP/Press Association Images; Fig. 6.7 Chip HIRES/Gamma-Rapho via Getty Images; Fig. 6.8 Bettmann/Getty Images; Fig. 6.9 CartoonStock Fig. 6.10 AFP/Getty Images; Fig. 6.12 © epaeuropeanpressphoto agency b.v./AlamyStock Photo Fig. 6.13 Keystone-France/Gamma-Keystone via Getty Images; Fig. 6.14 IRNA/AFP/Getty Images; Fig. 6.15 KavehKazemi/Getty Images; Fig. 6.16 NORBERT SCHILLER/AFP/Getty Images; Fig. 6.17 Getty Images; Fig. 6.18 AWAD AWAD/AFP/Getty Image; Fig. 6.19 KavehKazemi/Getty Images; Fig. 6.20 KavehKazemi/Getty Images; Fig. 6.21 GettyRAMZI HAIDAR/AFP/Getty Images; Fig. 6.22-/AFP/Getty Images; Chapter 7 Q2 source D Chinese Propaganda Poster collection, International Institute of Social History (Amsterdam).